Do You QuantumThink?

"This is not your usual ponderous self-help book but a delightful fun read that opens a door to a life of living in the moment armed with the power to create the future. Dianne is able to define what is not definable, to allow us to tap into the universal mind, to re-define ourselves and the world around us in a way that empowers rather than defeats us. This book should be required reading for all literate human beings."—**ROY BLACK**, Attorney and Network TV Legal Consultant

"In her own inimitable forthright, brilliant and charming way, Dianne Collins moves us all beyond our small worlds into a life filled with new possibilities. It allows the reader to go safely where they have never gone before. And then bring that new reality into relationships with everyone from mom to the boss. This voyage on the road to discovery is fun, eminently readable and most importantly it works!"—**GAIL EVANS**, *New York Times* bestselling author of *Play Like a Man, Win Like a Woman: What Men Know About Success That Women Need to Learn* / Retired Executive Vice President, CNN

"With QuantumThink, Dianne Collins has distilled the essence of the work she and her husband Alan have been doing over the years to create a new understanding of how the world works for those fortunate enough to have been coached by them. As one of those 'Wake Ups,' as she would say, whose life was incredibly enriched and enabled through their teachings, I strongly recommend you read the book, undertake its recreations, and see the world with new eyes. Both it and you will be far happier and successful as a result."—**MORLEY WINOGRAD**, Former Senior Policy Advisor to Vice President Al Gore and Executive Director of Marshall School of Business Institute of Communication Technology, University of Southern California / Co-author, *Millennial Makeover: MySpace, YouTube & the Future of American Politics*

"*Do You QuantumThink?* is beautifully designed and written for readability by everyone. Important ideas to be shared and pondered—and acted on."—**ERVIN LASZLO**, Founder and President, Club of Budapest international think tank / Author, *Science and the Akashic Field*

"We are all looking for a creative breakthrough of some type—whether it is at work or in our personal lives—and Dianne provides the key to that breakthrough. By reading her words and practicing the recreations, you quickly realize that our creativity has been limited by the mechanical working of our own minds—minds that have been preconditioned to think that the past dictates the future, that developments are always continuous, that we all are separate and that choices are limited (you can have "either" this "or" that). This book will make you smile and laugh. More importantly, it will help you strip away your preconditioned thinking and allow you to access your own power to create a truly worthy life that fulfills your unique purpose."—**KEITH COWAN**, President, Strategic Planning and Corporate Development, Sprint

"Even if you consider yourself already a great thinker, Dianne Collins will get you to 'next' in your own thinking, brilliantly in the best way possible—so you take further command of whatever 'success' personally means to you now. *Do You QuantumThink?* is a seminal work, arriving at the perfect time in this defining moment of reinvention for all of us, bringing relief and real answers."—**CAROLE HYATT**, author and founder of Leadership Forum and "Getting to Next"

"Do You QuantumThink? is an engaging and thought-provoking exploration of how we think, and provokes an awakening to the power of the mind to shape and create our interrelated personal and work worlds. Anything that quotes and draws lessons from Albert Einstein, Jesus Christ, and Jimi Hendrix is surely worth active inspection and reflection."—**ALAN BARNES**, Partner, Accenture

"There are very few originals in life—Dianne Collins is one of them. When I first heard about her work regarding QuantumThink, I knew in my soul that she was on to something. If we expect our world to evolve in a positive way, we must adopt a powerful new way of thinking. Dianne's distinctions on how to do this provide a blueprint for all to use that is both dynamic and user friendly. I knew this would have a profound impact on my life and it continues to do so."—**FRANKIE BOYER**, award-winning talk show host, The Frankie Boyer Show

"Wow, Dianne. You've written a wonderful and necessary book for those of us *on the path*. I'm thinking I may need another New Agreement in the Workplace—QUANTUMTHINK! The universal wisdom you have shared with us is both timely and timeless."—**DAVID DIBBLE**, Spiritual Teacher in the Workplace / author of *The New Agreements in the Workplace: Releasing the Human Spirit*

"There is no book—of the thousands upon thousands on the shelves today—which so clearly gives us access to harnessing the power of thought to create our reality as this one. *Do You QuantumThink?* is the pre-eminent manual for living in the 21st century ... a must for creating a life of one's own design."—**CYNTHIA GREENAWALT-CARVAJAL**, Contributing author to the *New York Times* bestseller, *Masters of Networking* / Senior Partner, Vision-Source Consulting, Inc.

"QuantumThink is a revolutionary process that has supported me in the transformation of my life. Thank you, Dianne, for the contribution you are making."—**DEBBIE FORD**, *New York Times* bestselling author, *The Dark Side of the Light Chasers* and producer of *The Shadow Effect* interactive movie

"We have all learned that our own perceptions create our existing reality. Now Collins helps us unlock our perceptions by challenging the way we use our minds. She has us touch on the deep topics that shape our human experience and raises our consciousness of a new world view."—**RICK SMITH**, Managing Director, Accenture Leadership Consulting Practice

"As I read this book my mind started percolating with energy and excitement recognizing it was being expanded right into a new world view. This book is an essential read for anyone wanting to form new neural pathways to higher intelligence and receive the real truth of how to create your reality. This book is Genius, thank you Dianne Collins."
—**RACHEL LEVY**, LMHC, The Love Coach and Director of The Sacred Space Miami

"Dianne Collins has had an immeasurable impact on my career, family, and life. Her QuantumThink Distinctions are truly powerful and insightful. They reveal basic truths and wisdom—ancient, modern and universal. Her associated 'Recreations' have allowed me to challenge and improve the way I think about my life and world. Through Dianne's brilliant work and coaching, I now own the way I think and feel about my life to a degree I never knew was possible, and so many of my hopes and dreams have been realized on the path to conscious awareness."—**BOB BICKERSTAFF**, VP, Consumer Data Products, AT&T

"*Do You QuantumThink?* is mandatory reading for the 21st century. When I need to 'quantumthink' personally or professionally, I have copies strategically placed at my home and office for instantaneous inspiration."—**DAN SCHMIDT**, CEO, JDS Companies

"Dianne has truly mapped the way across the bridge from what many have called 'An Inner Journey' to simply living your most authentic self today and everyday. As Dianne states, '… it is about generating a new condition for your experience of life.' This book is uplifting to your mind and spirit in a light, fun, friendly format. Whatever your background, *Do You QuantumThink?* is a dance into your consciousness."
—**DEVRA ANN JACOBS,** founder of *Mystic Pop* Magazine

"*Do You Quantum Think?* is the quintessential book for making the shift from an outmoded way of perceiving the world into a new evolution of thinking. Dianne Collins has done a masterful job helping the reader distinguish between antiquated thinking and quantum thinking."—**JARED ROSEN,** co-author of *The Flip: Everything You Think Is About to Change*

"Dianne Collins has found the missing link in this wondrous world of thought and creation. This is the 'how to' book, the roadmap, to taking your outrageous dreams and turning them into living reality. *Do You QuantumThink?* explains what's been stopping us and then gives us the tools to achieve the life we want."—**PHILIP CARROLL,** Managing Director, Benchmark College, Sydney, Australia

"*Do You QuantumThink?* unlocks the door to infinite possibilities, guides us to rediscover the miraculous, and awakens us to our greatest potential. Dianne Collins gives us life altering tools to achieve what we truly want for ourselves. Dive into this book and tap into a wealth of wisdom."—**LISA DELMAN,** author of *Dear Mom, I've Always Wanted You to Know: Daughters Share Letters from the Heart*

"What is most striking about this intriguing new book is the author's practical approach for transforming our ordinary thinking into wisdom, a goal of many of the world's spiritual traditions. Dianne Collins' concept of QuantumThink is at once contemporary and ancient, practical and philosophical. For most of us, our hearts and our minds conflict, but Collins skillfully interweaves the two."—**NATHAN KATZ, PH.D.**, Director of the Program in the Study of Spirituality and Professor of Religious Studies at Florida International University

"Dianne has created a new context of thinking for me with QuantumThink. This book provides a simple and powerful way for living life at a level that is extraordinary. I find myself creating new awareness for living. This is the end of the search for self and the beginning of living in the 'conscious.' The principles are universally applicable in life, be it spiritual, personal, business or family. QuantumThink is a new way of thinking that transforms our perspective for living each moment consciously, powerfully, and present."—**DOUG McCRAW**, President, Peregrine Partners Group, Investments and Real Estate Development

"At a time in history when our ability to actually influence events seems impossible, Ms. Collins suggests that we ARE the influence affecting our reality. '. . . in an observer created reality you will find what you are looking for.' Dianne Collins nudges us into the rabbit hole and then supplies us with the tools to make sense of it, from clues to avoid our automatic habits of thinking, to learning the principles that enable us to create. How refreshing! The possibilities are infinite. So much so that one could believe a CHAMPION wins, even on an 'off day'!"—**BRUCE E. FRAZEY,** CPA and Attorney / Former President and CEO, KC Masterpiece Barbecue & Grill Restaurants

"Dianne Collins is revolutionizing our definition of thinking by presenting it through the mist of quantum experience. *Do You QuantumThink?* allows us to know the expanded borders and infinite possibilities of the quantum world. We break free of the conditioning that has for so long kept us away from our natural fluid values of clarity, focus, peace, gratitude, innovation, and courage. A must read for anyone who is on the path to present moment living."—**FAYE MANDELL**, author of *Self-Powerment: Towards a New Way of Living*

"QuantumThink is interesting and different yet relevant to so many aspects of life. These are tools, concepts, and distinctions that you will use every day to help you wake up and distinguish when automatic actions or reactions (rather than consciously chosen ones) unnecessarily limit your sense of opportunities, options, or even what is possible. Frankly, I was surprised by how many of my thoughts, beliefs, and decisions were the result of unconscious habits or predictable patterns of behavior. Even this single distinction can make a material change in your life, if you let it. Do yourself a favor and give it a chance."
—**HOWARD GETSON**, President and CEO, Capitalogix, an intelligent response to the market

"Dianne Collins' book, *Do You QuantumThink?* will *excite* and *inspire* you!!! It will expand your mind to limitless horizons, and enable you to fulfill dreams you never before imagined. I want everyone I love to have this book because I believe it can change your life."
—**PEDIE WOLFOND**, Artist, Toronto, Canada, www.pediewolfond.com

Do You QuantumThink®?

Do You QuantumThink®?

New Thinking That Will
Rock Your World

DIANNE COLLINS

SelectBooks, Inc.
New York

QuantumThink® is a registered trademark of Breakthrough Energy Systems, Inc.
This edition published by SelectBooks, Inc.
For information address SelectBooks, Inc., New York, New York.

First Edition

ISBN 978-1-59079-074-8

Cataloging-in-Publication Data

Collins, Dianne, [date]
  Do you quantumthink? : New thinking that will rock your world / Dianne Collins. -- 1st ed.
    p. cm.
  Summary: "The author presents QuantumThink®, her system of thinking that contains twenty-
two principles and practices combining ideas from quantum science and spiritual insights"--
Provided by publisher.
  ISBN 978-1-59079-074-8 (hardbound : alk. paper)
  1. Creative thinking. 2. Quantum theory. I. Title.
  BF408.C5825 2011
  153.4'2--dc22
                        2010000120

Interior design by Janice Benight
Part I opening photo: "Sun Awakening" by Dianne Collins
Part II opening image: "The Creation of Adam" section from the Sistine Chapel fresco by Michelangelo

Manufactured in the United States of America
10 9 8 7 6 5 4 3

For Alan
The love of my life
My best partner in every way
Because of you,
I was able to get this out to the world.

Contents

FOREWORD
by Fred Alan Wolf, Ph.D. (aka Dr. Quantum)

Albert Einstein once said, "We can't solve problems by using the same kind of thinking we used when we created them." Considering that the discoveries of quantum physics have only recently been brought to the attention of common people primarily through the inventions of devices that quantum physics itself has made possible, such as the modern computer and the laser which made possible recording vast amounts of data on new forms of everyday devices, it is already apparent that quantum physics has changed our thinking regarding our technologically advanced world. We now see, practically instantly, what's going on around our world as if it was happening around our corner.

Yet although quantum physics has certainly entered our technological mindset with a bang, few of us have any idea of its potentially more significant impact on our consciousness of ourselves and those around us. Dianne Collins has fully felt this "quantum" impact and as such has dedicated her life to the teaching of others how learning some basic principles of quantum physics can also impact their lives and change their thinking so that solving the problems that our old way of thinking have created becomes possible with a new way of thinking called and invented by her "QuantumThink®."

In a nutshell: So why is understanding the quantum universe important? Because it excites a feeling of delightful deliciousness—life takes on a new vision. First, you find out why it is that you may think the way you think and what conditions have arisen to make you feel that way, and then you can find out how to change them. It inspires a deeper way of inquiry. Asking yourself deeper questions opens up new ways of being in the world. It brings in a breath of fresh air. It makes life more joyful. The real trick to life is not to be in the know, but to be in the mystery.

The old adage *what you see is what you get* appears to apply to the world we see all around us. However, we little appreciate that a different way of observing complementary to the adage exists. It states *what you see is what you expect.* These adages may appear to be saying the same thing, but the two are really quite different. That difference arises from understanding some principles of quantum physics and spiritual practice. Our appreciation of these principles will help us to grasp conceptually what it means to quantumthink.

To accomplish new thinking, we first need to look at how and why the world is not as it seems. This helps us grasp the quantum physics principles involved, particularly how observation changes the world. Next we need to see how and where we lose our ability to think clearly, and why this naturally occurs as a result of our desire for objective or "out there" stimulation. This helps us grasp the spiritual practice principles involved.

Most of us take it for granted that we see the real world. Of course we know that much more of the world exists than what we see with our eyes. There are worlds of sounds, smells, tastes, skin sensations, and thoughts. Although those worlds may appear to be distinct because they appeal to different sense organs, we nevertheless take it for granted that each sense organ only picks out from the world-in-total a particular aspect of that world that registers on that particular sense organ. We rarely consider that any other world exists, although we have learned from the practices of science that the world consists of far more than just that world we sense with our normal senses.

How different is the world of quantum physics from the everyday physical world that we experience using our normal conditioned senses? As a physicist I have learned that it is very different; however, the difference may not be easily appreciated by nonscientists. The quantum physical worldview leads to observations often very dissimilar from the world we ordinarily see. Usually the dissimilarity is difficult to see in everyday life. According to quantum physics principles, there is no reality until that reality is perceived. This means that the world cannot simply exist independently from the means used to perceive that world. We call this *the observer effect*.

This effect, long unsuspected in the physics before quantum physics, first came as a big surprise to the early scientists who discovered it. They saw, at times much to their dismay, that any time they attempted to perform an observation on an atomic or subatomic system, the tools they used to make the observation appeared to introduce uncontrollable errors into their measurements. They were as the adage pictures, "bulls in the china shop" when they attempted to make such refined measurements. However, they soon realized that it wasn't the tools that made the errors in their determinations, but that they had stumbled on a very stubborn part of nature herself. Like a mysterious fan dancer, she always kept part of herself hidden. But when asked to reveal herself, she demanded that each observation, regardless of the measuring tool employed, make its mark on the thing being observed in a completely irreversible and often unpredictable way. Whether they liked it or not every observer ended up disturbing the thing he or she sought to look at. This observation went far beyond eyes alone, and included any sense a human being used to observe from listening to tones coming from an instrument such as a Geiger counter, or watching dots on a flashing oscilloscope. Since anything revealed by observation depended on the observers' choices, *nature* demanded that we must be an integrated part of *herself*, even though our minds sought to believe that a natural and physical world existed objectively separated from us.

Because we usually don't pay attention to ourselves in the perception processes involved in observation, our immediate experience will not appear to show that our actions of perception changed anything. To our unsophisticated minds it just seems we make errors. However, if we construct a careful history of our perceptions they often show us that our way of perceiving indeed changes the course of our observations and even our personal history. Further examination shows that by making different choices, not only would our perceptions of the outcomes change, but also the very things we were observing would also exhibit traits that would not have appeared had we not looked for them.

That may make sense to you when looking at something new and deciding what it means. But you may wonder, "I'm not actually changing reality, am I? I'm just changing my interpretation of reality."

The answer is often difficult to appreciate, but as surprising as it may seem, you are changing reality simply by observing it. In the world described successfully by quantum mechanics, ultimately and fundamentally observers affect the universe whenever they observe it or anything in it. If we refine our ability to see by looking at atomic and subatomic processes with sophisticated instrumentation the differences would be quite magnified from our normal way of seeing and would appear astonishing to our minds.

Physicists' observations of nature taught us a new principle of physics exists in the world. As I simply put it the principle states, *what you see is what you expect.* By choosing one way to see the world, another equally likely aspect of that world becomes hidden. Physicists have carefully made a map of the way our expectations alter our perception of the world. They noticed that there were always two complementary ways of seeing.

Let me give you an everyday example. Suppose you are a student of music. Undoubtedly you learn how to listen to music, particularly how to hear rhythms, motifs or themes, and the notes different instruments sound. While listening to a particular piece of music, you can find yourself listening to particular instruments, say the violins or the trumpets, and by focusing your mind you can pay attention to each note played, and to the beat of the music. Or if you wish you can pay attention to the theme or the blending of the music into a whole. You find from your listening experiences that you can't do both at the same time. In fact paying attention to themes alters your ability to hear notes, while paying attention to notes alters your ability to hear the melodies. This alteration in your observing ability illustrates a principle of complementarity that exists in listening ability.

Take another example. While you are speaking to someone, you most likely find yourself not paying attention to the individual words, consonants, or vowels you use, while you focus on the meanings and nuances of your sentences. However, at times, you find that you must stop speaking and momentarily search your memory for a particular word. Maybe you notice that once you find that word you have to go back and reconstruct your sentence all over again. This illustrates how a principle of complementarity exists in your thought processes.

Probably the most astonishing fact that emerges from a quantum physical study of matter and energy is that a complementarity of our choices affects the results we do observe in a manner similar to the examples shown above, yet somewhat differently. In other words what you choose to observe can not only nullify your ability to observe another complementary aspect, it can render it nonexistent. The difference tells us that what you observe not only hides the complementary aspect from your sensory awareness, it renders it imaginary altogether. It would be as if when you listened to a symphony's melody being played by a grand orchestra, the individual orchestra members disappeared into a sea of sound. But when you decided to listen for the violins, they popped out of the sea while the symphony's melody stopped to make room for your appreciation of the violins' parts.

This quantum physics complementarity principle was made well known more than ninety years ago by the wave-particle duality that showed up in quantum physics and equally mystified its discoverers. That mystery persists to this day and provides a basis for our understanding of modern technology and as you'll see in this book a new way of thinking that will bring a joyful appreciation of the mystery that is you.

Note to Readers

Uppercase is used throughout the book in the QuantumThink distinction titles and for principles directly related to them. Uppercase use is found, for example, in the word "Intent," which is a key principle of the quantum world. The purpose is to use the visual cue of uppercase letters to become familiar with the main principles.

PART I

Wake Up

1

SITUATION
Now

Come in real close to me now, because I am about to become your best friend.
You know what best friends do. They tell you things no one else will dare. Out of
their love for you. Okay, so here it is.

It's a whole new world out there.

Big revelation, you chortle.

And it's not going back to the way it used to be.

(Did you really think it would?)

Okay here's more.

You have no idea how to think for this new world.

This is no fault of your own. We've never been in this situation before. You know
what I mean. Kids know more than parents; you can't understand half of the ads on
TV; the two-party systems (pick any country) have blended into blur. Jewelry is
worn *in* the body, not on it; companies worth billions one day and less than nothing
the next rule the world; and people in jeans and dreadlocks discussing stock trades
have replaced the Perfect Guys in Suits.

"They" are trying to sell you food that Mother Nature didn't grow, and are building space stations for your future home when you're not ready to move. People
touting themselves as compassionate are waging war, while young people blow
themselves up with their parents' consent in order to kill even younger kids. The
information superhighway has no traffic signals and probably never will. Things
move so quick you can't keep up. Furthermore, you're not sure you want to.

Quantum physicists write books on spirituality, government intelligence uses
psychics, and your mortgage broker is now a holistic healer. While you're trying to
figure out who'll be the next *Survivor,* live television audiences are conversing with
dear departed loved ones, and all these ladies are sitting around watching Oprah
every day getting enlightened, while you're still convinced intuition is a woman-
thing. All this is so mind-boggling you can't even think. Precisely my point.

(Drumroll. Enter ... your new best friend ... That's me, remember?)

Old thinking isn't going to cut it in this new world. Hold on to your hat, Friend.
It's time to QuantumThink.

Good, you're still here. I had to say all those things to cut to the chase for all of you bottom-line people.

Okay, so *do you* QuantumThink?

Don't worry about whether you do or not. That was just to entice you so you would be intrigued enough to pick up this book. Hey, don't be insulted—I just wanted to have a chat with you. This may appear as a book in one dimension, but it is really me, a real live human being person over here, talking with you over there, wherever you happen to be in this moment of reading.

Perhaps we don't know each other in the ordinary sense of knowing our personalities and personas or meeting each other physically, yet we can know one another at our essence. What we *can* know is that we are kindred spirits working together on the planet in these very tenuous, both terrifying and terrific times, to co-create a reality that each of us knows is worthy of the most beautiful and brilliant aspects of our humanity, despite mounting evidence to the contrary.

Anyway, you don't have to be concerned about the answer to the question *Do You QuantumThink?* because as you read this book you are QuantumThinking. The important question is *why should you* QuantumThink? There is only one reason. To have a great life. That's it.

Not tomorrow. Not next year. Not when you get everything worked out or the world becomes a better place. Not after you sit on a mountaintop for twenty years contemplating right living. Now.

~~~

This book isn't going to tell what you should do, how you should be, or the way the world should be. It is not going to analyze your psyche or why your past made you who you are today or who you wish you weren't. It isn't going to tell you how to make your productivity higher, your employees more empowered, your money increase, or your relationships work. It is not going to tell you *how-to* do anything to make you richer, thinner, happier, or enlightened.

Wait, don't leave yet!

Now the fact that you may get any of those results, or whatever else you want in life, and much easier and quicker than you thought possible—is likely to happen. But it isn't going to happen because I tell you *how* or what you *should* do, and certainly not what you should think or how you should think.

It will happen because you have *access* to your power to create. It will happen because you will know the workings of your own mind, the way your own consciousness works to generate your world and your experience of life. It will happen because you are aware of a more accurate and expanded view of reality, universal laws that have been underground and out of sight. It will happen because you experience living and thinking from a foundation at the heart of ancient spiritual wisdom now being verified by 21st century science. It will happen because you are QuantumThinking.

Getting what you want in life will happen because you are tuned in to the way reality actually works and the part you play in it, rather than continuing to live in the *illusion* or perhaps *oblivion* that has plagued our culture until now. Illusion means *erroneous belief.* Oblivion means *forgotten.*

A great contemporary spiritual teacher, Gurumayi Chidvilasananda, advises,

> *"If you want to talk to somebody, talk in such a way that your statement provokes contemplation instead of an argument or a challenge or a useless debate. Let this very conversation be one that takes you to the Truth."* [1]

I am not here to prove anything to you. This is not a book to agree or disagree with. (This lets a lot of pressure off both of us!) I am here to speak from my heart to yours, from my mind to yours, soul to soul. At some point you realize we are really one and the same being anyway, so you can consider reading this Self-reflection.

I am not here to tell you something you don't already know at some level of your being. If you didn't know it, you wouldn't be able to relate to it. I am here to presence the more authentic reality you are already sensing, feeling, thinking, or at least wondering about (maybe you're ignoring it).

How do I know this? Because you and I are here sharing the same planet at the same time. One of the great paradoxes of life is we are each uniquely different and yet we are all the same. Whether you are a wealthy mogul who has amassed a personal fortune, or whether you are 16 years old and looking at your future; whether you work in a factory or in construction; whether you're an entrepreneur or educator; doctor, lawyer, artist or programmer up all night writing code; cultural creative or compassionate conservative; celebrity or 15-minute-fame wannabe—this undeniable fact remains the same for us all:

We are in a time of evolution unlike any we have ever witnessed or known, when what must evolve now is human consciousness itself—our own mind and awareness.

Boldly Go Where You Have Never Been
A Voyage Into Your Very Own Awareness

When you hear the word "quantum" you might think of science. QuantumThink is not about science; it *is* about how the discoveries of science shape the way we think. It is not just about "thinking." In many ways it is designed to take you beyond thinking. It is not just learning new ideas; *it is about generating a new condition for your experience of life.*

We are talking about a larger happening, a new stage for our humanity. You and I know it is time—the world is dramatically shifting. Yet, it may not have occurred to you that *it is also the moment for you to shift to a higher state of evolution yourself.*

In this book we present the biggest ideas of the universe as they *relate* in your ordinary everyday life. These principles do not belong to me. They belong to the wisdom of "Infinite Intelligence," that which defies description, is beyond labeling, and transcends definition. Were you thinking you are outside the laws of nature and the cosmos, that you are just an anomaly, an unexplainable accident taking up residence on Earth without paying rent? You are not only *on* the Earth, you are *of* the Earth. This is not biblical language I am speaking. This is natural law. You and I are part and parcel of the physical system of Earth.

You "hang on to your hat" because we are going for a wild ride, a virtual voyage from which there is no return, an adventure into your own awareness. We travel via a route that extends in all directions in space-time and beyond, unrestricted by any historical knowledge or theoretical future.

It may not be all neat and tidy and fit your conventional logic. (It probably won't.) You know how the mind starts in … *I like this, I don't like that. I agree, yes. No, that's wrong. I wish she would do it this way. Why doesn't she get to the point? I love the way that's written. Give me the bottom line. Give me definitions, I like things more clearly defined. Examples, can you give me some examples. Too much talking, too little talking,* and so on and so on.

Lacking mastery, our minds are like this, incessantly chattering away our judgments and opinions and interpretations. There's nothing wrong with this in and of itself. The only point is that it erodes our present-moment awareness. And it is in the state of present-moment awareness where we learn, gain, benefit, develop, expand, and evolve.

‿‿

You are about to have a most powerful experience that will alter your experience of life for the rest of your life. Yes, that's pretty audacious. But that's okay, it had to be said. You may be asking why you would want to alter your experience of life. Your life is just fine, thank you. Okay, I'll tell you.

We have in our culture what we call "grown-ups." That means a person who was once small in size and age, and now is bigger and older chronologically. It's not enough anymore to simply be a grown-up, or even a potential grown-up. It's time for a new culture of *Wake-ups.* "Wake-ups" are people who have been asleep and woke themselves up. Wake-ups can be any age, and of any culture. You're human? You qualify.

Wake-ups are people who wish to awaken from the outworn, conceptual reality and absurdities of everyday living that in our minds don't make sense, in our hearts don't hold true, and in our souls no longer work.

Think about it. We kill each other in the name of the Most Holy, presume politicians to be liars and crooks and then entrust them to lead us, turn guard gate blockades into residential status symbols, pass blasé through elaborate airport security checks just to go on holiday, and produce television "entertainment" that proves the more deviousness you can perpetrate on your fellow companions, you'll not only survive, you'll become rich and famous and get a book deal.

Saints and sages throughout the ages have admonished us, *Wake up!*

Outer circumstances can wake you up, but that's no fun. On the contrary. (Witness the infamous 9/11 debacle and its aberrant offspring.) Imagine ... you are in a nice comfortable sleep and the alarm shrills. Not very pleasant. Now imagine you are in a nice comfortable sleep and you awaken with the morning light. Instead of setting the alarm, you set the Intent for that in your own mind, in your own consciousness, and it happens, *naturally*. You generated your own awakening. *That's* nice.

We have lots of circumstances that can wake us up that are the alarm clock jolt: disease, destruction, disaster. And on another level, embarrassment, humiliation, reprimand. None of it too appealing.

Another problem with being awakened by an external force is that it's too easy to fall back asleep. You know, just hit that snooze button and you're back where you were. Look around. The flags are down. Immediately following 9/11 politicians reached across ideological aisles of separation to literally *hug*. People around the world were united for a brief yet momentous instant of recognition of humankind as one. American flags were flying, two at a time from car windows. People willfully slowed down to let you in the lane. They looked at you with presence. You connected with them. *Later that month* ... the flags are down. Try to fight your way into the next lane in rush hour traffic. Touch the snooze button and you're back to sleep. You see what I mean about Waking Up.

<hr/>

Sometimes we must notice what's happening in the outer world to reflect our inner state back to ourselves. **It's no secret. The changes we are feeling and seeing now are revolutionary. Actually, you could say they are** *evolutionary.* In a few short years our entire world is different. It's global. It's instant communication and access to all information, 24/7. We are more interconnected and interdependent than ever. The unrelenting pace of change, infinite choice, and unfathomable uncertainty are signs of our systems and cultural ways reaching their limits, beginning to crumble and fade away, making room for a more workable culture to emerge.

Everything is intricately interrelated: our ecology to our economics, our economics to our politics, our politics to our fears, our fears to the confusion and questions of our youth, and the questions of our youth to the continuance of life.

On the other side we also see the changes related to our invigorated strength in uniting, to the opportunities of building societies anew, to the passion to create a future brighter than would be possible predicated on patterns of the past. There is much to acknowledge in terms of miraculous accomplishments, and still a long way to go when you think of the continued unrest in so many areas, the suffering of millions, tragedies of spirit, of humans' inhumanity to humans and to our Mother Earth herself. And if you think this doesn't affect you and me personally, daily, you're kidding yourself.

We've all become pundits at pointing out the shortcomings and wrongdoings of ourselves and our fellow humans (especially *them.*) We're still treating each other as separate, still reacting to our differences, still treating Earth, host organism of our life, like it doesn't matter what we do to her, still behaving as if national boundaries are absolutes rather than arbitrary agreements, still operating in the Fear mode, stockpiling weapons for power in the name of the lord or our country.

If we are not killing people physically, we kill them off in other ways. We gossip about them, denigrate them, persecute them, sue them, prosecute them. We morally destroy them. We make them pariahs, damage their reputations, ruin their lives and the lives of their families. All in the name of *right*-eousness—or TV ratings. This isn't just about "them" either. Spiritual path notwithstanding, don't we subtly kill off a little spirit in our loved ones every time we snap at them, criticize them, resist them, or simply don't listen when they speak?

A modicum of common sense will tell you we need to start thinking in a new way. Pre-9/11 we were overwrought and overwhelmed. Now we're frightened to death and stymied for solutions. Decisions we make now set the trajectory for decades to come. Yet, plausible, satisfying answers elude us in every area of life, from personal relationships to world conflicts to the deeper questions of meaning and purpose.

Despite visible hints of a new world culture and a burgeoning quest for spiritual connection, the pull of the old world prevails, an Either/Or world of separation that crescendos in confusion, culminates in conflict and keeps our collective sanity in check.

All right, then, aren't we ready for a new spin on this?

Suppose there is nothing actually "wrong" with us. It's not that we *want* to be derisive and divisive. Consider that we have simply been caught unawares in an automatic negative spin, in an inaccurate, limited view of reality that until now has been undistinguished and never brought to light.

The dilemma: We're living in a Quantum Age trying to use Industrial Age thinking and it's not working. The picture is moving ahead and the sound track isn't keeping up. We're out of sync with the nature of reality. What's worse, we don't even know it.

Let's not get too somber here, not to worry. You don't have to attend the Hogswart School of Magic to transform yourself from a muggle to a wizard. What can bring relief? QuantumThink. Well, yes. *Naturally.*

~~~

QuantumThink is a new system of thinking that has come through me.

Okay, back up a minute—"come through me"—what does that mean, I'm a channel or something? You and I and every one of us are channels of some knowledge or wisdom, born with distinctive gifts and talents we are here to give to the rest of us. *Wisdom distribution channels*, you could say.

You may think you are here to amass wealth and spend it on yourself and your family, and try to build up a protection shield from all the ills of the world "out there." (Hey, why not? It's a multidimensional universe of Infinite Possibility and all that may be in there, too.) Still, each of us has a unique purpose, and when you discover yours, life becomes so much easier and definitely more fun.

Anyway, we'll get to *that* (Your Purpose) later. For right now, let's just say I got the cosmic tap on the shoulder and was told to get this out into the world.

～～

Changing the world ... one thought at a time ... *Sigh* ...

I don't think so.

Can you imagine the agony of such a task, not to mention the utter impossibility of it?

QuantumThink is a new *system* of thinking. A system of thinking is beyond a creative or clever idea. A system is a whole, a gestalt, a field. You get everything, all at once.

We live in a universe of systems and our everyday world is comprised of systems. Yet, it doesn't occur to most of us that we *think* in one system or another.

When you drive to the grocery store or the local marketplace, every system along the way is shaping your actions. The door of the house or apartment you are walking through to get outside, the road system with its speed limits and red and green stop and go lights, the sequence of the aisles in the supermarket—all these are systems. Even the food options we have available to us are a result of a complex of systems, from growing methods to government regulations to marketing and economic systems.

A system is like a vortex. Once you're in, it takes you with it. If you try to drive outside the road system, you'll only get so far until you are forced back inside the system.

This is why when you try to change something, the change often doesn't work or doesn't last. Even a novel idea or the most brilliant plan is likely to get swept into the powerful force of the existing system. When you QuantumThink you do not attempt to change the current system; you think in a *new* system.

QuantumThink deals with the system of all systems for human beings— consciousness itself. The operating system in your computer is what allows for all the other applications to work. The "operating system" for human beings is our own mind.

~~~~~~~~~~~~~~~~~~~~

QuantumThink-Wave
Thought, Consciousness, Awareness, and Mind

There is something that precedes thinking yet is simultaneous with it and that is conscious awareness, or consciousness. **What is consciousness?** You don't need anyone to tell you what consciousness is because you experience it yourself directly. Just for a moment, right now ... become aware of what you are aware of. Watch your own thoughts. Become aware of your own awareness.

Consciousness as we speak of it here is that aspect of ourselves (of life!) from which all else springs forth. That place which is unbounded, from which all ideas and attributes derive, but which has no limiting attributes or descriptions itself. It is free, unbounded, and that which enables us to know anything at all because in essence it is *awareness*.

The place of silence that the great Beings speak of is that place where we are aware of awareness itself. To even speak of consciousness, however, requires thought—words and meaning expressed through language. In this way, consciousness becomes individualized as your mind. This is what we mean when we speak of mind.

~~~~~~~~~~~~~~~~~~~~

Imagine the scientific principles governing our awesome technology applied to the human mind—to your own thinking. The principles are here ... *waiting for us.*

~~~

Reality's changed, Dude.

"Everything you now know about the universe and its laws is more than likely to be 99.99% wrong."
> —Dr. Fred Alan Wolf, *physicist and author*

Imagine waking up one day and discovering that everything you thought you knew about the nature of reality and the way life works was, well, ... *wrong*! Incorrect. Null and void. This is no imaginary story.

Why was Albert Einstein named the Person of the Century by *Time* magazine over revered political and spiritual icons such as Ghandi and Mother Teresa? Einstein's discoveries literally and fundamentally altered our entire picture and understanding of reality. A *new world view* is emerging. In many ways this "new" view has been around forever. We simply haven't been aware of it. We've been glued, bleary eyed, watching a single black-and-white station when digital cable has arrived.

However real the world of "solid" objects and "fixed" circumstances may seem to our ordinary five senses, the fact is we are living in a multidimensional universe that has been spoken about for thousands of years in the perennial wisdom of our spiritual traditions, and is now being verified by modern science. Ours is a universe comprised not of solid physical objects, but of energy continuously in flux, vibrating frequencies, always moving and changing. We live in a world comprised not of dead or inert matter, but of intelligent living systems, whole systems—a world not restricted by old concepts of time and space, but a world at its source beyond space-time. Sounds abstract, yet this amazing reality is reflected all around us in our technology.

We construct parallel worlds in the virtual dimension of the Internet, TV, and movies. Energy medicine is becoming a standard. The focused light of lasers is used to penetrate human membranes and bore through metal. *What is invisible to us,* radio waves, microwaves, and hair-thin glass fibers carrying communications through pulses of light, *has transformed the world.*

Just think ... If not for this revolution in science you and I wouldn't have the chance to complain about people using cell phones in restaurants or attend a wedding in space via videophone. We couldn't witness a war across the world, collectively contribute a billion dollars over the Internet to our brothers and sisters in need, or download 10,000 of our favorite songs into an MP3 player that fits in our pocket.

Relativity and quantum science have altered our "outer" world. But what about you and me? Our technology has indeed surpassed us. We know the word *holistic,* we can repeat the noble declarations: *We are One, do unto others ... judge not ...* but mostly they're just concepts because we don't *really* live that wisdom.

People are ready to make changes. *Yet there are ways of thinking—firmly established patterns of relating and deeply ingrained beliefs embedded in our culture—forming the condition from which we attempt to make these changes.* Einstein's edict, *the problems we have cannot be solved at the same level of thinking that created them,* has become a modern day mantra not just because it makes sense; it has never been more relevant.

2

PREMISE

As you think, so you become

In television writing, a premise for a story is proposed, and people ask you, *Then what?* (what happens next), *Who cares?* (why should I care), *What's at stake?* (what are the consequences; what will I gain or lose). Our Intent is to keep addressing those questions. All right, then ...

Why Should I Care?

What makes our thinking so important, anyway?

When we observe ourselves, what do we see? We are all human beings here on planet Earth. By a great, mysterious force most of us refer to as Divine, we have been granted the gift of life. Okay, now what?

What do we really want? You could answer this on a personal level, and what we each want would take a different form, or you could answer this on a universal level that everyone could relate to. Either way, the answer is obvious: We want what we want. Whether you yearn for spiritual awakening or material gain, emotional satisfaction, or all of the above—we want our desires fulfilled. We seek results. We want our life and the world to work, and work well.

Whether you seek peace of mind and a state of happiness and tranquility or a feeling of excitement and enthusiasm about being alive every day when you open your eyes from sleep; whether you long for a mansion or a modest home with a white picket fence; whether you yearn to be a political leader, business mogul, sports icon, or remain anonymous; whether your passion is to save the whales, end world hunger, or be the reigning queen of hip-hop, the basic fact is—we all want what we want.

The question becomes: how do we get it? The logic is simple. In order to create what you want in life, you would have to know something about what enables us to create anything. We are not speaking in terms of the ultimate Divine creation but in the realm of our everyday human affairs; an ordinary person's ability to create what he or she desires. What *does* enable us to create anything?

Thought creates reality.

As you think, so you become.

As I was growing up, along the way I learned, *thought creates reality*. The mastery traditions proclaim this: *As you think, so you become*. The Buddha said, *All that you are is a result of what you have thought*. The Christian and Judaic Bibles read, *As a man thinketh in his heart, so is he*. In the Upanishads, the *rishis*, holy men of ancient India, teach: *One's own thought is one's world; what a person thinks is what he becomes*.

Thought creates reality. I began to see this studying philosophy in graduate school. People would ask me, *Why study philosophy? What are you going to do with that? What's the good of it? What's the use of it?* At the time those questions rattled me, but it soon became a bit of a cosmic joke because when you study philosophy you discover that thought is the foundation of everything, from the small individual action and idea, to the large collective reality. Every one of the institutions we live within—our educational, governmental, judicial, economic, and health systems—regardless of what culture you reside in, all begin, are sustained, and end in thought.

Our predominant habits of thinking shape our actions and generate all of our results. The mind, an individualized form of the all-pervasive consciousness from which thought derives, is the great instrument of life. What fills our consciousness—our thoughts powered by intent, the meanings we ascribe to those thoughts, and our emotional responses to those meanings—gives us our moment-to-moment experience, determining our actions and our outcomes.

～～

Thought creates reality. I pondered, I mused, I contemplated this. *Thought creates reality? Well, okay, how does it do that?* I wondered. And furthermore, if all you had to do is change your thoughts to change reality, then why does the world still look like it does, with all the conflict and war and poverty and hunger and endangered species and the rest of the problems that seem to endlessly hang around?

It's not as if we don't *know* what to think and what to do. Spiritual and practical wisdom from every tradition has been available to us through the spoken and written word since time immemorial. Shelves of mega-bookstores are lined with how-tos, techniques, and formulas for living, instructing us what to do and how to be.

If all we have to do is change our thoughts to change the world, then *with six thousand years of wisdom available to us at the click of a mouse, how is it we are still not living it?*

These vexing questions propelled me to search for a real *access* to creating a life that is joyful and sublime. And what did I discover? **One vital, crucial key has been missing: We imagine we think freely, but we don't.**

3

REVELATION
The myth of choice

Yes, *of course*, we could alter reality with our thinking, that is, *if* we were in command of our thinking.

As much as you and I love to fancy ourselves independent thinkers, consider that your thinking is not random. Like everything in this vast universe, *our thinking takes place in a system*, as a system, based in the reality current we are traveling in known as our "world view." A world view is simply that: the way we view the world—our ideas, notions, and beliefs of what we hold to be true about the nature of reality, including what's possible and what's not, including what we are capable of or not.

Our world view comes to us through the discoveries of scientists and other thinkers whose job it is to investigate the nature of things and how they work. Then they come back and tell the rest of us of their findings. They invent new language that filters into our common language shaping our thinking and outcomes in ways we're not even aware of.

Take the idea of a *quantum leap*. The phrase first entered our language around 1927, a few decades after German Nobel Physicist Max Planck discovered that energy did not move smoothly and continuously as previously believed but instead moved in packets of "quanta" in discrete, unpredictable light bursts he called *jumps*. Now we use "quantum leap" to mean an abrupt change discontinuous with the past, a giant leap. Today someone says, *Wow, that was a quantum leap*, and we know exactly what they mean.

Our world view not only shapes what we think; it *allows for* what we are even *able* to think. Were you *able* to think about a quantum leap prior to 1927? Okay, you're too young for that, but you get my drift.

Even though a world view seems philosophical and distant from the everyday and is typically not even spoken about in daily life, the beliefs we have about the nature of reality shape our entire way of life and allow for what's possible in our life. If someone told us prior to 1971 (more like 1995 for most of us) that a virtual world wide network would revolutionize daily reality, *shaping* our entire way of personal communication, connectedness, and commerce, we might not have even believed it.

We imagine we think "freely," unaware that our thinking is shaped, guided, conditioned, directed, *programmed* by this background version of reality that we collectively organize ourselves around, invisibly and silently serving as the context of our lives.

14

Okay, would-be television writers, go ahead and ask: *why should we care?*

We should care because our "current" thinking is shaped by an *old world view* based in assumptions about the nature of reality that are largely inaccurate or limited at best! Not only that, since the old world vision was of the universe as *machine* (forgive me for saying this), in many ways our thinking and we have become automatic and mechanical, too.

We imagine we think freely, but we don't. We live in the illusion that we are consciously choosing our thoughts, that we have mastery over our minds and actions. We have the *possibility* of choosing, we have dominion, we have sovereignty, yes, we're in charge. But to the extent that we are conditioned by a limited world view and don't realize it, to the extent that we are automatic and are unaware of it, we are not actually at choice.

Mechanical "thinking" shows up subtly everywhere. Many opinions are this way, as are many of our beliefs, interpretations, aversions, and attractions. Think about a machine. Once it is set up it just runs on its own.

Did you ever intend to be one way, but you cannot help but notice you're acting some other way? You want to be sweet and loving and cheerful—to your mother, your boyfriend, your associate, your wife—and instead you notice you are irritated, agitated, resistant, not loving and pleasant at all. Or, you think of yourself as kind and benevolent. But a friend says something you don't like and you *automatically* strike back or want to retaliate. You desire to be guilt-free, liberated from "shoulds" and "ought-tos"; however, you're very clear that this free and easy state is eluding you. Do you imagine you are at choice in these situations? You wouldn't *choose* to feel guilty, would you?

On a global scale, haven't you ever wondered why everyone wants peace, but we still have wars and have actually built an entire complex industry and world economy and international relations around the intentional goal to ally, to attack, destroy property, and kill people *en masse*? (I realize in another context these decisions are "justified" because we are under attack or fear we are under threat of attack. We're simply looking at the discrepancy in "thinking" here.)

All those thousands and millions of holiday greetings proclaiming "Peace on Earth." Sit-ins and stand-ins and bed-ins and naked lie-downs all in the name of Peace. Beautiful, moving expressions. We are "choosing" peace, yet the wars continue. Call these cultural habits our *collective* automatic and mechanical ways.

We are conditioned to stimulus-response. The advertising industry uses this to great advantage. Imprints. Like Pavlov's famous dogs conditioned to activate a particular behavior by associating it with a bell, you like the girl's leg stepping out of the car, you buy the car. There is nothing wrong with stimulus-response in and of itself. Actually, this is one of the great faculties of our mind. For instinctual and biological survival, the automatic mechanisms are essential. However, without *awareness* of this mechanism, you are truly not at choice. When we are in the automatic stimulus-response, knee-jerk reaction, not only is there no *independent* thinking; in a very real sense, *there is no thinking going on at all.*

～～

Are you sitting there telling yourself you are immune to old world view automatic conditioning? None of us want to think of ourselves as "mechanical" and really, it's not personal. I know you like examples so I'll show you a few.

Why does $39.95 appeal to you more than $40? Is it really because you are saving five cents? When something doesn't go your way, do you *automatically* blame something or someone else? When you are on holiday, do you find yourself spending half the time comparing it to where you went last year rather than enjoying where you are "now"? Are your decisions run by the minutes on the clock or the balance in your bank account or the numbers on the right side of the menu? When your health needs attending to, do you *automatically* go to the conventional approach, even when *it is known not to be a cure,* ruling out other healing modalities? (Do you even *know* of them?)

Anyway, it doesn't really matter what examples we use. The point is to just notice all the ways we behave or "think" automatically, even when those actions don't even make sense.

I realize this is not a particularly appealing idea, that in many ways we're functioning on autopilot and that for the most part, choice is a myth. *Fret not, friend.* This is good news! When you see how our world view has conditioned us to react to life in automatic, limited, and mechanical ways, you breathe a sigh of relief, knowing *it's not personal, it's cultural—a stage of evolution we now have the opportunity to transcend.*

4

REALITIES
World views and you

Context is everything.

Dr. Phil, advises, *Get real*. But what is real? It depends. As much as we would like to pin things down and get certainty, there is, in fact, no "way that it is" out there, outside of your given perspective. Reality is Context-dependent. Context is a space, a frame, a perspective, a lens. The overarching perspective is our world view—the ideas, beliefs, and notions we live by, often without even realizing it. A world view is a powerful context shaping everything we think, everything we do, everything we create.

Every one of us wants to feel we have command over our life. If Reality is Context-dependent, doesn't it behoove us to check out the context we're living from? To contrast the classical-mechanical world view with the quantum world view is to grasp the magnitude of the opportunity before us. When you examine how the old world view has shaped our thinking, our attitudes, and our actions, our outcomes and our institutions, this is a form of waking up. You experience a big "Aha!"

When you are aware of the principles and can distinguish between systems, you expand your perspective. You liberate yourself from the constraints of old world view conditioning. Authentic choice becomes possible.

Consider that whatever reality current (world view) we are traveling in, we are going to be subject to the "laws" of that system. Until you can tap into the distinctions of our emerging new world view, you have little access to the benefits of a quantum reality.

Even though the principles are operating, they're not operating for *you*.

> *"Quantum theory is a completely different picture of reality so it should concern us all but it is hardly known outside physics and chemistry and not even properly understood by many in those fields. Yet if, as I hope basic science becomes part of general awareness, what now appear as the paradoxes of quantum theory will seem just as common sense to our children's children."*
> —STEPHEN HAWKING, *Science in the Next Millennium*
> *Remarks at the White House Millennial Evening, Monday, April 26, 1999*

"Common sense to our children's children"? We don't have to wait *that* long. *Experts say* (I love that phrase; it covers so much territory) ... experts say it can take fifty to a hundred years for scientific discoveries to reach the public mind and awareness. Quantum principles will filter into our culture and into our thinking— *eventually*. When you QuantumThink you take things into your own hands—now. You consciously condition your own thinking, of your own volition.

If you are sitting there with a fervent desire to get right to the QuantumThink distinctions, go ahead and skip to Part II of the book. That will work. Or you can stick around for a few other conversations I thought you would enjoy, starting with a real quick primer of old world view/new world view characteristics. It will reveal to you the dramatic differences of these realities and you'll be amazed at the ways each system of thinking plays out.

Our concern is not so much to learn the details of the science or even that any of this is fascinating. Our interest here is intimately personal: What can this mean for us in our relationships, in the ways we connect and the quality of our communication, in our approaches to accomplishing, in our moment-to-moment enjoyment and peace of mind? Think about those important aspects of *your* life as we take the tour.

A real quick primer: Old World View/New World View and why we should care

The Industrial Age and its mechanical marvels were made possible as a result of the classical physics that began in the 17th century with Sir Isaac Newton and continued to develop throughout the 19th century. In this *classical-mechanical* (aka "old") world view, only "matter" mattered, the seemingly solid physical-material reality we glean with our ordinary five senses. You can imagine how science began with that. You're a scientist sitting around on the Earth, looking up and out at the world around you, wondering: what's it all about? Look around you now. What are you aware of? Things around you; things that appear separate from us.

Theirs was a science based upon absolutes, certainty, and prediction: a linear, logical, rational world of solid objects reducible to their constituent parts, fixed objects that moved only when an outside force was exerted on them. There was always a "cause and effect" behind every action—the world as a perfect clockwork machine. If we could analyze the parts and figure out how they worked together, we could predict and control everything.

Also during the 17th century the French philosopher, René Descartes, best known for his famous conclusion, "*I think, therefore I am*" strengthened the idea of separation and parts by declaring mind and body as *separate*, that each of us are isolated egos inside our bodies.

Why should we care? Because a world of fixed and solid objects renders us powerless victims in the face of fixed circumstances. In that view we are destined to be the effects of whatever unchangeable forces happen to come our way. (TRANSLATION = YOUR WIFE, YOUR BOSS, YOUR PARTNER, ARE NOT GOING

TO CHANGE AND THERE IS NOTHING YOU CAN DO ABOUT IT.) We should care because an Either/Or world of predictable outcomes drastically limits the possibilities. (TRANSLATION = INFINITE POSSIBILITY HAS BEEN DOWNSIZED.) We should care because A ONE-DIMENSIONAL VIEW OF REALITY HAS NO SOUL.

Quantum Relief

Fortunately for us, early in the 20th century along came Einstein and relativity and the proponents of quantum theory to make discoveries that surprised the world and unearthed many of the earlier "truths," turning the old world view topsy-turvy.

Scientists began to prove in the laboratory what sacred texts have revealed and what many of us have felt in our hearts and souls—that the universe is a multidimensional unified whole, and that all of us and everything are intricately interconnected. There are distinctions, but no real separations; just whole living systems interpenetrating one another in an evolutionary dance of energy and information.

If the classical world view saw the universe as a giant Machine, the quantum world view sees it as a giant Mind.

In the quantum view, there is no static or absolute reality. (TRANSLATION = WE ARE NO LONGER STUCK WITH THE WAY THINGS "ARE.") Everything exists as Infinite Possibility (with certain probabilities). Exactly which possibility manifests is dependent on the Observer. (TRANSLATION = DEPENDENT ON YOU.)

Objects are not solid as we perceive them to be with our ordinary five senses, but mostly empty space; fluttering with fluctuations of energy. (TRANSLATION = REALITY IS MALLEABLE.)

Matter can exist as a wave or a particle. (TRANSLATION = "OPPOSITES" ARE BOTH TRUE, AND AT THE SAME TIME.) Particles are not particles, but are more like tiny vibrating strings. (TRANSLATION = YOUR "VIBE" REVERBERATES OUT TO THE WORLD WHETHER YOU REALIZE OR NOT.) Chaos is self-organizing. (TRANSLATION = YOU DON'T HAVE TO WORK SO HARD TO GET THINGS "RIGHT.") Energy moves backward and forward through time. (TIP: THROW OUT YOUR OLD CONCEPTS OF TIME.) Energy does not flow smoothly in a straight line path, but "leaps" in bursts from orbit to orbit with no pathway in-between. (TAKE A QUANTUM LEAP. *RELAX*, YOU ALREADY HAVE.)

Your mind may be jumping to, *well, I know about quantum reality*. Perhaps you are a student or a scientist, even. You've read the books of brilliant quantum physicists, perused the proofs, and studied theories of the greats. You've been in workshops, seminars, and conferences of visionaries expounding the quantum domain, exalting its implications. You've meditated and cogitated and surfed websites and saw the movie, *What the Bleep Do We Know?!* five times over, or whatever way you've heard this.

Despite vast resources of knowledge about the quantum reality, your thinking and mine have been conditioned (read: programmed) by the old world materialist, mechanistic view that continues to dominate our consensus society. **We are living in a quantum world, but unbeknownst to even the brightest and the best of us, our thinking stubbornly remains industrial age quality. Until you can make this distinction in yourself, you have information, not transformation.**

Context is everything. If you are living from the context of the old world view, *and you are unable to make that distinction in your awareness,* you are going to be shaped by the "laws" of that system, by default—just because it's already "there."

Consider that at an earlier stage of our social development, we needed to learn to observe, organize, categorize, analyze, formula-ize, even predict and control. In many arenas, we still need to do this. We couldn't survive without those aspects of ourselves. It becomes problematic when we get lost in the illusion that one slice of reality is the whole pie.

Reality Bites
A Taste of the Classical World

The classical-mechanical view has served us up a taste of reality a là:
I'll take Matter, sliced; keep the Spirit on the side, and hold the Soul.

Imagine how those "facts" would shape our thinking and the way we are with one another. A world based in physical sensory data means I can know only what I can see, hear, touch, taste, or smell; no knowledge beyond the senses is available or *real.* You are separate from me, and my mind is separate from my body. We see things and each other as separate, our differences as points of contention. We live in life compartmentalized: business and personal, management and labor, spiritual and material.

In a world of solid objects we attempt to manage our results by *force*—pushing or pulling on circumstances (people, emotions, things) to get something to happen. There is nothing I can do about "fixed" circumstances except try to change them, or at best, adapt myself around them, a victim of circumstances.

Decisions are automatically swayed by the boundaries of Either/Or persuasions: English or Irish, Democrat or Republican, Liberal or Conservative, Muslim or Jew. In a world of *parts,* we say we have to "balance" personal and professional life like a scale. Add more time here, less time there, or get "more quality time." In this view, we may never be able to balance the parts enough, or even know that we had, if we could accomplish it!

Either/Or thinking embroils us in conversations of dubious merit—in business, whether to focus *Either* on the so-called "hard" results of profit and production, *Or* the "soft" areas of vision and values; in politics, having to over-generalize or make inept decisions because you are pulled to have to side with *Either* one party *Or* the other.

We are reluctant to commit to a decision until we can see the *predictable* future result. We want to know in advance: How is this relationship going to work out? What will happen if I accept this job or invest in this new business or decide to marry? We want to *determine* beforehand: What if I take a stand on an issue, a vision I have for myself, or for the world at large? If time moves in one direction only, once an event has taken place, there is nothing I can do to alter it.

We live oriented around one dimension of the physical when reality is multidimensional. We make decisions from obvious options even though we live in a world of Infinite Possibility. We're attempting to use ordinary logic, linear thinking, and the confines of chronological time in a world that's become time-less and spaceless. We struggle for certainty when the very *essence* of life is its *un*certainty.

The classical-mechanical world view has conditioned us to draw conclusions and live from those conclusions as if they are "absolute truth." Now we realize our everyday world is not absolute. According to scientists, there is no objective world "out there" separate from us to be described, analyzed, and pinned down. It is a world of Energy In Flux, always shifting and changing, and we creatively interact with it. Reality is Context-dependent. We are the ones shaping what we see based on whatever *we bring* to our observation. Physicist Fred Alan Wolf says it this way: *"There's no 'out there' out there."*[2]

No Wonder!
Aha! Awareness

When you realize how a classical world view has shaped us, so many things become clear. Your "aha! awareness" prevails. You gain a cosmic perspective. You gain a *comic* perspective. When you grok how all the confusion and confounded-ness have come about, you lighten up about it.

When you realize that the materialist world view has oriented us around the physical as the only thing "real," you can understand how words like *soul* and *spirit* and *heart* and even *love* have been taboo in corporate and professional milieus. Even with the recent trend toward "spirituality in the workplace" you comprehend why in many companies people are still uncomfortable with their mention.

When you live in a universe of parts rather than wholes, and are not living the reality of Holistic & Holographic systems, you can see why we have focused on *effects* rather than getting to the *source* of problems. You fathom why our judicial systems make pariahs of people who have gone out of harmony with themselves and society and outcast them even to the point of executions, killing them like it was nothing, rather than getting to the *source* of what conditions in society are causing the deviant criminal behaviors in the first place.

When you understand that our institutions are born from the outdated idea that *matter* is fundamental, you begin to understand why Western medicine, as brilliant and groundbreaking as it is, has primarily focused on the physical body, rather than on our multi-dimensions, including energy, subtle energy, spiritual, and mind influences on health. You can see why medicine was led to focus on isolated parts or singular chemicals of the body rather than on integrated whole systems.

When you distinguish the characteristics of the old world *reductionist* view that "the whole is equal to the sum of its parts," you get insight into how holding things as separate and disconnected might enable the ambiguity of killing people who have committed crimes while fighting vehemently for the rights of unborn fetuses or cells in a Petri dish.

You glean that a reality system based in the physical dimension would condition us to make judgments about and even reject others just because they look or think or act differently than we do.

When you see that we've been embedded in a world view of *parts* and *separateness*, you sense that the erroneous notion of being separate could lead to equating differences with antagonisms and result in the unabashed lunacy to think that just because *you* believe something that it is "absolute truth." You see how this *fiction about the nature of reality*—that we are separate from one another—could be the source of a horrific movement to kill off people of all religions or cultures other than your own, whether killing them off physically or spiritually.

This is not in any way to condone or justify crimes against humanity or nature. This is simply to distinguish how a reality system gives rise to results that we are so accustomed to, in many cases we literally don't see them. Distinguishing makes us aware of them. Understanding these outcomes (effects) at their source does raise the possibility of being able to educate and generate an enlightened society.

When you realize the extent to which we live ensnared in dry intellectual "concept"—rather than from an awakened heart in touch with the conscious experience of spirit springing forth from our soul—you can understand how a distorted world view has cultivated a humanity who willingly devotes billions of dollars to weapons of mass destruction and organized, strategic killing while devoutly quoting the scriptures. You can see why the total disconnect exists between the *illusion* and the *actuality* of the way we are being. When you begin with a fundamental premise that is out of harmony with universal natural law, it is logical you would end up with confused and incoherent ways of being. The commandment *Thou shalt not kill* didn't come with a footnote citing exceptions.

～～

The medical paradigm, our business cultures, our legal, political, and judicial systems are all construed from this limited model, the classical thinking of times long gone by. There is nothing right or wrong with any of this. It is simply how the classical-mechanical reality current affects us. One thing seems haltingly apparent: *this old world view has reached its limit of effectiveness.*

TV writers everywhere, I hear you. *What are the consequences?*

~~~

Turn your world inside-out, upside-down, and backwards... it just might work.

When you begin to think in whole systems and witness the interconnectedness and interrelatedness of everything, you literally get a new lease on life.

As you think, so you become. For years it was only underground. Now scientists are beginning to concur. The ill health situation is reaching proportions that demand it. When you are at the effect of negative habits of thinking, it affects your health, the economy, and industry.

Contemplate this vicious cycle.

Lacking mastery with your own habits of thinking, fear may arise. Fear of loss (of job, of health, of lifestyle, of partner, of life) generates an automatic reaction to hold back spending (of self expression, of energy, of money, of love, of joy), which results in lower demands for goods and services, which means decreased profits and less investing, which means securities markets plummet.

Bear markets lead to wide-scale layoffs and fewer job opportunities, which generates more fear (due to lack of mastery over one's mind and thinking), leading to emotional stress which can result in increased ill health, which means mounting medical costs that fewer people can afford, leading to overcrowded clinical facilities, which leads to inferior quality health care, contributing to more stress, now in health practitioners as well as in patients. More stress means more illness, and the whole cycle perpetuates itself to no good end. Add to that the proliferation of drugs to treat and/or suppress the *symptoms* arising from these illnesses, with their accompanying litany of "side effects" (that read like your worst nightmare), rather than dealing with the problem at the source, which would enable not only a cure, but prevention. And the beat goes on.

It turns out that what you think is not just interesting or even important; what you think is *vital*, that is, *necessary to the continuation of life.*

> *"The fact is that harnessing the power of your mind can be more effective than the drugs you have been programmed to believe you need."*
> —BRUCE LIPTON, PH.D., *cell biologist, author of* The Biology of Belief

~~~

Socrates was wise enough to figure out, *"The unexamined life is not worth living."* Not because you have to distinguish yourself as some kind of deep philosopher, but because if you don't examine your life, "you" are not truly at choice—life is living you. It is useful to distinguish these things because it wakes us up. We examine the consequences of classical-mechanical thinking habits from *a new context of workableness.* The idea is that from an expanded perspective we can just look, sans reactions, without taking offense or criticizing anyone or anything, to see how things came about. I can't resist poking a *little* fun, though, just to keep us entertained. (If we don't laugh, we'll cry?)

There are plenty of striking examples of similarly "scary" inside-out, upside down and backward cycles once you stand back and look from the whole.

How about the brilliance of manufacturing SUVs that require even more oil in a time when oil is at a premium and continuing to damage the environment, not to mention incite national animosities and international atrocities? What about political leaders disregarding pleas of leading scientists urging development and investment in clean and renewable energy sources—so we don't have to resort to drilling to violate the last vestiges of natural beauty and pristine life, uproot peaceful indigenous peoples, attack and destroy wildlife and precious rainforests that are the source of oxygen and remedies for sustainable health, damage the ozone layer and further upset the already endangered ecological balance of the planet? Gee, ignoring the facts and research really makes a lot of sense, doesn't it? All the profits your company, your political campaign, and you are making from all this are *really* going to do your grandkids a whole lot of good when their Earth's life-sustaining resources are dwindling and they have a hard time breathing. Think this is a stretch? Consider that only a decade ago, the bottled water industry *didn't need* to exist.

How's this for an inverse oxymoron: *organic food*? Paying premiums for organic food? Shouldn't all our food be "organic"? Why do we tamper with food so it creates toxicity in our bodies and clogs our arteries, furthering the ill health epidemic? Inside out and backwards. Willful manufacturing of pesticides and chemicals messing with the fragile human ecosystem. Farmed fish now poisoning nature's own. Defenseless animals that end up on your dinner plate and in your body after being raised in environments of unimaginable filth and disease. Manufacturing products, chemicals, and fuels that cannot be properly disposed of and integrated back into the energy systems of the Earth.

And if you are sitting there thinking you don't really "care" about any of those things, how would you like your precious delicacy, chocolate, made impure by using cheaper vegetable oil instead of pure cocoa butter as a key ingredient? Yes, this is what manufacturers are working on getting approved, folks. No more natural chocolate as you have loved it, and most people won't even realize it happened as there's a fancy name on the package because government standards won't allow them to call it "chocolate" anymore.

Mismanaging the birth, life, and renewal cycles of all the Earth's resources, the bounty we have been entrusted with, squandering away your fortune. Environmentalists, people who are aware and dedicated and looking out for our host, Mother Earth, are often held with disdain, as counterculture. Upside down and backwards. To paraphrase John McEnroe, *We cannot be serious!*

The great master, Jesus, taught: *Forgive them for they know not what they do.* Now we can have true compassion for ourselves and for one another, realizing that these are all outcomes of mechanical world view conditioning and that mechanical reaction to life is not actually at choice. Choice is only possible with awakened awareness.

When you realize that so much of life has become mechanical and that mechanical means unconscious in the sense of being unaware and automatic, you can understand how we have merely endured these glaring, blaring inconsistencies, feeling hopeless to do anything about them, though we're tired to the bone and weary to the brain of our same old problems. We speak here not of your private set of ideas and beliefs; we are talking about a backdrop of our world stage that has been centuries in the making.

When you understand that we have attempted to improve things using the *push-pull* force characteristic of old world view thinking, you can see why worthy solutions have eluded us. You cannot edict the family of humankind, a global family that would not violate one another. You cannot establish the feeling of brotherhood by forcibly conquering disagreeing nations. You will never impose stiff enough fines, or dollar amounts large enough to have big business produce foods that are safe and healthy to eat, and keep our oceans and our air and lands pure, free of pollution and dumping. There will never be a legal suit award large enough to prevent unscrupulous business practices. You *cannot legislate Peace* that would be enduring.

Okay, had enough "real life examples" of old world view "thinking"?

My purpose is neither to rant nor cast aspersions, but rather to cast light— together with you right now—to realize that when we expand our world view and our thinking it's possible, essential, and as you will discover, *actually quite easy* to move beyond the current state of affairs. The vortex of the old world view is powerful, but not indomitable. When you distinguish the *limits* of your thinking, you have choice. Viable possibilities appear right before your eyes.

Fortunately, there is a magnificent gift of life that is at the heart of life itself, and that is its ability to grow, expand, evolve, and bring about transformation resulting in new life forms and greater possibilities. As human beings we *are* that life dynamic. With consciousness and Intent we can direct ourselves to our ability, our power to alter the world, our personal worlds and the one we share. A new world does not happen through force; it is brought about from a naturally awakening state.

When we realize that mastery of our own thinking and being is fundamental, paramount—the alpha and omega—the picture becomes perfectly clear: *Only a culture of Wake-ups will do.*

New World View Thinking
Vive la différence!

How do we think for a world where change is not only constant, it is constantly accelerating? How do we relax when the complexity of choices and demands appears overwhelming? How do we remain centered when uncertainty compounds daily?

When you expand your mind and thinking, miraculous things do happen, quantum leap style. That means there is no logical pathway to how these transformations occur. They are instantaneous. We call them *quantum occurrences*—wonderful things that happen outside your ability to provide an explanation using conventional logic.

What is life on Earth like when you are QuantumThinking? You transcend your limited experience of time and go from overwhelm to relaxed alertness. You are comfortable with change because that is the nature of life. Instead of resisting or merely "embracing" change, you actively work with it. You use change to your benefit. You are no longer daunted by uncertainty; in fact, you appreciate it, knowing that it is only because of things not being firmly in cement for all time that you and I can fashion ourselves and our circumstances anew.

When you are QuantumThinking, you learn how to be healthy from all your dimensions. You are able to transform negative energy experiences into positive ones, instantly, because you know how to work with subtle energy and emotions. You can create contexts that give rise to things working and working well, regardless of how dismal or hopeless they may appear at first blush or on the surface. You establish a different relationship with Time and you accomplish more with less effort. You find yourself *listening* to people, your kids, your parents, your partner, like you've never heard them before and this makes for amazing relationships. You will most likely be supremely grateful to environmentalists for taking an active interest in looking out for your home, Mother Earth. Yes, all this does happen. And guess what else? You restore your sense of humor. Of course, you already realize that.

Quantum physics indicates that there is no "way that it IS" out there—that our "knowing" affects our reality, that our Intent affects our reality, that the Observer shapes the reality. We live no longer in a limited world of fixed Either/Or options. We have entered the world of Both/And, the world of Infinite Possibility. We've moved from a world of fixed, determined certainty to a world of uncertain, probable possibilities where we, as the human observers, are shaping what we see in our "Observer-created Reality."

In the quantum age, we are no longer victims of unchangeable, fixed circumstances. We are reality-generators in a quantum field of Infinite Possibility. If nothing is absolute and reality is Observer-created, then as the Observer, I am the force in my world.

Sounds good! Except for one thing: merely *knowing* all this won't make any difference in your life. No knowledge in the world, no matter how accurate, how profound, how exciting, how divine, even—none of it makes any real difference until and unless you can *live* it.

5

WISDOM
Knowing it and living it are worlds apart

"Everyone else is waiting for eternity and the shamans are saying,
'How about tonight?'"
—ALBERTO VILLOLDO, PH.D., *author and teacher of energy medicine*

It's Time for You to Become Shamans

On the summer solstice of the auspicious year 2000, at a conference in Mérida, Mexico, my husband and I had the good fortune to be in the company of the respected and honored shaman, Hunbatz Men, the Mayan Elder known as the "Day Keeper," or "Keeper of the Knowledge." In traditional cultures, "the knowledge" was handed down by word of mouth from generation to generation. This is how their wisdom was kept alive and passed along by the ancestors.

A *shaman* is considered to be a person of great wisdom, tapped into the many dimensions of reality, adept with the dynamics of the energy and spirit realms, tuned into cosmic laws and esoteric knowledge of the soul as well as the physical domain. Most importantly, a shaman knows the way the multi-dimensions of reality work together.

One day nearing the end of the weeklong conference, Hunbatz Men, a light-hearted spirit, assumed a more serious posture than usual. He walked up to the front of the room and said he had a message for us. Through soulful eyes born of infinity, slowly and deliberately, he looked around at each one gathered there. Palpable silence filled the air. Finally, he spoke. *"Shamans are people who live in wisdom. And now, it is time for all of you to become shamans."* A command so simple yet so compelling, it penetrated, his words reverberating. *Time for **you** to become shamans ... **Live in wisdom** ... **Now.**

What wisdom? The eternal wisdom that every great being and all mastery traditions speak of and teach. The quest for truth and beauty that scientific discovery and artistic creation make visible in the outer world so our rational minds can grasp the sanctity of our collective genius. The wisdom so simple—compassion, kindness, love, service, appreciation, gratitude—that we take it for granted. The special brand of wisdom that comes uniquely through you, entreating you to give it away to others.

What does it mean to live in wisdom?

"Information is not—nor ever was—wisdom."
—Catherine Ann Jones, *screenwriter and author of* The Way of Story

In my library I sit surrounded by a sea of knowledge. Books, tapes, articles, CDs, DVDs. Amazing thinkers, researchers, practitioners, masters. Of what do they teach? Of what do they sing? Each in the way of their calling all point to the same thing: To be in the experience of one's own divine nature, to live the highest humanity one can bring to bear on our situation here on Earth. To express our talents and make our contribution. To cooperate in harmony with all living creatures, cosmic law, and sacred duty. To pray, to play, to live each day in gratitude for the bounty we are given. To keep uncovering how this *Great Mystery* works. To rejoice in bliss simply in being alive.

The difference between merely recognizing wisdom and actually *living* it is vast. We can know the wisdom as information; we can even teach the wisdom. But until we integrate the wisdom, become the walking embodiments of wisdom, dare we even call it wisdom?

～～

"Why comedy? Because there is definitely something funny going on!"
—Swami Beyondananda, *The Cosmic Comic*

Why should we care to break free of our old world view conditioning? If you go around preaching to your friends how one shouldn't judge, and then you get on the phone and start gossiping away your lunch hour, you can see how the automatic habits usurp your own desire to live in wisdom.

You cannot be on a spiritual path at your convenience. Have you noticed how we sometimes do that? All of sudden, you find yourself oh-so-certain about your judgments. Or your circumstances become difficult and you think, so much for the power of Intent and all that jazz. Static on the wisdom channel. These are the times to *really* live the wisdom. Living in wisdom doesn't mean you have to be serious and somber. Catching yourself "in the act" and being able to laugh about it will free you. If you "believe" you are joyful and enthusiastic (because of course you know you should be or want to be), but *in practice* you habitually moan and complain, you can chuckle while you remind yourself that this is like sleepwalking and imagining you are awake.

～～

"I am awake."—Buddha

When we think of wisdom we picture the old man with the long white beard and flowing white hair who has finally lived enough years to warrant the appellation "wise." We encounter a child we deem to be wise beyond her years and we call her an "old soul," like she's been around awhile. We have tended to associate the acquisition of wisdom with the passage of time. Yet, wisdom is truly Beyond Time. Enlightenment happens in an instant.

It is often recounted that when the Buddha was asked if he were a god, an angel, a man, what was he? he replied, *I am awake.* The word "enlightened" stems from the Indo-European root *bheudh* meaning, "to be aware, to make aware," and from the Sanskrit, *bodhati*, "he awakes." Every time you wake yourself up in the moment of catching yourself in the act of your mechanical ways, you are living in wisdom. Awakening can only be a direct, personal, present-moment experience.

~~~

"Have you ever been experienced?"—Jimi Hendrix

Once in a while you hear a voice in your head and it makes perfect sense. It's life altering. It's a high. It's *wisdom*. Wisdom scintillates. It has life force. You feel it tingling in your body. It's your own voice. You think, *Wow, where did that come from?* And that's a good question.

When wisdom comes alive in you, you recognize it. Though you may not be sure how you know it, wisdom is the voice of "truth" within you that emerges triumphant amongst the monotony of opinions, beliefs, aversions, and interpretations—the clear sound of something undeniable.

Where does wisdom come from? Is it stored somewhere in your body or in your brain? Cutting edge scientists say no. The brain is a connector, a receiver, a transmitter. Consider that your entire physical body is a sensing organism that enables you to experience the messages, the meanings, the wisdom. No one has ever found wisdom inside your body or your brain. Then *where does* the wisdom come from? Consider that it is less a "place" and more a "connecting to" or a "tuning in" to the field of all possibilities we call Infinite Intelligence.

Wisdom originates outside of space, time, and matter, yet it is expressed through us in space, time, and matter. Whether you call it the wisdom of your soul, spirit, mind, or heart, when the light of wisdom comes streaming in, you realize that you are a connecting point to the ultimate Intelligence beyond the limits of our mind to fathom, the "Force" that can't be contained and cannot be doubted. As classic comedic actor, Stan Laurel, philosophized to his sidekick, *"It's bigger than both of us, Ollie."*

We live a personal life and a transcendent life simultaneously. Personal life is defined by the specific roles we play out as mother, son, architect, businesswoman in the epic film, Planet Earth. The *transcendent life* is the experience of universal awareness beyond our mundane roles. Many of us have forgotten the transcendent aspect of ourselves. When you live in the experience of being a connecting point, a wisdom channel, you relax. The sense of separation is over. The idea that you have to do it on your own happily fades into the sunset. When the personal and transcendent integrate, wisdom comes alive. In the moment it arrives it's alive … *in you.*

<hr>

Living in wisdom—a noble idea, or who we are?

How do you tune into wisdom? Do you wait until you have a lucky moment and the wisdom shows up? Or is it possible to *consciously, with awareness, choose a life of wisdom*? To live in wisdom is to activate your Intent to live that way.

Maybe *living in wisdom* is not just some noble idea but an aspect of our very being, as natural and essential to us as feeling or thinking. Think about the alternative: *not* living in wisdom? We've seen how that continues to play out in the human drama. What about for you personally? If you are not consciously connecting to wisdom, then what are you doing? What are you working on (or not)? What is your direction? Yes, it's true: Wake-ups (aka QuantumThinkers) live in wisdom.

People yearn for spiritual connection. This is wisdom we want. What if you and I live fulfilled only when we live a life in wisdom, when we *experience connection*? As Hunbatz Men heeded, it really is time for us to become shamans.

Before you get all hung up on that word *shaman*, consider what it really signifies. Let's extrapolate the meaning to our modern lives. *Shamans are people who live in wisdom.* Consider that you cannot "know" wisdom; you can only *be* wisdom.

To live in wisdom means you are aware and responsive to the multi-dimensions of life. To live in wisdom you need knowledge of universal principles. To live in wisdom means you know how these principles work together. To live in wisdom means you use this knowledge as a way of life. To live in wisdom is to have steady wisdom. To live in wisdom means to live in an awakened state beyond mechanical conditioning, in a state of clarity that enables you to connect. To live in wisdom is to *be* the wisdom. Wisdom is only alive when it's alive in you.

<hr>

The QuantumThink system of thinking is not something you merely read nor is it more information to add to your already full storehouse. It is not a new "truth" for you to believe. *It is a direct personal experience of an expanded reality and natural laws at the edge of our knowledge that awakens wisdom within you.* You don't just learn these laws, you imbibe them; you integrate them as a way of life. You connect. You cannot do this conceptually. You cannot do this through your rational understanding. You cannot do this by believing it. It only happens in *your own* experience.

"If there were such a thing as sin, this would be it: to allow yourself to become what you are because of the experiences of others."[3]
THE VOICE OF GOD *in Neale Donald Walsch's book,*
Conversations with God

I could tell you that scientists have proven that we have a nonlocalized mind (that is, not "local," not located in place or space) that can "see" into any corner of the world from anywhere when trained to do so; that children being born today have an advanced level of awareness and intelligence and even a different DNA, and that they are more aware than their teachers and parents in many cases, and that this has also been substantiated.

I could tell you there are energy fields around the body and that people who have developed a gift for seeing or sensing them can discern disease in the energy field before it manifests in the physical body and can work with you to eliminate it right there. I could tell you that the proper use of color, light, and sound can and does heal.

I could tell you that any psychotherapist or psychiatrist who does not understand how the mind gets programmed by language may unintentionally reinforce the very behavior he or she is trying to change.

I could tell you that it is proven in science that the heart's electromagnetic field is five thousand times greater in strength than the field produced by the brain and, in fact, this concurs with what spiritual masters have taught—that the mind is not in the brain; the mind is centered in the heart and transmitted through every cell in the body.

I could tell you there are empirical scientists studying ancient sacred texts and writing about the importance of the inner spiritual journey, and that it is a proven fact of science that meditation and specific breathing practices improve health, mental acuity, and state of mind.

Furthermore, we could list all those studies that prove these facts in an appendix at the back of this book. And then you might say, yes, okay, so ...?

Whether you have opinions about these facts, whether you have skepticism and doubts or totally reject these facts, or whether you embrace these facts, saying "yes, tell me more, I want to know these things" in any case, we could say to our *opinions* or beliefs about them, *so what?* Unless you can *access* these principles in the everyday world of you, your relationships, and your work, it really is, so what. Until you *experience* the value of the knowledge, it really is so what.

Scholars and researchers debate whether consciousness is energy, whether it's light, or whether it is something else altogether that we haven't yet identified. Perhaps we'll never be able to "define" it because its very nature is indefinable. If reality is, as scientists and sages say, Observer-created and constantly in flux, then the goal to find a fixed definition may be superfluous. We may not ever be able to define consciousness; however, we can distinguish the way it works. Whatever it is, as you QuantumThink, you *experience* the creative power of consciousness for yourself. Living the wisdom is not just about having an experience—it is being aware enough to *distinguish* the experience you are having.

~~~~~~~~~~~~~~~

QuantumThink-Wave
Living Wisdom Contemplation

When you distinguish what you do, what you do becomes knowledge.
When you distinguish what you know, what you know becomes wisdom.
When you distinguish your wisdom, you are living it.

~~~~~~~~~~~~~~~

All right then ... thousands of years of wisdom and still not living it? Now we have a plausible reason *why* ... We see how an old world view has conditioned us. And we're clear about *what* ... It truly is time to be shamans. The big question is always ... *how?*

How do we awaken ourselves and think and live from an expanded perspective? If we haven't done it yet, since the beginning of recorded civilization, how does it happen now?

We live in a world of technology based upon discoveries about the nature of reality that are barely one hundred years old, yet we think and live according to principles of an outdated version of reality that is nearly four hundred years old. Realizing it's not just a question of adding more information; what will have us *living the wisdom* of our emerging new world view? How do we make the switch?

From a new world view, consider that "how" might not be the right question.

~~~

I hear you, scriptwriter friends ... *what happens next?*

We arrive at a monumental juncture in our adventure.

6

LEAP
The path of no path

"There comes a point where the mind takes a higher plane of knowledge, but can never prove how it got there. All great discoveries have involved such a leap."
—ALBERT EINSTEIN

Leap Before You Look
You can't get "there" from "here."

You come to the proverbial fork in the road of your life. Humanity stands at the crossroads alongside you. It's time to make a choice. A Big Choice. You can continue to go along with your "old" way of thinking and limiting cultural beliefs you have grabbed onto (many unknowingly) and feel comfortable with (or not), or you can take a new direction. Only we're not on a road. So how do we get there?

Right here, right now, we step into a new reality. Except it's not really a step. It is a leap. We jump systems. We take a literal quantum leap in consciousness to the new world view reality and *look and live from there.* There is a very good reason for this.

You cannot see a new world view from the perspective
of an old world view.

Try to experience the world of a butterfly if you are a caterpillar. You are this creeping, crawling tubular fuzz, restricted to grounded surfaces and probably not traveling too far from home. Now you want to *experience* the reality of this beautiful gossamer winged creature flying high above the ground sometimes, like Monarch butterflies, for thousands of miles. Can't do it. Different reality.

You cannot "see" a new world from the perspective of the old. How can you learn to work with subtle energy if you believe matter is solid? How can you think from Infinite Possibility if you believe what you know now (any of it) to be "absolute"? How can you live the wisdom of compassion for your closest *mates* if you are asleep to your own automatic judgments? You cannot live in an expanded world view from the perspective of a more limited one. At best you will be looking at it through the old filter.

This is the dilemma, isn't it? Because all we have is our current (i.e., old) view to begin with. So what can we do? We take a quantum leap in consciousness. You leap to the new world view reality system and start looking and living from there.

33

It's a quantum leap because there is no pathway or direction you can trace; *there's no how-to.*

〜〜〜

When you walk along a traditional path to a body of knowledge, it typically takes time to get there. It is step by step, incremental. To QuantumThink is to go the route of the quantum particle, the way of no path. Analysis and reason will not get you "there."

When you take a leap to a new thinking system and look *from* there, the whole reality shifts all at once. There is no leading up to a quantum leap. Rather than something that happens gradually over time, a quantum leap happens instantaneously.

"Quantum leap" refers to the fact that a particle of energy can be observed in one moment inside the center of an atom and observed outside of it in the next, *with no observable pathway of the movement* of the particle. It changes orbits. It goes from one energy level to another without passing through any intermediate levels. The energy is said to "leap" from one place to another, without a linear or detectable route.

Reality is Context-dependent.

A shift in context is like this. It is a literal quantum leap. The new science has shown us: Reality is Context-dependent. There is no reality separate and apart from the context in which you are seeing it. When you begin to QuantumThink, you are coming to life in a very different context, a different framework and set of principles than what we could say has been the "default" context, the one that has just been here, automatically. When you QuantumThink you are choosing to think and live *from* natural laws and principles of an expanded, up-to-date view of reality. The key word in that sentence is *from*. You leap first, and *then* you look. You live from quantum principles. The new context shapes your actions and your results. You can't get "there" from "here."

Get hip: Life moves in quantum leaps.

It might seem inconceivable to a mind steeped in (remember, a 400-year history) linear logic to consider that in one moment you are in one world and in another moment you are in another, and there is no way to trace how you got there. The idea of this goes beyond ordinary common sense. And that is precisely the point. As Einstein said with characteristic flair, *"There comes a point where the mind takes a higher plane of knowledge, but can never prove how it got there."*

Only a quantum leap will do. There is no how-to; you may not be able to "prove it" using conventional methods. However, you can *experience* a quantum leap in consciousness. It's effortless. I'll show you.

Experience a Quantum Leap in Consciousness—Right Now

Imagine where you are located in this moment. Typically we identify ourselves as located within our physical body looking out at everything around us. This is our normal perspective. We stand on the Earth and we look out at the stars and the moon and the rest of the cosmos from this apparently individual body-centered perspective.

Okay, now imagine it is the other way around. Imagine yourself outside of yourself looking back at yourself. Imagine yourself outside the Earth looking back at the Earth, like the astronauts do when they rocket into space.

If you did this, you just experienced a quantum leap in consciousness. Admittedly, that little exercise didn't transform your world. However, if you did it, you definitely altered your perspective. We have these mind leaps all the time. It's just that we aren't *consciously aware* of them and they are not necessarily intentional and with purpose. When you QuantumThink you take a deliberate quantum leap in consciousness to think and live *from* new world view principles; your perspective of reality and the world shifts, *just like that.*

~~~~

People wonder why they struggle with attaining their goals. It helps to know the dynamics of creation. We exist in *whole fields* of energy and intelligence. Shift the context and everything in the field shifts with it. If you're a ten-million-dollar company and you want to be a one-hundred-million-dollar company—if you continue to think like a ten-million-dollar company "trying to get *there* from *here*," it could take you an excruciatingly long time to reach your goal, if ever. Actions and outcomes are consistent with context. When you take a quantum leap, you start thinking from the perspective of a one-hundred-million-dollar firm. Then the actions you take, your decisions, the resources you attract, your clients, and your creative pulses all take a different direction in sync with "hundred-million-dollar thinking." When you work from context, you work from the *source* of results. Context is a state of being. Quantum principles are not cause and effect. In a quantum world, movement occurs in quantum leaps and nonlinear connections happen. They are field effects.

I'm sure you've experienced quantum leap moments in your life when monumental transformation occurs. One day you're a single man or woman with a lifestyle to match. The next day quantum destiny comes your way while you're out grocery shopping, unsuspecting, and you meet "the one." Your life shifts in an instant. One day you are one of tens of thousands of people walking around Hollywood, script in hand, lonely, forlorn, frustrated, and the next day you get a deal that rocks your world. (We all love a good Hollywood moment.)

Life occurs in quantum leaps. In this monumental moment for humanity, do we really have time for incremental step-by-step change? Why wait when you can take an intelligent, conscious leap in your own thinking? *In an old world view, circumstance rules. In a new world view, Intent rules.* Context is everything.

QuantumThink is not about learning a novel idea or a clever innovation and trying to employ it. This is about leaving the old reality system in the dust. There's nothing wrong with old world view thinking. It's just that every model, every world view, has its inherent limits. Don't worry … the old classical system isn't going away. In a quantum world of Holistic systems, all systems are included in the whole. You don't get rid of the "old" view; you include it in a larger all-encompassing one. You are *expanding* your view. You move from a world of Either/Or to a world of Both/And.

～～

The ironic thing about empirical scientists is that the really great ones are aware of the limits of the current scientific method and theories. Albert was tuned in. That's probably why people love him so much. A humanitarian heart with reverence for the mystical, he realized that not everything can be proved with the current technology and measuring instruments. At some point we acknowledge the creativity that invented those instruments and the Divine Intelligence we're connected to, and when we do, we lift ourselves beyond our conventions. When you tune into the operating principles, the dynamics of creating and the power of your own Intent, the fruits of your own experience become your proof. *Good … you're seeing this. I can feel it.*

Think of it as El Niño of Human Consciousness

While strolling along the world-renowned trendy South Beach area of Miami Beach, Florida one fine day, my husband and I encountered two gents from Thailand who were working for the Asian Institute of Technology preparing people and commerce leaders for unexpected changes El Niño brings about. Rather than focusing on remedial action, what they do is forecast the changing patterns that will result from it, and they create actions and industry around *what will be*. In effect, they start with the result. They work on building the new, rather than attempting to restore what *was* and will be no longer.

What is El Niño? A disruption in the entire oceanic atmospheric system in the tropical Pacific, the warming of the waters due to two trade winds heading the same way but coming from opposite directions. Meteorologists familiar with El Niño will tell you it is not a force on its own. It is one of many influences in the complex inner connectivity of the oceans and the Earth's atmosphere. Nor does it cause any one specific weather event, but rather fits into the overall view. This coming together of forces of nature does not cause but influences upheavals in the status quo or in the way we expect or predict things should be going.

Let's say "El Niño of human consciousness" has arrived; human trade winds and heated waters bringing about unpredictable occurrences of not just changes in weather but of an irrepressible climatic shift. In the actual El Niño the effects can be earth shattering, however in El Niño of human consciousness, fortunately, we can influence the shift.

To QuantumThink you take a literal quantum leap in consciousness. You start with the result. Rather than look *at* the new world view principles from your current perspective, you look and live *from* them. You jump systems. You go from caterpillar to butterfly with no chrysalis in between. No struggle necessary. It's faster than the speed of light. What can be faster than the speed of light?

7

MIND

Passport to heaven

"... the search for enlightenment or nirvana beyond this mind is impossible. There is nothing outside of it."
— GEOFFREY SHUGEN ARNOLD, *Zen Buddhist Sensei* 4

Your mind is your life.
And, You are not your mind.

Your mind is your life. Yes, I know it looks like all that stuff "out there" is your life. Yet, your mind is your life. Everything that seems to be experienced "out there" is experienced by the mind. Regardless of what is going on outside of you—that home, that relationship, that job, those people, the look on someone's face, this book—*how you think about* those circumstances is giving you your experience of life.

There is nowhere we experience life other than what we are conscious of in any moment. You don't have to take my word for it. You can verify this for yourself right now. What can you experience other than what you are aware of in this very moment? Examine your state right now. Are you relaxed, hurried, impatient, at peace? Are you happy, enthusiastic? What is the state of your mind now?

The power of mind is formidable. Think of what happens when you arise. One day you feel exuberant, vibrant, thrilled to be alive. The next day you feel down, a little melancholy, or maybe even depressed. Your outer circumstances are the same. Nothing has changed. Same home, same school or job or business, same wife, husband, girlfriend or roommate. Same amount of money. Same world situation. Yet, your experience of life is totally different. Such is the power of mind.

People tend to associate the mind with the intellect, yet the mind as we are speaking about it is the individualized, personal aspect of the all-pervasive consciousness. The mind in this sense encompasses *whatever you are conscious of* including:

thoughts
emotions
feelings in the body
revelations of the heart
yearnings of your soul
mystical experiences
experiences of insight and awe

wisdom that comes through you
the sense of the sacred,
the ineffable, indefinable infinity responsible for all of creation—
all of this is experienced by the mind.

~~~

The mind is the great instrument of life, an inestimable gift. If someone gave you a rare and precious treasure, how would you treat it? You would learn its workings and the proper care and use of it. You would seek the best way to maintain its value and put it into practice. You would be attentive to it. You would hold it in high esteem.

In our culture we have a lot of attention on taking care of our body, but not so much on taking care of our mind. Yes, we have traditional education, but that is not what I mean by taking care of the mind. Nor are we talking about the psychological whys and wherefores. We're speaking about the mind as a creative force.

We can distinguish between thinking as an action of intellect and thinking as an act of conscious creation. Thinking as a creation act always involves conscious Intent, the willful and deliberate focusing of attention, energy, and awareness. Your intellect can analyze what you think *about* your partner, whether he or she is kind or caring; however, your Intent is what influences, colors, and conditions what actually happens in the total field of your relationship.

~~~

As you think, so you become. Acts of consciousness are our forces of creation. There is a general unawareness about the way the mind works to generate our reality. We haven't addressed this in conventional education. It has received scant attention by science. Yet, the power of mind and its faculties are awesome.

The power of mind is awesome. And … you've got the power.

Our thoughts affect the molecules in our bodies and are therefore strong determinants of our health. It is well documented though not completely into mainstream awareness that your mind changes your body chemistry, enhances or diminishes your immune system and your brain function; it even alters the way your DNA responds.

Clinical studies have shown that people who *thought* about exercising by imagining flexing their biceps as hard as possible five times a week actually increased their strength by 13.5 percent after a few weeks, and maintained the gain for three months after the training stopped.[5]

Research on the effects of group consciousness with people experienced in Transcendental Meditation found that people peaceful within themselves can lessen and/or prevent the measured incidence of violence and crime within a specific geographic area when trained to focus with that Intent. According to physicist,

John Hagelin, this decline happens because "the *field* of collective consciousness has a radiating influence, as quantum physics has shown that fundamentally nature is comprised not of particles, but of waves traversing nonmaterial fields."[6]

The hybrid feature film *What the Bleep Do We Know!?* made famous the experiments of Japanese doctor and researcher, Dr. Masaru Emoto. His studies with frozen water crystals demonstrated that people adept with the use of their conscious thought were able to turn deformed crystals of swamp water into beautiful healthy crystals with the power of their mind alone.[7] Regardless of his would-be detractors, Dr. Emoto's seminal research suggests the vibratory nature of language and meaning and its interconnection with matter. Written words placed on containers of water had significant effects on their water crystals according to whether the words were positive or negative: *You make me sick* or *I love you.*

Why should we care? Our bodies are 70 percent water, our brains 83 percent water. The Earth is 70 percent water. Our thoughts have a consequential effect on our physical health, our emotional state, and the way we develop throughout our lives.

This isn't a bunch of "new age hooey" either. Listen, the time of that stuff is over, those ridiculous comments spoken from pure ignorance. (Ignorance is not derogatory; it simply means uneducated, unaware or uninformed, or in many cases, ill-informed). This is not about "alternative" anything. The more accurate and updated view of the nature of reality is supported by an abundance of scientific evidence. Which, by the way, I am not going to go into in this book. If you want the evidence, you can refer to the Endnotes and the Bibliography. We have other things to focus on—the matter of our own awareness.

~~~

"The word 'consciousness' implies more than just energy and information—it implies energy and information which is alive as thought. Therefore we are bundles of thought in a thinking universe. And thought has the power to transform."
—Deepak Chopra, The Seven Spiritual Laws of Success

"I cannot recall all of the people who reported to me during my twenty-seven year management career. Nor can I remember the jillions of college graduates who came to my office for a job interview. What I can remember is that regardless of their job experience or their university degrees, most of them were not trained to think. Were you?"
—Al Rothstein, Retired Paramount Television Executive, author of A Hands-on Manager Is an Oxymoron

Thinking Gets a Bad Rap in Our Culture

Thinking gets a bad rap in our culture. This kind of thinking about thinking is mistaken due to limited thinking. As in most limited conclusions we make, it is simply due to a lack of distinction.

When you QuantumThink you think Fully Dimensionally. What is it to think *Fully Dimensionally*? You think with your heart. You think with your soul. You think with your intellect. You think with your body. You think with your spirit. You think with your divine nature. There is nothing left out when you live in the awareness of the multi-dimensions of life.

Thinking is given a bad rap by the focus on connecting to the heart. *Get out of your head!* people say. *Stay in your heart.* Awakening of the heart is a wonderful thing, sacred, and definitely required for Wake-ups, though it doesn't have to happen at the expense of thinking. There are people who are now pro Emotional Intelligence (EQ) and anti IQ. Why make one more or less than? How can you leave any of it out? It's just the Either/Or mechanism doing its number on us.

When you expand your knowledge of reality, you learn that the mind is centered in the heart and operates in every cell of the body. You learn that making a coherent connection between the heart and the brain is essential to expanding consciousness, effectiveness, and wisdom. You realize the mind is expressed in every cell of your body. Then you don't need to make limiting remarks or Either/Or decisions that restrict your experience of life, like "thinking *or* heart." You expand your joy as you expand your knowledge of the way the dimensions interconnect. Yet, you also realize that the source of what creates is mind. This is an aspect of what it is to be a modern day shaman.

Some people think the mind is not too important, because what *really* matters is beyond the mind, beyond thinking and beyond language—the place of wordless silence. Still another of the great quantum paradoxes of life: **Your mind is your life *and* you are not your mind.** When you ask yourself who is the watcher, the witness of the mind, it is evident that we are that pure awareness doing the watching.

Clearly, we can never fully express the eternal, mysterious nature of existence in words alone, yet any attempt to capture reality is nevertheless encased in thought, language, and meaning. Language is the way human beings relate to the world and make things real. If you think, "beyond thought," even that is a thought. The idea of anything—of soul, of spirit, of heart, of the sacred, of the void, of the silence—is only possible because we can think those thoughts and express them in language.

Say all you want about going beyond the mind, but the fact is we still have mind to deal with.

> *"Truly speaking you should respect the mind. Pain and pleasure are in the hands of the mind."*—SWAMI MUKTANANDA

What's on your mind?

When we ask the question, what's on your mind, it seems like a casual kind of question à la Twitter. Yet, when you consider that what is on your mind is giving you your experience moment by moment, this question takes on new significance.

The power of mind is formidable. During a teaching I attended with His Holiness The Dalai Lama, he reminded us that no matter how comfortable one is physically, the physical cannot override the mind; however, the mind *can* override the physical.

Your mind is your life. I know it doesn't look that way to the world of our ordinary sense perception that separates our world into parts, into inner and outer realities. The sages say, *The world exists on the screen of your own consciousness.* Scientists tell us we live in an Observer-created Reality, that there is no "objective" reality out there, that reality is a function of our own observing it to be so. There is no separation between you and what you observe. You don't need a sage or a scientist to tell you this. What fills your mind gives you your experience of life. If this is the case, then what's on your mind becomes of keen interest.

What you think about expands. So it behooves us all to be vigilant about what we think. For the most part, we don't do that. You may have certain affirmations you practice. Maybe you stick them on your desk or your wall. That's good. But what about all the thoughts in between?

The plot thickens …
Nonlocal Mind

"There is no space between minds and souls though their physical vehicles may be far apart."
—*Paramahansa Yogananda*, Metaphysical Meditations

Yes, thought creates reality. But the picture is much bigger. The power of our mind is *literally* beyond our imagination. One of the most significant discoveries of science today is that we live in a nonlocal universe and *our minds are nonlocal*. What does it mean that we have a "nonlocal mind"?[8] Our mind does not end at the edge of our body, or even at the edge of our brain. In fact, the mind is *not located anywhere* in the ordinary way we think of space because the mind does not have that kind of spatial existence. Since the mind is not located anywhere, it exists everywhere. Another quantum paradox. You may balk at such a statement, but let's explore the possibilities.

The nature of mind exists outside of ordinary space-time limitations. This is why you can watch a movie and actually *feel* like you are there in the hills of Tuscany enjoying a balmy day strolling through the vineyards, or cry real tears as your favorite leading lady gets reunited with the love of her life.

There is a famous physics experiment that has been replicated many times since it was first performed in 1982 by Alain Aspect and his team at the University of Paris. Basically it shows that once subatomic particles have been together in a meaningful relationship, "entangled" as it's called in quantum science, the particles are in instantaneous communication with one another regardless of how far apart they are physically. Whatever happens to one instantly affects the other. The "problem" some physicists have with this is that it means that communication can travel *superluminally*, faster than the speed of light. Imagine how *this* scientific discovery might shape our thinking.

What can travel faster than the speed of light? Your very own mind. Using ordinary logic alone, if mind exists outside of ordinary space and time, then the effects of mind can be instantaneous as well. Hmmm … is a "quantum leap in consciousness," no pathway, no traveling in between, beginning to make more sense? Or at least you are starting to understand why you can't get your ex-boyfriend out of your mind. Quantum entanglement, anyone?

～～

QuantumThink is not about science; it *is* about *how the discoveries of science shape the way we think.* QuantumThink assures us that we can develop our own thinking to be in sync with the latest scientific insight. (Even if you prefer to take all of this as metaphor, if you allow yourself to be a true scientist—to experiment, remain open and see what develops rather than being set in what you think you already know, you will pleasantly surprise yourself.)

Let me jump out of those parentheses to say again: the mind is not to be confused with the brain. As we go along and you begin to distinguish what it means to Live Fully Dimensionally you'll see that the brain and the mind belong to different "orders" of reality. When you realize this and can make these distinctions, so many things become clearer. Reality is multidimensional. The brain belongs to the physical, and the mind belongs to the virtual. Consider the brain as a conduit of consciousness, a transmitter-receiver.

Our nonlocal minds do not exist in the physical dimension; therefore, the mind is not restricted by ordinary space or time. What makes the nonlocal faculty of mind powerful is that we can both access information or knowledge that is not local to us, and we can transmit information and influence things at a distance from us.

Implications of the nonlocal mind reach far and wide. Our minds have the capability to see across the world when trained to do so. In scientific research this activity is called "remote viewing." During the Cold War years, physicists Russell Targ and Hal Puthoff trained agents for the CIA to see in their minds the buildings of the Soviets, to determine where objects were located and how things were laid out. They put the natural interconnections of mind to practical use.

American physician, Dr. Larry Dossey, devotes himself to "reinventing medicine" by introducing research that proves "consciousness occupies a significant place in the origins of health and illness and that nonlocal mind affects healing." In what he calls Era III medicine, his books present scientific evidence to show that "not even common diseases can be understood without taking into account the manifestations of a patient's mental state, emotions, thoughts, attitudes, and perceived meanings."

We are immersed in a field of living intelligence, a field of mind. We can and do influence things at a distance from us through nonlocal mind connections. Your thoughts affect you, the people around you, the world at a distance from you. We are in a continuous exchange of energy and information. How do you know when someone is going to call you, and in fact, they do? We call it a "coincidence"; however, when you QuantumThink you use the faculties of nonlocal mind as a way of life.

You can imagine that becoming adept with the nonlocal abilities of mind, being able to influence things at a distance from us, provides us easier ways of accomplishing things in this world where life is increasingly complex, demands are great, and chronological time is a precious commodity.

In a universe whose basic nature is Holistic & Holographic, that is, comprised of whole systems interconnected and interrelated, a nonlocal mind makes logical sense. If everything is connected as one whole, then in a very real way, even beyond the Internet, *our minds are also interconnected—not just with one another, but with the whole of life.*

<hr>

We are in a live-substance universe. It has life force; every cell, every atom, every quark. You and I are the shape-shifters, the meaning makers, the heartbreakers. Mind is a most powerful creative faculty in our live-substance universe. If you have negative thoughts and allow yourself to indulge in them, you will have a negative experience. It's that simple. You will affect your brain and body chemistry, which translates into your "mood" or your emotional state. Your state emanates beyond you; it broadcasts out to others. You affect the field around you. You might just as well have a good or pleasant thought so you (and others) have a desirable experience.

This is what I mean by the crucial, vital, essential idea that we have the opportunity to shape our reality once we are aware and awake enough to interrupt the mechanical habits that come from old world view conditioning, leap to and look from new world view principles, and learn to use the dynamics of creating, ours by birthright.

TV writers, are you ready? There *are* consequences. People create the exact condition they don't want because of ignorance of these principles.

The sages say *the world exists on the screen of your own consciousness.* What we focus on expands. We add mass to that which we hold in our awareness. Consciousness is a live dynamic of being, a *creative life force*, the clay of reality that we get to sculpt. Lacking awareness of this fact and with little mastery with our mind, we will tend to keep in place the very things we don't want.

Good intentions notwithstanding, we want to be slim but we have all our attention on being fat. We want to be rich but we think of nothing but our debts. We want to realize God but we're set on thinking of ourselves as sinners. We want to live free of substance addictions but we insist on relating to ourselves as lifetime addicts.

The mind is so powerful that it can create something "outside" itself to be more powerful than itself. In fact, don't we do this? We make the circumstances outside of us more important: what we imagine someone else thinks of us or what the economy is doing or the stock market. We give those things dominion over our state. In our automatic reactions to mechanical meanings, we fall into the trap of classical world view conditioning. Aren't you glad you're a QuantumThinker so you'll be able to catch these things in yourself?

~~~

Our institutions and collective bodies are also subject to the effects of the mechanistic world view and natural laws of mind. Have you heard the expression, "If it bleeds, it leads" referring to which TV news stories should be run first? Generally speaking, the media has become conditioned to focus on what's wrong, what's going wrong, and what went wrong—assuming that people thrive on conflict, adore the gore, and it gets high ratings. Viewers actually scorn and deride the idea of producing "positive" news stories. Like they're unimportant or it's too sappy or boring to be positive. And of course, the ratings would go down. And they certainly will go down, until we develop a culture of Wake-ups who have conscious choice in what they broadcast, what they condition their minds to, and what they want in their news and entertainment. If you think we are currently at conscious choice in these matters, you're fooling yourself. Yes, the Suits are making decisions, conducting marketing studies, polls, and focus groups. That is to be expected, that's their job. But conscious choice is a whole other thing.

> *"Creation is what one sees and is aware of and this is within oneself."*
>
> VASISTHA, *venerated sage of ancient India*

~~~

What fills your mind becomes your world. What would happen if we developed enough mastery with our collective consciousness that we would enjoy watching stories and reports on how we can have things work, as a collective culture? How would our society transform if our media focused on *what works* about our government, our politics and our social programs? You think this is Pollyanna-ish? Great! A perfect "QT moment" to check the limits of your own beliefs.

I realize there are TV programs that present the wondrous discoveries, inventions, and genius of humankind and nature, and what they can mean to us. We call those "specials." Watch any typical daily news show today from a context rather than content perspective and the negative downward spiral is overwhelming. Instead of focusing on the specifics of the story (that is, the content), consider: what is the news network's Intent (context) in the way they are reporting on that story?

Daniel Goleman, the Harvard Ph.D. who brought the importance of Emotional Intelligence into the limelight, points out, "Research in psychology has focused far more on what goes wrong with us, depression, anxiety, and the like—than on what goes right with us. The positive side of experience and human goodness have been largely ignored in research ..."9 What you focus on expands. When you focus on negativity, you get more negativity. When you focus on depression, you get more depression. When you focus on what is working, you get more of what works.

Do you want to fill your consciousness with low grade or high grade stuff?

We're using examples of what happens in our collective consciousness, but the idea here is for you to look for yourself, personally. What are you filling your consciousness with? What are you broadcasting? When you develop mastery with your own mind, it isn't that you have to avoid the good, the bad, and the ugly. Enjoy the thrill of blockbuster blow-ups, crashes, and shoot 'em ups if that's what turns you on. It is that *you do not have to have your consciousness be hijacked by it*. Wake-ups are hip to what's going on, in themselves and around them. An awakened consciousness is more powerful than programming.

QuantumThink-Wave
We are simulcasting reality.
What are you broadcasting?

Like radio, TV, and the Internet, we are always broadcasting our thoughts and therefore, our state into the world. Collectively, we simulcast reality.

What are *you* broadcasting? Watch and listen to yourself for a day, even for an hour. You'll discover what you're broadcasting.

What you focus on expands. Fill your public media with constant talking about drugs and you will surely get more drugs. Focus on disease and pharmaceuticals in umpteen TV imprints weekly, and guess what we're conditioning? Fill the airwaves with terrorism and the collective consciousness adds mass to terrorism and the feeling of fear that fuels it. Fill your consciousness with fear and you help keep terrorism alive. Before you get annoyed with that comment, think about it for a moment. There can be no terror without fear because there would be no one to terrorize.

Sages and saints have admonished us, *Wake up!* Good advice, don't you think?

Thought Creates Reality Echoed through the Ages

"... the Kabbalist has long known that thought controls all manifestations of the physical reality."
—*Rabbi Philip Berg, author of* To the Power of One

" ... financial freedom begins not in a bank but in your head with your thoughts."
                                    —*TV financial guru and author,* SUZE ORMAN

Can you imagine what society would be like if our schools taught at the youngest age how our minds work to create reality? What would it be like if students learned to interrupt the automatic and mechanical, and stay centered, serene, and alert, with the Intent to live a life of mastery? Shouldn't this be in the public awareness?

As you think, so you become. If our mind gives us our experience of life, if thinking generates results, why isn't this knowledge taught in our school systems? Well, now you can understand why, if you are constrained by the limitations of a matter-based reality (i.e., the old world view), learning about the power of conscious thought creation *would never even enter your "field" of reality or study.*

It is vital now for future and current leaders to be able to think in a new way. Okay, this is not your typical business book. Even so, consider that **access to the source of what creates** is as essential to mastering results as are the best, brightest, and boldest strategies. Despite a preponderance of scientific evidence about these fundamental dynamics of nature, knowledge of new world view principles has pretty much remained underground, hidden from the river of humanity we call *mainstream.* The literature is available, though. It always has been.

～～～

The power of mind to generate reality from Intent in the form of thought, energized by emotion, made manifest through feeling and an inner knowing, has been addressed throughout the millennia in the sacred texts of India, the ancient scrolls of the Essenes, and the mystical teachings of Kabbalah. Variations of principles of mind are taught by yogis, avatars, and shamans; integrated into the work of coaches, counselors, and consultants; popularized by business people, financiers, and visionaries; verified by scientists, physicians, and practitioners.

In the past, people held "thought creates reality" as self-help jargon or mumbo jumbo. As leading edge researchers investigate consciousness today, we realize that the effect of human intentionality on physical space and the influence of mind on matter go beyond a motivational ploy to pump yourself up so you can "get a life."

The list is long of luminaries who have tapped into this core creation principle: *As you think, so you become.* Why? Because it works. Sometimes. Well ... actually, it works all the time. So why don't we always get the results we expect? Whether we are creating the realities or selecting them out of the Infinite, it is always a matter of being aware in the moment so you are truly at choice. If you want to accomplish what you truly desire, *you eventually end up on the path of all the great ones who have ever lived.*

8

MASTERY

A moment-by-moment proposition

"... the same mind that is the cause of suffering is also the means of attaining the highest happiness ... One who has made the mind pure, strong and still is able to accomplish anything."
—SWAMI MUKTANANDA, *Siddha Yoga Meditation Master*

The Masters
Golf and Beyond

Throughout history there have been certain persons known to have reached higher, supreme levels of consciousness—cosmic consciousness, as it is sometimes called, achieving Self-mastery or Self-realization. They are considered to be *perfected beings*. The rest of us here on Earth revere these people, sometimes pray to them, see them as God, even. What is it about them that has the rest of the world society hold them in this light?

Without speaking a word, their very presence or essence enables you to experience focus, clarity and well being. They emanate a transcendent awareness that pierces through superficialities. They transmit inner peace and a profound heart connection that enables you to feel it, too. They exude a purity of being. They can shake us up by providing the contrast that reveals the dissonance in our own being. This is considered grace, to show us where we need to grow. They maintain a state of equanimity, unwavering even amidst harsh circumstances. Surely, *they* lived in wisdom. We call them *masters*. What did they master?

The great beings hailed from various spiritual traditions, diverse countries and different eras, yet they stood on common ground on this message: *that you and I can attain their state.* Meditation master, Swami Muktananda, made a point to tell his students that the scriptural and philosophical texts of India never speak about attaining God; they speak only of purifying the mind. If our own mind is the very essence of life, *what there is to master is our very own mind.*

<hr style="width:10%" />

We are enamored of mastery. It's alluring. We're captivated by it. Why do we love the Tiger Woods, Michael Jordans, Pelés, Agassis, and Federers of life? They are not simply champions; we consider them masters of their sport. What distinguishes a champion from a master? Their state. Regardless of circumstances, whether they win or lose the match, masters maintain an unquestionable, undeniable *presence*.

You can become proficient in golf or tennis, fly fishing or Texas Hold'em, public speaking, painting or yoga. You can learn all the techniques. The golfer in you knows that in the defining moment when you're standing on the green about to make a putt that determines the outcome of the match what is paramount is the state of your own mind.

When you know your mind as a creative instrument of consciousness, an incredible faculty that literally gives you your experience of life and determines your outcomes, then you want to put some attention on it. You want to make sure it is clear and serene, that you have discipline and mastery over your own thinking.

Perhaps talent is inborn; however the Intent to master the talent is a conscious act. Mastery of the Self transcends talent. When you have an Intent for Self-mastery, you elevate your own state, you perform in a rarefied realm. Self-mastery is much different than mastering a sport. The virtues kick in. The more masterful you are within yourself, the greater the mastery you can sustain in your spiritual attainment, in your profession and in your relationships.

Relationships and Mastery

Relationships. A big subject. I admit it. I thought if I put "Relationships" as a heading, you would be sure to pay close attention to this section. *Why should you care* to choose a life of mastery? May I present this way-too-common scenario.

You're in a romantic relationship. Everything is going along wonderfully. You're in heaven, blissed out. Then one day she does something you don't like. You tell her about it. She isn't too happy with your opinion of her. In fact, she says you're all wrong about this. Your reaction: more judgments about her. Emotions boil. Up comes all the things (that have ever happened since you met) that she doesn't appreciate about you. Now your mind is going crazy. *This isn't working. I'm not happy. She is pathetic. I've got to get out of this. How did I ever think she was the one?* Meanwhile, she is having similar high-pitched mind chatter about you.

What happens next? Unless you can quickly, in that moment, (or soon thereafter) (a) *wake up* and realize: both of you are in automatic, mechanical reactions that you are not actually "choosing" despite how "real" the circumstances feel and how "right" you think you are about how "wrong" she is; (b) interrupt the reaction; and (c) return to your greater Intent to have the relationship work—if you are unable to garner any or all of the above, then guess what: You're out of there. It's Over. It's likely that neither of you wanted The End, yet lack of mastery with your own mind allowed the circumstances to decide for you. There is no deep seated psychology here for you and your friends to analyze to death. *It is truly a simple matter of waking yourself up in the moment.*

To achieve mastery with your mind means freeing yourself of whatever binds you. In the QuantumThink system we adapt a term from science, "Least-action Pathways,"[10] to indicate the automatic patterns and habits that limit us. A Least-action Pathway is the path the energy takes because it has been that route before. A Least-action Pathway has no conscious awareness involved. It is strictly stimulus-response.

Life is in flux, never ceasing, always moving. Something is being created all the time. You are either consciously creating with awareness or you are defaulting to mechanical ways, many of which (you realize by now) you did not choose. Like using a computer, you choose the settings or it defaults to its own. Lacking mastery with your own mind, habits of thinking and habits of relating, how can you expect to freely create and *sustain*, anything?

Certainty in an Uncertain World

Scientists tell us this universe is at its core a world of uncertainty. In every moment, in any moment, what can show up? Are you ready for it? Are you prepared? Are you confident? Whether you're on a tennis court or a job interview, negotiating a business deal, getting married, or sitting comfortably in your home while a fierce storm brews hundreds of miles away, one thing you can count on is that unforeseen circumstances *will* arise. Click your way over to any news page on the Internet for the daily "uncertainty report." Perhaps you need look no further than what pops up in your personal life. The question is how will you deal with the circumstances?

To be masterful, to be at real choice, one cannot fall victim to one's own reactions, uncontrolled behaviors and automatic tendencies. The paradox of mastery is that it is *a practice*. It takes a willingness to notice how you are actually being rather than living in a bubble of illusion. The moment to practice is any moment. When you learn the laws of mind which are the basic laws of creation itself, and apply them in the moment, you experience certainty in an uncertain world. When you master your mind, you master your life. Mastery of the mind is not mind control or behavioral conditioning born of a cause and effect world. We are speaking of mastery that gives you freedom and a sense of your own power. In that state of equanimity, you are centered, you have clarity, you are effective. Whatever happens, you are fine.

"Force is experienced through the senses; power can be recognized only through awareness."
—DAVID R. HAWKINS, M.D., PH.D., Power vs. Force

Is my Intent to convince you to *choose* a life of mastery? What do you think? Of course it is. Yes, altruistically I want you to have the best quality life you can have. And yes, I do have an ulterior motive … a passion for the collective world to work. I want to hang out with awakened souls. I want you to be awake enough to nudge *me* when I doze off.

Without conscious Intent, life can be drab. You can sing by rote, or you can sing with Intent. You can touch with a mechanical gesture, or you can touch with Intent.

You can listen routinely, or you can listen with Intent. You can "love" conceptually or you can love with Intent. You might be able to get away with a lot of things going through the motions. But mastery can never be rote, mechanical or routine. A life devoted to mastery is a life of passion. It's an inspired existence. You cannot fake mastery. You can't wing it. If you don't choose it, it's not happening.

What could keep us from a life of mastery? Can you guess? Another quantum paradox: *knowing*.

~~~

"A Superior Man is cautious about jumping to conclusions about that which he does not know."
— CONFUCIUS

Special Segment
QuantumThink for Know-It-Alls
From Hubris to Humility

This is a special segment for all of us who already know everything. Okay, in a very important sense, we all already *do* know everything; at least we can see from the nature of our nonlocal mind that we are *connected* to all knowledge and all knowing. But this section is for that part of you who fancies yourself too smart, too rich, or too cool to QuantumThink.

"There are more things in heaven and earth than are dreamt of in your philosophy."
—Hamlet to Horatio in SHAKESPEARE'S Hamlet

I have a friend of more than twenty years, Iris Saltzman, who is an extraordinary clairvoyant and astrologer. People with this gift were called "seers" in earlier times. Clairvoyant means clear seeing. It is of interest that in English "voyant" looks similar to the word "voyage." You go somewhere to see something. Clairvoyant means to go there in the invisible dimensions of subtle energy, spirit, and mind.

At one point people thought clairvoyance was new age weird stuff. Some people ignorant of the facts still do think of it that way. In serious scientific experimentation clairvoyance is called *remote viewing*.

Anyway, Iris used to give talks and readings, psychic "demonstrations" in her school where she would tell her audience, *if you are going to come in here to prove for yourself whether or not this* (her psychic ability) *is real, you might as well go home.* She was interested in having people use her counsel in the right way, to benefit themselves and confirm what they were already sensing. Iris makes an important point. If you have to spend your time proving that you have such faculties of mind rather than learning how to make use of them—you miss the opportunity of discovering what you can *do* with that capability.

The purpose of QuantumThink is to experience a system of thinking that you are not familiar with to see what it makes available to you. If you do things the way you have always done them, think the way you have always thought, learn the way you have always learned, organize information the way you have always organized information, arrive at conclusions the way you have always arrived at conclusions— then what can be new for you?

Get In Touch with Your Inner Know-It-All

I once joked that I could have called this book *QuantumThink for Know-It-Alls*. A TV producer friend savvy in marketing seriously suggested I do. That might have appealed to the insatiable appetite for something ever more "edgy." However, I chose to structure the title as a question *Do You QuantumThink?* to invoke a contemplation when you look at the book sitting on your table or your shelf; a reminder to keep awakening ourselves. The Indian sage credited with developing yoga, Patanjali suggested one way we can awaken is to recognize when we are asleep.

Since we all have a little of the Know-It-All in us, (some more than others) I thought it would be useful to identify the Know-It-All "types" so we can get in touch with our inner Know-It-All. Joking aside, it's an opportunity to take a look at your own limits. Where do you stop? Where do you close off? Where do you not even allow yourself to get in the game, let alone become masterful? Can you imagine any of the masters thinking they already *know*?

~~~

Know-it-all #1   Independent

I don't need anything and nobody needs to teach me anything.
I already know or I'll figure it out on my own.

Some people think if you go to a coach or a guru or to any type of "outside" learning or development, that you are weak, you need help, something's wrong with you. You can't think for yourself. You are searching, seeking, troubled.

Do you know anyone who thinks that way? Self development is for the *other* people, the "lost souls." What about you? Are you relating here? Do you feel you do it all on your own? This is just another outcome of old world view conditioning: the *illusion* of separation.

What do you suppose you have ever done on your own? Look around the room you are sitting in, the computer you are using, the food you are eating, the clothes you are wearing. How many people went into the making of your outer garment? The people who planted and harvested the cotton, the weavers, the dyers, the manufacturers, the designers, the advertisers, the marketers, the drivers of the trucks who shipped it, the list goes on. We are all so interwoven, yet we don't realize it because we live in our own little edited version of reality.

"Self-help" is perhaps an unfortunate nomenclature (Who thinks of self-help as cool? Yeah, right.) for wisdom that comes through our fellow humans, wisdom that enriches us. It's a Both/And world. We're interdependent and we're independent. You can discern what is valid for *you* and what works for *you* when you open yourself to new knowledge.

Know-it-all #2 Superior

I understand all this, I get it, but the other people won't.

There is a strange thing people would sometimes say to me regarding my work and my writing, "You've got to dumb it down so the masses can understand." *Whoaa ... hold everything.* Who are the individuals that belong to the amorphous "masses"? How are we sectioning "them" off from rest of us non-masses?

Then there is the classic, "You've got to write it so an eighth grade intelligence can understand it." Someone once said that about newspaper writing and it stuck. Like the 1,400 hundred years of the erroneous Earth-centered universe believed by the astronomer, Ptolemy, the "eighth grade" comment became "truth" in our culture. Can you imagine being in a conversation with someone and the person says, "Oh, by the way, I can only understand at an eighth grade level, so can you please speak to me that way?" From another angle, why the disparaging allusion to eighth graders? There is a lot that eighth graders can teach us today. The point is when something strikes a universal chord *everybody* gets it, eighth graders and octogenarians and everyone in between. Remember what it takes to be a Wake-up: you're human, you qualify. So Mr. or Ms. Superior, get over yourself.

> **"Your reality, sir, is lies and balderdash and I'm delighted to say that I have no grasp of it whatsoever."**
>
> —BARON VON MÜNCHHAUSEN

Know-it-all #3 Rational

I'm rational and none of this quantum stuff is real or logical.
Do you have any peer-reviewed, double blind studies to show me?
I only believe what I can see and touch and what has been proven
by empirical, classical science.

These are the die-hard old world view thinkers, the strict "materialists." If they can't see it, they don't believe it. As Deepak Chopra has pointed out, our perceptual apparatus is not so trustworthy to be definitive about what's real. Think about it. Right now you are on a globe in space spinning at a rate of 1,470 km per hour and orbiting around the Sun at a speed of 107,000 km per hour. Do you experience the spinning or the movement?

Some of us wait for scientific proof of Psi or ESP (extra sensory perception) to even concede its existence, while others are *just using it,* considering it a natural phenomenon that facilitates results and decisions. This is typical of how an old world view has taught us to deal with knowledge we don't understand. We whisk it away with a sweep of ignorance. If we ask which system is the "right" one, the scientific or the intuitive knowing, we throw ourselves straight back into the pitfall of an "Either/Or" world. We can embrace both. Appreciate and honor the science and appreciate and honor the self-intuited knowing. Use them to enhance each other. The genius of science is that it verifies what we have an inclination or sense of, and then further develops practical ways of using those proofs to benefit humankind and other Earth dwellers. The genius of intuitive knowing is to apprehend insights and revelations that can be placed before science to work with. The genius of intellectual knowing is to determine ways to make all of it work together.

In this book you are "the scientist" and you are the spiritual seeker. You are the skeptic and you are the ingénue. You are the cynic and you are the earth angel. A true scientist remains open to whatever he or she may discover. Another one who calls himself a scientist may only be looking to prove what he thinks he already knows. What he thinks he knows is called a theory. In the midst of looking for evidence of his theory, if something arises that does not fit his picture, he calls this an anomaly. A true scientist uses his theory to guide but is not attached to the outcome; he is open to what serendipitously unfolds.

> *"The absence of evidence does not mean the evidence of absence."*
> —SHIRLEY MACLAINE, *actor and author*

When something doesn't match our current model, it doesn't mean that it isn't real or valid. In many cases it simply means we haven't yet developed scientific instrumentation that can view it or measure it. Perhaps what we think of as "a miracle" is simply something that happens that we don't *yet* have a logical explanation for because we aren't aware of the operating principle that has it work.

Physicist Peter Russell states, *"There is [currently] no way of measuring consciousness; therefore, there is no scientific evidence for consciousness."* Does this mean that what we refer to as "consciousness" isn't real or doesn't exist in some way? (If you are going to reach *that* conclusion, there are a few good therapists I could recommend.)

Know-it-all #4 Humble

I'm not smart enough, I can't understand the words,
and science is not my cup of tea. I already know enough.

Sometimes we will discuss subjects and use words that may have your mind automatically resist. For some people science and scientific discoveries are the area where your mind will turn away. For others of you it may be the use of certain words and language or unfamiliar ideas like "guru" or "shaman." How often do we venture out from our own comfort zone to explore?

A guru is a teacher who brings one "out of the darkness into the light" of knowledge. In certain cultures in a particular understanding, finding a guru to be in relationship with is considered the ultimate grace. What's so intimidating about *a word*? For others, your automatic and mechanical resistance will be to ideas that don't seem to jibe with yours. Why allow yourself be stopped by *an idea*?

> *"In the beginner's mind there are many possibilities; in the expert's mind there are few."*
> —*Zen Master SHUNRYU SUZUKI*

Know-it-all #5 Intellect

*I'm a Harvard, Yale, Wharton Business School
(or whatever) ... graduate. I most certainly know.*

You listen to pundits and experts and academes on TV and the radio, and you think, *wow, she's brilliant; he's articulate.* A person has three college degrees and graduate degrees and speaks seven languages. We see that person do something foolish and we're astonished, saying, *how could she do that? She's so intelligent. She's a Rhodes Scholar!*

With the greatest respect and reverence for education and the effort and energy it takes to garner depth of knowledge and earn degrees, in the realm of awareness and mastery of the mind, these facts are not necessarily relevant. You may be well equipped to rationalize your point of view because you are educated, you are erudite, you can cleverly create with words and you have a nice palette of facts to paint with. None of this, however, makes you a Wake-up. Intellect gives you information; awareness gives you choice.

Intellect often masquerades as awareness, but there is a vast difference between the two. An *aware* individual probably wouldn't have committed the foolish act in the first place simply because they were awake to what they were doing. Imagine all these brilliant, educated people *also* becoming awake and aware. *Muy rico!*

Know-it-all #6 Lightworker

*I'm a lightworker. I live this way;
I teach these principles. I already know them.*

Greeting and salutations to you who are committed to a seeker's path with an Intent to live the highest and be a beacon for others. As you realize, to live in wisdom takes vigilance with your own mind.

Many of us get seduced by our own spiritual knowledge and mistake that for mastery. Through self examination and self inquiry, and honesty with one's self, only then can you know if you live that which you preach. Does your "higher knowledge" keep you in a state of judgment about others who allegedly lack this knowledge? Or you're in a "mood" one day and you tell your friend who reminds you that you can shift in an instant, "Oh, please don't give me that stuff right now." We cannot be on the spiritual path at our convenience. Whenever you think you've "arrived," you can take that as a clue that you're ready to go to the next place of awareness. Transformation is not a one-time event. Mastery is a moment-by-moment proposition.

Know-it-all #7 Devout

My religion tells me everything I need to know. I already know.

It's lovely and uplifting to meet persons devoted to their faith, which gives them reverence for the sacred and a commitment to live the highest virtues. The question is: Are you devoted to the divine or are you devoted to the dogma? If doctrine becomes dogma, when ritual becomes rigidity, and when belief becomes exclusionary, such "devotion" causes separation and becomes an impediment to authentically living the very virtues one espouses.

The sense of the sacred takes diverse forms. Have you ever contemplated what makes some people connect to Jesus, others to Mohammed or to the God of Abraham, still others to Krishna, Oshun, Hunab K'u, Lao-Tse, or Buddha? Though we mention just a few, there are thousands of religious faiths and spiritual practices and hundreds of designations for God. The Creator (or creator principle, however one thinks of it) apparently assumes infinite forms beyond comprehension.

There is a popular expression, "practice what you preach." Enlightened clergy and followers would concur that God cares about the *entire world*. We are speaking about mastery here and that means not merely preaching and not just practicing either. Mastery means *embodying* the core messages, living and breathing them beyond your individually adopted or parochial beliefs.

Picture yourself climbing to the highest mountaintop to meet God (God always meets people on mountaintops). God instructs you to direct your gaze toward the panorama of creation, a universe teeming with boundless varieties of species, atmospheres, land terrains, celestial bodies. Can you imagine that God then takes you by the hand, looks into your eyes and tells you to limit your own horizons? It would seem a little inconsistent with God's plan, to say the least, for any of us to think we already know everything just because we have read the scriptures of our choosing.

You can tell if your devotion is working by the results it generates. Does your interpretation of scripture cause divisiveness and separation? Do your beliefs create upsets for others? Are you "sending people to hell" with your interpretation? Are you equipped to make such determination for another? You take your teachings to a higher level when you go beyond the blind faith of stale convention and contemplate them in their purest form. Consider that this is when you resolve to live the wisdom.

QUANTUMTHINK-WAVE
From Hubris to Humility

What do you think you are absolutely so sure about that you will not open yourself to an idea that doesn't seem to fit with yours? When you reach the point of "it's possible I don't know" as a perspective to look from, the possibility for mastery arises.

One evening at a party I met a charming, intelligent, convivial yet rather feisty gent in his 30s who was asking me about QuantumThink. When I told him we make the distinction between our mechanically conditioned thinking and thinking from new world view principles, he was insulted. He said I was presuming that people don't know these things. I told him *au contraire*; that everyone has all knowledge available at some level of their being. I asked him if he thought he was at his peak level of awareness and he answered unflinchingly a definitive, *Yes*. Yet he was ready to pounce on everything and anything with his judgments and opinions, with little awareness of how his own views limited him from possibilities *in that very moment*.

Know-It-Alls and Masters. Hubris and humility. Hubris means *overbearing pride or presumption; arrogance*. Humility means *not prideful; modest or showing respect*. Can a Know-It-All attain the state of a master? Sure, why not. What you focus on expands.

Did you recognize yourself in any of the above? Let's not take our know-it-all-ness too seriously. The Know-It-All types are simply outcomes of a classical world view that implies *we have to know so we can predict and control*. Forget about embracing your inner Know-It-All. Just awaken it. When you do you'll have some good laughs with those who know you and love you anyway. Besides, maintaining the Know-It-All front can prove a bit stressful.

Okay, we got through that section. A little challenging, yes? Anyway, it's established. You're in the QuantumThink field.

> *"Masters have more distinctions in their art form than other people."*
> —ALAN COLLINS, *Master QuantumThink Coach*

Can you really *make a difference?*—*The Effects of Mastery*

You hear so many people say, *"I want to make a difference."* Honorably and admirably we contribute our time and money, talent and expertise, caring, compassion and celebrity to those in need. These actions do make a difference. One wonders: can we *really* make a difference, one that forever alters the course of events?

Consider that the greatest contribution each of us can make is by becoming a *perfected being* ourselves. Or at least strive toward that state. Maybe that sounds too lofty for you. Yet isn't this the essence of wisdom teachings and what all the great beings have attained?

You can only give at the level of which you yourself have attained. The quality of your contribution is a function of your own state; your state of mind in the moment as well as your state of evolution and spiritual maturity. Your gift is what you emanate. How could it be otherwise?

Mastery is a personal state and a personal choice. The *effects* of mastery reach far and wide. Contemplate the possibility even for a moment: our collective consciousness is out-pictured in the world in our ideas and inventions *as well as in our mental habits and our emotional states.*

Do our collective emotions affect the reactions of Earth herself? Crazier things have been said, scoffed at, and later proven to be true. Can global mind change affect global climate change? As you come to know the nature of mind that idea may sound quite sound, indeed. We are not separate from Earth. Just as thousands of organisms take up residence on our bodies as their host organism, Earth is our host.

In ancient spiritual literature "water" symbolizes our emotional life. It is commonly known that emotions influence the cells and chemical reactions in our own bodies. We witness "natural" disasters intensifying and emotions rising along with them when people succumb to fear, anger, and despair.

It is worth considering that planet Earth is a living entity responsive to our collective consciousness. When you think and live from the Holistic & Holographic principle you realize there are distinctions, but no actual separation between our inner and outer life. Consider that our collective consciousness can and does alter the course of affairs.

In times of crisis people blame the government, the nongovernmental organizations, the media—anyone in the path of their pointing finger. The press, the politicians, the police, and each one of us are all simply individuals who are either willing to become Wake-ups or not, willing to go beyond conventions and ineffective old world view thinking or not, willing to choose a life of mastery or not.

What if political and government leaders committed themselves to a life of mastery? Suppose all the customer service people you ever got through eighteen automated voice prompts to reach, created a conscious Intent for mastery? What if you chose in this very moment to dedicate yourself to your own mastery? How would it shape the world? Mastery is not about reading the script perfectly, performing "the rulebook" with excellence, or being great at implementing political strategy. Mastery is a presence of mind you bring to everything you do.

We quote from many whom we think of as great. Or maybe they weren't so great, but they said something good once in a while. When do you become the person you want to quote? Mastery is about you awakening to your own greatness, to your own magnificence. It's about becoming the icon of your own life.

Mastery is a state. All outer results reflect your own state. Your mind affects reality. Your mind creates reality. Your mind holds reality in place. What there is to master is your very own mind.

~~~

All right then, let's review.

We're in a new time. It's a different reality.
We have been functioning in a limited view.
Systems work other than we thought.
It is a time of evolution of consciousness itself.
This evolution takes conscious choice—of the individual, the organization, the institution, the collective.
It cannot be an intellectual exercise. It's not about information. It is a practice.
It's a direct personal experience moment by moment of your own Self awakening.
You can do it. It's easy.

9

METHOD

The art of distinguishing

What's good about this cereal?

Cereal manufacturers are clever. They strategically place messages on the box so while you are sitting there crunching away all those nutrients and fiber, your eye just goes there. On the box of my favorite cereal they tell you "what's good about this cereal." I love that they just tell you that straight out so I thought I would do that, too.

What's good about this book? Aside from being enlightening, comforting, entertaining and truly a pleasure to read, this book gives you a way "there." It gives you an immediate access to QuantumThink your life. We're not saying, *hey listen, you should QuantumThink. We are saying, here, you can QuantumThink. Here's the system. Here are the 21 principles (distinctions) and here are the practices (recreations).* You really didn't think I was going to leave you without a method after all this, did you?

It's all about the access

The mysterious little silver box that the computers on our network check in with to wirelessly connect to one another and the Internet is called the *access point.* QuantumThink is an access point. If you can't access the wisdom of expanded thinking so it *connects* for you in your life, what's the point?

We're so near Part II of this book, "Live the Wisdom," where you delve into the QuantumThink distinctions. Let's discuss. I want you to get the max, the full tilt boogie. You realize by now QuantumThink is not a how-to. You aren't going to get the 10 steps to entering a new world view. You *are* going to become adept at The Art of Distinguishing. **What's good about The Art of Distinguishing?**

To distinguish is to bring awakened awareness to an idea or a situation in a way that broadens you and alters your experience forever. When you *distinguish* something it becomes real for you. "Distinguishing" gives you immediate access because it can only be done "live" in the present moment. Distinguishing wakes you up.

Reflect back a moment: Until we distinguished "old world view" and "new world view" as reality systems that condition the way we think, you may not have given attention to the idea that thinking takes place in a *system*, and that we can condition ourselves to think from an entirely different system. And now, *voila*, a few chapters later, it's happening.

Distinguishing makes something new available to you *in your experience.* Distinguishing "new world view thinking" opens the door for you to expand the entire way you relate to everything in your world. This is the power of a distinction.

~~~

The Art of Distinguishing
The Distinguishing of Art

A novice photographer looks through the viewfinder of a camera to take a picture of his friend in a park. All he sees is his friend, the "subject" of the photo. He doesn't notice the tree behind his friend, appearing to grow out of his friend's head, or the people in the background or the messy lunch table to the side of him. He doesn't notice the way his friend's face is shadowed or how the colors of the sky look. The resulting photo is no work of art. LATER THAT DAY … The novice enrolls in a photography class. A distinction is created for "composition" which includes the all-encompassing aspect of actively looking at every millimeter of that frame, seeing the whole of it, studying every part of what he sees through the viewfinder, every corner of it, designing what he places in the picture, noticing how the light and shadows affect it. Composition includes the Intent in taking the photo, how the graphic components line up or relate to one another, and the feeling the image evokes.

The distinction, "composition," has opened up a whole new way of seeing for this photographer. Never again will his sight be focused solely on the person standing in front of his lens, the main subject. He will see all of it and how it relates to his overall photo. He has learned something that he *won't have to try to remember.* It has become his natural action. Even without a camera, he will see how light changes colors and hues, he will discern patterns in nature and on the streets. He has transformed the way he views the entire world, from this moment on. This is the power of a distinction. It becomes part of you and it expands you and continues to open new worlds.

Distinguishing: A New World View of Learning

Since energy is not fixed, scientists study not the energy in itself, trying to define what it is; instead they examine the way the energy behaves. Distinctions are not static either. Distinguishing is a *new world view of learning* because it is alive and dynamic and continuously unfolds. Distinguishing is not the same as describing. A description gives you the *concept* of an idea. A distinction gives you the *experience* of the idea. When we live by definitions we can get stuck in them, and nothing much new can happen. As you contemplate the QuantumThink principles, the important thing is not to get an exact definition; the important thing is to get to something you can relate to and something that *works.*

In our increasingly complex world, distinguishing is one of the most important things we do. By distinguishing "awareness" from "intellect" for example, we glean why "knowing" the concepts has been insufficient to actually integrating wisdom, and we can see that by distinguishing *awareness*, we connect to the boundless state of choice.

When you distinguish instinct, intellect, and intuition, and the unique way each one works in your own experience, you strengthen your ability to make beneficial decisions. Researchers might be able to define which areas of the brain get activated when instinct, intellect, or intuition are in play, however, that information alone may not be much help to you in making decisions. When you distinguish *in your experience* that instinct helps us survive, intellect enables us to logically work with concepts, and intuition connects us non-locally to all intelligence—you make confident choices. Experience becomes transformative when it is distinguished. Undistinguished, it fast fades out of the picture—out of the field of *conscious* awareness—a fleeting memory at best, a blip on the screen of life.

> *"Disneyland will never be completed. It will continue to grow as long as there is imagination left in the world."*
> —WALT DISNEY

In distinguishing, *you* are the one generating, discerning what something can be, and what it makes possible. In contrast to a "definition" you do not need to end up with a fixed, measurable quantity or conclusion. Walt Disney did not *define* theme parks; he *distinguished* them in a way that continues to unfold imaginative, awe inspiring experiences for millions of people around the world, well beyond his physical presence. This is the power of distinguishing.

~~~

A QT Moment
Had one lately?

Since The Art of Distinguishing is a present-moment phenomenon, it becomes a natural wake up. This is good. Even when you are *aware* of QuantumThink principles, you are subject to the default system running the show until you can make a distinction in your own thinking *in the moment it occurs*. Our clients in the Philippines affectionately dub this *"A QT Moment,"* the moment of awakening when they see something so clearly that it shifts their experience.

Suppose one day (for your sake, sooner rather than later) you look at your mother or father and realize they are just *people* doing the best they can at their own level of awareness and self development, and all of a sudden you have tons of space for them. Your heart is open. They can do no wrong. You are having A QT Moment. You experience extreme gratitude and appreciation for the efforts your parents put forth to support you in your life, even when what they think or say or do doesn't match your pictures of "how they should be." This awakening with your mother or father extends over to all your relationships. When you see people, not as ill-intentioned but simply caught in their own automatic ways and cultural conditioning (i.e., in

Least-action Pathways) you naturally release your judgments and embrace compassion. Your parents don't have to change. (What a relief!) *Your* presence and new context for how you see them instantly alters the relationship. This is the power of The Art of Distinguishing. This gives you access to living the wisdom.

The realm of awareness is often called the "subtle" realm. "Subtle" is defined as *"finely distinguished, refined; hence, penetrating and pervasive."* When you practice exercises of awareness, the results are pervasive. A leap in one specific relationship penetrates *all* of your relationships.

QuantumThink distinctions are purposefully simple but not simplistic. Pablum, it isn't. Cereal wakes you up in the morning. QuantumThink wakes you up anytime.

Cereals are plants that yield edible seeds. You imbibe QuantumThink multidimensionally to nourish your mind. As you read each distinction and as you practice each Recreation you experience *living wisdom*. Like any practice you exercise regularly, the intelligence integrates. You will *be* the wisdom.

To QuantumThink is very simple. It only requires your presence. You being present to what is being said. As you read you have the opportunity *in every moment* to become aware of the routine habits and limits of your own mind. When you *distinguish* the limits of your thinking, you move beyond them. It's instantaneous and it's practical. There is nothing theoretical about it.

Hmm … wait a minute … It does require one other thing: your Intent to have something happen for yourself. The QuantumThink system is for you to take the leap, expand yourself beyond conventional thinking, outdated beliefs, and automatic habits. It is for you to become masterful in your own life as a result of knowing and working with universal principles of what actually does create your reality. The rest is up to you.

~~~

> *"Our minds are not just along for the ride in an impersonal universe. Instead we define the fabric of reality at a fundamental level with the choices we make, the things we choose to see or not see, and most importantly our intentions in each moment."*
>
> —FRED ALAN WOLF, *quantum physicist and author*

QuantumThink is based in a fundamental tenet of quantum physics: there are no absolutes. "Reality" exists as *waves of possibility* until we "observe" it into form. Since nothing is fixed and Reality is Context-dependent, we have the opportunity in every moment to create a context that shapes our outcomes. "Intent" is tantamount to a context that shapes reality. Whenever you undertake anything that is important to you, it is wise to ask yourself, *What is my Intent here?*

"Intent" is not positive thinking. While it is always a good idea to generate positive thoughts, QuantumThinking is not positive thinking. My husband likes to say positive thinking is like spreading jam over peanut butter and pretending you've got a jam sandwich. You take a bite and the peanut butter sticks to the roof of your mouth.

Intent is a creative dynamic. It is neither true nor false. It is an invented context you are choosing to live from to shape your experience and results. If your current (peanut butter) idea of yourself is that you are not good with details, when you see that this is not the "absolute" way that you are, you can create the Intent that you are good with details. Neither of these statements—that you are bad with details or that you are good with details—is more true or false than the other. It is a question of which statement (context) would you rather live from? While "positive thinking" may or may not transform your experience, Intent is a dynamic that *does*, providing you are not attached to the idea that the "peanut butter" (your current thought about something or someone) is cemented for all time.

The most important dynamic in every moment or any venture is your Intent. In life we are either creating consciously with awareness, or—the default circumstances are creating for us. Even if your Intent is simply to explore and discover what pleasant surprises await you, I invite you right here, right now, to create your Intent for what you desire as you expand your way of thinking.

～～

What's good about this book? You can open it anywhere anytime you want to tune into your own awareness. To QuantumThink is to *experience* a walking, talking, living meditation. When you meditate, you close your eyes, and you bring your focus within. You experience the peace and light of awareness we refer to as *consciousness*. This is presence. In ancient yogic and Buddhist traditions it is called the "witness." You may also notice your mind is flooded with thoughts that float in and pop out like bubbles from a child's toy wand. But what happens when you open your eyes from meditation? To maintain a state of peace and presence, you simply become the watcher of yourself and your thoughts *with your eyes open, during all your activities.*

> *"The moment you start* watching the thinker, *a higher level of consciousness becomes activated."*
>
> Eckart Tolle, *spiritual teacher and author of* The Power of Now

It is known in modern brain research that our brains build new neural network connections and gain greater coherence when we expand ourselves through new thinking, through connecting to a higher octave of heart-centered mind, and through establishing ourselves in "meditative" brain wave states. When you live in a state akin to meditation you remain connected to the state of unbounded awareness that quantum physicist, John Hagelin, refers to as the "core unity of all life."

When you meditate you enter a restful state and re-charge yourself, like placing yourself in the cosmic charging station. You come out of meditation fully refreshed with your energy renewed. Imagine that you could live in just such a continuous state of revitalization. It is possible.

> *"Let's not be too logical."*
> —ISSEY MIYAKE,
> *world renowned fashion designer*

How to Read the QuantumThink Distinctions

QuantumThink may be novel, but it is not a novel. You read one chapter at a time, that is, one distinction at a time. You contemplate it. Savor it. Immerse yourself in it. Practice the Recreation. Then you move on to the next chapter. And it's so simple. It's easy. All you do is stay present, awake to your own awareness, with an open mind. (Re-visit the Know-It-All types in the Mastery chapter if you forget.) If you have moments when you find you cannot stay awake and aware while reading, it's best to stop. Go do something else. Come back when you can. Be careful driving.

The distinctions are purposefully simple because the Intent is to awaken awareness. It is not about learning more stuff; it is to become aware of yourself, your habits of thinking, your habits of relating, and your habits of emoting, so you can be at masterful choice in your life. Yes, emotions can become mechanical, too. Complaining, moaning, criticizing could just be automatic habits, whether your own or your friend's. After all, you wouldn't *choose* to complain and moan, would you? Well maybe sometimes you would, just for fun.

When you present anything of this nature people always want to know, *what are your credentials? What qualifies you to do this?* Even if I have in my background thousands of hours of study (which I do), even if there are thousands of people who have been in our teleconference programs who continuously benefit from being QuantumThinkers (which there are), the *only* thing relevant is what *you* experience as you read and as the QuantumThink distinctions show themselves in your life.

You don't have to be concerned about "figuring it out." This allows you to access other aspects of your multidimensions. As you read the words, tune into your own presence. Notice what arises in you from the depths of your own being. Allow your wisdom to surface. An amazing thing happens when we're quiet within. You hear things.

Establishing a state of natural tranquility and joy

Being established in a natural state of tranquility and joy, the state from which all masterful performance derives, takes practice. The Recreations are for this purpose.

> *RECREATION = "refreshment of mind and body; diversion; amusement. Any pleasurable exercise."*

The Recreations presented at the end of each QuantumThink distinction are practices for the mind and awareness that "re-create" the distinctions for you in your life. The Recreations change your life. I say that only because they do. It isn't the Recreation that does it; it is you. They just give you the key, the clue, the cue. Most of them take literally no time at all. You practice them in the midst of your ordinary activities. Even if you never again do the Recreation, it's in your repertoire. Like a song you learn, you can pull it out and sing it anytime.

> *"It's tough to make predictions, especially about the future."*
> —YOGI BERRA

Quantum systems are not deterministic; you cannot predict precisely what will happen. You *can* however, influence the field of probability with your Intent. You will likely experience peace of mind, increased focus, a relaxed spirit. You may notice yourself naturally relating more effectively and even masterfully in a reality where continuous change, uncertainty, and upheavals have become status quo. Perhaps you already experience yourself lighter than before you picked up this book. (Let me know.)

Whenever you put yourself into any experience outside of what you ordinarily do, you give yourself an opportunity for an expansion, an illumination, another perspective—or shall we say ... *many* perspectives.

From 3D to FD
Living Fully Dimensionally

While we're here practicing the method, The Art of Distinguishing, I thought it would be a good idea to distinguish something of great importance, and that is, Living Fully Dimensionally. Living life FD is acknowledging that everything we deal with on a daily basis has existence in many dimensions simultaneously. *Why should you care?* You want to create the life you desire, yet, until you begin Living Fully Dimensionally, you can't even begin to get at what creates reality.

You and I live in many dimensions of reality simultaneously. The old world view has focused us in one dimension: the physical, a 3D reality of "matter" that we can see, hear, taste, touch, and smell. The Internet is moving us along in this area, but there is so much more to consider when we think of what it might really be like to be Living Fully Dimensionally. Like anything else, if you don't have this in your awareness, until you *distinguish* it, it is not your reality.

Right now you and I are relating in the *virtual* dimension, a realm beyond the limits of ordinary time and physical space. To a mind that is used to things in a particular way, it may seem odd to say that you and I are related in this moment. We are in fact very much related as I write and as you read. A case in point: if you begin reading this like "information" to understand or remember, the Intent for both of us (Waking up) will have gone awry. This means I have to stay aware of *you* as I write. The moment I stray, the moment my mind wanders off on its own trip, what happens to our connection? *Click.* It's like going off-line. The connection is lost. (By the way, you *are* with me now, aren't you? Just checking.)

In a more encompassing view of reality, the virtual dimension is a valid way of knowing our world and one another. *In fact, most of what we "know" in the world, we know virtually.* Think about it. The celebrities and world leaders in the public eye whom we talk about with friends and family over dinner, have opinions about, and vote for or against—we know them mostly from electronic video images and sound bites. Much of our emotional experience in our relationships takes place over the telephone and the Internet, and through text messaging that is "here" one instant and gone the next. We participate in the virtual dimension all the time. We simply haven't acknowledged its importance in the same way that we do our ordinary physical world. The earlier materialist world view put forth the idea that matter is fundamental and that the physical is what's real. This leaves out quite a bit.

What is invisible to us—subtle energies, thought, emotions, principles, spirit, and fundamental consciousness itself—play a grander role in our experience and outcomes than we have been taught. Traditional education has not addressed the relationship of physical matter to the dimensions of energy, mind and consciousness, and what we call "spirit" or "life force." We have never learned in formal schooling how to work with subtle energy, the faculties of our nonlocal mind, and the way our minds manufacture reality.

◦◦◦

This book is a virtual dialogue between you and me and all the others who are reading it and will read it, and all those who have contributed to it by sharing their wisdom with me directly and otherwise. When we come together like this we create a *conscious* quantum field—a field of awareness, a field of intelligence and of energy, of connection, a *mind field*. Call it what you will, the fact is, we can and do affect one another.

Although we are conditioned to relate to life through ordinary sense perception, there is much more to our reality than meets the eye. We exist in *fields*. A field is not visible, yet we are connected through it. Most of the fields we pass through during the day are chaotic and unfocused. Walk into a shopping mall, the office building where you work, a grocery store, (okay, maybe around *food* we get *a little* more focused), and you will experience what I mean. When you bring conscious focus to a field, it becomes coherent. In science "coherence" means *waves coming together in focus.* In a coherent field the power of Intent intensifies.

Physical and social scientists have divergent ideas about what "the fundamental field" is. Some say it is consciousness. Some say it is light. Some say it is energy. Some say it is love. Others say we don't actually know what it is, but that it is definitely nonmaterial. When you are Living Fully Dimensionally, you think of it as *all of the above.* Consider that the question, *What is the field?* may be the wrong question. It limits us to old world view thinking of a fixed "way that it is." If reality is multi-dimensional, then the field itself manifests *all* of these aspects, and probably some we haven't discovered yet.

We can learn a lot from the Internet. It is nonlinear. It is infinite. It is non-locatable. It's a Both/And world—the nonpareil of individuality and interconnected unity at the same time. It equalizes people and companies in spirit, large and small. It is a 24/7 operation functioning in real time and it's timeless. It out-pictures humanity and reflects us back to ourselves: from the vile to the sublime, from mediocrity to ingenuity, from the inane to the brilliant. The Internet isn't a "thing," it's a field.

We're not used to relating to one another through a field; we're not accustomed to thinking this way. Yet, you and I and all the others who are imbibing QuantumThink are tuning in together and generating a conscious mind field and by virtue of our collective Intent this field is powerful.

"Our experimental work ... has provided robust evidence that human intention, properly applied, can significantly influence physical reality."
—WILLIAM A. TILLER, *Professor Emeritus,*
Stanford University's Department of Material Science and Fellow to the
American Academy for the Advancement of Science

What is Living Fully Dimensionally? Acknowledging that everything that we deal with on a day-to-day basis has existence in many dimensions simultaneously. In a world of Infinite Possibility we could distinguish any number of dimensions. In QuantumThink we distinguish seven:

♦ the **Physical** dimension that is obvious to our senses, the world of everyday people, places and things;

♦ the **Energetic** dimension of electromagnetism, subtle energy fields and forces that we may not see but we can **feel**, including emotional energy;

♦ the **Virtual** dimension of **mind**, consciousness and all extensions of mind including technologies like the Internet;

♦ the **Spiritual** dimension of **heart** and life force, where we experience inter-connectedness with one another and with the whole of life;

♦ the **Cosmic** dimension of **nature**, of natural laws and universal operating principles that function throughout the universe and within each one of us;

♦ the **Esoteric** dimension of the **soul**, of meaning and purpose and stories of evolution and prophecies;

◆ the **Divine** dimension of the **sacred**, that ultimate mystery maker and/or force of creation responsible for All That Is, encompassing all dimensions and also transcending all of them.

> *"In this new world you and I make it up as we go along, not because we lack expertise or planning skills, but because that is the nature of reality."*
> —MARGARET WHEATLEY, *author of* Leadership and the New Science

As in any distinction, Living Fully Dimensionally is an *invented* distinction to give us access to living the full richness of life, seeing how all the various dimensions work together. All seven dimensions are always present and integrated even though we have tended to emphasize the physical, have a special time for the spiritual, gloss over the cosmic or leave that to scientists, pay little heed to the energetic or reject it outright, and often ignore the esoteric or consider it's only for mystics.

Brainy Stuff

What are the consequences of not Living Fully Dimensionally? When we don't distinguish between dimensions, we end up in limited and limiting dead-end or debilitating Either/Or debates.

Creationism versus biological evolution, for example. Creationism, the story of the creation of the universe as expressed in the Bible, addresses a context within the *Divine* dimension, while biological evolution addresses itself to the development of the *physical* dimension. "Both" of these "And" other interpretations have their own value and place when you see life Fully Dimensionally. In the Both/And quantum world seemingly contradictory views have validity in their respective places—and others hold a valuable place as well—in our understanding of the universe. In QuantumThink we address conscious evolution from the *virtual* dimension and the role of our own awareness in it. Formerly disparate disciplines are converging with new discoveries of evolution such as research scientist and biologist, Bruce Lipton's groundbreaking work in uncovering the unquestionable effects of mind on evolutionary biology at the cellular level.

The way our brain has developed over millions of years tells still another story of evolution. The highly respected thinker and world renowned advocate of evolutionary child-rearing practices, Joseph Chilton Pearce points out that each new evolutionary development of our five-part brain includes and incorporates the intelligences of the older/lower parts. We have evolved: from an ancient Reptilian reflexive brain wired for survival; to the limbic system where emotions register; to the neocortex that enables us to organize data and use ordinary logic and reason; to the more recent pre-frontal lobes and the newly recognized brain in the heart—the areas of higher intelligence and of love, acceptance, and joy that continually move us toward well being.

> *"The idea that we can think with our hearts is no longer just a metaphor, but is, in fact, a very real phenomenon."*
> —Joseph Chilton Pearce, *author of* The Biology of Transcendence

Joseph Pearce teaches us that *we are designed for transcendence*, destined to reach the state of the great masters, and that anything that interferes with that transcendence, such as the inconsistencies of modern culture, causes a resistance to this natural inclination for something higher. The resistance to the "high road" throws people into violence, activating the Reptilian reactive brain that is driven solely to survive, and at all costs.[11] Just realizing what he is implying, and seeing the violence prevalent in children and teenagers, is enough to convince any reasonable person of the necessity to start Living Fully Dimensionally.

There is indeed more than we have imagined in whatever "philosophy" and set of limited beliefs our Either/Or culture has thrust upon us. By the way, it is of no avail to think of this as "relativism." That's the old world view mechanism attempting to categorize and stick a label on that which defies pinning down. We're engaged here in a new world view of learning, The Art of Distinguishing, to extend our vision, to make something else possible, to create our shared society in a way that works, for everyone.

When we are Living Fully Dimensionally we truly can give up the exorbitant waste of time and energy spent in these Either/Or debates, battling to decide which of the limited viewpoints is going to "win" out, and instead start providing a more expansive way of thinking for ourselves and for our young people. After all, isn't this what education is supposed to do—*expand* minds?

Relationships: Let's Get Fully Dimensional

I know. You want a sexier reason than "evolution" for Living FD. How about *relationships*? When you Live Fully Dimensionally, you have a crystal clear understanding of your relationships. Can you imagine that? Yes, *really*, no kidding. Like anything else, if you don't get your relationship going consciously, you are throwing yourself into the daily drama of: *Is this relationship going anywhere?* How will Living Fully Dimensionally come to the rescue?

Let's say you can't help but notice that you and your partner are strongly attracted physically and emotionally, but you still feel there's something missing. Now that you have the distinction Living FD you realize it's not that the relationship as a whole isn't working; it's just that in the spiritual dimension there's *nothing*—it's not happening. At least *not yet*. Or you meet someone and you feel an immediate, deep soul connection, but later discover there is no mental affinity and few common interests to share. This might appear rudimentary now, yet not so patently obvious when it plays itself out and you're in the throes of emotional confusion. This happens not just in budding relationships, but in marriages of twenty years and more. You want to know the way to put some spark back in your relationship? Living FD. It's electrifying.

From this moment on, now that you have this distinction about the many dimensions you participate in with your relationships, you'll naturally see where your dimensions hover. You'll astound yourself with your own relationship wisdom. When you distinguish this *with your partner*, you can choose which dimensions you want to develop together, or not. This makes for fascinating conversation. Let's get Fully Dimensional. You are going to *love* The Art of Distinguishing.

~~~

People today ask one another, *Are you spiritual?* It's all so very hush-hush. When you look from the fullness of reality, isn't it laughable to leave anything out?

Enlightened business leaders know that the relationship of "spirit" to employees being happy translates to profits. When people experience a connection to the spiritual place within themselves—the place of *life force*—they are energized, they feel good within themselves, they're inspired and free to create. They authentically relate from the heart—to one another, to clients and to customers. The "money" (translation: effective, productive, brilliant work that brings profitability) follows, because money, a tool of exchange in the physical and virtual dimensions, is also an expression of creative and spiritual energy.

When you are Living Fully Dimensionally, things that once appeared problematic from a one-dimensional old world view become non-issues. You see the whole picture. You don't have to get stuck in Either/Or squabbles. Instead you are merrily (and wisely) creating contexts that have things work. Freeing yourself from the antiquated one-dimensional reality (the physical only) is what makes this possible. Now you can see why you can't even begin to get at what creates your results until you begin Living FD. No single idea or theory gives us the whole picture; and every single cogent idea and theory provides valuable wisdom to the whole.

Living FD is simply a lot more fun. When you realize that *everything we live with has existence in every one of these seven dimensions*, when you begin to give equal weight and equal importance to all dimensions of reality we are living in and learn how they operate, it is *Wow*; life is so much richer. This is the power of a distinction.

~~~~~~~~~~~~

QUANTUMTHINK-WAVE
7 Dimensions for Living Fully Dimensionally

Take a mind stretch. Select any subject or area of life and consider how it manifests in each of the dimensions.

Physical Dimension~Senses
material aspect of ordinary objects and
our bodies and ordinary sense perceptions

Energetic Dimension~Feeling
forces and fields including emotions, electromagnetism,
subtle body emanations

Virtual Dimension~Mind
mind, consciousness, thought and all extensions of mind;
the Internet

Spiritual Dimension~Heart
life force, spirit, experience of interconnectedness
through the wisdom of the heart

Cosmic Dimension~Nature
natural laws and universal operating principles
that we discover and learn to use

Esoteric Dimension~Soul
meaning and purpose, stories of evolution, soul's journey

Divine Dimension~Sacred
All That Is, ultimate mystery responsible for all of creation,
encompassing all the dimensions and also transcending them.

~~~~~~~~~~~~

What's good about this book? You become adept at The Art of Distinguishing (you've already begun). You free yourself from your edited, abridged version of reality. You go from living a bland 3D existence to Living Fully Dimensionally.

What happens next? TV writers everywhere know what makes a story great are great characters, and what makes characters *great* characters is dimensionality. We've released ourselves from the stranglehold of a one-dimensional story. Time to write a new one.

10

STORIES

As the human drama turns ...

"*According to High Initiation,* **it is written that the wisdom of the cosmic light will return.** *When the human race begins to slip into the darkness of ignorance, oblivion, and despair, it will be the wisdom of the seven brothers of our Father Sun that will shed the great light of wisdom in order to awaken the powers that have remained dormant in human beings due to an erroneous form of education.*"

—HUNBATZ MEN, *Mayan Elder*
From Sacred Text by the Maya Mysteries School

I

We love stories. We are brought up on stories. A wonder and pleasure of being a child is when your mother or father, nanny, guardian, or guru sits by your side and tells you a story. Story hour has the aura of a sacred, magical space.

We live by stories. Bedtime stories. Stories over dinner. Stories in novels. Stories in movies. Stories on "reality shows." Stories we eavesdrop on as talk show hosts converse with their guests. We collectively watch the same soap opera on TV for fifty years and more. The characters mirror our daily dramas and emotions, albeit exaggerated versions.

Great beings, writers and artists all tell stories. Are their stories true? Maybe, maybe not, but they do have some impact on us. They inspire or teach us, they enlighten us, they forewarn us. They open our hearts, cause us to think, and move us into action. Their stories touch our souls.

You're reading a book and you're waiting for the author to tell you his or her story. You want to know, *How did you come to write this? What led you to it?* You may have noticed I haven't told you my story. That's because the story of this book, the story of QuantumThink is really *our* story. It goes like this.

～～～

Once upon a time a group of people known as the human race appeared on an amazing, breathtakingly beautiful celestial orb they called Planet Earth. At first they had all their attention on surviving the conditions of the planet. They didn't see themselves as separate from the planet so they lived in harmony with the forces of nature and natural resources that they knew kept them alive. They were quite an ingenious people, very industrious and had been granted by birthright unlimited creativity so they continuously developed their outer life, something they called civilization. After they had handled the essentials of survival and security, they advanced themselves in art, music, sports, science, and technology. One marveled at what they brought forth to the planet.

They felt things profoundly. When they looked up at the stars and the moon and the sun and the never-ending sky, they knew there was something, some force, some great intelligence that had to be in some way responsible for all of creation. They made up lots of stories about what they thought the ultimate creator was. Some of them even eschewed all the creator stories; their story was that it was all just a fluke, happenstance. Even so, something mystical referred to as "the sense of the sacred" was felt deeply by each one in his or her own way, though it could never be limited or explained by words alone.

The humans had a lot of questions. They were curious. How did they get there? Why was there existence rather than none? Who was responsible for this great mystery? Now that they were here, what were they supposed to do? They pondered these questions and many people wrote their thoughts about them. They documented sparks of wisdom in their great books, some of which became widely known. The fundamentals of the wisdom most people agreed upon: *Love one another. Be kind, compassionate, honest, and respectful. Take care of each other and the Earth Mother.*

So this was a good lot, the humans. Yet with all their accomplishments, progress, and even with their wisdom books, there was one thing that they were never able to do: they could not get along with one another in harmony and peace. In the beginning they had been sensitive and intuitively experienced the answers to such things. Each within themselves was capable of knowing the truth of existence, but they started to get so wrapped up in the external world they forgot to go within and connect to the Great Intelligence that they were part of. They became enamored of the outer physical creation and got lost in the illusion of separation. They started relying on others to tell them what to do and how to be and what to believe.

The humans would read the wisdom books and make up their own interpretations. But since these books were written by many different people and revised over hundreds and sometimes thousands of years, the modern generations of people didn't understand the language of previous centuries. They began to misinterpret the great wisdom. They began to see their differences as frictions and they invented good and evil, haves and have-nots, allies and enemies. They created a world of great separation. They made up rules and regulations that included some and excluded others. They clutched on to their belief systems and they argued over which view was "right." Even though in their hearts and souls they sensed the true underlying reality of unity, they no longer allowed themselves to live in the experience of that wisdom. They had lost touch.

They became mechanical and fought about the concepts that they themselves had created. Not only did they fight collectively, the energy of the anger filtered into their families. Many of them fought with their wives and their husbands and their children. Their fear and anger affected the conditions of the planet Earth herself. Earthquakes and draughts and floods and hurricanes became frequent and fierce, mirroring the angry conditions amongst the people. They lost sight of their connection to one another and the living system they were part of.

Once in a while, when something terrible happened that affected all of them, like a devastating storm or seaquake, they would come together to help each other. But when things returned to "normal" they too would return to their old ways. As much as they had advanced the practical aspects of living, after thousands of years the humans did not advance *themselves*. Even though all their great teachers had told them the single most important thing is to love one another, they allowed themselves to live with prejudice, in judgment, and even in hatred. The odd thing is they didn't see themselves that way. They believed they were kind and loving and fair minded even though their actions belied that. They remained unaware and asleep to the wisdom of their heart. They even developed a killer disease known as "heart disease" that reflected this condition.

And so the Earth people fought with one another for millennia, at first with basic weapons and since they were keenly inventive, they kept developing more advanced ways of killing one another until one day they came to a realization: too many of the nations had enough weapon power that one of their leaders could at any time on a whim order the command and wipe out whole countries. And since the activities and people and creatures on Earth were all interdependent, any one disaster could ravage life on Earth.

Meanwhile in their great books the answers were still there, but they no longer understood the messages. They didn't understand that what they called "evil" simply came from the illusion of separation that they perceived as differences played out as adversarial forces. They didn't get, even though revered masters told them straight out, that the divine kingdom was within them. Some books said certain groups were "chosen people." They had forgotten that all people who would choose to master their divine nature were "the chosen" because they were choosing to live the highest.

Things got so discombobulated that the humans feared the world would end, and they began to make up stories about how "the end" would come. Various "interest" groups who sectioned themselves off from others each had their own version of why things were the way they were. They would tell of horrific things to come, and then they would say who would come and save them (only *some* of them would be saved, according to their stories) and who was going to be in charge afterward. Of course, they all had entirely different stories, so which story was true? (Each group was sure *their* story was the real one.)

Anyway, it was looking very bad for the people of Earth. Many succumbed to fear. Their fear brought out greed and they tried to hoard riches for power so they could protect themselves and bully the other people. They did things that violated natural law. They built structures without regard for the land, they poisoned the waters, they polluted the air, and they raped the forests and ravaged natural resources. They even planned to build "defense" stations in outer space. They clung onto myths that did not serve themselves and the greater good. They were sadly out of sync with nature, inside and out, as if they had fallen into a deep stupor that prevented them from realizing what ills they brought upon themselves.

<center>~~~</center>

There was a story that became quite well known that one of their respected early Greek philosophers told. The story was that there were people in a cave where a streak of light came in and made dancing shadows on the walls of their cave. The cave dwellers mistook the shadows for reality until one day someone found the way out of the darkness of the cave and discovered a whole different reality—a reality much grander, more illumined and magnificent than the illusory one they had been living in.

Like the people who found their way out of the darkness of the cave, a few Earth people began to see the light. They sensed there was something more to life than the shadowy reality of the cave. They called themselves Wake-ups because when they woke up they saw the reality behind the illusion. They knew they had been given a precious gift. They realized they were all part of one whole majestic living system and that they were here to look after the planet and one another. The Wake-ups checked around and found out there were other people who also realized this. Then a few more, then more, and more and more.

Earlier some of them had believed some force or great being would come along some day and save them. They began to wonder: what if no one was coming to save them? Besides, what would they be saved from? Themselves! When they saw that it was *they* who had to save themselves from themselves, it became a day of delight and laughter. Maybe that was the real message of the masters. When they realized this they once again appreciated the wind against their skin, the sea that took them on adventures, the endless sky that lit up with sparkling jewels they called stars. With new eyes they looked upon one another with reverence as brothers and sisters of one human family. Their scientists began to prove in their labs the core wisdom: the unity of all.

They experienced deep gratitude for what the Earth Mother gave forth freely and abundantly: water to drink and air to breathe, fruits and vegetables to eat, rubies and diamonds and sapphires to enjoy, rain forests teeming with natural remedies to maintain health, oceans that contained untold wealth. They knew they were being taken care of by The Great Spirit and that it was a partnership, this life. They also had to do *their* part.

They would have to give up their familiar complaints about one another. They re-interpreted the stories that divided them and had made them enemies. They saw that if they didn't take the words literally the wisdom stories divulged the clues to getting along with one another. Even though when they looked at each other they saw differences with their eyes, in their hearts they knew they were all part of the same human tapestry. When they read the great books with their heart and soul and an expanded mind everything became crystal clear.

And so magnificently and courageously the Earthlings who had been on the brink of disaster saved themselves from themselves because they woke themselves up. They took a giant leap out of the dark and limited cave of their old ways of thinking into the light of awareness and began to create a splendorous world. They had already been given everything they needed by The Great Intelligence. They had been imbued with the power to create. They could write a new story ... and they did. *The End ... and A New Beginning.*

Maybe we're just like the movie moguls—looking for a good story.

So how did you like our story? Well, *of course* I made up a happy ending. What did you expect? We can do that you know. We've been making up the beginnings, middles, and endings all along. Maybe we are just like the movie moguls—looking for a good story.

Since the dawn of recorded history accounts of creation and of our purpose here on Earth have proliferated as we search for a story that can make sense of our lives and of life overall. The golden thread that runs throughout the fabric of humanity is the path of "seekers." What do the seekers seek? Answers to the perennial questions and a connection to an ultimate creator or creative force, the source of existence, an inkling into the Intelligence so awesome that no one of us can even begin to fathom it, though we persistently try and we query.

Who am I?
What is existence?
Is there a God?
What am I supposed to do here?
What is my purpose?
What is happening now?
What will the future bring?

We've developed many stories around this seeking. One website references "over four thousand two hundred documented religions, churches, denominations, religious bodies, faith groups, tribes, cultures, movements, [and] ultimate concerns."[12] That's a *big* number of stories, 4,200. And we take our stories very seriously, so seriously in fact that there are serious arguments around them. That euphemism is putting it mildly. Of course if you have paid even a glimmer of attention to what's been going on for the past few millennia, you know this.

All religions and faiths have their own story, as do other peoples who do not find a need for the concept of God in order to live a purposeful, loving and compassionate life. There are fables and myths and parables and allegories with hundreds of different gods and goddesses, demons and saviors. There are as many interpretations of scriptures as there are groups who study them. Scholars change the interpretations over the years, as do clergy "in charge" of declaring such decisions. Though some arrive at a general consensus, there is no widespread agreement. Even within what are classified as the world's major religions and philosophies there are vehemently opposing viewpoints.

If you have a universal viewpoint to bring people together while honoring our differences, some will label you a "secular humanist," or accuse you of "relativism" (can you imagine *that*?) and these are not compliments, dear friend. Prophecies are numerous and as diverse as belief systems. One website classifies the prophecies of "the red people, the brown people, the olive-skinned people, the black people, the yellow people and the white people."

So what's a person to think?

One of my editors read the statistic on the forty-two hundred registered religious faiths and asked me: "Is that *relevant*?" I smiled to myself. Let me ask *you*. Is it *relevant* to be aware that there are thousands of "stories" depicting belief systems and as we well know from the daily news, they are not all in agreement? Is it relevant in the context of having life be great for everyone to pose the question: How do we deal with this when you realize that lacking mastery with one's own thinking, the differences have kept us from cooperating toward a coherent society? Is it relevant to remind ourselves that just because we think or believe something, it might not be the absolute truth, or at least may not be "right" or appropriate for everyone? Is it relevant to suggest that not any one group of us has cornered the market on spirituality?

These are not necessarily topics we want to have our attention on, especially when you are anxious for your own *personal* expansion and creation of a great life. But let's face it; sometimes we have to. This is the field that surrounds your life and mine. There are distinctions and there are physical distances between us, yes, but according to science, in this universe of whole interconnected systems there are no actual separations. To QuantumThink it is necessary to look from the whole. We condition the fields of energy and intelligence we live within. Those fields condition us in turn. Is it relevant to take a look at *what we are allowing to condition us*?

I'm grateful to that editor because perhaps what she was really asking on your behalf is: *What's religion got to do with it?* What does all this have to do with learning to QuantumThink? **QuantumThink is about expanding our way of viewing the world so we can create more efficiently and effectively with the highest**

respect and reverence for all of life. When we are trapped in any mechanical shell of cultural conditioning we tend to allow our beliefs, our rules, our politics and our outdated laws to supersede our humanity.

Religious and other beliefs tend to be deeply engrained, passed along by the ancestors from generation to generation, often without questioning. For example, in certain religions "suffering" is believed by some to be a kind of grand noble act. The fact that many great beings have suffered does not automatically equate to suffering being a desirable ambition. And why would you want to allow yourself to be convinced of such an idea?

During the researching and writing of this chapter I agonized over it because I didn't want to offend anyone's beliefs about religion, heaven, hell, nirvana, or otherwise. Then I finally realized: if you want to be offended that is your choice. Of course it's good to acknowledge that you are actually *choosing* to be offended as distinct from merely mechanically *reacting*. After all we are here to QuantumThink and that means you wish to live a conscious life.

Whatever your personal belief, please know that this discussion is intended to honor and respect, not to disparage. I am not here to agree or disagree with anyone's beliefs. My only Intent is that our life here on Earth works at the highest aspect of our nature. Sometimes that takes expanding our vision by questioning what we have automatically accepted in the face of unworkable and even tragic outcomes of blind unexamined acceptance.

~~~

"Never discuss religion or politics in polite company."

An informal caveat popular when I was growing up was never to discuss politics or religion in so-called "polite company." I suppose because people are so strongly attached to their political and religious views it tends to frazzle nerves and fizzle friendly relations. Resistance to others' beliefs is generating global incoherence. In science "incoherence" means waves out of phase. In the body, incoherence results in disease because the cells aren't harmonizing with each other. Some religious leaders are arriving at the conclusion that non-acceptance of other people's beliefs is not really working. This is not to say accept others' beliefs as your own; it is to say, acknowledge and accept that there are other beliefs as valid as your own and that people are entitled to practice their traditions in freedom so long as they do not harm others. Hallelujah for small revelations.

A Heavenly quantum occurrence.

While I was writing this chapter television journalist Barbara Walters did an ABC TV news special called *Heaven* where she interviewed leaders of various faiths and belief systems including a Jewish rabbi, an Islamic scholar, an evangelical preacher, an Islamic failed suicide bomber, a Baptist pastor, the spiritual leader of Tibetan

Buddhism, an atheist leader, authors, actors and others. As you watch the show what is contained in this chapter comes alive in the flesh for you, seeing all the different beliefs and how an individual seems convinced that *their* belief is "the one." Though most adherents are friendly and kind, incomprehensively the terrorist voices the intent to kill people in the flesh while a few other religious advocates attempt to wipe people out "spiritually" by declaring all who have another religious preference other than theirs are sure to end up in hell. Either way, doesn't it seem ungodly and maybe even a little insane to think that you are doing God's work by going around killing people off in any dimension?

So I thought maybe we could start discussing these things *politely*. Have a real dialogue beyond the old world view-conditioned *Either* my way *Or* yours. Get a little more creative, go to a higher place. The Cognitive Science Laboratory at Princeton University ("WordNet 2.0") defines "indoctrination" as "teaching some-one to accept doctrines uncritically." Indoctrination without critical thinking can be deleterious to a civilization and bad for your health.

Chiune Sugihara, the Japanese diplomat consul to Lithuania who acted outside of "official orders" to courageously assist thousands of Jews escape horrific, tortuous deaths by Nazis stated, *"You do what's right because it's right."* Chiune used critical thinking.

> *"To tell the truth, having the instructions, I thought of them over and over again. Through the night I finally concluded that humanity must come to the first place more than anything else."*
>   —Chiune Sugihara, "Decisions for Life 1983"

As Chiune Sugihara said and did, maybe you do good—beyond all rituals, beyond all conventions, beyond all rules—you do good because it's the right thing in support of all people. Are you going to get an eat-all-you want buffet in heaven not only without paying money for it but without gaining weight? It's not for me to say. (Isn't that kind of an Earth-bound thought anyway?) Look in your heart. Look at the world. The question is what are you going to do about it?

Whether you believe there is heaven and hell here on Earth, be it in your state of mind, or someplace else, the fact is: we are all on this Earth, together, in this time.

It might be worthwhile to ask yourself not whether you are going to heaven or hell, but rather, it might be time to ask yourself how we all make it together coher-ently and harmoniously on this planet in this lifetime. And who knows … if there is reincarnation, the idea of a soul or spirit taking form again in the sense of a renewal of energy and life, or if there is another "place" in another dimension you are en route to, then doing things "right" here and now just might turn out *heavenly* for you.

Hey, hey, hey, let's not add another "complaint" without coming up with a solution. From a new world view it's a Both/And world. Can you hold your beliefs for yourself and allow others to hold their beliefs without ill will or retribution at any level? You can master yourself. Maybe that's all there is to it. An interesting contemplation.

~~~~~~~~~~~~~~~

QUANTUMTHINK-WAVE
Doing what's right because it's right.

Do you do what's right because you fear the consequences if you don't do it, or because you are going to get some sort of "reward" if you do? Or do you do what's right simply because it's "right"?

~~~~~~~~~~~~~~~

What can we learn from King Tut?

The celebrated young Egyptian pharaoh, Tutankhamen (King Tut) exhibit is traveling around the world to various museums. Once you bring yourself past the weirdness of digging up people's burial sites and opening their coffins to check out what their trip was, you see the "story" of this 3,500 year-old past. A genealogy is shown indicating it is questionable who Tut's father was, but historians venture their best guess. Then you see that the person who they *think* was his father but there is no real proof so they are really not sure—anyway, you also see that this previous pharaoh, King Akhenaten (known as the heretic pharaoh) decided to change the system of gods they believed in. He determined there was only one god to be worshipped, the sun disk. And that was that. He changed what people were to believe in. After all, he was the king, you know. And then when Tut came into power he decided to change it back to the many gods the Egyptian culture had worshipped previously. Even though Tut changed it back, Akhenaten's idea of one god "had legs" as they say in the movie business, as it is said to be one of the precursors of modern monotheism.

Now if you think this sort of thing happened only back then in antiquity, one person changing beliefs for the other people, that is; pardon me for saying you are mistaken.

A case in point. Many people have what we call "mystical experiences." A sense of awe about life itself when you connect to that Great Intelligence, when your heart is so open and you experience a love so profound and the connection so real, the ecstasy of the infinite unboundedness of it all is experienced directly. Many times throughout modern history someone had one of those revelatory epiphanies and imagined they were "The One" through whom God was speaking. (Where would that leave Neo in *The Matrix*?) And then what happened? He or she started a new religion. Have you ever thought about how many new religions are started every time someone has a mystical revelation? How wonderful that in many nations we do have the freedom to worship as we please. Yet does that make every new religion "the one"? Is God speaking to some of us but not all of us? Let's get some critical thinking going here, friends. Watch the Barbara Walters *Heaven* show with critical thinking and you might see that the way we have dealt with religion and beliefs isn't exactly practical and not even logical. If you are already critically thinking about such matters, examining for clarity, thoroughness, and fairness, then all I can say is … thank you. And God bless.

Prophecies or Patterns?

In the midst of an unpopular war in Iraq, a woman of Jewish descent said to me, resigned about the war and state of affairs: "The Messiah is coming, and then it's the end of the world anyway." I am not certain she actually believed that story. She was simply explaining what had been told to her. Many people today subscribe to their own version of an end time around the story of human evolution at this particular moment in the unfolding of the Universal Drama. There are various versions of this. The Christian version with Armageddon as the site of the final battle between good and evil. It is said that at the low point in human existence Buddhists await the arrival of Maitreya to come five thousand years after the original enlightened being known as Buddha. There are others, a Rostiferian version, an Islamic version, a Hindu version, a Bahá'í version. Since the current cycle of the Mayan calendar is said to end in the year 2012, some believe it to prophesize "the end of the world."

Despite the kaleidoscope of tales, the major religions and the prophecies of the indigenous peoples appear to agree on a few things: There will be signs (not such positive ones) when the world is coming to an "end point" and afterward each one's version of the "promised one" ("messiah") arrives, and following a few battles with the other religions, one reigns triumphant, the others fall away, and eventually (it takes a lot of years they say) there is peace on Earth. Or something along those lines. Despite their cognitive dissonance, the prophecies concur on one thing. They predict that it gets worse—*real* bad—before it gets better. The darkness before the dawn thing.

Did God play a bad joke on us?

Let's see … if God were playing a bad joke on us, what would the "bad joke" be? (If you don't like the term or the idea "God" fill in whatever word pleases you that refers to the ultimate creative force). If we take the prophecies to be "the way it is" or in this case, since prophecy is of a predictive future nature, "the way it *will* be" the bad joke would be that we have no say in anything, no control over anything, no ability to advance and develop, and no real creativity. The bad joke would be that the prophecies were determined absolutely and that's it. But nothing in the universe gives evidence of such pre-determinism. There are reliable patterns yet everything is in constant and continuous motion and change. The planets move around the Sun yet the entire galaxy is shifting. Electrons move around the nucleus of the atom yet their paths are not fixed. Every one of the trillions of cells in your body and mine are undergoing continuous process changes and re-patterning can occur. Whether mechanically conditioned or consciously chosen, in the human realm we make decisions that affect things. What is *absolutely* determined and "fixed" in our world?

> *"I have noticed even people who claim everything is predestined, and that we can do nothing to change it, look before they cross the road."*
> —STEPHEN HAWKING, *cosmologist*

If God wanted us as pre-determined we would all be God's robots, mere puppets. Is this what you truly believe? Prophecies are considered to be revealed knowledge, that is, revealed from Divine source, what we can call the Great Intelligence. Did you ever consider that what gets prophesied is *projected* from whatever *habitual patterns* of behavior are currently being observed in the culture? It's like going up to a teenager and saying, "You know if you keep acting out your anger in destructive ways, you are going to end up having a life in prison." That's a prophecy based on the way things are going now. But it's not an absolute. The teenager can alter his ways, take a higher road, improve his character, and alter his destiny. And so can we.

If you go online and search on "prophecies" you'll be deluged with Web writers wanting to convince you absolutely of how what is going on today—war, pestilence, disease, and nature's furies of fire and floods—is evidence of what their scriptures predicted. They're saying, *"See, see, this is what God said, and so it has to get real bad and then the messiah will finally show up. You see, it's already happening"* they tell you *"this is it, the end times."* Well, friends, it's an Observer-created Reality after all. If there are no "absolutes" we can take a different cut at this.

> *"There is nothing either good or bad but thinking makes it so."*
> —SHAKESPEARE'S Hamlet *(or was it Francis Bacon's?—wink ...)*

It's an Observer-created Reality after all.

Consider that prophecies are *"possible* futures" (again, based on currently discernible habits), *not absolute* ones. What we focus on expands. You activate the field and forward manifestation with your attention and Intent. Just as people activated the so called "truth" of a flat Earth and a geocentric galaxy, millions of people over many centuries can hold "realities" in place, even when those "realities" aren't pre-determined *or even factual.*

One can understand how we would come up with "the fallen condition and being saved from evil" story. Yet, if you get caught up in literal or questionable interpretations you might give yourself (and others) an unpleasant ride with all of this. Your mind is your life, remember. However you hold this story in your own consciousness is what is giving you your experience. It will shape your actions. It will determine the circumstances of our outer world.

<center>~~~</center>

The essence of all the stories comes down to the "struggle between good and evil." It is that we have come to the fork in the road where we choose good over evil, life over extinction, the united brotherhood of humanity over divisive separation caused by perceived differences—where we have to choose to take a leap of faith in consciousness or we will destroy ourselves.

Consider it's a case of which came first, the chicken or the egg. Do things *have to* get bad in the world because that's when the prophecies say we'll get saved? Or do conditions get so bad because we believe the old stories and fall victim to them until we find ourselves on a downhill slide? And then when things get so bad in the world that we can't stand it anymore, we wake up and realize either we really can make the shift or else we're sitting around waiting for the messiah to do it for us.

Movie moguls like the stories of good and evil. Social scientists might say that the dark themes in books and movies are the way we express the "shadow" aspects of ourselves. Most audiences like when good wins out over evil because underneath it all people seek the highest and want the best. The way they think we arrive "there" is another story. Anytime you are *against*, even with the noblest intentions and in the name of the highest virtues, you perpetuate the "good and evil" mythology. A mythology doesn't mean something is false; it means this is a story we choose to live by. We know more now, folks. It's time for a new story.

Consider that it is the end of the world *as we have known it until now.* Suppose we really are in a time of evolution unlike any we have witnessed or known, and as we evolve ourselves and our own consciousness, our inner and outer reality is truly *new*, different than what we experience now. The Indian scriptures say this entire universe is a *play of consciousness.*[13] This "reality" came about—why not another one that we have never known?

In his book, *The Universe in a Single Atom*, temporal and spiritual leader of Tibet, His Holiness The Dalai Lama discusses his feeling that the ancient Buddhist teach-ings that describe the nature of things such as atoms need to be updated where appropriate in light of the more accurate and precise scientific discoveries of today. What great wisdom he teaches us by his own example to acknowledge and take action when there is re-writing to be done even of the most revered texts of his own tradition that have stood for thousands of years. When you uncover new knowledge, it's time to revise the story.

What story are you living in? Have you ever thought about it? Have you ever questioned its efficacy? What re-writing is appropriate now in your life? What "antiquated facts" have you been living by that need to be updated? Yes, you can write a new story, my friend. You wrote the one you're living now (or "someone" or group of "someones" wrote it for you). You can write a story about how you broke free of crusty old stale beliefs. Reality is not what we once believed it to be. Our heart is 60 percent brain cells, not just a muscle. Our DNA is not fixed nor is our mythology.

II
A New Mythology: A Different Story

"If we worked on the assumption that what is accepted as true really is true, then there would be little hope for advance."
ORVILLE WRIGHT, *aviator and inventor who,*
with his brother, WILBUR, *built and flew the first airplane*

There are lots of new stories arising today. Some say this Earth is a large classroom and we are here to get our lessons on our way to Self-mastery as we evolve toward manifestation of our highest godlike nature. Great thinkers today envision a different kind of future consistent with the idea of The Great Shift that many indigenous cultures refer to. The *new* story is we have come to a place of a leap for all of humanity, a grand quantum leap in consciousness to a higher state of being of such scale as we have never witnessed or known. *No child of the cosmos left behind.*

Futurist Barbara Marx Hubbard proposes an "emergence" of a Universal Human, one that finally matures from adolescence to adulthood. Social scientist Willis Harmon said a Global Mind Change is underway, changes in our images of reality, a power of consciousness beyond any economic, political, or military power. Earth scientist and visionary author, Gregg Braden, proposes the "awakening to the zero point," when we reach a state of energetic "stillness" that enables a restructuring of human consciousness such that The Great Shift happens. Cosmologist, Peter Russell, proposes "a white hole in time" when a dramatic opening of critical mass in higher consciousness occurs all at once and pulls all of us into the white hole of awakening. This author (your friend) is saying that a literal quantum leap to a *new world view thinking system* can bring about the shift quickly and easily.

As far as mythologies go, the idea of a Great Shift definitely sounds like a better story to me. What about you? In our Observer-created Reality, you and I have the amazing opportunity to choose. Would you choose to live the lowest or most dismal vision? Would you choose to live a mediocre vision? Does *old world view* thinking have you attached to the "absoluteness" of troubling prophecies or can you see deeper into the symbolic meanings and brighter possibilities of a human species imbued with the power to create? In any event we need to be in the state of a Wake-up, free of automatic and mechanical thinking, to make any kind of choice.

The 19th century French writer, George Polti, put forth the idea that there were basically thirty-six dramatic situations in stories and that everything else was more or less a variation on those themes. The notion of thirty-six was accepted and has stuck in dramatic theory, even though *Polti himself said* that the number of themes could be more or less and explained that this is simply how *he* categorized them. This portrays the way we latch onto a theory and stay within the same old monotonous dramas.

Suppose we could leap beyond the good and evil thing altogether and move on to another kind of reality where we aren't pulled to be "against" anything? Spiritual teacher Ginger Chalford points out that we have been "stuck" in the good and evil myth. Like anything else, that story of good and evil and their ongoing battle, is not an absolute. Hey, I realize this is so far from anything we have known in our good and evil structure that we can barely hear it, let alone embrace it. Yet, it is possible. And not to worry, it doesn't mean life becomes homogenized and boring.

Can you imagine a world where we were not dealing with the current problems of poverty, hunger, crime, bigotry, war, dictators, and disease? Probably not. Yet there is some resonant field for it. John Lennon's "Imagine" is one of the most often quoted song lyrics where essentially he asked us to imagine just such a world. In the past we have called that "utopia," an unattainable state of perfect harmony or Heaven on Earth. (Heaven is allegedly someplace *else*, right?) The quality and nature of everyday living would be so different than what we have now that we cannot even envision it within the limited scope of our mind's eye in this moment in space-time.

Every time you have these thoughts, *"... it will always be like this ... (the girl's naïve) ... there'll always be war (poverty, hunger) ... that's human nature ..."* stop yourself right there and remember what creates and sustains reality: your own mind, your own thoughts, our collective consciousness. When the war machinery appears too entrenched, when the national cultures look too disparate, when the religious beliefs appear too unyielding, recall to yourself: who is creating those thoughts and holding them in place?

The bottom line is ... when you heighten your consciousness you don't tend to do things like pick up weapons and kill one another. It doesn't make you unpatriotic. It doesn't make you unsupportive of men and women in the military. It simply creates a different kind of reality. Albert Einstein stood for such a new reality. One week before he passed away he signed his last letter to Bertrand Russell where he agreed to place his name on a manifesto urging all nations to give up nuclear weapons.[14] Maybe not yet a full fledged different reality of the type I am speaking about here, yet a beginning spark. Of course, Einstein like Ghandi gets labeled a "pacifist" in our current story line. And the "others" who believe in war get labeled as "hawks." Is the desire for peace a bad thing? Let's get over the labels already, fellow actors and playwrights. *Way* too old world view.

Many people are working on a new reality, such as acclaimed author, Marianne Williamson, who along with others is petitioning the U.S. Congress to initiate a cabinet level Department of Peace. *(Think of the possibilities; from a new world view, context is everything.)* Justice activist attorney Van Jones, along with others seeks to transform a retributive punishment-based justice system to a restorative system based on reconciliation, healing, and rehabilitation. Quantum physicist Dr. John Hagelin is actively investigating the use of group meditation practices toward generating peaceful, stable resonances in hot crime-ridden cities. These projects may sound crazy or be looked upon as impossible by the stale and crusty among us, yet these are real and practical actions and innovative contexts that are gaining credibility and momentum.

The meditation master Swami Muktananda had a wonderful teaching. He said the purer the vessel the better you can hold the energy of a higher awareness. The "real" stories (i.e., daily living) all point to one thing: go out of balance with wisdom and basically you're screwed.

When you are tuned into cosmic laws, you know how to take care of the lands and resources and people and your own health. And guess what, you do! Collective reality is by consensus agreement. What were once problems vanish because people no longer activate that level of reality. The bottom line is … when we become Wake-ups, the way we function collectively is transformed. What if it really is that simple?

God did not play a bad joke on us. Pre-determined mechanical puppets would be much too boring for God and nothing God does is boring. God gave us free will so he/she wouldn't be bored with the show. We have free will. We have been granted creation principles. When you wake up to them you can use them.

Dr. Brian Weiss, the Yale psychiatrist renowned for his work in regressing patients into knowledge of "past lives" to eliminate phobias,[15] has also documented that *people can alter their future by altering their actions in the present.* Dr. Weiss points out that since many different futures are possible the determining factor is our own choice. In his studies with groups he has asked over five thousand people including experienced clairvoyants to look ahead to see what Earth would be like one hundred, five hundred, one thousand years from now. A significant percentage of people saw that in one thousand years into the future we would have an idyllic peaceful world of lush greenery and harmony. Why wait?

Since we are quite literally the creators of our reality, we could get our world to that new state, yet we cannot fathom how it would happen and can't imagine from our current viewpoint what such a reality would be like. Cutting edge science is proving over and over again that our consciousness plays an essential role in the outer world of matter. The indigenous shaman cultures know that we "dream" our reality. In a universe of Infinite Possibility, why not dream something more appealing into view, now?

What does it mean to live in an incredible, miraculous information age such as ours? With so much communication and transmission capability whatever effects we focus on today are going to be magnified. Everyone is always so concerned about how things are going to be recorded in "the history books"; did that president or this prime minister do a good job or a bad job? What about Now? Re-write the Present, and the Future and Past take care of themselves.

> *"Do not yield to misfortunes, but advance more boldly to meet them, as your fortune permits you."*
>
> VIRGIL, *poet of ancient Rome*

The point is why should we wait, like feeble, fearful victims for the *ancestral* automatic and mechanical thought pathways to hit? We can intervene. We are in a time of evolution unlike any we have known when what must evolve is human consciousness itself: our own mind and awareness. The irony of an evolution in consciousness is that *it must be chosen, consciously.* Think of it as an experiment in human kind. Yes, I spelled that as two words deliberately to remind us … to be kind.

One of the facts I learned during my research is that the term "Rapture" does not appear in the Bible, neither the Old or New Testaments. It is attributed by scholars to a 19th century Irish Anglican priest, John Nelson Darby, who broke with the Church of England and founded his own sect. He coined the term "Rapture" from the Latin *rapere*, meaning "to be caught up" or "snatched."[16] Many believe that they will be "snatched up"—carried away to heaven from this Earth by a savior, who will leave the rest behind. Yet, if you think of the meaning of *rapture* as being carried away by an expression of an ecstatic feeling, you might give new meaning to traditions and ideas such as this one.

Whether or not one "being" is coming to save you, who knows? What we do know is we can honor the spirit of "the messiah" in our very own consciousness. Perhaps that is what we are destined to tune into. When you pray, when you read scriptures, when you communicate directly with whatever you call Divine, when you invoke the spirit of whatever archetypal hero, god, or savior you relate to, when you meditate and contemplate to establish yourself in the state of the clear light—*in that moment*, where does the messianic spirit exist? In your very own Self.

Philosophers have combed their minds to find "proofs" of the existence of God. If God, by definition, is unlimited and metaphysical we can use neither logic nor physical measurements to know or accurately "describe" God. That's about the most logical statement I can make about it. Regarding questions of the existence of

"God" people tend to rely on faith. One definition of "faith" is *"Belief that does not rest on logical proof or material evidence."* From a new world view we can go beyond "belief" to an inner knowing. If God is light, if God is consciousness, if God is love, if God is infinite creativity, kindness and compassion, then we can *know* what we mean by God in our experience. The teaching is that we are made in the image of God. If God is creation, and we are reflections of God, then *bingo*. According to any kind of logic, in some important sense we are creators, too.

> *"The purpose of the Creator in creating the human being was for his highest creature to live his or her life according to true human nature, which is to realize the potential of the "image of God" which lies within every human being."*
>
> —Torah interpretation

> *"God created man in His own image, in the image of God He created him; male and female He created them."*
>
> —Genesis 1:26–27

> *"The 'creator of the world,' basically, is the mind."*
>
> —Philosophical questions on Creation, H.H. THE DALAI LAMA

QUANTUMTHINK-WAVE
Who or what creates your reality?

Perhaps the most important task for each one of us is to ponder this question. Whether you are of the belief that your soul chose the exact conditions into which you would be born, or whether you are of the belief that God decided for you, or whether you think that your existence is simply a random blip on the cosmic radar screen—the fact remains: We are here on this Planet Earth in this Milky Way Galaxy in this never-ending cosmos, and we can in fact create, generate and invent. This world is a playground of creation. We have been imbued with the ability to create. To discover and become adept at the laws of creation, to use this knowledge in the highest form with awareness in the purest state: This is our task now.

Art imitates Life

A characteristic of what we consider great art is that it can be interpreted on many different levels. This is what makes it so rich. The same could be said of our stories.

A story like *Alice in Wonderland* can be seen as a fantastical, fanciful children's fantasy, a symbolic allegory that tells us about how our minds work, and as a political statement from Lewis Carroll, born Charles Dodgson. At the time he had to deal with the new discoveries of science in a cryptic way, hiding his message through fable.

A story points to a deeper reality beyond the capability words alone can express. In Buddhism they refer to this as the finger pointing to the moon. If you mistake the finger for the moon you miss the true nature of the moon.

Master spiritual teachers use symbols from one tradition to another to show they indicate the same meaning. The Bulgarian Master Omraam Mikhaël Aïvanhov compares, for example, the Father, Son and Holy Ghost trinity of the Christian Bible to various branches of the Sephirotic Tree of Life in Kabbalah, the chakra system and fiery Kundalini energy of the Indian tradition, the symbol of the caduceus in medicine, and the laser in technology.[17] They all point to a similar purpose. They are blueprints, guideposts illuminating our path. We are here to manifest the highest so that all may enjoy the gift of life and all of creation whose principle force is love—God, Light, Love, the Tao, the Void, however you wish to relate to it. There are many energetic and spiritual techniques that have been developed for reaching such heights, some that have been taught for millennia in what are called "mystery schools" where initiates into a particular teaching or school were the only ones privy to the information.

It used to be that "the knowledge" was passed along orally only to those elite and privileged and/or mature enough to receive it. Not any more. It is said that the time has come for the "mysteries" to be revealed to all. You and I are the ones who must expand to meet the world we are co-creating. Enlightenment is not a belief. It is simply waking up to your true nature.

> *"In the deeper reality, you know absolutely who you are and what your purpose is. There is no confusion or conflict with any other person on earth. Your purpose in life is to help creation to expand and grow."*
>
> Deepak Chopra, The Book of Secrets

What can we learn from the stories in scriptures? The Old Testament says there will be an Exodus where all will be free. According to the Old Testament, God chose the descendants of Abraham through the line of Isaac and Jacob, the ancestors of today's Jews, as the people through whom he would reveal himself to the world. God therefore freed them from slavery in Egypt and led them into the Promised Land. (Is this the reason Jews have had so much difficulty? Other people wanted to get to the Promised Land, too?)

Could the "Exodus" be the freeing of ourselves from the "slavery" of old beliefs that don't work, never have and never will? What if the "Apocalypse" simply refers to the breaking down of the illusory reality we have been living in, the disintegration of the divisive "sin" of separation. Could the Promised Land be symbolic language for the enlightened state?

~~~

"Everyone wants to understand art. Why not try to understand a song of a bird, why does one love the night, the flowers, everything around one without trying to understand them."

—PABLO PICASSO

When you read all these inspirational quotations that get sent to you over the Internet you are bound to receive one that compares your life to a work of art. As Picasso intimated perhaps we're not here to "understand" it all; maybe we're here to create the stories and be aware that we can make up new stories and just love our stories. The art of life is painted and the music of life is played with the all-pervasive consciousness that becomes your mind and the collective mind and objectifies itself in the out-picturing we call our world.

Anne Frank, youngest and most well known victim of the Holocaust, endured the cruelty of a conceptual society so far separated from heart, soul, and spirit that they became like video game robots positioned to kill without remorse. Still, she wrote in her diary: "... *in spite of everything, I still believe that people are really good at heart.*" We activate the field with our intent and our intentions. Let's activate *that* field.

Suppose you do good not because you'll suffer the consequences of a legal system or of a wrathful god, not because you will get rewarded in another place; you do good because it's "right," because *that works*—for everyone. Could that be true mastery? If you cannot master yourself, how can you master anything in the outer world or any "other world" either?

"When science sees consciousness to be a fundamental quality of reality, and religion takes God to be the light of consciousness shining within us all, the two worldviews start to converge."

PETER RUSSELL, *cosmologist and author of* From Science to God

Stories are created to reveal something to us; higher truths or truths of our being. We have more knowledge now. It's time for a new story. As a culture of Wake-ups we can alter the individual and collective destiny of ourselves and this Earth. *We can write a new story and live by it. It has already begun.* Even if you are not so interested in the bigger picture as you are in yourself, I know one thing for sure: You can still appreciate some awesome moments of light.

11

LIGHT

One quantum moment can change the world

Spiritual master Omraam Mikhaël Aïvanhov taught that light is a living spirit; light is a conscious entity. He said that light wants to reach us to elevate our consciousness but just as the Sun cannot pierce through dense clouds in the sky, when there are clouds in the atmosphere of our being, the light cannot reach us. When the clouds dissipate through awareness and purity of your own thoughts and emotions, you have such clarity that a single moment of effulgent light can alter the entire direction and quality of your life.

A Little Bit of My Story Sneaking in Now

A *USA Today* newspaper article hangs on a wall in my office. The headline reads:

All the answers for all time in one tiny package.

The article speaks about the wonders of quantum physics and that quote refers to the "quantum," the tiniest unit of measurable reality holding so many answers within it. Since life is Holographic (the whole of it is contained in each part) you could imagine that we have tiny moments when you see all the answers for all time in one tiny package, for your own life and for life itself. Yes, I have had such quantum moments. I'd like to tell you about one.

One day early in my writing aspirations, to make what I thought would be "easy money," I was attempting to write romance novels, the kind of light and pleasant love stories that are simple (so I thought) and short, and I was having trouble doing it. I couldn't understand why I was having so much difficulty. *I'm a decent writer*, I thought. *Why is this so hard for me?*

In a delirious moment beyond frustration, I declared to my cousin, *I'm stuck. I can't do this. I'm going to call up Isaac Bashevis Singer and ask him what to do.* With her hysterical laughter still ringing in my ear, I brazenly picked up the phone and called Isaac Bashevis Singer. He answered the phone himself. When I heard his voice and realized I had just dialed up a Nobel Prize laureate in literature to ask advice on writing a romance novel, (was I nuts?), I blurted out, *"Isaac, you don't know me, but I need your help!"* Isaac Bashevis Singer, a man of great curiosity, was intrigued. He said, *"A philosopher turned marketer turned writer? This, I've got to meet."*

And meet we did, the next morning over coffee on a street named after him in Miami Beach. We chatted for a while. I had a zillion questions about him and his writing and what it was like to receive so many awards for his art form. He told me he didn't think so much about the awards because people always want to know how good the *next* creation is going to be so he had to concentrate on that. I learned much from his wisdom. Finally I poured out to him the woes of my own writing dilemma. He listened intently, piercing, steel blue eyes twinkling in my direction. Then he leaned across the 50s' diner table and whispered loudly in his enchanting, thick Yiddish accent, *"In order to write junk, you've got to have a junky soul."*

In one tiny moment, an answer for all time. It was the jolt I needed more than the strong diner coffee. Of course! *You can only do what is true to you.* Seems so obvious now, yet how much time do we spend doing or attempting to do that which seems logical but is definitely not in accord with who we are? I should tell you that Isaac immediately clarified that his reference to "junk" wasn't directed toward or disparaging romance writing in any way. He had simply stated the message with his inimitable poignancy and passion to make the point to me so it penetrated deep. (And did it ever.) I knew I could only do what resonated in my soul, what I am uniquely here to do. The light was on. One Quantum Moment with Isaac changed my life from that point on … *forever.*

<hr />

How amazing would it be if young children were taught to know that they arrive on Earth with a unique purpose. In our own way, each of us grows up sometimes feeling like a stranger in a strange land. You look around at the absurdities in the world and you are appalled. You have private thoughts like *No one understands me. Am I the only one who sees this? Does anyone else feel this way?* As a youth you are wondering what's it all about, Alfie, but in a reality focused in physical matter we're not talking to 5 year-olds, 15 year-olds or even 55 year-olds much about other "matters" like meaning and purpose.

Then what happens? A person in your life, someone in the throes of their own unaware mechanical Least-action Pathway—a parent, a teacher, a counselor—inflicts their "trip" on you, tells you you're stupid or you'll never make it, or you should give up acting or music or astrophysics or whatever form your dream takes that doesn't fit their picture. "Wretched Self Syndrome" sets in and molds your experience for the rest of your life. We can all give that one up now.

Wretched Self Syndrome—It's got to go.

This is a perfect time for us to discuss Wretched Self Syndrome because, basically, it's got to go. I adapted the term "wretched self" from a teaching of the meditation master Swami Muktananda who said, *"The biggest sin is to think of yourself as a wretched little creature."* Isn't this a wonderful idea—to give up thinking of yourself as lowly in any way? From a new world view perspective, Reality is Context-dependent. Think of the life you would have if you live from *that* context—that is, suffering from Wretched Self Syndrome. (By the way, quite a widespread phenomenon amongst us humans.) Muktandanda called this "the biggest sin." You can see why he said that, if you think of all of us as divine creations, whatever you consider "the Divine" to be.

Some people think of us as *aspects* of God and since God is by definition omnipresent, that is, everywhere all the time pervading all things, this interpretation makes sense. Others think of us as *children* of God, and if God is the original creative force from which we are born, then this interpretation makes sense also. Some people do not find a need for the concept of God in order to acknowledge the primordial essence of the universe. Even if you are agnostic or atheist and you have high morals, ethics and standards and feel you don't need a belief in a God, or even if you think of yourself as your own God—the point is that in any of these divine scenarios it's not only inconsistent to think of yourself as a wretched creature; it is truly *ineffective*, abundance of "sin" propaganda notwithstanding.

Chase the clouds away

When you begin to watch your own thought patterns with awareness, you are likely to find that much of what you think and do is automatic. This is not a bad thing in and of itself, just something to notice. Besides, now you have a perfectly good explanation for why we are so mechanical and automatic, (old world view conditioning) so you're off the hook of thinking of yourself as a wretched little creature who is "not right" in some way. Not being "wretched" does not mean we're not responsible. After all, we've been endowed with create-ability.

One of our automatic habits is that we spend so much time and energy and effort talking about what doesn't work, we miss the point that we have the power to create something that works ... for everyone. When you get access to the laws of creation in your Self, something really interesting happens. You realize that you, along with others, actually can generate a new reality. We don't have to be stuck with this one. Maybe you don't have to spend your whole life trying to get rid of something that you picked up from someone else. You don't even have to make excuses or rationalizations for it either.

If we do in fact create our reality and keep it in place by what we continue to hold in our consciousness, isn't it possible that you can literally give up deeming yourself "recovering" or "co-dependent" and *slip into something more comfortable* as they say in the movies, or in this case, more *comforting*, more empowering, more enlivening. Why not drop the labels that doom you to failure of any kind? Why do we have to be stuck with *that* convention?

"Quantum physics is the physics of possibilities."

—AMIT GOSWAMI, *quantum physicist and author*

Question Reality

Next to the quantum article in my office is a hologram bumper sticker on my credenza window that I like to keep directly in view, "Question Reality" just in case I forget. Now you can Question Reality in a new way. Instead of asking with scorn or in despair why is this *this* way, and why is that *that* way, you can question the reality of its workability, its efficacy. You can ask: Does this still work in light of what is going on today? Why do we have to keep *that* convention?

In the movie, *About a Boy*, the boy lives with a single parent, his depressed mother. The boy realizes in this situation that two people (he and his Mom) aren't enough; you need backup. So he befriends a man he likes and though he doesn't convince the man to become his stepfather, he does become "extended family" in friendship. That was one creative young dude. And it works. The idea of an extended family where people come together to interconnect in kindred groups not restricted to or by the traditional family unit is in essence, an expansion.

Various groups want to stake their claim to "family values" and narrowly define what that is. A consequence of limited thinking regarding the family structure stigmatizes children with the cultural conditioning that "they could have problems as a result of being from a divorced family," and turns them into an ice-cold statistic. Divorces and children in divided homes being a cloud in your life? Why do we have to be stuck with *that* reality?

Given the number of families who have experienced divorce and re-marriages, it makes sense to have that situation become workable and healthy. The extended family is essentially a new reality, another possibility. What about creating a reality where all the "ex" wives and "ex" husbands, all the children from another marriage learn to love and respect one another, as part of our culture? Something like the REMIX on a CD recording. You take the original soundtrack of Destiny's Child, and you add in JayZ, and you come up with something else great and exciting, using the same musical foundation. (If you don't know what I'm talking about, consult the nearest kid.)

So imagine this: you learn the natural laws at the edge of knowledge today that we each have access to that enable us to generate, create, and manifest reality. Then you realize you have the power to generate something more workable. All we have to do is learn to think in a new way. And you are already doing that. *Cool.*

I say "at the edge of our knowledge" because one of the things we realize is that the nature of life is to grow and evolve and change and expand and transform itself—so we can never be so arrogant as to think that any bit or body of knowledge is the end point.

A more workable world begins with each one of us. Through each of us we broadcast a collective reality. We're connected. We affect one another and the whole. We condition the field with our predominant habits of thinking. Thoughts are not fixed containments. They infuse the energetic realm. The thoughts we hold in place personally shape our experience of reality, and what we hold in our minds collectively sustains the shape of our world. We're a global broadcasting station.

Without clarity on the radio of our being, you know what happens. There is noise. However, we can come together consciously, with awareness, with the Intent to have something sublime happen. What does this affect? Everything. It affects your moment-to-moment experience, the way you relate with your partner, your child, your parents, your associates, your customers, your pets, yourself. It affects what you allow yourself to have and be—your approaches and relationship to success, economic status, degree of self expression and creativity, your understanding of your purpose on the planet. It affects the way we view politics and politicians, health and health care practitioners, corporations and corporate leaders. Through you, it affects the world.

Light giving light.

In our world we have a lot of candlelight vigils to show our support or to honor an event or someone of importance. In the Olympics there is a ceremony of passing the torch. Each one honored with the task of holding the torch lights the next person's until the final torch is lit at the top of the Olympic stadium for all the world to see. The whole world united in light. These are symbolic.

Planets are visible because of the light they reflect from the Sun. The play of light and shadow creates a photograph, enabling us to see things in a particular way. The inner light is the life sustaining force. It is the light of consciousness, of awareness. It is the source of our experience.

In initiatic schools where students come for spiritual teachings, it is said the master or guru lights the light of the student or disciple with her or his own light of consciousness. The light of awareness is another kind of light that once illuminated shines brilliantly, eternally. The light of awareness is a great gift we can bestow on one another.

At the close of his performances musician and bearer of light, Julius "Happy" Zebede gathers his audiences to form a circle connecting hand in hand with one another in a meditative moment. When he senses they are deep in the experience of the heart, he breathes slowly into the microphone and tells them, *"Take it to the 7-11."* He means you don't reserve your light and your love for special occasions or group meditations; you take it with you to the neighborhood store, to the streets and you give it. As the songwriters wrote, when you turn on your heartlight, it shines wherever you go.[18]

> *"You have to have an alertness to deal with the unexpected."*
> —CLYDE TOMBAUGH, *American astronomer*
> *who discovered the planet Pluto in 1930*

The one essential ingredient in all of this is *you*. It isn't about you seeing the bigger picture or understanding it; it is about you *being* a force in it. As we awaken ourselves we clear the static on the radio of our being enough to tap into the knowledge. Without standing on a soap box or sounding like a Pollyanna the fact is when we achieve some mastery with our own thinking and our own mind, we become beacons of living wisdom and literally alter the world.

You got to have heart.

Everyone fell in love with E.T. the Extra Terrestrial, the image of his heart light "turned on" etched indelibly in our happy memories. When athletes achieve a challenging feat, they tap their heart. When a person has a spiritual awakening it is said he or she had an opening of the heart. Awakening begins with an awakening of the heart.

> *"The true division of humanity is between those who live in light and those who live in darkness. Our aim must be to diminish the number of the latter and increase the number of the former."*
> —VICTOR HUGO, Les Misérables, *pt. 4, bk. 7, ch. 1 (1862)*

We as a humanity and as individuals have an opportunity now that is unprecedented. We have entered a new world view, an expanded reality, laws and principles which when they come into our awareness make new human beings of us. It is a time of conscious evolution. It is a time of awakening of which great saints and sages foretold. This is no longer restricted to the elite few or spiritual intelligentsia. Thinking from a new world view transcends all categories of interest groups, activists, poll groups, ethnic this or that, or media slant. It is a leap beyond the barriers of our differences and separations.

> *"Unity should not be mistaken for uniformity."*
> —SWAMI VIVEKANANDA

This is about all of us realizing what it takes to think for an entirely new reality, regardless of age, gender, creed or ideology. It's time for the Traditionalists, the Moderns, and the Cultural Creatives to converge in a higher octave of awareness. Maybe we can't control life the way 17th century scientists once believed, but we can surely direct and dance with it—*if* we understand how it works and *when we master those natural laws and principles in ourselves.*

We have been thinking according to a system of reality that is largely inaccurate. When you contemplate this for a moment—you can get a good laugh. And since that view is a mechanistic view of reality, you and I have developed a lot of mechanical habits too. (Are you laughing yet?) Why should you and I be laughing?

You know what comedians do. They distinguish something in a way that lets you see the absurdity of it. Even though it's "real" in the sense that it's going on, that some quirk of human action is actually happening, when you hear their routine you can't believe that we humans actually are behaving that way. It is *funny* in that context. Let there be light-heartedness about all of this.

～～

Our most brilliant scientists and thinkers today are devoting their life to elucidating the core principles that we have been so misguided about: how we have discovered that we were looking at the materiality (the atom) and not the space, how we have been studying the particles and not the waves, how we have been focused on the parts and not the whole system, and how we have been focused on the outcome of consciousness and not the source of the materiality that is actually consciousness itself. It's like a great big cosmic joke. The cosmic comedian is giving us a great big wink. A new world view is emerging. The irony is that "it" is emerging and we are the ones who are bringing it forth.

> *"You must be the change you wish to see in the world."*
> —Mahatma Gandhi

If thought indeed creates reality (which it does), then when we can achieve mastery with our thinking, really with our own mind, we can transcend our levels of discontent, discontinuity and discouragement—and begin relating to one another in the wisdom of love, interconnectedness, and mutual respect, truly living the wisdom of universal spiritual traditions we have revered and aspired to throughout the ages. We can dance in this evolution of the life force, either unconsciously, rendering ourselves flotsam and jetsam on the sea of life—or consciously, with the awareness of our own power and the role we play in it. The choice is up to each one of us to make.

So, dear friend, what's it going to be? Crisis-awakening or Self-awakening? Rejoice. You and I get to choose.

～～

Wisdom of The Tao
Finesse instead of Force

There are many paths to Self-awakening. Whatever path you take, it is good to choose to consciously awaken. The Tao is a philosophy spawned in ancient China and attributed to the sage, Lao-Tse. "The Tao" prefers not even to be called a philosophy and certainly not a religion. It is simply referred to as "the way." The Tao teaches *wu wei*, action through inaction, effortless action which basically means finesse instead of force. Go with the flow. From the perspective of a new world view, there are no "accidents" in the universe. The fact that you picked up this book and are reading these words means you are ready to *be* the light. You're in the flow. The tiniest flame illumines an entire room.

Is QuantumThink "the Truth"?

Despite the fact that "seekers" seek "the truth," whether something is the truth or not seems to be an appropriately "questionable" question, given that our world is creative, always in flux and Observer-created to boot. Perhaps a more valuable question to ask is: Does it work? What will work now? Does QuantumThink work in your life? You are the sole determiner of the response to that question.

The point is: What if you and I and all of us started thinking from these distinctions, from whole systems—realizing that our minds are entangled (connected) and affect one another and the space (fields) we reside in? What if all of us could become masterful co-creators of our reality by thinking in a way more consistent with natural law? What if this really works?

Anyway, my dear friend, it is going to happen. You are going to evolve. The question is, will it happen through crisis awakening or conscious awakening? Are you going to wait for the universal force to do its thing and wallop you over the head one more time, or do you want to do it *consciously* and become a Wake-up instead of a mere grown-up?

> *"Here's to the crazy ones, the misfits, the rebels, the troublemakers, the round pegs in the square holes ... they push the human race forward ... because the ones who are crazy enough to think that they can change the world, are the ones who do."*
>
> —STEVE JOBS, *co-founder, Apple*

It is time to go to the next octave with this. Take, not the proverbial, but an actual real-life, real-time quantum leap. Get hip. The world as we know it is reaching the height of unworkability. We can do something about this. It begins with the awareness that the nature of life is to be awakened, to evolve. How long can we go against the laws of nature? Thinking and living from the expanded reality of a new world view makes this possible.

It begins with each one of us. It only requires waking up. Waking up *from* our own automatic habits, and waking up *to* an expanded reality at the edge of our knowledge today. To become aware of how light becomes thought becomes energy becomes manifest. To be a modern day shaman means to learn the principles, to use the principles, to be the principles. To become a Wake-up may be a lot easier and quicker than you ever dreamed.

> *"Baby, if I could ... change the world."*—ERIC CLAPTON

We've been talking about the bigger picture here, however, even if your only interest at this point is *"me, me, me, me, I, I, I,"* or as my cousin, Ro, and I refer to it *"Enough about you, let's talk about me, me, me, me, I, I, I."* Even if you do not yet experience the epiphanies, the unity of the entire universe, I know one thing for sure: You can still appreciate some awesome moments of light.

> *"Our lifelong quest is to find our way back to the eternal light from which we are born."*
>
> —LISA R. DELMAN, *author*

Remember this now as you delve into the QuantumThink distinctions. They are here for us to integrate and Live the Wisdom. When you go to a restaurant you don't order everything on the menu in one sitting. When you read the QuantumThink distinctions although they are interconnected as one system you take each one on its own. Enjoy the experience of the awareness you bring to yourself and the fruits of your actions infused with your "new mind."

My wish for you as you read and QuantumThink is that you experience at least One Quantum Moment of light. It is my Intent that you experience many more than one—and more than anything else that what you get from this book is a profound and loving awareness of and connection to your very own Self and your power to create your life and your world in the highest, exactly as you desire. If reading this book stokes that fire within you, then my wish shall come true.

If life is fundamentally uncertain and we can live comfortably with the uncertainty instead of trying to lock everything down into place, then life becomes an amazing adventure. The certainty comes from knowing the principles and universal laws that are operating within you. The certainty comes from mastering what it is to be uniquely you. The certainty comes from an inner knowing, faith in the sanctity and majesty of the miracle of life. The certainty comes from knowing that you are here to enjoy the wonder and the light of your own awareness.

~~~

I've enjoyed our chat and trust that you have too. I said I would be your new best friend and tell you things. Even with thousands of years of "evidence" to the contrary, you don't have to be stuck with "the way it is." Understanding all this is nice, but experiencing it is the only thing that really matters. That's the purpose of the rest of this book. You can expand your view. You can interrupt the mechanical, conceptual habits and condition yourself to think in sync with the laws of physics as we know them today and as the great beings before us have known in the poetry of their own era and culture. You can QuantumThink. You can become enchanted with the faculties of your own mind. You can elevate your spirit and revitalize your soul. You can create a new world. It can shift in an instant. You have everything you need. The creation principles are born in us. *The most powerful force in this world is the light of your own awareness.*

"What is this precious love and laughter
Budding in our hearts?
It is the glorious sound
Of a soul waking up!

—HAFIZ, *Sufi master and master poet*

PART II

Live the Wisdom

QuantumThink®
The System of Thinking

*QuantumThink
is a system
of thinking*

*comprised of
21+1
distinctions.*

*What
do the distinctions
distinguish?*

*A different nature
of reality*

*expanded
beyond
the consensus reality
we have been accustomed to
in our culture,
yet a reality more consistent with our true nature,
what has been known by ancient wisdom
and what is being uncovered by modern science.*

*As you read
and tune into
each distinction
remember
each one is complete in itself
and each one belongs
to the whole
of the
system.
As you read, as you contemplate, and as you practice
you experience this and you know it.
The wisdom is living because
the wisdom lives in you.*

QuantumThink-Wave
Where do You begin and end?

One auspicious evening we were fortunate to be in the company of a Native American Indian, a teacher from the Chippewa-cree tribe of Montana and western Canada for whom they say mythology is a way of life rather than a fictional history.

The way he introduced himself was striking. He made no reference to himself as an individual nor through any descriptive phrase that would "label" him. Instead, he spoke of himself in terms of the whole of the entire history and wisdom and teachings of his people as it had been handed down for generations from the elders of their tradition.

We can contemplate this: He did not exist for himself merely as a separate individual, a member or "part" of the Chippewa-cree tribe. He *was* the tribe, the wisdom, the tradition, the mythology. It wasn't even like he was *connected* to it or them; it was that he *is* it—*all* of it. (You can imagine it took quite a little while for him to introduce himself!) It wasn't that you couldn't distinguish his unique personal expression in the world. Obviously you could. It was that he related to himself in a much greater, grander and all encompassing perspective.

Here was a living presence of a core characteristic of a new world view, the idea that the universe exists in patterns of relationships, interconnected and interrelated, everything enfolded in all of it within **one** ever expanding, ever evolving *whole*, unrestricted by limits of time or physicality. This marvelous being known as Brother Ron is an electrifying reminder that a new world view is not a function of the time period you live in, but of the awareness you live within.

1 Holistic & Holographic

I am you and you are me and we are we and we are all together[19]

Do you ever deeply experience the Oneness of All, the unity in everything and everyone in this vast universe?

Perhaps you feel it as you stand silently gazing at the moon gleaming brilliantly amidst a star filled sky. You are caught breathless at the sight of a pristine lake, or you fall to stillness while perched on a mountaintop surrounded everywhere by spectacular snowcapped peaks. During these moments the experience of oneness is so profound that words cannot match their majesty. We call them mystical experiences. They're described as transcendent awareness beyond the ordinary way we relate to the world. We yearn for these experiences of unity. Have you thought about it? Let's explore further in this first distinction, Holistic & Holographic.

Scientists seek a unified theory, a theory of everything that will account for all the forces of nature working harmoniously together as one grand system. Where does such desire for unity come from? Consider that the experience of *wholeness* is a vital aspect of what it is to be alive. People go around saying, *We are One. All is One.* But what does it really mean?

Scientists who investigate the nature of reality tell us that everything exists as one continuous whole. Even though we see distinctions there are no actual separations.

This may seem simple and obvious however this is a quite different view from the philosophy and science of older times. In previous centuries the thinking was that "the whole was equal to the sum of its parts." A *reductionistic* universe meant that everything could be *reduced* into separate, constituent parts.

The new view of the world that we're exploring is to see life as one whole with no separations; the universe as Holistic & Holographic.

Holistic means: Everything is interconnected and interrelated. Everything impacts everything else. You take one small action and that action ripples. Even though you may not see all the effects of that action—it may be invisible to you—still that one action affects the whole.

Holographic means: The whole is contained in every abstracted part no matter how small the piece. This comes from a hologram, a three-dimensional image made with laser light. When the original negative is cut into pieces, no matter how many pieces or how small the piece, each piece contains the image of the whole.

From an old world view thinking habit focused in the physical world of matter, the universe does *appear* as a world of differences and separations. In this limited perspective, we look separate from one another and objects look separate from us. You and I appear to be separate from the entire "outer" reality that we refer to as the external world. Old world separation thinking has conditioned us to divide, analyze, and see our lives in parts.

In the past we have tended to compartmentalize life: business and personal, mind and body, material and spiritual, and so on. We tend to see only what *we* are working on, only what we are accountable for when we do our work. We are generally not looking from the totality of things, from the whole of our company or how whatever we are doing in our job fits into the overall purpose of the business. We don't typically have in our awareness the interconnectedness and interrelatedness of what *we* do—to all the rest. Even in relationships we tend to make a decision or judgment about a person based on one isolated "separate" interaction.

Yet today we realize that all of creation is characterized by wholeness and unity. The whole is present in every smaller aspect of itself. Leading-edge scientists concur that there is an underlying field where all matter, energy, and information are connected and that this unified field is the basis of all thought and of all experience in what we perceive as the outer world.

Astronauts experienced this profoundly when they went to the moon and looked at Earth. They didn't see countries; they didn't see divisions. They saw one globe. Every person on Earth was enthralled with the famous picture of their planet photographed from space, now an icon of our space age culture. Foremost authority on mythology, Joseph Campbell proclaimed that this picture began the new myth of our time. He said, *"When you see the earth from the moon, you don't see any divisions there of nations or states. This might be the symbol for the new mythology to come. That is the country we are going to be celebrating. And those are the people that we are one with."*

If you are allowing yourself to fall prey to the concerns of Either/Or thinking you might object to this, asking, "One country? What about individuality? What about uniqueness? What about the fact that we do live in a world of countries and ethnicities and differences?" The sage advises: let's not mistake unity for uniformity.

Contemporary physicist John Hagelin clarifies this for us, *"The universe is superficially diverse but fundamentally unified."*

～～～

The universe as a system of whole systems interpenetrating one another is not a new idea. The oldest and most honored Eastern wisdom teaches that all reality is a single principle and that we are here to realize one's unity with that principle. Ancient mythology and wisdom traditions taught this and looked at the forces of nature as living entities to be in harmony with. Indigenous peoples from around the world revered the Sun, knowing that it is through the heat and light and energy of the Sun that we are kept alive. This is not something we are necessarily aware of in our modern life as we stroll through our wonderfully convenient supermarkets and select what our food sustenance will be for the day. Yet it is fundamentally the light from the Sun that nourishes us by way of photosynthesis with plants. We ingest vegetation directly or indirectly through other animals who consume the vegetation. These are not mere concepts but actualities of our interconnectedness.

Poets, mystics, and musicians have expressed this big idea for us. The whole is everywhere reflected in every other aspect of itself. The 15th century Indian poet sage, Kabir said: *"All know that the drop merges into the ocean but few know that the ocean merges into the drop."* And British poet William Blake surely envisioned the Holographic nature of life when he wrote:

> *"To see a World in a Grain of Sand; And a Heaven in a Wild Flower,*
> *Hold Infinity in the palm of your hand; And Eternity in an hour."*

Think of it: the silicon element in a grain of sand found in abundance in the Earth's crust is the exact same silicon in semiconductors that has become the "world" of technology, communications and commerce of today.

American poet Walt Whitman experienced the intrinsic interconnectedness of a Holistic world when he wrote: *"For every atom belonging to me as good belongs to you."*

In QuantumThink our main concern is how we can use the latest discoveries to shape our thinking and elevate our results and mastery in life. As we distinguish the Holistic & Holographic nature of creation from various angles and perspectives, the message penetrates and becomes real for us. You will be happy to know that these poetic phrases inspired from direct personal experience are borne out in modern physics.

Even in the physical world of matter while there are distinctions there are no actual separations. What we perceive as empty space between objects, though invisible, is not empty at all. We are connected through the field, the field of intelligence, of energy, of awareness. Scientist and philosopher Ervin Laszlo refers to this field as the A-Field, the field of all knowledge, information, and energy. He named it that after the notion of the *Akashic* records, the idea of a nonmaterial "library" that records everything that has ever happened or will happen in human experience. Laszlo says what's remarkable about this A-field is that everything that happens in our universe *informs* everything else.

From the tiny quantum particle to the larger macro world of objects and us, the "quantum hologram" refers to the discovery that the event history of all matter is continuously emitted. In quantum holography, each body emits and absorbs the complete information about that body on a continual basis.

QuantumThink distinctions are not here to fill you up with interesting facts but to bring your awareness to these things and to universal laws underlying our nature so we can think and live in accordance with nature, effective and fulfilled. Holistic is not just a word we use to describe alternative health methods or organic foods. It is a principle operating throughout nature and that includes you and me.

People say they want balance in their lives. You can see that if you try to measure all the "parts" of your life you might not ever figure out how to make them balance.

How would you do it anyway? One part work, two parts family? Three parts self, four parts others? Balance as it refers to parts may be asking the wrong question. When you view your life as a totality you will no longer need to "balance the parts" because you realize the many ways you can live an integrated and harmonious life.

～～～

Yes, the idea of wholeness is not really a "new" idea. What would be new is integrating it into the way we think and the way we live. In one of his most memorable songs Reggae music genius Bob Marley suggests very simply that we are "one love, one heart" so why not just "get together and feel all right." Perhaps the reason we haven't just gotten together as one human family to "feel all right" is that despite the hopeful concepts and affirmations that "we are one," except for those rare mystical moments, we truly haven't *yet* been thinking and living that oneness.

You can notice all the ways that thinking in parts and in separation shows up in our lives. Because of separation we think of haves and have-nots, we have economic policies that consider only the more developed or wealthier nations' perspectives and just envelop the others within it, we manufacture things that don't harmonize with and follow nature's ways, we deal with health by isolating one chemical. You take a drug to lower cholesterol. But how is that drug affecting all the other bodily systems, the whole system? Popular integrative medicine pioneer and medicinal herbs expert, Dr. Andrew Weil tells us there is a vast difference between the whole plant and an isolated plant derivative. From a single derivative he says, "The body has no choice how to respond."

You put in landfill to hide the garbage. What is that toxicity doing to the soil and how is it affecting the water? What is that water doing to us who bathe in it and drink it. Think about it. They want to create a beach on the shore of the Hudson River in Manhattan but who will swim in that water? Slander of people in the public eye masquerades as news because of separation thinking. We have separated matter from spirit and you are well aware of all the problems that has caused! Separation thinking may cause us to get divorced too easily, give up friendships when we don't really want to, and give up activities we love because we don't see how to fit them in to our compartmentalized lives.

Consider that it is your *state* not the "parts" of your life that throws you off balance. In her book *Biomimicry* science writer Janine Benyus urges us to mimic nature's processes to create solutions. Nature doesn't tear things apart; nature functions in whole systems. When you are thinking from wholes you are thinking coherently. It is known that when we experience the underlying unified field of awareness, our brain and heart activity gain coherence. Brain and heart coherence means improved mental ability and peacefulness. Though you can distinguish your inner and outer worlds there is no actual separation between your inner experience and your outer life. Consider that we desire the experience of unity because we require it for our well being. To live Holistically & Holographically is to align with natural law. When you are in tune with nature which is also *your* true nature, life becomes so much more satisfying and you function with ease. Connecting to our unity means we are just plain happier.

〜〜〜

If you are overwhelmed by the number of items on your To Do lists you can begin to look from the whole and see the interconnection between all activities. Then you can take *multidimensional actions*. "Multidimensional action" means one action accomplishes many results. You shift from wondering "How am I going to get all this done?" to "How are these various projects and activities connected? In what ways does the work in one area contribute to and further my progress on the other areas?" (This is not the same as *multitasking*, the term from computing science which means many applications or different actions are happening simultaneously.) A multidimensional action is an integrated action. You are thinking Holographically. One action you take has many results because you intend it that way. It is seeing unity in diversity. You do this deliberately *as a conscious act*.

You want to learn to use the Internet *and* you want to spend quality time with your child *and* you want to get information for a product you want to buy. You combine these three desired results into one action. You ask your son to teach you how to use the Internet by researching the product you're interested in. It seems so obvious yet to think this way as a conscious act can relieve your overwhelm and fill you with excitement in the creativity and joy in the accomplishment.

〜〜〜

Within the ever-evolving unfathomable complexity there are unifying principles throughout nature. Perhaps you have heard the expression whose "truth" has remained with us since antiquity: *As above, so below.* Everything in the universe reflects everything else from the "heaven above" to the "earth below," from the macro world of the cosmos itself to the micro world of single celled organisms, subatomic particles and everything in between.

As above so below doesn't necessarily imply mirror-like images or symmetry; it also includes what is known in new geometry as "fractals," irregular patterns that are self-similar and resemble the whole, like leaves on a tree. Patterns in the macrocosm are woven throughout the microcosm. The orbit of an electron around the nucleus of an atom is reminiscent of planetary orbit. A galaxy's spiral is repeated in a snail shell and in the cochlea of our own human inner ear. Earth is 70 percent water and our bodies are approximately 70 percent water. Our blood contains roughly the same amount of salt as the ocean's salt solution. Respected physicist Richard Feynman thought *"the most remarkable discovery in astronomy is that the stars are made of the same kind of atoms as those on the Earth."* Can there be any question about our unity? We are comprised of the same elements—carbon, hydrogen, oxygen, nitrogen—of everything else in this universe born of the same stardust.

Research scientist James Lovelock named the Earth *Gaia*, the Greek name for the Earth goddess, to signify that the Earth is alive—a whole living, breathing being. You are not separate from this being. Just as millions of tiny living organisms find their abode on our body, so do we find our abode on hers. Just as our body is comprised of trillions of cells, so each of us is a cell on the body of Mother Earth, comprising what cosmologist Peter Russell calls "the global brain." Realizing we are all aspects of the same being and the same consciousness shines new light and deeper significance on the scriptural edict, *"Do unto others as you would have them do unto you."* At the fundamental level of existence we "are" one another. Of course we may not like this idea as we go through our day and our minds start clicking away their automatic judgments about "the other" people we encounter. Then again we are here in QuantumThink to take ourselves to a new place with all of this. Since we are higher on the conscious level than the single celled organisms, we can interact with one another as well as with our host in more conscious ways.

Consider ... everywhere you go is your living room. When you are in a public place do you ever think of the person who is coming in there after you, the person you may never meet physically, the person who uses the ladies' or gentlemen's lounge after you, or the housekeeper who cleans your hotel room after you leave? What about at home or in your office? Do you consider what trail you are leaving behind with no thought as to how others will experience the kitchen or that room after you have been there?

How are you treating your host organism, Mother Earth? When you're not living the wisdom of a Holistic & Holographic reality you might think preserving the rain forests or keeping the Earth's atmosphere in balance are "good causes" to get behind, or contrarily you might think the whole "green" thing is ridiculous and rationalize that it's nature's cycle to use up its own natural resources. However, when you truly see from the whole you awaken to the fact that we are completely dependent on Earth's well being for our own well being and the sustainability of human life.

Cutting edge thinkers today are activating the Holistic & Holographic distinction in their work presenting integral theories and integral studies, whole brain technologies, and whole language learning to illustrate the benefits when we live Holistically & Holographically, in tune with nature and our own nature.

What about you and me? Each of us has experienced, scientists concur, and sages assure us that looking from a larger, multidimensional perspective everything in creation and everything on Earth exists as one interconnected whole. Suffice it to say, like it or not, believe it or not, the fact is we are intrinsically, intimately, undeniably connected physically as well as through the energetic, mind, and spiritual dimensions. What does all this mean? Our own nature is singular, expansive and unbounded. The quantum paradox is, we experience and express an individual mind and collective mind simultaneously, yet at our core consciousness we are *one*.

We could say we are "quantumly entangled." *Quantum entanglement* is what physicists named the phenomenon that particles that appear to be separate in one sense really are not separate at all because when one particle is stimulated the other one has an identical reaction to the stimulation, even when they are long physical distances apart. There is an instantaneous exchange of energy and information. If we are quantumly entangled with everyone and everything else, then guess what: each aspect of our own personal life is also entangled and affecting and informing every other aspect of our life.

This is excellent news. This means if you effect a transformation in one area of your life it will transfer over to all areas of your life.

Sacred wisdom teachings tell us *the cause of suffering is separation*—whether it is separation from one another, from our purpose, from the unified field or from the source of creation. What has held us in the grasp of the illusion of separateness is the old world view focus on the physical-material dimension. You don't need the teachings to prove this; you can see it for yourself. An old world view has conditioned us to see our distinctiveness as differences and we have used our differences to keep us separate and too often at odds with one another. We separate ourselves by age. Young people don't want to hang around with the old folks and the old people say get the kids out of here they're too wild. We separate ourselves by looks, by money, by power, by ethnic, cultural, and religious differences, and even by illness and wellness.

Looking from the whole, from a global perspective, does *not* equate to having our diverse, imaginative and colorfully exotic differences become homogenized, blended into a nebulous, tasteless stew of humanity. On the contrary. From a new world view we use our uniqueness. In fact, we come together *because of* our distinctiveness. A global perspective does not mean you give up what makes each person and each culture unique. Rather, you see them inside of a larger perspective and how they together comprise the continuously in-motion mosaic of humankind. Can you imagine what the world might be like if we all began to *appreciate*, in the true sense of that word, *value*, one another's differences?

Unless we begin to look from the whole, from an integral perspective where we see the connections between what is going on in our lives and in our multidimensional bodies, how can we expect to achieve the balance, health, and harmony we long for? Until we learn to think, look and live from the intelligence of a world that is at its source a universe of whole systems, how can we expect to sustain peace and maintain economic viability for all? The sooner we begin living in the integrated experience of the world as a unified field, regard our consciousness as a unified field, and understand the physical Earth and ourselves as aspects of the same living entity—the sooner we take a quantum leap in our reality to one of cooperation, respect, and appreciation, one of love, honor, and gratitude.

The modern business practice known as "systems thinking" examines how the flow of business processes fit together as *whole systems*. Yet if you are not considering the *big* Holistic & Holographic picture, you could end up with the opposite of the result you desire. You create a business process. Look at all the phone recorded instructions designed to eliminate a worker's time that at times appear to be insane.

How many people just click on "zero" to speak to any person because it takes longer to sit through the menu options or because they don't understand them? When you think from whole systems you even become consciously aware of where the light switch is placed on your wall, not just according to electrical code, but does it make sense in terms of how you'll be using it?

If you are in business, examine for a moment something you are working on now. From what perspective are you looking at it? Take it out one perspective larger, and then again, and consider how what your organization does affects other departments and the company as a whole? How does seeing the largest perspective alter your decisions and actions? You will find this exercise extremely refreshing! Looking from the whole alters the way we deal with the well being of ourselves, our organizations, our planet, and even the galaxy.

In QuantumThink we go way out to the farthest reaches of the universe, and then we come back to our everyday world. We don't have to get overwhelmed by the "bigness" of it. To experience the genius of Holistic & Holographic is to take a literal quantum leap and experience it in your own life simply in the most familiar everyday activities. How does this work in our relationships and in our work? How can it affect our creativity and our state of mind?

When you live the wisdom of a Holistic & Holographic universe, you start to think a lot differently about everything. Perhaps you take note of how the animals you are putting into your own body are treated and what kind of conditions the farmers are growing your fruits and vegetables in. You may start to care whether our scientists and governing decision-makers are aware of the critical function of rainforests in regulating the Earth's atmosphere, controlling the rainfall, in providing natural health remedies, and millions of life supporting species—not because you're on a bandwagon or supporting a political ideology but because its nature's system and we need to be aware of how it works best. Looking Holistically & Holographically is to see how it can work for a company's financial viability *as well as* for the planet. It's a Both/And world. Surely the universe is greater than the sum of its parts.

We are connected through the multidimensions of the unified field. What is the nature of that unified field? It is deliciously free, infinitely creative, and naturally blissful. Imagine it: the fundamental state of human beings is bliss. Perhaps that is why Joseph Campbell's gentle imperative, *Follow your bliss,* resonates with us so deeply.

So how is your mind doing right now? Notice if you are having any automatic thoughts placing limits on that statement that our fundamental nature is bliss. Would you want to live other than experiencing the bliss of being alive?

In this world we celebrate freedom in many different ways. Countries celebrate freedom from constraints, such as Cinco de Mayo and Independence Day. It seems natural to want the freedom that is inherent in creation itself in the very nature of consciousness. When you live the wisdom of Holistic & Holographic in your own life, you free yourself in many ways.

Chaos theory enthusiasts love the idea that *"a tiny alteration in any initial condition of a dynamic system will bring about a change in the whole system."*[20] One of the originators of chaos theory, meteorologist Edward Lorenz used the example of a flap of a butterfly wing to illustrate that a small effect like that could change a weather pattern bringing notoriety to "the butterfly effect." Regardless of controversy of whether butterfly wings actually do affect the weather, the point is made. Translate this to say for us: a tiny shift in your life can affect the whole of your life. In QuantumThink these shifts are shifts of awareness.

〜〜〜

What will give you the experience of living Holistically & Holographically? We can do this in many ways. To begin, we can do it in the Recreation practices. We want to begin to look from the whole of our life and see that how we are in one area impacts the rest; how any one aspect of what we are doing or not doing is actually *present* in all the rest.

Sacred Geometry expert Bruce Rawles reminds us *"The sphere is an ultimate expression of unity, completeness, and integrity."* Perhaps we aren't shaped like spheres, we're more like fractals, however we do have a sphere of influence based in the expression of integrity in our own life. We tend to think of integrity in the sense of morality, but integrity truly signifies being whole or sound. When we think of something being whole it has a quality of soundness, of making its own sense, so to speak. We could say it this way: it is complete. Nothing is left out, nothing is hanging out; there are no loose ends.

When you view your life as one whole you want to make sure it has this quality of soundness, of being complete. One incompletion, one blocking or thwarting of energy flow can affect everything. Being complete and whole doesn't mean "finished." It just means the energy is balanced. There is a sense of equanimity. *You know where things stand and you are okay with it.* In this state, you are free to create the new. Since QuantumThink is about creating the new, we are starting off with getting complete.

Again, this does not mean *finished.* In this *state* of being complete you are energized and free to create.

As soon as you experience your own life as Holistic & Holographic you can distinguish that wholeness anywhere you place your attentiveness and awareness, in the macrocosm or the microcosm. Create a state of peace with the circumstances in your life by being whole and sound and complete. Connect to the place in your soul where you experience unity. This is accomplished in real time, in action.

We no longer have to compartmentalize business and personal, mind and body, spiritual and material, and attempt to balance the parts. Living from the Holistic & Holographic nature of reality means the parts are inseparable. We experience our lives as integrated and coherent, a rich symphony harmonious and whole.

When you are living in a state of wholeness with no loose ends or fragmentation, you experience being free. The Intent and purpose of the following Recreations are for you to experience being "whole and complete" as a way of life.

When you are free, not only are you free to choose wisely, you also clear the atmosphere around you which frees the way for attracting what you want in life. Saying it is one thing. Living it is the point.

⌒ QuantumThink Recreation ⌒
Live the Wisdom of Holistic & Holographic

ONE»Experience Wholeness as Integrity. Create wholeness by having your life be sound and balanced and complete. This Recreation has three aspects to it. First, make a written list of everything in your life which you experience as being incomplete, the things that are nagging at you and therefore using up your energy. Then complete three items and notice how that affects you. As you write the list and complete three items, contemplate how being complete moment by moment permeates the whole of you. Read on for discussion.

1. Write a Completion List. Write a list of everything in your life you are "incomplete" with, that is, whatever is nagging at you, pulling your energy, attention and consciousness away from being present and focused. Put these on the list. (Note: This is a completion list, not a "to do" list.)

Places to look: Physical Environments, Relationships, Technology, Communications, Business, Health, Finances, Recreation, Relaxation

Really take a moment and write it all down. You will be amazed at how just putting this list on paper or in a document in your computer will be an experience of completion and free you. Your list is finite. There is an end to it. Just putting these things on a list on a piece of paper to file away for the future will give you a sense of completion, of soundness, of centered wholeness.

Some examples of what might be on the completion list: Clutter or mess in car or office or room, phone calls you need to return, taxes that need to be filed or paid, stocks and bonds to buy or sell, change of address or other information that needs updating, items you'll never use again that need to be discarded or passed along, communications you need to address in your relationships, health appointments you need to make, diet or exercise regime you have been meaning to start. All of this "pulls" on other areas of your life because everything is interconnected and interrelated.

2. Complete three items on the list. There are various ways you can complete things:

    a. Do it. (The obvious yet not always the appropriate way.)

    b. Eliminate it. (Get real. Admit and decide you are never going to do it because you have no commitment to it and eliminate it.)

    c. Deem it "complete" exactly as it is now. (You are the one who gets to say.)

    d. Schedule it short-term or further in the future. (three days, three months, or three years.)

    e. Delegate it to someone else. (If you're in a position to do that, ask nicely.)

    f. Hire someone to do it. (There is an expert for any service you need.)

    g. Re-contextualize it. (From a new perspective what you thought of as incomplete actually isn't.)

    h. Any other way you can create completion.

3. Contemplate how your life is one interconnected whole; it is Holistic & Holographic. As you write your list and get yourself complete, contemplate how even the smallest incompletion belongs to the whole and impacts the whole of you; and contemplate how being whole and complete, moment by moment, also permeates the whole of your life. Each area of your life is related to all the other areas of your life. All of you is always present in every situation. Be aware of this as you write your list and get yourself complete.

TWO»Just for one day imagine the Earth as your living room and treat it that way. See if you can leave any place more "conscious" than you found it. Even if you cannot bring yourself to picking up a stray paper or aluminum can from a lawn or the floor of a public place, just think about doing it. Notice how becoming aware of this affects you.

THREE»Consciously create one Multidimensional action. Accomplish several results with one action. Enjoy the game of it.

For extra Holistic & Holographic fun, watch the video, *Powers of Ten*.[21]

QuantumThink-Wave
"Truths" And Consequences
How Do You Know What You Know?

How do you know what you know? Did you ever think about this? Aren't your actions based upon what you know? If so, then how do you know what you know? We don't mean you learned it from your parents, or in school or from friends or from your own experience. Really the question is, how are you *related* to what you know? Is what you know *the truth*? Is it *a belief*?

In Philosophy, there is a fancy word for the study of how we know what we know called "epistemology." Philosophy always has these big words that scare people away. You don't have to be intimidated by a word, you know. Anyway, we are engaging in our own epistemological conversation right now. Isn't the purpose of Philosophy what it brings to us in our lives everyday?

Whatever your country of upbringing, you probably learned that the ancient astronomers had an entirely different idea about the structure of the cosmos than we do now. In the 2nd century the astronomer, Ptolemy, put forth the idea that the Earth was the center of the universe. We can imagine it was perfectly logical for Ptolemy to think this during his era, considering there had been nothing invented as yet that extended our human capacities for seeing.

This idea of an Earth-centered universe was believed—probably held as *the truth*, to be *the way it is,* for a very long time, by a lot of people. In fact, according to our documented history, this was held as the truth for fourteen hundred years! That is one millennium plus four centuries.

And then … the "truth" changed. Copernicus came along in the 16th century and showed that the Sun was the center, and the rest, as they say, is history.

A "Truth" Trip in Disney World Aboard "Spaceship Earth"

In Disney World in Orlando, Florida you can take a ride inside the AT&T exhibit, "Spaceship Earth," where you journey through the history of communication. You travel 40,000 years in a 15-minute ride, brilliantly accomplished inside an architectural giant, a striking, shimmering, silver 180-foot high geosphere.

What you see is that the first recorded communications were the cuneiform carvings on the walls inside the cave of Cro-Magnon man. You see right there that whoever made those first carvings was recording their interpretation from that person's perspective, from what they were able to perceive, interpret and give meaning to, inside the system that equated to their "reality" at that time.

As you travel along in your little cart winding through the darkness inside the massive globe, you pass by the lighted exhibits: the Egyptian hieroglyphics, the Phoenician alphabet, the Gutenberg printing press, the plays and paintings of the Renaissance. Then you journey through the age of inventions: the telegraph and the telephone and the radio, and all the way up through TVs, videos and computers, the Internet and global networks, and electronic space communications—all the different ways we human beings have ingeniously invented to record and transmit our communications.

At the end of the ride you realize, as my husband, master QuantumThink coach, Alan Collins, astutely noted, *"Well, that ride just showed us there's a little of the cave man in all of us."* He said it jokingly, yet there is something significant in what he says. Much of what we have held as our "truths" are meanings that have simply been passed along to us; different people's interpretations along the way, based on what worked for them during their era.

We point to this just to remain alert to the fact that when new evidence is revealed or uncovered, when an interpretation ceases to be of value to us, we do have the capability to operate from a new view of things. We don't always do that. Perhaps we become enamored of our ways (nice way of saying we are "attached"), or perhaps we are simply unaware that ... **It's an Observer-created Reality.**

2 Observer-created Reality

What you bring is what you get

Who is the authority in your life?

Okay, this is a trick question. Obviously, you are. As you contemplate what is explored in QuantumThink, you look to see how it works in *your* life. This is a trip, a virtual voyage through thinking. The purpose of it is to see what it can make possible beyond what we already know, to open up vistas for all of us. Though we may reference "authorities" in different fields, clearly you are the final word in your own life. Or are you? The trick is to see where, up until now, you really have *not* been the authority in your own life, even though you have assumed you have been.

Where have you not been the authority? Wherever there has been a lack of awareness, an automatic nature to things, mechanical, unthinking reactions which have not given you what you wanted. Wherever there has been a lack of distinction. Perhaps you have not in those moments known, in the deft words of the legendary sage, Vasistha, *"The world is as you see it."*

Every time we say something with authority as if we know "this is how it is" we are shaping our reality, crystallizing it. The way you see something in every instance is entirely up to you. When you see someone as stupid, *you* are creating him or her that way. When you see a person as brilliant, *you* are creating him or her that way. This is so simple. Yet, it is the most profound awareness we can live.

This realization is echoed by science. It's called "the observer effect." Reality as we see it is shaped by our own Observation. In fact, nothing exists for us until we Observe it. This truth has been experienced by great beings. You and I can be great beings. We can experience ourselves as the Observers in our Observer-created Reality. We can be the authority in our own life.

~~

"I can't believe that!" said Alice. "... one can't believe impossible things."
"I daresay you haven't had much practice," said the Queen.
"When I was your age, I always did it for half-an-hour a day.
Why, sometimes I've believed as many as six impossible things before breakfast."[22]

This passage from *Through the Looking Glass* by Lewis Carroll, who took his famous Alice on mind-boggling trips through Wonderland, suggests to us the quirky character of the quantum world.

You might say the primary Intent of QuantumThink is to transform your thinking from the mind of Alice to the mind of the Queen. So what before appeared seemingly impossible or not believable now becomes quite the ordinary habit of life, based on the characteristics of the new world view and the dynamics of how it works.

As we go along you will find that what we have generally accepted in the classical world view as "the way things are" is not that way at all. This is why contemporary quantum physicist and author, Dr. Fred Alan Wolf, declares undauntedly, *"Everything you now know about the universe and its laws is more than likely to be 99.99% wrong."*

The distinction, Observer-created Reality, is a life-altering example of how our knowledge of nature's laws has changed. **An Observer-created Reality means: reality as we see it is always being shaped by the way in which we observe it.**

It doesn't appear to be this way, looking from an old world limited by our ordinary five senses. It seems as though there is some objective reality "out there." It seems that what we see, the objects we see, the people we see, are separate from us, and further, it seems like we can accurately describe the way things are. We say things like *my professor is stuffy*, or *my wife is scattered*, or *my boyfriend is selfish*, or *my manager is hard on his staff* or whatever it is you deem to be the so-called "truth" about *the way it is.*

It looks like the physical circumstances "out there" are immutable, absolute quantities that behave in a particular, predictable way. Even the dictionary promulgates the old world view definition that *circumstances* are *"... determining factors beyond willful control."*

It seems like what we have to do is manipulate ourselves around those "fixed" circumstances in an attempt to get our way or to achieve the result we want. Said simply, it looks like we have to change the circumstances. We think we have to get someone we love to change so they are more like *we* think they should be. We think we have to change our job so we will be happy. We think we have to have more money so we will be more relaxed. We think we have to get a new boyfriend so we can have a better relationship. Even the thoughts you have in your own mind can be considered another circumstance or set of circumstances that you think you have to fix or change. Maybe in an Observer-created world it's not that way at all!

What we are looking at here is that there are circumstances, and then there is the matter of how we are *related to* those circumstances. **It is in this relationship, in the relationship of ourselves to our circumstances that our power lies.**

Let me explain what shifted this.

In 1927 the physicist, Werner Heisenberg, was attempting to measure a particle of energy, and what he found was that he couldn't measure both the velocity and the position of the energy at the same time. He could measure either one on its own, but never both together.

Further, he found that the instrument he was using to perform the measure-ment had an effect on that which he was attempting to observe. From this came the now well known Principle of Uncertainty that in essence states you can never get certainty. You can never get an objective and "absolute truth" about what you are observing because nothing is ever standing still or static, and the instrument of observation is always altering what is being observed based on its own inherent attributes. The instrument through which you are looking is *always* influencing and shaping what you see.

This effect, called "the observer effect" has become a central fact of the quantum world. Later, scientists further discovered that human consciousness itself as an instrument of Observation is actually shaping what we see, as directed by our *Intent*.

Intent, the focus and direction of our purposeful attention and energy, is therefore, the primary dynamic of creation for human beings.

Remember, we are living in a Holistic world, meaning there is no separation between the instrument doing the observing and what is being observed. What we see only exists that way because of how we are looking at it, because we ourselves are a part of what we see. As an abstract notion, this looks like the impossible world of the queen, but when we bring it out the abstract and you realize how this works in your life, the impossible will become quite ordinary for you, albeit quite miraculous in terms of how you can use this principle.

Prior to this notion of an Observer-created Reality scientists looked at the phenomenal world, that is, everything external to us, as having a fixed, static, and objective nature. They considered that the nature of reality is that it could be identi-fied and described. With quantum science that notion was completely dispelled. It was found to be *not* true. What they found is that the objects that we perceive as solid or fixed are not solid at all but are fluctuations of energy, always in motion. In fact when an object is observed under a high-powered microscope scientists discovered what's there is mostly empty space.

～～～

What can all this mean for us in our lives? The nature of reality is not fixed, but mutable. It can be changed, it can shift. It is not absolute. Reality is not just out there, separate from us, waiting to be described by some super-human who "knows" the correct description. The quantum Observer-created Reality means we actively participate in what shows up in our experience. Everything exists only as a "cloud of infinite possibility" until an Observer brings it into existence through the very act of Observation. You and I are human creators. Our own human conscious-ness is the creative force. We are not separate, discrete objects who happened to be dropped on the surface of the Earth to stand by and watch what's going on—we *are* the play. We are the actors, as Shakespeare eloquently wrote, on this great stage.

He did not say we are puppets; we are the protagonists—we are the ones fashioning the drama.

The quantum realization is that we *have a choice* in what we are seeing; we have a choice in the experience we are having, in the result we are getting because there is no separation between the Observer, (ourselves) and the Observed.

When we use the word Observation in this distinction, we are not speaking about the act of seeing with the sensory perception we know as visual. Observation belongs to a multidimensionality which is greater than just seeing. Observation is what you hold in your awareness. Observation is a creative act. It is you *participating in* what you experience and call your reality. What you bring is what you get.

Since our interpretation of what we see is what gives us our personal experience moment by moment, examining *what we bring to our Observation* becomes very important.

~~~

What do we mean by "what we bring to our Observations"? What *do* we bring to our Observations? What *do* we bring to our Observations of other people, of the situations we are in, of what we see going on in the world at large? What Observations do we have about ourselves and about what's possible?

Mostly what we bring we are not even aware of. We bring our automatic reactions, we bring our thoughts, ideas and notions based on habits and concepts conditioned by the classical world view, from the past, from our culture, and from our upbringing. Automatic reactions are not thought through. We bring our interpretations, our meanings, and the conclusions we have reached about "*the way things are,*" about the way the people in our life are, about the way people are with each other, about the way our company is, our government is—whatever you have made up your mind about ... *absolutely.*

Though these automatic conclusions and interpretations are in the invisible world, they are not necessarily being spoken; still, they are always there with you shaping what you see, and most importantly, creating the results you are getting.

This is all very abstract, so let's bring it home now—to Mother.

Living in an Observer-created world means that lacking awareness, you bring all of your judgments and conclusions about "the way your mother *is*" with you into every single interaction with your mother. Your judgments and conclusions are part of every conversation or thought you have about your mother, even when your mother isn't present. This is subtle because it is in the "invisible" background. If your mother is acting "different" one day, you probably see it as a fluke; that is, it is an exception to your "rule" about your mother.

Our acts of Observation are creative and participatory. These acts of consciousness take the form of thoughts. You have a thought. You give that thought meaning. That meaning gives you your experience. Your action is shaped by it. Your results are the outcome of your action, which was shaped by the meaning you gave to your thought. Semantics? Not really. What's more ... your automatic meanings affect the people in your life.

~~~

Think about it. If you go to visit a client, and you have made a judgment about that client that he is difficult to deal with, and you are going into his office with a less than respectful attitude toward that client, how do you think that is going to shape how you are with him? How is that going to shape *his* experience with you? How is that going to shape the results you get with that client?

Consider that you may not feel authentically related with that person. You may be judging him, and he will likely experience being judged. Though he may not be able to articulate it, he will feel it. Remember we exist in fields, we are connected through the field. The interaction may be strained, not easy. There may be resistance. You may not get the result you wanted from the meeting. In an Observer-created Reality, when you walk in with "difficult client," you walk out with "difficult" outcome. What you bring is what you get.

The Good News and The Bad News are The Good News

So what do we get from all of this for ourselves? Consider that you and I are shaping our experience of reality 100% of the time. This is happening either with our awareness, or without it. Now this is great news. Why? Because if reality is absolute, and you have made negative absolute conclusions about people and situations, conclusions that do not serve either you or them well, then you are going to be stuck with it. Because if it's absolute, there's nothing you can do to alter it. The definition of absolute is that it is true for all times, in all instances, and it is unchangeable. On the other hand, if you and I are living in an Observer-created Reality and we have an awareness of this fact, then *we have authority* in the matter of how we are going to shape our reality. With this awareness comes true and authentic *choice*.

Ask yourself: What do you bring to your Observations? Look at your professional life. What do you bring to your meetings? What judgments and conclusions have you already made about the people you are meeting with? If you are a student, what Observerations do you bring to your classrooms? To your attitude toward your teacher? To your approach to studying? To your examinations?

If you are a single woman or man, in search of that "right" person to be in relationship with, what conclusions have you made about men or women that you are bringing with you as your personal and "absolute truth" every time you meet a new person?

If you live with other family members, what conclusions are you bringing to your conversations with your wife or your husband, or as a parent, with your children? What silent conclusion are you living in about your son or daughter that will no doubt shape his or her future? Until you start to bring yourself present to the fact that your statement *"My son is a slow learner"* may not be the "truth" about your son, consider that your actions, *and his,* are going to be shaped by that Observation.

What about the meanings you have given to *yourself* about what you are capable of doing, having or being? You can't possibly be present to something new, something novel or unknown, if you are bringing your fixed conclusions with you. In an Observer-created Reality, *you will find what you are looking for.*

What's possible in an Observer-created Reality?

The dynamic of "what creates" in an Observer-created Reality is the Intent of the Observer. When we use the word Intent, we are speaking about it in a very specific way.

An Intent in this sense means one that is *consciously* created, with awareness in the present moment. What's possible when you know you are living in an Observer-created Reality is: if you are not getting a result you want, you can create a new Intent, and you will alter the result.

〜〜

In order to create a new Intent, you would first have to become aware of the interpretations and conclusions that are already present, causing the predictable outcome. When you bring yourself to this awareness, you have choice. In the moment of awareness, you have real choice. You can shift your experience. In fact, you can shift your entire relationship with someone just by realizing it's within your power to do this. You can practice this awareness anytime, anywhere, with anyone.

Notice when you have reached a definite "conclusion" that is giving you an unwanted experience. Then, create a new Intent for how you would like to think of that person or situation, for how you would like your relationship to be, or how you want to experience it.

For example, suppose you have a thought that your manager doesn't value you or your work. Imagine how that thought "I am not valued" would make your feel. Think about how that would color your experience of your job. Now, realize that in a quantum world of "no absolutes" that your thought is not the truth. It is just a thought. Next, create how you would like your manager to experience you and your work. Your Intent might be stated like this: "My manager experiences me as someone producing brilliant results." Now you can live from *that* context, which is another word for Intent. Imagine how that will shape your relationship with your manager going forward.

Very important to note: creating from Intent is not "positive thinking." Positive thinking is something like trying to cover over a thought you believe is "the way it is" with another thought that amounts to wishful thinking. Creating from Intent is a totally different domain. It means you realize as Werner Heisenberg and many other scientists and sages have realized: reality is not absolute; reality is alive and being created all the time by virtue of the way we relate to it, by what we bring to it.

To create from Intent is to choose a new context to live from. You no longer have to blindly accept a disheartening reality that is there simply by default. Instead you can create a most appealing and uplifting way to relate to the people and circumstances in your life.

<center>~~~</center>

Using the power of Intent consciously is amazing. In fact, you are creating all the time. The difference is you have been doing this *without* awareness. Without awareness of this distinction, the default Intent automatically kicks in. You can shift your experience of your son or daughter or parent or partner, right now, without even being physically together with him or her. I invite you to do this.

You can do this in any situation, not just with another person. You can shift your experience of driving in traffic. You can shift your experience of stressing out during your work, or anything else you choose to alter with the conscious use of your Intent.

This is so simple that when you realize you can do this, you become free. You may even be laughing right now at this cosmic joke, the idea that you have been stuck with downward spiraling conclusions *that are not the way things are.* And all you had to "do" is become aware that from a new world view, reality is not absolute. Just because you have a thought doesn't make it the truth!

Intent is a field-effect dynamic. Intent is not a "cause and effect" process. You will not necessarily see a direct straight line linkage between the act of your Intent and the result of it in the world. Intent doesn't work in a mechanical way. Intent is the active dynamic of creation. Consider Intent as the focused, directed attention of your awareness and energy. Intent, as distinct from intention, is not a course of action toward a singular goal; Intent is an ongoing, ever-present force. Rather than an end-state to reach, Intent is always in effect.

Since everything exists as energy fluctuating in varying frequencies, consider that your Intent sets up a resonant field. Intent sets up probability waves in the field of Infinite Possibility. This means that your Intent sets up a probability for any number of beneficial outcomes to attract your way—whatever resonates with the energy frequency of your Intent. You cannot use Intent in a way that is manipulative, in the sense of forcing or push-pull. Intent establishes *the nature of relationship* between you and the other person, a relational field, like a field of attraction that activates all the probabilities consistent with your Intent. Dr. Wolf says it this way, *"When my intent is clear, pathways appear as if by magic, taking me from one place to the next. Certain connections get made; key phone calls come in."*

⌒⌒

In the moment-to-moment activities of daily living we don't often stop to consider or create: *What is my Intent with regard to this situation or this person that I am in a conversation with, right now?*

That reality is Observer-created could be the most compelling and far-reaching insight of the new science. It synchronizes with what has been part of the ancient wisdom teachings of India for centuries. The sage, Vasistha, taught, *It is only when the division between the seer and the seen is given up, only when the two are "seen" as one substance, that the truth is realized.* The meditation master, Swami Muktananda advised, *The world exists in you, as you.*

The good news is you are free to create. The bad news is you can no longer blame the circumstances. Translation: It's not his fault, her fault, their fault, its fault, or the fault of your upbringing. This is also the good news because if the circumstances have the power in your life, then guess what—you don't.

It isn't that there aren't circumstances out there you are interacting with. Your mother is there doing what she does. The traffic is there. The stock market is there. Your management is there. Your own mechanical conditioning is there. However, we transform our experience of the "what" we Observe when we shift the "how" we choose to Observe it. Happily, our outcomes dance along in step with our Intent.

Let The Magic Begin!

When you begin living in an Observer-created Reality, the magic begins. When you realize that your mother *is not* that way (no absolutes, not even for her), you are free to *create* her as the most fun, loving character you know, someone totally committed to you having a great life, regardless of what she does or says. That last phrase beginning with "regardless" is key.

When you authentically live from your new Intent you have a different experience. When your experience shifts, you radiate a different attitude, a lighter energy which in turn resonates with the environment and other people. The "circumstances" shift. It's like magic. You'll think your mother changed. Perhaps she will, but don't count on it. Anyway, it will no longer matter.

Please don't take my word for it. After all, you are the authority here. Experiment with this yourself and watch what happens. Let the magic begin!

◈ QuantumThink Recreation ◈
Live the Wisdom of our Observer-created Reality

ONE» Shift a predictable outcome by consciously creating your Intent in the moment. Notice the automatic judgments and conclusions you have about someone in your life which you have been holding as "the way it is" about that person. Then, create an Intent for this person with regard to your relationship with him or her—an Intent that actually alters what happens between you.

Do this in the moment with at least one person, such as an associate, a customer, a family member, a friend. Be bold. Practice this with a person you think you already "know" that *this is the way he/she is*. Watch what happens when you can authentically notice that your old conclusion is not the truth and that you can genuinely shift yourself by your own conscious choice to do so.

You can create an Intent for your relationship, for the intended results, for an unknown, unforeseen unfolding, for any or all of the above. Allow yourself the pleasure of what unfolds when you are meeting with people, consciously, and awake to your relationship with them.

Just the act of noticing when your thinking is fixed, rigid or mechanical will be freeing for you. Remember, when you work in the area of consciously creating your Intent, the results are quantum; you can expect the unexpected. Expect to be pleasantly surprised, and even amazed!

———

TWO» Watch a movie that illustrates Observer-created Reality. A few movies that beautifully demonstrate the Observer effect:

Joe Versus The Volcano with Tom Hanks and Meg Ryan

Being There with Peter Sellers and Shirley MacLaine

Life Is Beautiful with Roberto Benigni and Giorgio Cantarini

Groundhog Day with Bill Murray

QuantumThink Contemplation
What is the basis for your acceptance of something?

This is a very good question to be in. Do you accept something because a lot of people have reached a consensus of opinion? That would be based on numbers. Do you accept something because someone you respect told you so? Do you accept something because someone has proved it to be repeatable in a science laboratory? Do you accept something because it appeared on TV or in the newspapers?

How do you know whether to accept something or not? From the perspective of an Observer-created Reality, you can look in your own being. Now this gives you a lot of authority, because the nature of your being is that it is One with Infinite Intelligence. If you look into your own being, you will know exactly what you need to know.

As we embrace this distinction, Observer-created Reality, the entire world shifts in an instant. Hmmm … well, at least after we all learn to master all the automatic habits of our own mind. Okay, we still have a way to go. But at least we are off to a great start for opening ourselves to Infinite Possibility!

QuantumThink-Wave
Imagining the Unimaginable

We have a dilemma, a conundrum, a perplexing predicament. We are attempting to envision the Infinite using an instrument that is finite—the human mind. At least, in a given moment in space-time our mind *appears* to be limited as to what it can see or even envision. Herein lies another great paradox: the mind is infinite yet typically works in the finite, within defined limits and edges. Choose a topic of interest to you and in this very moment, pause and think of everything you can about that topic. There are edges.

Even so, the very nature of our universe is Infinite Possibility. The quantum view tells us that every moment contains an Infinite number of possible outcomes, one of which manifests according to the Intent of the Observer. To the finite aspect of our minds, to envision something Infinite is unimaginable. Yet, QuantumThink demands of us that we imagine the unimaginable.

Consider the "new" star that was recently discovered in our galaxy[23] so big it would fill all of the solar system within the orbit of Earth (which is 93 million miles from the Sun), and so powerful that it has the energy of 10 million suns, the brightest star ever observed in our Milky Way galaxy!

The energy of 10 million suns? When you hear about things like this, doesn't it seem so far from our reality? How do we even begin to envision one star 93 million miles "big"? John Noble Wilford of *The New York Times* wrote: "Actually, a star so big and bright should be *unimaginable*, according to some theories of star formation."[24]

This statement exemplifies precisely what we are talking about. When scientists discover something they didn't know—"that shouldn't be"—it requires them to recast their theories about the way things work. This is what happened to physicists when relativity and quantum science came into view. It didn't "fit" the current theories.

What about for us? What theories do you have that need to be recast? As we QuantumThink, we probe phenomena that you might think "should be" unimaginable according to your own theories of "the way things are."

The question is: If this star is *that* big and *that* bright—how is it no one ever noticed it? The writer from *The New York Times* solves this for us, *"But there it is, near the center of the Milky Way, long hidden from the human eye by vast dust clouds and its magnitude only now revealed by the Hubble Space Telescope, using a camera sensitive to the infrared light that penetrates the clouds."*[25] According to astronomers, because of the massive dust clouds that absorb the visible light of the stars, we know less about the center of our own galaxy than we do about more distant ones.

Magnificent metaphor. We can play with this; take it as a clue from cosmic intelligence. We speak about the realm of the invisible, the realm that our eyes *cannot* see. We can distinguish another dimension of the invisible; what *seems* to be invisible, that is, what we *can* see, but what is not presently in our view. You know ... the part covered over by the dust clouds formed by the turbulent eruptions of our own mind. Sometimes we just don't see what is right in front of us. We illuminate with our awareness. By clearing away the dust clouds stirred up by our own mental conditioning and habitual ways of being, we alter what becomes possible in our world. To think from Infinite Possibility is like this.

3 INFINITE POSSIBILITY
Would you have it any other way?

In many ways trying to grasp the quantum view of the way the universe works takes us *beyond the limits of our mind.* The dilemma of inquiring into what it is to go beyond the mind is that you have to do that using your mind. Since we use our minds to think, how do we imagine what it is to transcend our own thinking, using the limits of our own thinking to do it?

In his poem, *Relativity*, English poet and novelist, D.H. Lawrence described his experience of the quantum world this way:

> *"I like relativity and quantum theories because I don't quite understand them,*
> *and they make me feel as if space shifted about like a swan that can't settle,*
> *refusing to sit still and be measured;*
> *and as if the atom were an impulsive thing*
> *always changing its mind."*

So while it is very exciting to explore these new insights about the universe, at the same time it presents us with so much that is a conundrum, a puzzle, for us.

Scientists tell us we live in a universe of Infinite Possibility. Each moment contains an Infinite number of possible realities. They also say the universe is Holographic, meaning all of it is always present is every aspect of it. How can something be Infinite and be wholly present at the same time?

This is mind boggling to say the least. But let's come out of the ethers back to Earth because we said from the start we are here, not to learn science, but to explore how the discoveries and insights of science impact our own thinking and the possible results we can create in our lives. Let's explore how living from a context of Infinite Possibility can quite literally transform our lives.

Our minds are finite in the sense that they are limited to what we can "see" in any given moment in time. Then how do we imagine what it is to think from a "new world view," to think from a world of Infinite Possibility? How do we imagine the unlimited with a mind which is limited?

Albert Einstein wrote something that can shed some light on this matter of going beyond the mind.

> *"Physical concepts are free creations of the human mind, and are not, however it may seem, uniquely determined by the external world. In our endeavor to understand reality we are somewhat like a man trying to understand the mechanisms of a closed watch. He sees the face and the moving hands, even hears its ticking, but he has no way of opening the case.*

> *"If he is ingenious, he may form some picture of a mechanism which could be responsible for all the things he observes, but he may never be quite sure his picture is the only one which could explain his observation. He will never be able to compare his picture with the real mechanism and he can never even imagine the possibility or the meaning of such a comparison."*[26]

Like Einstein's man with the closed watch, you can imagine that you could go beyond the mind, but you cannot imagine what that would be like. Reality is Multidimensional. There are forces and principles working that we can access, that we can tap into. Even though our mind may not quite understand *how* they work, what we *can* know is *that* they work.

To our ordinary minds something either exists or it doesn't, because from the classical world view existence refers to what is physical. We don't think of the world of possibility as existing. We hold what isn't there as nothing, as having no existence. There is either something or nothing. This is thinking shaped by a classical world view—the world of an Either/Or reality of one dimension, the dimension of physical matter, that which we can glean with our ordinary senses. In a classical Either/Or world, something either exists or it doesn't, because "existence" in that world view means the physical material world.

Yet, one of the most eye-opening insights we've learned from physicists of the new science[27] is that the total universe consists of both the actual physical world whose existence is obvious to us, and it also consists of the *possible* world whose existence is unseen. The possible world has existence.

In the new world view we move beyond the limits of an Either/or Reality to the world of Both/And. *Both* the possible *And* the actual worlds exist, and they exist at the same time.

So what can all of this mean to you?

Suppose for you, in the realm of your imagination, in the way you imagine yourself to be, you consider yourself to be a person of great generosity. But someone you know accuses you of being a stingy person. Who is correct? In a classical world view, the world of Either/Or, where only the material aspect of the world is considered real, that which is provable by "evidence," you would be one or the other. You would be either generous or you would be stingy. Because in the Either/Or world, both of these traits cannot exist at once.

Did you ever notice how we want to categorize people as being one way or another? Either they are generous or they're not. We think someone is nice or they're not. This is the way the classical view has conditioned our thinking, separating the world into parts.

We look into the world external to us, we collect the data, we analyze the data, categorize the data, and we make conclusions. We proceed to live those conclusions as the "truth" about *the way things are.* Then we compare and match anything that comes into our purview up against what we have already concluded. Isn't this the way things happen?

You go out for dinner with a new friend. The check arrives and your friend makes no attempt to offer to pay. You conclude he lacks generosity. Do you continue to hold that conclusion of this person in the future? Probably so. Until, of course, you distinguish this automatic mechanism working and recall to yourself it is an Observer-created Reality after all.

In a quantum world view our perspective is entirely different. If everything always exists, then generosity exists for everyone, including *you*. It exists in the *possible* world. Now the question is—does your generosity exist in the other aspect of the world, the *actual* world. Said another way, is your generosity *manifesting*?

From a new world view we don't end up classifying people as one way or another; as honest or dishonest, selfish or giving, stingy or generous. We can see **everyone** as the possibility of any human quality or attribute. Which specific trait or quality actualizes, what becomes manifest, is contingent upon the Intent of the Observer. This is really, really important: you can literally bring someone else's generosity into actuality *by virtue of your Intent to see them that way*. Intent is the dynamic of creation, the activation of the life force. Intent activates Possibility that originates in this quantum vacuum, the realm of Infinite Possibility. There is no absolute truth about the way a person is. There is only what you the Observer actualize by virtue of your Intent. *What you bring is what you get.*

～～

As you can begin to see, the possibilities are endless. Or, to put this in terms of this distinction, the possibilities are Infinite. Sounds good. However …

Even though we know that the nature of our world is a universe of Infinite Possibility, we don't necessarily *live* in the world of Infinite Possibility. In fact, often our everyday activities take the form of a "Least-action Pathway."

This term comes to us from science. A *Least-action Pathway* is the way of getting somewhere that takes the least effort, the least creative action. It is the established or habitual pattern from the past, the path the energy has traveled before. The more something takes the same path, the more likely it will continue to take that path. It becomes the easiest path because it has already been established. Least-action Pathways are neural grooves in our perceptual apparatus that keep the world static and unchanging for us. In everyday terms, we call this a "rut."

In contrast to Infinite Possibility as the limitless source of all creation, a Least-action Pathway is the route of the mechanical, the automatic, the non-thinking. You could think of our habits arising as a result of our Least-action Pathways. No new action has to be taken. The energy, thought or action will automatically go in the direction established by the past.

How does a Least-action Pathway show up in your life? In your automatic habits. What we mean by a habit is one that is automatic, mechanical, without thinking, one over which we have no mastery because we lack awareness of it; it's a reaction to circumstances. Think of the way it generally happens. A circumstance comes up, one which on the face of it is unfavorable to you. Your irritability unfolds. It is automatic.

You don't even have to try! Or you go to a store to buy a gift, or even to purchase something for yourself. Is your generosity unfolding?

Who hasn't had a thought that they wish they didn't have? Perhaps a disparaging remark against your wife, your father, or your child, or perhaps against a certain ethnic group or religious belief or sexual persuasion. Did you *choose* that thought? Where does it come from? Why is it crossing through your mind? This is what we mean by automaticity.

We all revere and aspire to the virtues of kindness, service, cheerfulness, temperance, joy, love, generosity, compassion. How many of us actually exhibit those qualities as our habitual way of being? It is not that we *are* one way or another; it is a matter of what we unfold. We are not speaking about some deep part of your inner being here nor is it psychological in any way. Careful not to give this any more "meaning" because it really doesn't have any. We are simply talking about habits that can be displaced by new habits. It all happens in awareness. All this takes is you noticing that an Observation you have is no more true than it is false. It is a question of what you choose to tune into. The entire fabric of a situation shifts when you shift.

You can see that our Least-action Pathways do not allow for any new possibilities. A Least-action Pathway does not even have any conscious awareness to it; it just happens automatically, unconsciously.

This automatic functioning is actually one of the marvelous functions of the classical world. The electro-chemical processes of our body work this way. When we perform certain repetitive functions, this automatic functioning is operating; when we are driving a car, or when we learn a language or when we learn to type or play an instrument. We don't have to have our attention on which letter on the keyboard to press, because of this mechanical functioning that doesn't require our full conscious awareness.

So in one sense, this automatic functioning is very useful. But on the other hand, if we want to generate something new, when we want to create from nothing, or innovate or invent; this requires our fully conscious presence.

Living from Infinite Possibility alters your experience of even the most personal and everyday activities you share with loved ones. A client said she took out Christmas decorations and was about to place them where she had always put them year after year after year. This year she brought the distinction Infinite Possibility into her awareness and decided to let her kids take care of the decorating. The children had fresh perspectives that not only livened up the season—just *allowing for the Possiblity* brought the family closer together.

When life becomes mechanical it becomes unconscious. To live in the world of Both/And, it is useful to know when automatic and mechanical is appropriate, and when conscious presence is appropriate for what we want to create. This is another aspect of the mastery we are after, being able to use our discrimination to travel effectively in both worlds.

We want to be able to think in a new way but we have no access to new thinking because this Least-action Pathway mechanism is automatically in gear. Until we become aware of this of course. Then and *only then* do we have any power to free ourselves from the automatic pathway and begin to use the creative dynamic granted us by virtue of our human birthright, the power of our conscious Intent.

What breaks the habit?

To operate in the world of Infinite Possibility you would have to become aware of your own Least-action Pathways, and interrupt or interfere with the automatic path. The two forces that enable us to interrupt the pattern are (1) *awareness* and (2) *intent*. We first become *aware* that we are operating in a Least-action Pathway mode and then we open to Infinite Possibility and create a new Intent.

Predominant Least-action Pathways of Our Culture

One of the most predominant Least-action Pathways of human beings is to operate from *What's wrong?* It's not like we go around saying, *what's wrong?* (though sometimes we do). It is more like a computer program, silently running in the background. It is a context that shapes our actions. You will smile at yourself (and all of us) when you look at this. We walk into a situation and tend to look for what's wrong. We go to see a movie or a play or dine in a different restaurant and we come out discussing what the director or the writer or the chef did wrong.

Even when things are going great, we are waiting for something to go wrong. What happens when something wonderful happens to you? You make a ton of money on a stock or you get a big promotion in your job or you meet "the one" you want to spend your life with and things are going fantastically well. The cultural Least-action Pathway kicks in: *This is too good to be true. This can't last.*

We live in the expectation that eventually, *something* is going to go wrong. Even with regard to our health and aging there is an unspoken Least-action Pathway in our culture that one has to get sick in order to die "properly," even though *good* health is our natural state. There is no "cause of death" in our culture that simply states "I am ready to go. I've finished here and I'm ready to make the transition." Yet that may be more viable and certainly more appealing than waiting for something to "go wrong."

A variation of this cultural Least-action Pathway is when we hear a new idea, a new or fresh possibility. You're in a business meeting or with the family or a group of friends. Someone brings up a novel idea. What happens? You are likely to hear why this can't, shouldn't, or simply won't work, or how you can prove this because it didn't work last time we tried it. Notice whether right now you are in the Least-action Pathway thought that "there's something wrong" with having this cultural Least-action Pathway! When you catch yourself in this type of automatic reaction, you can begin to grasp the cosmic humor of the Least-action Pathways. It is so freeing when you do.

Cultural Least-action Pathways aren't "the truth about the way we are." They are simply mechanical, non-thinking, unaware habits and patterns that have been established in our human culture. We are not even implying that the ways of the culture are "bad" or "wrong." What we are saying is that when you are unaware of the pull they have on you, you are not at choice, even though it *appears* as if you are. The Least-action Pathways can be so much a part of who we are that we don't even notice them. (Remember the dust clouds shrouding the star's brilliance?) Even when we think of ourselves as bright, alert, aware, and "with-it," the riptide of the culture catches us in its undercurrents and pulls us along with it. Before we know it, we have drifted miles from where we want to be.

Thinking Beyond Compromise

A gentleman we know, a highly educated, well-read, and widely traveled doctor with an active, inquiring intellect, wrote to us of a situation and concluded, "There are two sides to every story, and there is always a compromise." Unbeknownst to him, he framed for us an excellent and common example of thinking from an old world deterministic, reductionistic view. The world of that particular situation is reducible to its two (Either/Or) *parts*, or options, and there seems to be enough dissonance between the two options that "compromise" looks like the only answer or resolution.

To "compromise" means: *"to come to an agreement by mutual concession, usually involving a partial surrender of purposes or principles."* I don't know about you, but I don't know anybody who is happy to surrender their purposes or principles. We present this not to invalidate this gentleman's or anyone's notions of compromise, but to point to the extent to which even the most intelligent among us unwittingly take the route of the Least-action Pathway.

We can transcend the automatic and begin to live and think from a more accurate view of our world, a universe of Infinite Possibility. Consider that from a new world view, "compromise" is no longer necessary. Why compromise? We live in a world of Infinite Possiblity. Why give up what you or anyone else truly wants? There is *always* another possibility, another way of thinking about something, another way of seeing something that can satisfy everyone.

In an Observer-created Reality we realize we can create something else. When we *know* that the nature of our reality, the very nature and essence of our world is Infinite Possibility, we can alter our thinking. We can shift the context from which we live. We can live from a context of *what's possible?* We can generate a context of possibility and efficacy (i.e. what works best). It has to happen with awareness, consciously. Because the Least-action Pathways are so embedded and so strong. We can generate an even more powerful force with our own awareness and with our own Intent.

This requires catching ourselves in the automatic habit of looking for "what's wrong" and why this can't work. With conscious awareness and conscious Intent, we can shift the focus to *what's possible* and *how can we have this work*. This is the discipline of Mastery. It takes having vigilance over your own automatic ways of thinking and being, over your automatic habits.

Acknowledging your Least-action Pathways is not to give yourself a reason for reviving Wretched Self Syndrome or criticizing yourself or others or our culture in any way. It is simply to distinguish your Self from them.

Noticing your Least-action Pathway *in the moment it arises*, you are no longer identified with that action or habit. In that moment you become the watcher, the pure witnessing Awareness. Remember, the mechanical habits we have formed in the past come from having been brought up in and conditioned by a mechanical world view, of life evolved only to a certain point in time. Now we are in a new time, a quantum age. You have chosen to consciously evolve yourself. When you realize this, you can *relax!* There is nothing wrong with you. Knowing this brings you *relief*. Take a long, slow breath and drop those shoulders. You're fine.

Intent opens the way

Intent is the dynamic of creating. Intent is what opens the way. Awareness of your Intent frees you from the grasp of Least-action Pathways. When we are functioning in the limited world of our own Least-action Pathways, we are not even aware of Intent. Can we even call it "our Intent" if we are unaware of it? Distinguishing your Least-action Pathways is what enables you to *go beyond the limits of your mind in any given moment in space-time.*

When you see your own limits, you can bring yourself present to your Intent by generating what your Intent is. One way to do this is simply to ask yourself pertaining to any life matter or situation: What is my Intent here?

As we have been saying all along, you cannot do this theoretically. You cannot accomplish this conceptually. Thinking from Infinite Possibility is an act of present-moment awareness. When you catch yourself in your own limited thinking, when you notice your Least-action Pathways and give them no meaning *in the moment they arise*, you depart the mechanistic world of Either/Or options, and you enter the world of unlimited creativity. You clear the dust clouds of your own mind, and allow shining, shimmering brilliance to emerge. Are you ready?

⟨ QuantumThink Recreation ⟩
Live the Wisdom of Infinite Possibility

ONE»Observe your Least-action Pathways. You don't have to try to do anything with them. Just *notice* them. Simply notice:

◆ Your habitual ways of Responding
to requests, opinions, judgments, promises, etc. you receive from others

◆ Your habitual ways of Speaking
your mannerisms, tone of voice, attitudes, compassion, expectations, demands, kindness, love, or lack thereof

◆ Your habitual ways of Listening
your "pre-conceived knowing," your patience and space for people, your evaluations, opinions, attentiveness

What you are bringing into your awareness are the automatic ways, not your consciously thought-through ways. You could say that a Least-action Pathway is one lacking in spirit or life force or conscious awareness. Notice if you find yourself in a "habit" of reacting resulting in one of these states: agitation, complaining, worrying, criticizing, irritation, pressured, stressed, angry. If you find it difficult to admit these to yourself, it is probably because you have ascribed some undesirable meaning to it. (Probably a result of another Least-action Pathway.) When you realize these mechanistic ways of being are simply an outcome of a stage of evolution we can now transcend, you note them and move on with ease.

TWO»Just once today, when you catch yourself in a Least-action Pathway, shift it by thinking from Infinite Possibility and generating a new Intent. Create possibility in a situation where it would ordinarily look like you are going to have to "settle" or compromise. Rather than focusing on what's wrong and trying to fix it, create a new possibility from your Intent alone.

THREE»Explore Infinite Possibility by doing something that is "foreign" to you, far from what you would typically do. Read a magazine that it would never occur to you to read, or watch a TV show that you would ordinarily not tune into. Do something entertaining or creative that you have always wanted to do, but never seem to get around to it. Sing from the rooftop. Kiss your wife or your friend unexpectedly. Create a possibility for yourself out of these experiences, even if you never engage in them again. Allow them to expand your experience of life.

"The only reason someone is a genius and knows things you do not know is because he has opened his mind to contemplate the what-ifs, the outrageous thoughts, the thoughts of brilliance that go beyond the limited thinking of man."

—RAMTHA

QUANTUMTHINK-WAVE
The Mastery of Balance

People everywhere cry out they want *balance!* in their lives. Perhaps you are one of them. As society becomes ever more complex and the number and variety of choices burgeon, you may be experiencing the weight of personal and professional demands. What can enable us to "balance" all of it? We can learn from Michael Moschen, considered perhaps the most masterful juggler that ever lived, for whom the mastery of balance is essential. When asked what makes his mastery possible, he replied, *"Balance is not perfect stillness."*[28]

Picture the master juggler balancing spinning plates in the air. At the height of his Mastery, he is at the height of *presence*. He had better be, because for the juggler there is nothing to hold onto, nothing to pin down, nothing fixed, nothing still. There is nothing but his present state. The stillness is *within*; the ability to dance in that moment, in the words of the master juggler, *"... the ability to make exquisitely refined responses to unexpected change."*

For you and me things are not likely to slow down and they are certainly not going to stop. The very nature of our universe is Energy In Flux, continuous movement. What allows for balance may be something else entirely than changing the circumstances, attempting to simplify or downsize or get things all lined up and under control.

Consider that living in a state of presence where balance is experienced has nothing to with the circumstances. It is a state beyond space, outside of time, and independent of anything you already know or have ever achieved. This is the state of Mastery.

4 SUCCESS TO MASTERY
Knowing what to do in the moment and doing it

Here is a very interesting Recreation for you that you can begin right now. It is to practice Listening From Not-knowing. Can you imagine what it would be like to live in a state of "Not-Knowing"? If I ask you whether you think you are open-minded, I am sure you would say yes. Yet, as we have already begun to observe, each one of us has a whole history of automatic responses to people and situations that come into play every moment.

Our habits of thinking, our habits of relating, our habits of communicating are so much with us. The system in which we have been conditioned to think puts limits on what we hear, how we hear new ideas, and how we listen to each other. What is "already there" limits what's possible. We think we have an open mind, a blank canvas. But you can see from your own Least-action Pathways that this isn't so.

People have stood by the famous assertion attributed to 16th century statesman and champion of education, Sir Francis Bacon: "Knowledge is power." In view of our ever-changing, non-static reality—a world in constant flux, always moving, and unpredictably so—you could say we can no longer rely on what we "know" in the form of information as a source of power. The nature of information is that it changes so fast we can no longer rely on information alone if we want to be effective.

The question is: if we can no longer count on "knowledge as power," from where do we get our source of power? What *can* we count on so we can be our most effective in the midst of the upheavals and transformation surrounding us? How do we ensure our success in such an environment? Perhaps Success alone is not enough. Consider that what we are ready for now is to move beyond Success to *Mastery.*

If we want to develop a state of Mastery, a state of not relying on what we already know, we need to somehow be able to "Listen From Not-Knowing." So how do we accomplish this, realizing we don't come in with a blank slate?

You accomplish this by becoming aware, moment by moment, of your "knowing" mechanism. When you catch yourself listening as if you already know who this person is, what she or he is going to say, or you are listening as if you already know "the answer" you can just notice that you are doing this. You consider that *maybe you don't know.* And begin to Listen From Not-Knowing.

Imagine you are sitting in a meeting or perhaps having dinner with someone you know. Your companion is talking about a subject you are very familiar with. It's not *true* that you "don't know." However, it is powerful, enlivening, and expanding to consider that *maybe* you don't know. Think about this for a moment: when you "know" you close off serendipity. Serendipity is the faculty of discovering something fortunate that you weren't expecting. What can be discovered, what can you possibly hear from the other person when you come into the conversation with what you think you already "know"? When you Listen From Not-Knowing you connect to the realm of creativity, of ingenuity, of the ability to dance with what reveals itself to you. There is excitement in the air.

Just doing this *consciously* brings you into a highly present state, into the "now" moment. Then instead of being stale, you will be fresh. The moment will be alive. This is what gives you access to your own Mastery.

Have you ever been in a situation when you actually *didn't know*? You traveled to a country where you have never been, and you didn't know the customs or the geography or the language. The circumstances dictated that in this case you would listen from not knowing. However, this is not what we are speaking about here. We are talking about Listening From Not-Knowing as a consciously generated state.

〜〜

We refer to QuantumThink as "thinking for a new world," an expression by design replete with double entendre. It means this is a system of thinking you would need to generate in order to create a new world for yourself, whether your new world is for you, your family, your company, or the world at large. Also, since we find ourselves in a new world developing around us today, *thinking for a new world* also means we need to be able to think in a new way more suited to and more consistent with the changing state of affairs in the world.

This is the paradox of a new world view. In an Observer-created Reality we are *generating* the new world in the sense of bringing it forth, and at the same time we are generating our *relationship* with the new world that is emerging around us. In a Holistic world where we are not separate from the world, the dynamic of creating is a co-participatory dance. To be effective in this is to develop a new kind of knowing, a knowing that we can call *Mastery*. Mastery is knowing what to do in the moment and doing it without having to think about it. Mastery is timeless and formless. Mastery has to do with effectiveness in the moment called "now." *Now* transcends our linear concept of time. "Now" is like an electron; we only know it by what it leaves behind. "Now" is like that. As soon as you try to capture Now, it is already gone.

When we watch a master juggler, a martial arts master, or master athlete we can literally see the spontaneity of their actions, the "exquisitely refined responses to unexpected change." They aren't thinking about some facet of information and attempting to apply it in the moment of action. In the moment of action, they cannot rely on any of their successes from the past. Every moment is fresh; it is alive and it is new.

There is a timelessness to Mastery, and there is an ephemeral quality to it in that Mastery cannot be captured or measured. It has no form and no shape. It has no mass, yet we know it when we are in the presence of it. We sense Mastery as a state to be aspired to. Mastery is not a thing nor is it a personality trait. Mastery is a quality of being.

Mastery is knowing the appropriate thing to be done in the moment and doing it, whether that means a physical action, a speaking or listening action, or a refraining from action which itself is an action. It is the confidence and conviction that you can do this, consistently. A paradox of Mastery is that it becomes possible from a state of Not-Knowing. We consciously put aside that which we think we know for what we can encounter in the moment.

All of us have experienced successes in many forms throughout our lives. Since Success is, by definition, measured by what has already occurred it has a past-based frame of reference. You could say we operate in life from the background of our successes. We don't associate Success with limitation. Thus we are not necessarily aware of how our successes, as great as they may be, can actually narrow our vision.

When we operate from Success, we operate from what worked previously. We attempt to reproduce, copy, or replicate what worked before or we try somehow to improve upon it. We want the formulas and the how-to's so we can be successful again. But novel situations, changing circumstances and emerging challenges may require new thinking and innovative approaches. This is not to invalidate in any way the value of past experience and former successes. We're not looking at this from an Either/Or viewpoint. The ability to create formulas and mechanical processes in many ways make our lives easier. However, if we look *only* from what worked in the past, we will be limited by it.

On first reaction to this, you may be saying to yourself, *That's obvious. Of course I look at each situation in a new way.* But do you really? It is so important to keep noticing the automatic habits and Least-action Pathways of our cultural thinking as they show up in our daily activities. The "force" of our culture without even having to think about it is to do it the way we have always done it.

Remember the last time you accomplished something truly extraordinary? People ask you: *How did you do it? How were you able to get all those sales? What did you do?*

We want the formulas, the how-tos, the quick answers. Yet as you can see Success does not necessarily lead to Mastery.

Success is a reference external to us. It is reliant on circumstances outside of us measured by what has already occurred. Mastery is an internal reference that we generate from ourselves. It is a state of awareness that has us be at the height of effectiveness in the midst of and regardless of any and all circumstances. You have in your repertoire the successes of the past, but you live in a state of alert and open readiness; a focused presence of mind that enables spontaneous creativity and appropriate action.

We can see the results of Mastery. What we don't see, what is hidden from our immediate view, is the discipline that leads to that Mastery. A paradox of Mastery is that it is a *practice*, a moment-by-moment proposition. You establish yourself in the state of presence that spiritual teachers call *steady wisdom*. It is to put aside what you already know, to bring yourself to what Zen meditation practice calls "beginner's mind." What gives you access to that state?

Distinguishing Allows for Mastery

In today's world, we require a new kind of knowing and a different kind of learning. In QuantumThink we say the *new world view of learning* is mastering The Art of Distinguishing. To distinguish requires an awakened state. As you develop The Art of Distinguishing, you naturally move from Success to Mastery.

What is present when things are "working?" People have *distinguished* something. That is, they have brought something into their awareness in such a way that alters something in life, a situation or a result. Let's take "chaos theory" as an example. From old world view thinking, if you attempt to define it, you will find yourself in a quandary because if you research chaos theory in science and mathematics, you will find numerous definitions. You may not be able to define it; however, you can *distinguish* many aspects of chaos theory that could prove useful.

Even though things may appear chaotic and random from one perspective, when you widen your view, you may find there is a naturally inherent order within the chaos. You can stand in a busy train station, like Grand Central Station in New York City, and it looks like pure chaos at rush hour. But if you knew the scheduling and could see this in a larger perspective, you would see that every person is following a certain path and a certain schedule. It is actually very organized and systematic, even though the system does not follow an exact symmetrical or linear order.

What is the practical use of such a distinction? When you are aware of order in chaos as a *distinction*, rather than just feeling overwhelmed or confused you can begin to see creative solutions in chaos around you. You now know there is something systematic organizing itself to have this all work out and that allows you to start looking for the novelty, for solutions and creative additions that can be found as a result of the chaos. However, if you use chaos or *any* theory as a rigid formula, then what happens?

You try to make everything that happens fit into this new formula which you have now made into a "new truth" about the way things *are*. You have disintegrated the possibility of Mastery. Why? Because, you are no longer looking freshly from what will work now, what is wanted and best in *this* situation. Your thinking has become stale because you are relying on a theory or practice that worked before. And it may work again, but it may not work in *every* situation.

Distinguishing allows for unlimited possibilities where formulas can tend to close them down. If you aren't aware that what you are doing is *distinguishing* then you tend to go to the new manifestation as the new "answer," the latest and greatest thing to do, the new formula to repeat, the new "how-to." We're not saying that if something is worthy of repetition that you shouldn't use it. What we are saying is that if you cannot *distinguish* that this is what you are doing, you can become a victim of the new solution which often leads to disappointment. When you make something your new answer or belief system, you want to continue to keep it in existence so you may tend to justify its existence and look for reasons why it's the "right" solution *even when it's not really working anymore.* How often do we see this in our businesses and our governments?

David Bohm, the brilliant quantum physicist said *"Our ideas have to be vulnerable."* We get seduced by the fact that it worked so well in the past. But to really think from Infinite Possibility and from what will work *now,* in *this* situation, we have to be able to free ourselves even from the allure of our former successes.

~~~

The intent of QuantumThink is to have you tap into your creative force at its *source.* When you become aware of the source of the creative solution, you are free to think from what will work *now,* from what is best or right in *this* situation. This can be uncomfortable for people because the source of creativity is the free space, the nothingness, the field of all possibility. We want to rely on something solid, fixed, a foundation we can see or explain. Except in a quantum universe, there is nothing solid or fixed. Rather, it is the world of Infinite Possibility waiting to be actualized by the Intent of the Observer. There is nothing to hold onto here in the physical world, and that drives people a little crazy (unless you know yourself as a "masterful juggler," of course). For the adventurous spirit, the idea of this is truly heaven on earth because in this new world view, you have freedom *to,* as contrasted with freedom *from.* We tend to think of being free as escaping from something, but consider that real freedom is the freedom to create.

This state of awareness of your Self as the source of what's possible in your life is truly the most powerful state because in this state your access to creating is pure, unfettered by old conventions, habits, beliefs or pre-dispositions. When you engage in Listening From Not-Knowing you connect to your freedom to create at its source.

Remember, we are in the time of redesigning and restructuring our relationship with the world around us. This includes the people in your life. What would it be like for you to ride in the car with your child or your parent and listen as if you don't already know them? When you practice this with your friends you'll be amazed at what you're able to hear for the first time. You'll delight in the way you deepen the connection with clients when you Listen From Not-Knowing. You are connected in the quantum field. When you shift to this state, the other person actually *experiences being heard.* For most people this is **monumental.**

Listening From Not-Knowing does not mean that you do not have some piece of information. It does not mean that you didn't know something, and that you are now going to be open-minded and discover information you did not know at the outset. Listening From Not-Knowing means something quite distinct from that. Listening From Not-knowing is a demonstration of *living in the Unknowable*. It is Unknowable because, like Einstein's man with the closed watch, you know there is something working in the invisible though you can never know precisely what that is. So you don't ignore it; you work with it. You don't leave it out; you use it.

You "live in the Unknowable" even with the person you think you "know" so well, or the situation you imagine you have lived through a hundred times, or the street you have walked down a thousand times and yes, even with your very own self. All of it is in constant flux, different in every moment. If you are Listening From Not-Knowing, you will hear and see something unprecedented, something fresh, something exciting perhaps, something enlivening, something life-altering. This is what it means to move from Success to Mastery.

QuantumThink Recreation
Live the Wisdom of Success to Mastery

ONE»Continue to Listen From Not-Knowing as *a deliberate act of consciousness.* Watch what happens in your relationships when you Listen From Not-Knowing in the moment of being in a conversation with someone, or in the midst of a business meeting or during one of your classes at school.

You can practice this as you listen to or read items in the news that we automatically tend to have very strong opinions and conclusions about. Listen From Not-Knowing to the news and the people and the stories.

Practice this when you listen to pundits or politicians you don't agree with, or when you are exposed to a genre of music you tend to tune out, or when you listen to someone you think you know very well, such as your wife or your husband, your mother or father, son or daughter. Listen From Not-Knowing as your boyfriend or your business partner speaks. Practice this when you listen to someone outside of your culture or your ethnic background or your country, someone you have automatic judgments about.

TWO»As you are sitting with the person you live with or the person you work with or the person you see in school every day, *consciously* consider and realize: *I don't know this person, because this is a person of Infinite Possibility, changing and evolving all the time. This is a fresh moment. I can hear something I have never heard before from this person.* Listen From Not-Knowing.

THREE»Practice Listening From Not-Knowing with your own self. When you think you know something about yourself, Listen From Not-Knowing. Notice when you have reached a conclusion about yourself, for instance, that you are not good at public speaking or you are not athletic, or you can't understand science, or you don't enjoy shopping, or that you are shy. Pause and Listen From Not-Knowing *yourself.*

Today, listen this way to at least three people you think you know so well. Include yourself as one of the people. Consider that you are more than you think you are; beyond your fixed ideas, concepts and conclusions about yourself. Today, live in the realization that you can be powerful and effectively operate in the aspect of the Infinite we call the Unknowable. Watch for amazing surprises. Listening From Not-Knowing frees you in the moment from automatically conditioned responses. You move from Success to Mastery.

QuantumThink-Wave
As the Crystal Turns

Have you ever held a quartz crystal up to the sunlight and watched it change colors and hues as you turned it, allowing the light to reflect off its many facets? This is what we do as we travel around the new world that QuantumThink distinguishes. Through each one of the distinctions we examine the same phenomenon: the nature of our conscious life. The quartz crystal is a great graphic metaphor for consciousness because the crystal is colorless, transparent, multi-faceted, and acts as a receptor infused with life-force. As we cast the light of awareness on the many facets of consciousness it appears to us in ever-new dimensions of prismatic splendor. Like peering at the crystal, we can keep looking at the same thing but we can never catch it in exactly the same light. This is what makes it so captivating!

As we keep turning the crystal of consciousness it is good to ask ourselves why we're doing this. What's the purpose? What's the value of this? Remind yourself you are here QuantumThinking *to have something happen in your life*, something unpredictable and marvelous—something splendid and even majestic. Why not live in *that* Intent?

You may find yourself attempting to figure out the main points of this as you read, or compare it to something you have already done or studied. This is one of the predominant Least-action Pathways of the classically conditioned mind: to *compare* what we know from our past experience to everything we hear or read or see in an effort to understand. We may not be practiced in simply being attentive to what is being said without an evaluation or comparison or driven compulsion to know everything there is to know immediately or figure it out. Now you can put this habit aside and bring your full presence to what is being introduced. You can *discover* what emerges from the quantum field of your Intent. There is a conscious act of Allowing.

Sometimes you find yourself working so hard at something. From a new world view "to have something happen" does not mean forcing it or pushing it to happen. A tennis coach once told me, *"You're working too hard. Just stand back, relax, get your racket back, let the ball come to you, and swing."* Just as in tennis we stand back as the ball comes to us and Allow our multi-dimensional intelligence to make the perfect shot, just as we stand back and Allow the colored reflections of the crystal to surprise and delight us, in a voyage of discovery we stand back and Allow for what unfolds.

5 ALLOWING

It's bigger than both of us

It is said that the two statues you encounter at the door of the temple of wisdom represent the two things that both keep you from the truth and also lead you to it. They are *confusion* and *paradox.*

As you delve into QuantumThink and begin to explore the distinctions of our emerging new world you may find yourself at times confused. Confusion is good. Confusion means your mind cannot go back and check out what it is hearing to try to understand it, comparing it to what it already knows. Confusion means you have been thrown beyond the ordinary boundaries of your mind.

Confusion could be said to be the state on the perimeter of a quantum leap. A quantum leap transcends understanding in the sense of ordinary linear logic. That's why quantum scientists refer to their science with words such as "wacky world," "bizarre," and "quirky." When you find yourself in a state where your mind can't quite hold on or grasp what is going on, just allow that to be. This is not the world of manipulation and control. This is the world of Allowing, of Allowing for what reveals itself to you, and of Allowing yourself to follow its lead.

What about "paradox"? Paradox means something which seems absurd or self-contradictory, contrary to what you would be led to believe conventionally or with common sense. The world of QuantumThinking is paradoxical in many ways. One of the ways it is paradoxical is the idea that *context,* which is pure space, is the source of all actions and is therefore the source of all results. That everything comes from "nothing" doesn't seem to make sense. Today we know from science that what was once thought of as "nothing" or empty space is actually a high-powered energy state known as the *zero point* when energy seems to be at rest. What does this tell us? That stillness contains power seems contrary to common sense. Then again, as cosmologist Stephen Hawking mused *"… common sense is just another name for the prejudices we have been brought up with."*

Another paradox of the quantum world is that you can affect something at a physical distance from you using thought alone, with no apparent or logical connection between you and that which is being affected. In quantum physics this is known as the principle of *nonlocality.* Physicist-philosopher Danah Zohar describes nonlocality as "action without causation." She wrote this about nonlocality:

> "Perhaps more than anything else, quantum physics promises to transform our notions of relationship. The oneness of the overall system is paramount. It follows from this that the once ghostly notion of 'action-at-a-distance,' where one body can influence another instantaneously despite there being no apparent exchange of force or energy, is, for the quantum physicist, a fact of everyday life."[29]

What does this tell us? We can and do create outcomes without having a direct physical link to the outcome. The old world classically conditioned mind is always looking for the cause and effect relationship between things. We look for things to fit our linear logic to explain how something happened or how something *should* happen. We have a result we want and we want it to fit our pictures of the way we think it ought to come about. We don't realize how much we are in the habit of thinking this way and we're unaware of how we cut off new possibilities by staying in these limiting concepts.

If all you have is one viewpoint, if you only have linear logic, a material world, and a fixed concept of chronological time as your background reference for what is real or valid, you are going to be constrained by the limits of that system.

Linear time is specific; it's precisely measured. It moves in one direction, in a straight line, in increments. If all you have is linear time as your reference, when you want to produce a result and it doesn't fit into the time frame that seems logical to you, what happens? Either you would have to give up on the possibility of producing that result or you would attempt to manipulate around the circumstances to try to get it to happen. How will you accomplish a project due in one week that you logically think will take one month to complete? You would have to force the issue in some way. You would have to work harder to try to get it done. This is how the old world view has trained us—to work from existing circumstances and from ordinary logic that is so limiting that we are forced to give up or stress-out trying.

When you begin to distinguish the new world view you relate to what you are doing in an entirely different way. You don't try to fit nonlinear results into a world structured by time and the idea of "cause and effect." It doesn't work that way. You cannot fit the larger unbounded world of Infinite Possibility into a measured world of linearity. When you truly operate from the condition of the new world view not just as a concept, but as a part of who you are and the world you inhabit then you transcend the limited mind. You use "quantum logic." You learn to use nonlinear connections to attract situations and resources that you couldn't possibly see using ordinary logic.

~~~

The Swiss psychologist Carl Jung coined the word "synchronicity" to describe what we commonly call coincidences—a meaningful relationship or connection between two events that is not a result of a direct "cause and effect." Today we have more profound knowledge of such synchronicities because of the fact of nonlocality. Consider that nonlocality is an inherent characteristic of your own mind. Consider that you can influence and attract situations and information without having to be the local cause of them.

Though we aren't always aware of it and may not *see* it, we do influence things, events, and people at a distance from us. We already have experiences of this when we notice synchronicities in play, when two events become related when there did not seem to be any direct link between them. The most obvious one is when you are thinking about someone you haven't seen in a while, and that person "happens" to call you in that moment. Or when you need a particular resource, like a specific amount of money for something special, or someone to fix your computer, and somehow the money or the exact right expert shows up in your life "unexpectedly." When these nonlinear links occur life seems easy and more fun. Life has a feeling of magic to it. What you may not realize is that we can *consciously generate* these synchronicities and serendipity in our lives. We can create this kind of magic on a regular basis from the power of our Intent—if we allow for them to happen. When you know yourself as a multidimensional being you can intentionally access both the material and non-material aspects of reality. You can interact consciously with the forces that extend beyond sensory data and outside of linear time. In this there is what we call an Allowing.

In essence what we are focusing on is the matter of what creates our reality from the human realm of what it is to create. You are already aware that the central dynamic of creating results, what we could call the *active* principle, is your Intent. It is your consciously created Intent, created deliberately and with the awareness you are doing so. There is another aspect to the creation dynamic that we are calling the *passive* dynamic, and that aspect is the principle of Allowing.

We are all familiar with the word "allowing" however in this distinction we're using it in a particular way. As a *definition* allowing means "to permit to occur." Allowing as a distinction does not mean to "let things be as they are" or "let the chips fall as they may." As a *distinction*, Allowing is a dynamic, powerful faculty of the mind; an essential factor in creating from Intent. Allowing is not merely waiting for something to show up. Allowing is a passive yet conscious act of *calling something forth* from the quantum field, even though we can't see or know at the outset exactly what is going to show up. *The faculty of Allowing is an undetermined unfolding from the quantum field of probability, set up by a conscious Intent.*

Since our habit of thinking shaped by a deterministic world view is to want to know or figure out in advance how something is going to work out, most of us are not yet very adept in the practice of Allowing. Our tendency is to want to push and pull on the circumstances rather than Allow them to unfold, realizing that our Intent will inherently attract what is consistent with it. Allowing is a faculty that operates in Infinite Possibility, in the realm of the unimaginable where the mind cannot see—in the invisible dimension where forces, though they may be unexplainable to us, are in effect nonetheless. Even if you are unaware of these principles, forces, and laws, they are operating. You are affected by them because you are intricately interrelated and interconnected with all of it.

~~~

If this is beginning to sound like an advertisement for a new science fiction film, "unknown forces" and things, consider this. As scientists build better devices for viewing, such as the Hubble and Spitzer telescopes, astronomers say that *dark matter and dark energy,* which have never actually been *seen,* comprise more than 90 percent of the mass of the universe. What we can see is only 10 percent at best! What can we glean from this? Imagine that you and I can only see 10 percent of what is present in a given moment. However, we can work with the other 90 percent, the unseen, first of all by acknowledging its existence, and secondly by exercising the faculty of Allowing.

In a Holistic view of the world both what we see and what we don't see, the visible aspects of the world and the invisible aspects, are both always in play.

Even if we cannot see *how* things work, we can know *that* they work. Even though in many ways we are like Einstein's man with the closed watch, still we can participate and enjoy and benefit from the unseen and sometimes unexplainable dynamics. When you can tap into nonlocality and synchronicity and Allow them to operate in your life, it is so liberating! In our information society where communications are instantaneous and things are moving at light speed, we don't have the time nor do we have the capability to maintain control and produce results by having all factors in our immediate view. You can begin to see that confusion and paradox are good traveling companions on the QuantumThink journey.

~~~

What we are really doing here together is heightening our awareness. The purpose of this kind of awareness training is not for you to change everything you are doing. It is so you have choice. As we become aware of the automatic ways we react to situations, when we catch ourselves in a Least-action Pathway, it is in those moments we have real choice. When you are not getting what you say you want in life, heightened awareness and learning the distinctions of the dynamics of creating enable you to interrupt the automatic habits and access your real source of power to bring about the results you *do* want.

Allowing isn't unquestioned acceptance or belief. Allowing means you stay open and Allow for what occurs that could not have occurred were you to remain closed or rigid. Allowing means we don't have to push it and control it every minute. We don't have to manage every action.

Have you noticed that if you live with someone, or if you regularly relate with someone, such as a husband or wife, friend or child that you have established a kind of habit in the way you relate with that person? Perhaps your habit is to speak to your child in commanding tones, telling him or her what to do all the time. This becomes a habit, an unconscious, automatic habit. In the moment you notice you are doing this you have the *choice* to generate some other way of being with your child. You can create a new Intent right in that very moment, and Allow your relationship to express a whole new quality.

It is useful to begin as a daily practice *to notice the extent to which your own thinking is conditioned by the classical world view.*

Notice the extent to which you *automatically* reach conclusions.

Notice the extent to which you *analyze* things into parts.

Notice the extent to which you think *you already "know."*

Notice the extent to which you want to *predict* how something is going to go.

Notice the extent to which you hold back from committing yourself because *you want certainty* first about how something is going to turn out.

Notice the extent to which you think from a *self-center* rather than looking from the whole.

Remember that Intent is not a cause and effect, stimulus-response mechanism. Intent sets up a field of probability in a world of Infinite Possibility. Whatever resonates with your Intent attracts to you if you Allow it. Create the Intent, put everything in order for something to happen, and then Allow for what is unpredictable to emerge.

What this means is you can't always see the "how" of the result you desire. You can't see *how* your Intent is going to manifest in your life. You just Allow it to be, and you watch what unfolds. You can Allow yourself the joy of the surprise. **It won't necessarily fit your pictures of how you think it will happen.** Allow yourself the confidence in the principle and power of your own Intent. When you are in the practice of Allowing, not only are you open to results beyond the current limits of what your mind can envision—*you can expect them.*

⟝ QuantumThink Recreation ⟞
Live the Wisdom of Allowing

ONE» Consciously and with awareness that you are doing so, create a powerful Intent to set up a resonance for something you truly desire. Then consciously and with awareness that you are doing so, Allow for all the possibilities to reveal themselves to you. Allowing is always in a co-creative dance with conscious Intent. Become alert to these manifestations of Allowing, realizing your own conscious field as the source of them. See the relationship between your Intent and the nonlinear results that occur.

Put together everything we have distinguished thus far in QuantumThink:

that we live in an Observer-created Reality

that you shape your reality with the interpretations and Intent you bring to every situation

that you can interrupt your own Least-action Pathways, those automatic thought patterns and behaviors that are keeping you from creating new possibilities

that you can be open to Infinite Possibility, to what you never imagined was possible

that you can Listen From Not-knowing and begin to experience a state of mastery in creating results

In this context, generate your Intent and consciously with awareness, practice Allowing. Allow the Intent to fulfill itself without pushing or manipulating it to happen. Allowing doesn't mean you don't make plans or take action. You set the scenario for your play to unfold, and play your part in it by responding to the cues the environment provides for you. You deliberately watch for your Intent to unfold in the various ways that it does.

Tip: For this to work you need to be very clear about your Intent. It is like planting a seed. You plant the seed and nurture it. Then you watch the blossoming, the flowering, the unfolding of it. This is Allowing. You will notice ideas, people, emotions, opportunities, clues or signals—clear instructions, as if you were being tapped on the shoulder and pointed in the right direction. Allow yourself to be surprised and pleased with the results. Enjoy whatever unfolds, and dance with what presents itself to you. Even if it doesn't make logical sense to you, Allow yourself the adventure!

TWO»For one entire day, become aware of all the nonlinear results or "quantum occurrences" that show up throughout your day. Nonlinear means connections that are made that don't appear to be related in the ordinary logic of cause and effect or physical linkage. We call them *quantum occurrences*, amazing things that happen in your day; activities, resources, people and situations that come your way. You don't have to do anything in this Recreation except to be aware and awake to the connections in the nonlocal quantum field. In this way you become intimately related with your own faculty of Allowing, a faculty you can most assuredly rely upon in your role as a co-creator of realities.

QuantumThink-Wave
Let's Make Music

One balmy evening we attended a concert of a cellist friend when he premiered his new chamber music ensemble[30] at an intimate gathering in the Bass Museum on Miami Beach. The concert was played in a small room filled only with grand Old Master paintings so we were sitting very near to the piano trio. When you watch musicians you barely see with your eyes any communication between them save for a nod or two at the start of each movement. Yet the depth and breadth of their communication is evident in the music.

The sublime experience of music is a phenomenon unexplainable by pure logic or analysis, created moment by moment from the wholeness of their relationship. The different instruments resound as one. Synergy and synchronicity and serendipity abound. Music has immediacy. It's fresh and alive; it invigorates you. When music is being made the miraculous is present. Imagine such communication with the people in your life. In the family room or in the board room we are here to make music together. It happens naturally when you're Being In One Conversation.

6 BEING IN ONE CONVERSATION
Mind meld for best results

In the classic TV series *Star Trek*, Mr. Spock would *mind meld* to communicate with someone who did not speak the universal language or to delve deeply into their mind to learn more about them. He connected by physical touch on the person's face. *Star Trek* references are careful to point out that a mind meld is not telepathy but a shared consciousness. You don't have to be a Vulcan to mind meld. You don't have to physically touch someone to connect with them. It only takes Being In One Conversation.

Now is a perfect time to sit back, relax and take a deep breath. Why not? Let your shoulders drop naturally as you sit softly upright and breathe in slowly. Exhale gently and just be aware of your breath continually moving in and out in rhythmic motion. In this easy and natural way we bring our awareness to a single focus. Patañjali, the great sage of old attributed with systematizing the science of yoga taught if you want to be awakened, *focus on one thing*. To begin the practice of consciously Being In One Conversation, allow yourself to focus only in this conversation. If you find your mind drifting or freely associating into other conversations, just notice that, and bring yourself back to this one. Practice your own mastery in staying present by Being In One Conversation.

It's good to remind ourselves that engaging in QuantumThink is not just some intellectual exercise or a sophisticated fancy of dilettantes. We are here to wake ourselves up to the fact of a vast ever-changing reality that we only have one tiny window on at any given moment in time. We're examining how the world view we live in shapes our thinking and therefore conditions what we consider to be possible in our lives. We are connecting together to get at something that approximates some unseen truths about our life that can have us uplift the quality of our relationships and experience life the way we choose. To distinguish this is to approach something that is very subtle, yet its effect on us is so all-encompassing, so forceful in an almost transparent way. We keep drawing the distinction between the older, classical-mechanical world view and the new world view of a quantum reality and we do this so we can of our own accord, of our own volition bring this updated and more accurate view of the nature of reality into our thinking and into our lives. We do this to broaden our horizons, to expand our capabilities, to tap into more of our own creative power. We do this to increase our enjoyment of life. We can let go of habits and ideas we have become attached to, ways of being that have outlived their usefulness for us. We can gracefully step quantum style into our own power to live an enchanted life.

What are some of the habits we can drop? Thinking of communication as the transmission of information, thinking of listening as a skill, and thinking of a conversation as composed of two parts, the speaker and the listener.

<center>~~~</center>

One aspect of the new world view is that we live in a *relational* universe. Scientists tell us that everything in nature exists as patterns of relationships in continuous exchange with each other. Anything and everything that occurs in reality is a result of relationships. We could say it this way: everything that is accomplished, is accomplished through being related. As you begin to examine this you cannot help but notice that what is most important, essential to being related is communication itself.

In our culture we don't typically differentiate between communication as the transferring of information and communication as a function of being related. When people say they want "open and honest communication" in their families and in their companies, they are not talking about the mere transferring of data.

You often hear people say the most important skill to cultivate is the skill of listening. But the idea of "skills" is really an outcome of an old world view because skills end up looking like something to acquire. So we acquire this set of characteristics so we can classify and define what this "thing" called listening *should* be, and then we measure ourselves and others against this, to try to become better listeners. Perhaps *listening* is not really a skill at all. Consider that *listening is a dimension of being which we have never fully explored.*

Like everything in this universe QuantumThink is multidimensional. It is occurring on many different levels at the same time—energetically, mentally, and spiritually. By now you have probably begun to know its multidimensionality in your own experience.

What do we know about our current world reality? We know that from a new world view the fundamental aspect of reality is non-material. In contrast, the fundamental aspect of reality from a classical view is its materiality, i.e., only "matter" is real. Listening from a material view of the world is generally associated with "hearing." In the material world of the ordinary five senses listening is equated with perceiving the data, hearing the words that are spoken. In modern culture there is an expression "active listening." What does it mean? That you are being consciously attentive to the words being spoken. This is not what we are speaking about here.

Like the new world view itself listening is multidimensional. From a new world view listening becomes much more; it includes the invisible, the intangible, and the unspoken. What we don't hear and see are present and are as valid and significant as their physical counterpart in the sensory domain. It is listening not just with the ears, which give you the sounds of the words, and not just with the understanding, the interpretation or meanings you give to the words. It is *listening with your whole being.*

As you continue to read, "listen" not just to the words; listen with all of you. Listen with your whole being.

~~~

A Note On Communication ...

You relate to communication as a thing. As something solid, defined. Communication is not a thing in the same way that music is not a thing. When music is playing, where is the music? In the instruments, you say. No, the instruments are vibrating and the vibrating is causing sounds. Then, in the sounds themselves? Music is not just sounds. We don't say something is music when we hear just any sounds.

Music is non-locate-able. You cannot find music anywhere. Music is a relationship that exists in the "ether" between one person and another. You can't see what's in the ether. It doesn't exist in the world of perception. Sound exists in the world of perception, but music doesn't. You hear something, but music is a creation that occurs in the relationship between the person making the music and me, the listener.

Music is not in the printed notes on a page. That is just the representation of the form of the music.

Communication is expressed in the form of language, but communication is not the language. It is not mere words, or syntax, or grammar. Communication is neither the form of language, nor the sound of the words. Communication resides in the relationship between one person and another. Communication is not a thing. It is an amorphous living presence that exists in the ether, like music. Communication expressed through language, in the broadest sense of that word, is the music of the human form, of human life. Language is what creates our relationship to life—to everything in our life, and to each other. Communication is a creation that occurs in the relationship between people.

Language is the tool of creation for human beings; the letters are the notes, and the words are the musical phrases. There is also syntax, (the structure or word order), and grammar, (how the word is used); there are facial expressions and body motions and pictorial symbols and signs, but none of that alone is the communication.

The written notes can be seen on the paper, the words can be seen on the paper; but the music can never be seen and the communication can never be seen. The sounds of music can be heard, the spoken words can be heard; but the sound of the instruments is not the music, and the spoken words are not the communication.

~~~

We may not have ever examined to what extent the classical world view has conditioned the way we listen, and further, how the automatic ways that we listen shape, not only what we hear, but *the ways in which we have been conditioned to listen become determining factors of our results.*

One way we can begin to distinguish the various dimensions of listening is to make a distinction between the *context and content of listening.* In the new view of the world, *reality is context-dependent.* The results we get are always related to the context in which we are looking or operating from. Thus, a very important aspect of inquiring into listening is to be able to distinguish between the context and content of listening. Although we know these terms, *context* meaning the framework or space of something else to fit into, and *content* as the stuff that fits in, we don't ordinarily make a distinction between them in our communication.

Generally we find ourselves in content-oriented conversations. Something occurs and a problem or impasse arises, and we try to fix it by convincing someone to our point of view, or giving in to theirs, or doing what we call compromise. These are the parameters that have been conditioned by an Either/Or reality. Something is either good or bad, right or wrong, my way or your way, Democrat or Republican, English or Irish, Conservative or Liberal, developed world or developing world, and so on and so on ... and on and on ...

Why the resolution generally turns out to be one of the two options or a fragmentation of the two called "compromise" is that people don't have present in their awareness a distinction for *context*—the ability to step outside or beyond both points of view to envision a larger perspective. When we listen, we generally listen to *content*, the words the person is saying.

Have you ever been in an "I said this/No you said that" conversation where you and the other person are attempting to prove what each other actually said five minutes ago? This is listening to content. *When you listen beyond the words to the context* you might realize that what you both want in that moment is simply to experience your connection. In many instances the content becomes irrelevant.

When we think Holistically we listen from the whole and for the whole. We hear the content and at the same time we can listen for the context of what is being said. Both are happening simultaneously. Context allows for solutions that cannot come from the limits set by dealing only with the specific content of a conversation. For example, in politics when we listen *from content* we are likely to reach conclusions based on polarities, party lines or ideologies. But if we listen *from context* we might more appropriately look from the whole of what would work best for all people and all parties concerned.

To listen from context is to consider the Intent in the conversation: What is my Intent? What is his/her Intent? What is our Intent in this conversation? When volumes get louder and tensions rise as the conversation spirals downward into an abyss leading nowhere, you can pause. As soon as you ask yourself what your Intent is in the conversation you instantly experience a qualitative shift leaping yourselves out of the prove-it-to-me or I said/you said Either/Or endless loops.

When you listen for the context of what is being said you go deeper into the communication. The relatedness between people becomes profound. What will give you access to such profound communication? Being In One Conversation.

～～

A mechanistic world view has conditioned us to relate to things in parts, including our conversations, including speaking and listening. A conversation looks as though first one person is speaking and the other person is listening, and then the speaking and listening roles are reversed when the second speaker begins to talk. The communication is broken down into those parts. What it looks like is that I have a conversation I want to get across to you and you have a conversation you want to get across to me.

Suppose you are looking from a new world view perspective. In a Holographic & Holistic world there are no separations even though in the limited world of the five senses it appears there are. In the view from the whole everything is interconnected. Consider that there can only be one conversation going on at any one time between people. Two or more people are really sharing in one conversation, each one an integral contributor to the one conversation. If you knew the conversation as belonging to all, then even what the other person is saying belongs to you. Therefore, when the other person is speaking your awareness would be wholly with what the other person is saying. Think about how this might shape your relationships with people if you considered that the conversation belonged equally to all, regardless of who is speaking.

However, what typically happens when another person is speaking? We know you have the best of intentions and still, think of what typically happens. You are judging and evaluating what is being said based in what you think you already know or have concluded. You are preparing your retort, rebuttal, agreement, or disagreement. You are thinking about something else entirely; you are distracted. You are assessing the person speaking—their mannerisms, personality traits, physical peculiarities, etc. You are concerned about how you are going to get the result you want from this conversation and you are busy in your own mind constructing some plan to get that result. There is nothing bad or wrong about any of this. It is simply the way a mechanistic, analytical world view has trained our thinking process.

Said another way, *you are in your own conversation.* You are listening to your own inner dialogue. You are not really listening with the other speaker at all. You may have physically heard the words; you can even repeat them back. Parroting or mirroring back words is a mechanical action and we can do that easily. Consider that for communication to be present, there can be only One Conversation. Examine this in your own experience. As soon as you go into any kind of judgment, whether silent or spoken, the chasm of separation happens and communication comes to a halt—even though you may still be talking!

When this happens the conversation becomes fragmented. Its purity and its focus are scattered. The Intent may be thwarted. You may not get the result or experience the communication was designed to make possible.

Your friend is speaking with you about her innermost feelings of what she wants to do now in her life. Perhaps it is your daughter speaking with you, or your mother. She tells you what would give her the most satisfaction would be to teach children. For whatever reason you have for thinking this is a wrong decision your inner dialogue starts chattering away: *forget it; that's not for you.* Your friend (daughter/mother) continues on speaking from her heart and soul. Not only are you not *with* her, you don't actually hear another word she says. Nothing is registering other than your own opinions. The disconnect can result in a cold silence or it can lead to agitation because the speaker does not experience being heard. Think about when a young child approaches a parent who is otherwise occupied. The parent ignores the child thinking perhaps erroneously that this is "training" the child. The child gets louder, more intrusive, upset, and starts crying when all that was needed was to give the child a moment of Being In One Conversation. Listening with your whole being.

To truly own the conversation and to allow it to unfold and be a created dynamic between all parties means rather than scattering your attention by thought fragments you are being pulled by, you stay focused Being In One Conversation. You remain present with the conversation as it flows forth. You stay with the person who is speaking and with what that person is saying until the communication is naturally ready to move to the next person.

In show business there is an expression, "You're stepping on my lines." It means the audience did not have a chance to digest what was just said before the next actor came along on top of the last actor's speech with another dialogue. Conversations are living essences. Allow what is being said the space to breathe. Let the conversational wave penetrate.

When you are Being In One Conversation you are in a creative, evolving dialogue. Like most people you may be accustomed to sharing your opinions, feelings, and your responses to life or to a particular conversation. Most of us are not as practiced in participating in a conversation as a creative dialogue. In a creative dialogue rather than simply sharing what you think or feel based on your past experiences with little regard for what's happening in the current conversation, instead you are totally aware in *this* moment. You engage the faculty of Allowing to tap into the intelligence of the nonlocal mind field where unforeseen possibilities pop in. The conversation is fresh and alive and exciting.

Being In One Conversation includes diverse voices and ideas yet it is the experience of a co-creative force larger than all or any one of us. It is not adding *your* conversation to the conversation. It is *merging* in the one conversation. If you know that there is only one conversation, then *whoever is speaking, whatever they are saying, belongs to you.*

What is Being In One Conversation? When both people concentrate only on the conversation being spoken by one person. When each person puts aside his own perspective, views, judgments, and agenda to just listen to the speaking of the other as if it were he himself speaking, you are Being In One Conversation. The energy is focused. There is coherence. The listener can truly hear because his listening is not being scattered by his own thoughts. The speaker can really hear herself because she is not fighting the intrusion of a conversation other than the one she wants to have. In this way the One Conversation is fully energized by both people and the purity of purpose is preserved. Knowing what's next is obvious when this kind of listening is present. When you focus your awareness this way who speaks next and what needs to be said flows. Each one naturally builds on the conversation.

Life is not static; it is Energy In Flux. A conversation is alive, a living pulsating essence with a flow that gets directed by your Intent. A conversation has the power to unfold, to create, to evolve solutions and ideas and proposed actions that no one can see at the start of the dialogue. This is why we say communication is our access to an inexhaustible fountain of resources. For this you need focus and Intent. *You give your whole being over to what is being said.*

Every one of us, every person young and old desires to be acknowledged. We yearn to be heard. We want the experience that our presence counts. We want our contribution to be recognized even if the contribution is a comment or a look or a spirit of being. You want to make a difference for others? With presence of mind and awareness of these human yearnings, listen with your whole being. Practice Being In One Conversation. You'll make music together. The results will be melodious.

⬥ QuantumThink Recreation ⬥
Live the Wisdom of Being In One Conversation

ONE»Practice Being In One Conversation with at least three different people before reading the next chapter. When the other person is speaking just be with what is being said. Remember, you are co-participating in this dialogue which is really One whole evolving Conversation that belongs to both of you (or all of you). If your own thoughts try to sneak into the conversation, just notice that and let them slip away as you re-focus yourself on what is being said by the other person. You will know when it is your time to speak, and you will naturally build on that conversation. You experience it as a co-creation.

TWO»*Listen with your whole being* to the complete Beethoven's 9th Symphony. Listen to the entire 9th Symphony, uninterrupted, with nothing else going on. No TV, driving, or puttering around the house. Listen with your whole being. Give yourself **completely** over to the music. Just be with the music. Go where it takes you. Enjoy the ride.

QuantumThink-Wave
What's Taboo to You?

Wait …
Don't read this if you think Numerology is taboo, if you have fear of it,
or if you feel it is a subject you shouldn't address for any reason.

You're still reading. That's good. It means you are not at the effect of limited conditioning that would prevent you from hearing about an idea even if it doesn't fit into *your* reality schema. Feel free to read on because the point of this is not to convince you about anything having to do with numerology. This is an opportune moment for you to contemplate just how free you are to be open to hearing perspectives that don't seem to jive with yours. There are plenty of them out there.

To truly think in a new way requires going beyond restrictive habits of beliefs that might actually be in the way of your own mastery. In the very least, holding taboos in place can prevent you from opening yourself to what might be valuable from a conscious examination of *any* topic. Genius sparks from exploring uncharted territory.

Since we mentioned numerology we can use it to illustrate our willingness to explore what we typically don't know anything about really, yet avoid based on beliefs handed down from someone else's cultural prejudices. Numerology is fun to use because it can sting your "rational knowing" a bit. Numerology is called an occult science, the word "occult" meaning "hidden" or "concealed from view." In our culture, it has long been taboo to speak openly about anything even remotely related to studies of the occult or of the many other aspects of reality which are kept "hidden." We bring this up now to keep probing our limits, to see how open we really are. Where do *you* draw the line before you turn off your listening to an unfamiliar topic, especially a subject that is beyond what your "rationality" deems worthy of serious attention?

We are approaching Chapter 7. In the study of numerology, the number "7" is regarded as "the number of mystery relating to the spiritual and the hidden side of things." As we mention numerology, observe whether your mind has already started to make judgments: *Why is she talking about this? What has numerology got to do with the distinctions of a new world view? Numerology—she's going too far now.* Just notice if you are ready to put down the book. Yet if we speak about numerology in the context of let's say, mythology, you might be more willing to listen and look at it in a brighter light. Context is everything.

164 DO YOU QUANTUMTHINK?

Symbolically the number 7 is also said to signify the "Oneness" of the individual and the All, represented graphically in the two distinct lines which though they appear as separate line segments are actually one whole, forming the 7. Gets interesting, doesn't it.

In the book of numerology from which this information is gleaned the foreword makes a point of naming all of the famous people who have engaged in numerology[31] including the great American author and humorist, Mark Twain, members of British royalty, and well known opera divas, as if their association with numerology gave it the necessary credentials to warrant reading on. Don't we see this all the time in our world? The lesser accepted subjects or unfamiliar areas of knowledge having to be justified and given credentials through their association with celebrities, scholars, or other famous or respected individuals. This practice has even become a cornerstone of advertising strategy. What can be so intimidating about an idea that we would have to go to such great lengths to justify our interest in hearing about it?

There have been countless acts of violence and cruelty inflicted by the "high authorities" of the time upon those people who dared to speak a new idea or a new discovery. In both historical and modern times we're all too aware that people who are so stuck and fixed and identified with their beliefs will go to extremes to disparage, discredit, and aggressively attack ideas and people they don't like or agree with, even when those ideas sustain unquestionable scientific validation. It is a good idea to be mindful of beliefs we are attached to. We're not always "right," you know. Sixteenth century Italian philosopher and astronomer Giordano Bruno was burned at the stake for upholding Copernicus' "heretical" idea that the Sun is the center of our solar system. Think about it: it was *just an idea*. And it turned out to be true.

~~~~~~~~~~~~~~~~

In the ordinary course of daily living and working we are always dealing with perspectives that differ from our own. The grand paradox of being human is we are universally the same and individually unique. To QuantumThink is to look from the whole. How can we ever see clearly if we cannot be with divergent points of view and ideas? If you cannot let another's perspective into your world even for a moment of consideration how can you begin to approach any kind of mastery?

Consider that you can relax all taboos and just remain open and observant while you simultaneously engage in the conscious practice of noticing when and what you resist. In this way you place yourself in a highly aware state, the Perspective Of All Perspectives.

7 PERSPECTIVE OF ALL PERSPECTIVES
It takes all kinds

There are many ways we contribute to one another. One of the most powerful things we contribute is our own state. Regardless of what else we give or do for one another, every action is infused with our own state. We emanate our inner state across the table and across the world. Do you notice what state you are in when you're conversing with the people in your life? Are you truly able to just listen, perhaps to find value in what others are saying even when you don't agree with them? One of the most important gifts we contribute is our unique perspective. Yet, what happens to your state when someone's perspective does not mesh with yours?

People want to know how to achieve harmony when differences seem to be irreconcilable and diametrically opposed. "Tolerance" is proposed as a resolution to such matters. Though "tolerance" implies a benefic judgment, it is still a judgment that keeps separation in place. There is a powerful state that transcends tolerance, the Perspective of All Perspectives. When you live from Holistic & Holographic principles it isn't just being *respectful* of different beliefs, it is realizing that every perspective belongs to the whole system, playing an integral role, necessary for completeness. The Perspective of All Perspectives is not about having more information. As you break free of automatic thoughts that limit and rigid positions you've been clinging to, you are nearer the *state* of awareness that is the sublime source of All That Is, Infinite Intelligence.

We have discussed that in the world emerging around us things are moving too quickly and information is accumulating so voraciously and changing so rapidly that we can no longer rely strictly on information to "know" what to do or to make decisions from. The new world requires a new kind of knowing. We distinguish this new way of knowing as *mastery*. Mastery is a state of alertness and clarity in the moment. Mastery is a state of awareness that gives one freedom to move spontaneously, perhaps taking the past into consideration yet able to respond to what is needed and wanted *now*, in *this* particular moment, in *this* context, and moving into the future.

There are no techniques for mastery. It doesn't fit into a formula. It is not a function of a static body of knowledge. Mastery is a function of active awareness, conscious awareness in the moment. This state of being ready for masterful action, of having the confidence and conviction of knowing the appropriate thing to do in the moment it needs to be done, and doing it spontaneously without hesitation requires the state of *being present*. We could also call this "presence," presence of mind, presence of being.

We are attracted to people with a strong presence. We even remark that he or she has a "presence" about them. Presence is powerful, it is charismatic, it is magnetic. It is commanding. When powerful leadership is being expressed we sense this magnetic presence.

If you are not formally in a leadership position you may not think of yourself as expressing leadership. Consider that this is an outdated view of leadership. In today's world, each one of us is being called upon to express our own unique leadership. No matter who you are or what you do, whether you are a prime minister or CEO or whether you are a high school student or a homemaker, each one expresses leadership through their unique perspective.

Leadership expressed with such presence contains a quality of *attraction*. It draws to itself resources, favorable circumstances, and peoples' alignment and commitment. What we are speaking about here is not just a trait of someone's personality; we are speaking about a person's state, a way of being, a state that can be generated.

How does one generate such presence? What distinguishes presence? We suggest it is simply the ability to be in a state of present-moment awareness with whatever is occurring, with whatever is showing itself—ideas, people and their attitudes, changing circumstances and unexpected situations, and to be able to *be* with any of it while maintaining a state of equanimity. To maintain a state of equanimity means to be in a state of steady calmness; the state of being unperturbed. In this state of equanimity we are not pulled into the circumstances though we are aware of them. We maintain our clarity. We maintain a freedom to respond appropriately without getting swept up into the drama of the situation. We could call this quality being able to maintain the Perspective of All Perspectives.

~~~

When you go to a movie, you are watching the movie and you are experiencing the emotions the characters and the writer and the director are taking you through and you are getting involved, but you know it's a movie so you don't get swept away by it. You can look at it and see it for what it is while maintaining some distance from it. Certain spiritual teachers have called this "True Perception" because you are just seeing what is presenting itself without identifying with it *as* yourself. When you are not "identified" with a perspective, you're not automatically reacting to it. You are clear.

This is what it is like to maintain the Perspective of All Perspectives. It is the ability to notice all the different perspectives of the people in our worlds and to be able to view them and include them by looking from a larger all-encompassing view which can hold them all, even when a perspective seems to be dissonant or even counter-intentional to our own perspective.

Imagine that you could be open to any possible occurrence, any person or idea, any event or situation, as integral to the process that will bring about your intended result. Every view has value. This does not mean we lack discernment or that we are foolhardy or unrealistic. It means when we look from the whole, we can examine all of it, we can allow for all of it. We don't have to resist it. You never know … Sometimes the very thing you may resist or want to overlook could be the catalyst for an innovative solution or possibility. When you resist or automatically reject or fight against something you can miss an opportunity.

Aside from being able to maintain the state of equanimity that this perspective would give you, why would we want to maintain the Perspective of All Perspectives? It opens us to solutions and surprises beyond what is in our immediate view bubbling up from the realm of Infinite Possibility.

As we have discussed the new world view is the perspective of the whole. It includes what we see and what we don't see. It includes the invisible aspect and also the nonmaterial aspect of a situation, the mind connections.

In physics the principal of nonlocality deals with this aspect of what we don't see, what is "at a distance" from us physically. The principal of nonlocality means we can effect something at a distance without there seeming to be a direct link or apparent connection. You are thinking about someone you haven't heard from in a while and you turn on your computer and there is an email from him. Psychiatrist Carl Jung called these occurrences "synchronicity" wherever there was a meaningful relationship between two or more seemingly unrelated events. In everyday terms we have called these "coincidences." We think we just got lucky when something showed up that was good but unexpected. Yet these effects are real and valid.

As a scientific principle nonlocality is something we can consciously access. We have the power to bring about a result without our having to be the "local cause" of it, without having to see a direct linear linkage between one thing and another. One of the greatest thinkers of our time, Ervin Laszlo, tells us the remarkable feature of this universe is that everything that happens in it affects and "informs" everything else.

The intelligence in every cubic centimeter of this universe is vast beyond our mind's ability to conceive, brilliant beyond our imagination, and present beyond our immediate view. Yet this all-pervasive intelligence is never beyond our reach. This is nonlocality.

How certain events get related this way is not something that we can always immediately recognize. Unless we are looking from the whole, seeing life from the largest perspective that we are calling the Perspective of All Perspectives, we can very possibly miss something that may be related to a result we are after but don't immediately see the relationship of. This is why we suggest that to achieve a state of mastery requires developing the Perspective of All Perspectives. This is the ability to be open to the idea that *anything* that shows up is valuable even when we disagree with it, because it's likely to be a contributing factor in the result we want to produce, particularly when the result we are after is *unprecedented*.

Suppose you are in charge of creating a new marketing campaign for your company's innovative product. You and your team come up with what you deem to be the perfect slogan. Everyone is jazzed. The next day you are reading the industry news and find out your competitor has already come out with the nearly identical slogan. Will you and your team's passion be dampened? Not when you maintain the Perspective of All Perspectives. Momentarily unnerved you speedily regain your equanimity. You call your team and decide to re-group at the nearby coffee shop. You're sitting there and you casually glance at the woman at the next table reading a book with the *exact* word in the title that jumps out at everyone as the key to a much spicier slogan for the product. Nonlocality in action.

From the old world view of separation we tend to see an unexpected event as an interruption or an obstacle along our path. From a new world view of wholeness we look deeper to see the wisdom in this seeming obstacle showing up, knowing it is part of the whole picture and realizing there is value to be gleaned from it. When you live in the Perspective of All Perspectives you see how the seeming obstacle might give you important missing information, more time to think, or a novel approach and actually leads to something even better that wouldn't have presented itself were it not for the "interruption."

We start the process of creating a result by generating an Intent, and we Allow for the circumstances to attract to us the exact circumstances that will bring about the manifestation of our goal. Solutions and possibilities can be beyond what is currently in our sight. Most of the time they are! It is a universe of uncertainty and unpredictability; this is its very *essence*. Mastery means we are able to *be* with this uncertainty. Mastery means we can actually "read" the uncertainty and use it. We can do this when we can maintain our equanimity.

When you are established in the Perspective of All Perspectives, even when the circumstances do not match what you already think you know; even when they're not consistent with what has worked for you in the past, *you remain open*, realizing other possibilities may show themselves here.

⌒⌒

Now this *sounds* easy enough. We can grasp this as a conceptual knowing. However, to embody this, to know this as *your way of being,* is quite different than knowing this as information. Until we become masterful Self-Realized beings it is highly unlikely that we are all going to go about everyday in this ideal peaceful state of equanimity where we have perfect discernment, discrimination, and know exactly what to do. What stands in the way of our equanimity and clarity? Attachment. Clarity and equanimity are obstructed by those ideas and thoughts we develop an "attachment" to, either because we have an aversion to something, we don't like it and we want to avoid it, or because we *have to* have something a certain way ... *our* way. Being attached to a particular point of view can keep us stuck or limited. Being attached pulls you to have to argue for what you already think you know, for what you are attached to. It is as if you are identified with that viewpoint as "you." Being attached usurps being open to what can show up.

Take a moment now and bring to mind someone whose point of view you vehemently disagree with or oppose. Now allow yourself to just *be with that point of view until all the emotional charge has subsided*. Use your imagination and creativity and conjure up a valuable benefit and *raison d'être* for that

Perspective. How can you have it synchronize with your view? When you maintain the Perspective of All Perspectives you see that everything has its place.

What allows you to be present and alert to new opportunities and solutions that may attract your way by virtue of your Intent? Having the Perspective of All Perspectives of course. What allows you to have the Perspective of All Perspectives? *Being non-attached.*

Non-attachment is not dispassionate or non-compassionate. It is equal vision, equanimity, staying centered beyond positions of right or wrong, good or bad, my way or your way. In fact, being non-attached which enables you to have the Perspective of All Perspectives invokes deep compassion—for others as well as compassion toward yourself. Can you imagine being non-attached to having to be liked, having to be accepted, having to be approved of, having to be respected? What freedom that would surely give!

The Perspective of All Perspectives frees you from being identified with any single viewpoint and places you in the space of choice. To master seeing from the Perspective of all Perspectives we need to master non-attachment.

ᴏ QUANTUMTHINK RECREATION ᴏ
Live the Wisdom of the Perspective of All Perspectives

ONE»Practice non-attachment. The way to do this is to notice what you are attached to!

What ideas, knowledge, experiences, ethics you have an attachment to? Here is how you can tell you are attached:

you feel anger or frustration

you make others wrong

you argue for your position

you have little or no control over your reaction

you cannot find your equanimity center

TWO»In the moment you become aware of your attachment, to a way of doing something, or to an idea or opinion you have about something, allow yourself to step back and look at it from a place of equanimity. Consider that whatever is present whether it is your point of view or another person's *is just one of an infinite number of possible perspectives.* See if you can include other perspectives in the sense of just allowing them to be even when you don't agree with them. Notice how that shifts your experience. Notice how that shifts the outcome and the relationship between you and others.

QuantumThink-Wave
Change? Not A Problem

Sometimes our thoughts crystallize and then they fossilize. The thought becomes outmoded and is no longer useful. We grab onto concepts that are not the absolute truth; they are just repeated often. One of those concepts is about *change*. You hear people saying all the time *it's difficult to change*. Psychologists and other well-meaning professionals convince us by declaring: *People are resistant to change. People are afraid of change.* Alas and alack, a cultural Least-action Pathway is born.

People don't like to change. Is this "the truth"? From a new world view there is nothing absolute about an idea. If you truly want to create your life the way you desire, why clutch an idea that doesn't serve you? Change is the way of the universe. This is a universe of continuous motion, of energy in flux, of evolutionary and biological and chemical and electrical and spiritual processes. Nothing stands still. In fact we only know Time itself because of change. So what is the good of a concept lived as "the truth" that would have you believe you are "resistant to change"? When change is no longer an "issue" for you the most wonderful experience happens. You flow. You even glide.

Change itself changes. In another context we *yearn* for "change." As soon as we shift the context our experience transforms. Yes, we desire something different, something new, something that has never, ever been before. Consider that if something has never existed "change" does not bring it about. You can only change what already exists. A conundrum easily mastered as you distinguish Transformation As Distinct From Change.

8 TRANSFORMATION AS DISTINCT FROM CHANGE
Context is everything

In the science of mind it is said, *what you focus on expands.* Whether you think of this as universal law or not, at least it makes logical sense. You energize whatever you hold in your attention. You keep it alive and magnified. You want something new. But all you think about is the "old" thing you want to change. You want a blissful relationship. But all you focus on are the traits about your partner that irritate you. Perhaps you've heard the expression: *The more things change the more they stay the same.* In effect you keep in place the very thing you no longer desire. In an Observer-created Reality attention alone keeps something in existence. To create what we want in life we need to distinguish Transformation As Distinct From Change.

You could say that QuantumThinking is in the realm of Transformation As Distinct From Change. What does this mean? When we distinguish something, for example, when we distinguish a classical world view from a new world view, we are not attempting to *change* what is already present, i.e., the classical world view. We are simply *distinguishing* what is already present. The classical world view isn't going away. It is part of the totality of everything. It is included; it is part of the whole that we call our reality or our world.

Distinguishing it is like outlining it, highlighting it so you can bring it into focus and see it for what it is. When you distinguish what's present, that is, what is already there, you have a choice to bring in something new. It is like having a blank white page. Nothing is on the page. Then you draw a circle on the page and what you have done is you have distinguished the circle from the rest of the space on the page. You haven't changed the blank page itself but in creating a distinction, in this case, a circle, you have transformed the page. In distinguishing a circle you have actually brought something new into existence, something that wasn't there before. The circle existed in the realm of Infinite Possibility. It existed in the possible world, in the enfolded or hidden aspect of reality, and in distinguishing it you brought it into the actual world of ordinary existence. What you distinguished now becomes a whole new world of possibility. Now you've got a circle and you could ask yourself, *what can this circle be used for?* And it takes you off in a direction where you can start creating all kinds of new images and ideas just from that one distinction of a circle.

~~~

"Transformation" means to go beyond the current form. You aren't changing the current form. You are transcending the current form. Transformation brings about a new state of existence of something. There is a special quality to Transformation and that is: when a Transformation takes place it has the power to transform the past, the present, and the future in that instant.

Let's say you had a tendency or a trait you didn't like about yourself. Let's say that you consider yourself very angry. You think of yourself as an angry person. If you live in a reality system that is fixed, then that would be it. Who you are is an angry person. There wouldn't be much you could do about it except try to change your anger. So when your anger would come up, you would try to *not* be angry, or *tone down* your anger, or try to *figure out why* you are angry. Or in some way, you would be trying to shift or change or manipulate somehow this way that you are called "angry."

That would be dealing with the anger with old world view "deterministic" thinking. Your thinking would be shaped by the fact that you see yourself, first of all, as having a fixed characteristic trait called "angry person" and secondly, your attempt to change the way you are would be shaped by thinking that works mechanically, that is, you try to manipulate the parts of yourself around somehow so things work better.

As we've seen, the ironic twist in trying to change something is that the very thing you are trying to change *must be present* in order to change it. You can't change an angry person unless "angry person" is there to change. And then you have to work on it. You would have to work hard on it usually and it might take a lot of time. We are using the example of an angry person but this mechanism can be seen in any area of life where you are attempting to change something that you are sure "this is the way it is." Think of all the times you try to change something about the other people in your life. What about when you get frustrated because there is a situation at work that you want to change and no matter what you do, no matter how hard you try, it still seems to persist. If a desired result continues to elude you and "change" isn't really working, then what else is possible?

We can effect a Transformation. We have spoken about the new world view that *reality is context-dependent*. In the reality we just described we're operating from the context that being angry is a fixed attribute of a person. You could say that being able to effect a Transformation is the ability to generate a new context. Creating a new context alters the reality of it.

In the example of an angry person suppose you create the context that being angry all the time is just a habit that you somehow picked up. It doesn't really matter where or how you picked up the habit. It has just become a habit that up until now you have "known" in a state of unawareness. What is a habit? A habit is a pattern of action, thinking, or relating that is both automatic and has a quality of a lack of awareness about it. In terms of an automatic response, we mean that it is rather like a stimulus-response, a cause and effect reaction to something that comes up.

A habit can also be *consciously* generated, with awareness. We could distinguish this as *consistency in practice*—when it is conscious, desirable, and deliberately put into place. Consistent practice has Intent in it. It has awareness and it has Intent. But in this case we are speaking about something more like one of your Least-action Pathways, the automatic way you react to something without thinking and lacking conscious awareness that this is what you are doing.

When you can see your anger as a habit rather than as a fixed attribute of who you are, when you bring it into your awareness in this context, you realize that like any habit you have the power and the wherewithal to interrupt the habit. Furthermore, *you can displace the habit* of being angry with a desired habit. *You could consciously generate a consistent practice* of for example, appreciation and joy of whatever is happening, moment by moment. Even when it seems like what is happening isn't something you really wanted, you can still look for what you might learn from it and continue your practice of appreciation. You could consciously develop a practice of being joyful and this displaces your automatic habit of anger.

What happens the next time your angry habit shows itself? You notice, *Oh, there's that angry habit again.* Once you notice it, in that instant, in that very moment, you transform the anger. In the moment of awareness you step outside of your anger. You have gone beyond the form of it. Remember, Transformation means moving beyond the current form. Instead of identifying with the anger, you are now watching it. When you can watch it, you are no longer in it *as* you. You are seeing it as just a moving wave so to speak.

There is another aspect of this which is really important. In the moment that you begin to see your anger as just a habit that you have the power to displace with another consciously created practice—in that instant you also transform the entire past with regard to whatever *meaning* you have ever given to holding yourself as "an angry person."

A Transformation is a shift in your state. When a Transformation takes place it transforms the past, the present, and the future. This is consistent with the fact that in the quantum world things can move backward and forward through time. Our experience of life is no longer restricted by linear time. When you effect a Transformation in yourself you might even forget your former state, the "old" way you used to be with regard to any situation. You'll think you have *always* been this way. You'll imagine you have always been calm and centered and free of identifying with your anger. That is quite all right. Life takes place in the present moment. This is your life right now. Why not think of yourself as calm?

Can you see that in many ways, if you have been practicing the Recreations for each of the QuantumThink distinctions, this is what you have been doing? Every time you notice an automatic way you are thinking or being or reacting, in that instant you effect a Transformation. It isn't that one context or the other is more true or less true. The important question is: which context energizes what you want? Remember, in a quantum world nothing is fixed or absolute. *You* get to choose.

From our old world view conditioning we attempt to change what already exists. Thinking from a new world view you realize that what you focus on expands. Thus, rather than focusing upon what we don't want, instead we create what we do want. What you hold in consciousness is what you make real.

Every time you bring yourself to the state where you become aware of yourself as the Observer in an Observer-created Reality, you have distinguished yourself from any fixed set of attributes or circumstances that you have been identifying with. In the moment you just *notice* your anger, you have transformed it. You have not changed your anger. This is what we mean by Transformation As Distinct From Change. Without changing anything, simply by being able to generate new contexts, you literally transform your world. You cause a major shift in your actions *and* your outcomes which follow from your actions. One tiny step of awareness is enough. This is a remarkable gift we've been bestowed by virtue of our birthright. A leap in conscious awareness is all you need to transform your experience and alter your direction.

To give us a powerful relationship with our ability to effect transformation, we ask the question: *what effects a transformation?* If transformation is a function of being able to generate new contexts, then it follows you would have to first be able to witness the context that's already present. Just seeing what is already there. What do we mean by "what is already there" or what is "present"? What is the current context?

As you go about your day you can notice: *What am I listening to? Am I listening to what that person is saying or to what I am saying to myself? Am I judging? Did I get distracted or swept away by some mind-association? Am I operating in a conditioned automatic habit that I have been holding as "the truth"?*

Consider that this is true accountability. Accounting for what is present. When you are accountable for what's present, in that moment you have freedom to choose. If by chance a Least-action Pathway pops up and you find yourself judging your self or others, you can choose to Listen From Not-knowing. When you find yourself attached to getting your own way, you can choose to look from the Perspective of All Perspectives. When you notice a co-worker or a neighbor in an automatic habit of complaining or brooding, you can create the context they're just caught in a Least-action Pathway and bring light to that person in the form of your compassion. Each one is a context you are generating through practicing The Art of Distinguishing.

Remember, a statement of context is a statement *you* are bringing into existence. It is a statement of Intent and it is outside the domain of "true or false." There is nothing to either prove or disprove about it. It is a context you are *choosing* to live out of, a framework you are choosing to operate from, a context that allows for the unforeseen to show itself. This is Transformation As Distinct From Change.

Being In The Right Question

Another way of viewing context is to examine *Being In The Right Question*. Whatever we are doing in life is always in answer to a silent question in the background of our actions. The question we find ourselves in will lead us in certain ways, in certain directions, and to certain actions consistent with the question. If you ask yourself

"Does she really love me?" you are going to be shaped by the underlying context of your insecurities about your beloved. If you ask yourself "What are all the ways she demonstrates her love for me?" you can see that the underlying context is "she loves me" and will guide you to appreciate all the ways a person demonstrates her love for you.

Generating a new question as a new context that our actions spring forth from gives us entirely new results. This is another aspect of an Observer-created Reality. Just as a scientist is likely to discover what he or she is looking for (i.e., the scientist's actions and conclusions will be led by the nature of the question he/she is investigating) our actions will be shaped by the question we are in.

To determine whether you are going to get to the result you desire, you can ask yourself: *What question am I in?* When we discussed Least-action Pathways, we observed that one of the Least-action Pathways human beings have is responding in some way to the question, *What's wrong?* We go to a movie or a play or a restaurant. We come out and we're immediately in a conversation about what's wrong with it, what didn't work about it, what we didn't like about it, how the chef should have prepared the fish so we would like it better.

And we noticed how that kind of conversation also gets generated when someone comes up with a novel idea. Offshoots of the *What's wrong?* question crop up as we quickly expound upon why this idea can't or won't work or why we shouldn't attempt it. There is nothing "wrong" with any of this. We don't have to attempt to change our cultural Least-action Pathways. We could see them, for example, from the context of a comedy writer and simply get a good laugh at ourselves. Transformation As Distinct From Change turns out to be very useful.

Another question in the background of our actions is the question, *What should we do?* We have a problem or project proposed to us and we are instantly in the question, *What should we do?* There's nothing wrong with that question. We are simply examining what automatic actions we tend to take when we're driven by that question. *What should we do?* leads us to have to come up with an answer—fast. It leads us to select one of the obvious options we have in front of us or that our mind or imagination can quickly discern. It might even lead to making decisions by a majority vote, rather than by a consensus where everyone is fully aligned. It may lead us to compromise or settle rather than exploring what else is possible.

A New Question—A Different Context
Results Beyond the Predictable

How can we have this work for everyone?

Suppose we could create a new question to operate from, one that displaces both "*What's wrong?*" which leads to complaining or fixing things and "*What should we do?*" which drives you to find a quick answer. Suppose you posed as a contextual question: *How can I have this work?* And you could further ask this from the point of view of having it work *for everyone* including you and everyone else involved. How might that question lead you? Posing the question, *How can we have this work for everyone?* rather than *What's wrong here?* could alter your whole life.

There are an infinite number of Right Questions to be in. For the purpose of the Recreation we are posing this question because everyone can relate to it. *How can we have this work for everyone?* This question has the power to transform your experience and the experience of everyone around you. Instead of trying to get other people to change or the circumstances to change, you shift the context with this question. This is Transformation As Distinct From Change. This question has the power to alter the world.

☜ QuantumThink Recreation ☞
Live the Wisdom of Transformation As Distinct From Change

ONE» Being In The Right Question. Whatever comes up in your life in the next 24 hours, practice looking at it by being in the question, *"How can we have this work for everyone?"* and watch where it leads you. You don't have to speak the question aloud though sometimes it may be appropriate and useful to actually say it. You can simply hold the question as your Intent.

TWO»Notice what questions you are in as you go about the affairs of your day. If you find the question you are in is leading you in an unfruitful direction, then create the "right" question. The Right Question is any question that will produce what is most appropriate and workable in the situation.

THREE»For at least one day practice staying focused on what you want rather than putting your attention on changing what you don't want. What you want will naturally displace what you don't want. Remember, what you focus on expands.

QUANTUMTHINK-WAVE
Q&A: What Is a State Change?

Q: *You say we can change our state in any moment and have a totally different experience instantly, and that this is the beauty of conscious creation. Yet, this allegedly simple shift of state is sometimes more difficult than it seems it should be. The questions arise for me, why is it difficult? And how do I do it?*

A: Though in a very real sense the *why* and *how* questions don't matter, I will offer something in the attempt to appease the mind's infatuation with them.

Why is it difficult? Because of our conditioned automatic habits, the Least-action Pathways show up. Okay that's the "why." Now for the "how."

How do you do it—how do you make the shift in state?

Conscious awareness of the habit *as* a habit, and consciously choosing another Intent.

Q: *And that's it? That's all?*

A: Yes, that's it. It is literally a quantum leap in your own mind. You know the nature of a quantum leap is that there is no traceable pathway from one state to another.

Q: *I think I need an example here. Will you give me one?*

A: Sure. Think about when you were young (and maybe even still now) and your mother or your father wants you to do something. It could be anything. Maybe they want you to clean your room, or they want you to come out of your room and be gracious to their friends who are visiting. Maybe they just want you to give them a big hug and tell them you love them. You know what they want. Yet you just can't bring yourself to do it. What is your state? Resistance. And what's more, you know you're resisting. You can see it. You know what they want and still you resist. It is loud in your head, in your internal dialogue—yet you cannot seem to bring yourself to translate this very simple, oh, so simple, small, spoken or unspoken request of theirs into action. Something in you is refusing. You know if you gave them that hug and told them you love them, that it would be so easy, that it wouldn't cost you a thing. You know what a huge difference it would make for them and for your relationship with them.

So what's up? You're stuck in a Least-action Pathway. It's probably a cultural Least-action Pathway; it's not even personal. It may be resistance to authority or based on habitual judgments you have about your parents or their friends that you're sure you are "right" about. It could be a habit of "shyness." It actually doesn't make any difference whatsoever what the Least-action Pathway is specifically or "why" it's showing up. You'll never be able to determine "absolutely" what it is anyway.

Q: *What do you mean when you say I'll never be able to determine the cause of the behavior anyway?*

A: The "why" doesn't matter because all you can do is guess and you'll never really know for sure. It's an Observer-created Reality and nothing is absolute. The important point is to just see it for what it is: an automatic habit, and to know you have the power to shift it even when the old vortex is tugging at you.

Anyway, life takes place in the now moment. The question is always: what are you going to do about this "habit" now, in the moment it arises? What is your Intent in this situation?

Q: *Are you saying that changing my state is not really difficult?*

A: Precisely. It is like this example with your parents. You *know* you could have a state change and be generous and give them what they ask of you. The state change itself is not "difficult." It's a matter of choosing a new Intent. Naturally, you have to be awake and aware enough of your Least-action Pathway to see it and choose something else.

Let's say you feel yourself irritated or agitated or maybe even depressed. You know the one thing in life, perhaps the only thing you have total charge of and are in total command of is your own mind, your own state. Yet, like hugging your mother and telling her you love her (or whatever it is someone ever wants of you) you are just holding back. You just won't do it. Do you want to be so rigid with yourself? Are you so convinced that whatever thought you are having that is giving you your current state is so much "the truth" that you cannot shift it?

Q: *I guess that doesn't work out very well if you're committed to mastery.*

A: Right. Mastery implies freedom to choose with proper discernment. If you are automatically reacting, there really is no choice. It is a state of Unawareness.

Scientists tell us we live in a universe of uncertainty (no absolute "objective" reality), of infinite possibility (no fixed range of options), of energy in constant flux (we, as the Observers, are shifting reality all the time). This means you can create a different Intent; you can transform your state any time, any place.

Q: *So this is what you mean by a quantum leap in consciousness? It's going on all the time, so I might as well consciously choose it?*

A: Exactly. Just become aware of your state. The next time you find yourself agitated or anxious or angry, just notice: what is your state? In noticing, it will shift. It doesn't matter *why*. And it doesn't matter *how*.

Q: *I get this now. Thank you.*

A: Anytime. My pleasure.

9 4 ASPECTS OF KNOWING

Get this one—zzaaap! you're a master

When you create your Intent and your Intent doesn't appear to be manifesting, what do you do? Do you doubt the veracity of the dynamic of Intent? Do you question yourself and your ability to use your inborn power to create? Since the principle of Intent cannot not-work, how do we explain when it doesn't seem to bear fruit? For this we need to delve deeper into the relationship between creating and manifesting.

Modern scientists and ancient sages alike concur our universe is vibrational in nature. You and I and all objects are spinning complexes of atoms vibrating at various frequencies. How does this translate into everyday life? Resonance. We attract and manifest what we resonate. A great master said: *You can only manifest what you are conscious of being.* In an Observer-created Reality, the observer and that which is observed are one. As daunting as it seems to grasp this, each of us holds the world of our reality within our own being.

One could say in life we are either creating or reacting. We are either in a consciously self-aware act of creating or we are at some level in a less aware state of being in reaction to circumstances that arise. Both of these actions, creating and reacting, will manifest results, material and spiritual. It is apparent however that mastery can only be attained through the practice of *conscious* creating.

When you create consciously you are *one* with Divine Intelligence. There is no separation. You know this experientially with profound certitude. When you are simply in reaction to life it is as if you have a momentary lapse of memory. *You forget who you are.* You forget you are not separate from infinite creative intelligence. Your "knowing" is temporarily on the blink. Therefore, consider the closer you get to "knowing" your creation as an aspect of your own being, the higher your degree of mastery in manifesting results.

The purpose of QuantumThink is to *live* this in your experience: to know yourself as the creator of your reality by virtue of being an expression of the fundamental creative force.

~~~

Our ability to manifest our creations is intrinsically connected to our "knowing," that is, *in the way we are related to what we know*. Consider what you "know" as anything you hold in mind. Whether it's a person in your life, a goal you have, or a situation, there are various ways you can be related to what you "know"—that is, to how you hold it in consciousness. You can be related in Unawareness, Conceptual, Intuitive, or Participatory Knowing. Each of these 4 Aspects indicates your state, and therefore the quality of your connection to the situation, the person, or the goal. This is an unusual way of saying it; however, distinguishing which of the 4 Aspects of Knowing you are operating in is extremely powerful because it gives you instantaneous access to mastering your faculty of manifestation.

The "knowing" we explore as we QuantumThink are the characteristics of our emerging new world view and how they shape our thinking, actions, and results. The Intent of the 4 Aspects of Knowing is to transform your relationship to the new world view from a concept to your *experience* of it as the condition of your world.

Let's put this in the language of this distinction. Before you were aware of the distinctions between old world view and new world view thinking, one could say you were in a state of Unawareness with regard to them. When you become aware of the differences in old world view/new world view characteristics, you move from Unawareness to Conceptual or Intuitive Knowing. When you begin *living* the wisdom of QuantumThinking, you are in Participatory Knowing. At first this may appear abstract. Stay with it. You'll find the 4 Aspects of Knowing becomes ingeniously practical indeed.

Picture a real goal you have in your life now. Perhaps it is an investment deal, a business project, being accepted to your university of choice, winning a sports competition, inventing a new technology or creating a work of art. Your goal might be earning more money, achieving a particular body weight or fitness level, or attaining a higher octave of spiritual awareness. How are you related to this goal? Are you certain of its outcome or is it a distant dream? You might find it staggering to answer this question in this moment, however as we distinguish the 4 Aspects of Knowing not only will the answer be clear, you will be guided by it. As you peruse further keep the thought of your project or goal in mind. You'll discover a gauge to determine precisely the shift required if you are not yet manifesting the result you said you wanted. The shift is of course within you. Our outer reality is an out-picturing of our internal state. You can shift from a state of unawareness to awareness in an instant. In fact it can *only* be that fast.

The sage says: *You can only manifest what you are conscious of being.* Really contemplate this for a moment. Use your breath to take yourself deeper and relax into this contemplation. *You can only manifest what you are conscious of being.*

There is so much in this one statement. *You* can manifest, meaning you are the one manifesting or creating your reality. *Manifest,* implying that you and I have the power to manifest. *Only what you are conscious of being*—meaning the world exists within you, in your experience. That is why the sage, Kabir, says *Most people know the drop is in the ocean but most do not realize the ocean is also in the drop.* Your world exists in your own experience. Because of you the world exists. Because it only exists for you in your experience. So you see there is no separation between you and your experience of the world even though the way we use words, the structure of our language makes it seem separate.

This is another quantum paradox. Your experience of life is self-referral; it refers back to you in your mind, that is, in your own awareness or in whatever you are conscious of. In the statement, *You can only manifest what you are conscious of being,* this is essentially what this means. **The world exists in you and therefore, you can only manifest in your experience what you are conscious of.** What you are conscious of is part of you.

Wherever you are sitting allow the muscles in your body to relax. Again take several deep breaths to center yourself and focus your awareness. Listen inwardly with quiet alertness to the 4 Aspects of Knowing as we go through them one by one. Allow yourself to be with these thought forms without having to understand, evaluate or do anything with them other than read ("listen") and consider what is being said. Be in this conversation as if you have never been here before. In fact you have never been in this moment in time before. Be here "not-knowing" and Allow your connection to Infinite Intelligence to provide you with everything you need from this distinction.

~~~

The 1st Aspect of Knowing is Unawareness. This is the state in which we say we have no idea. In popular parlance, you are "clueless" and you are clueless that you are clueless. You have a total lack of distinction about something. You don't see it. You don't "know" it. Something exists, an idea exists but it does not exist *for you*. It is outside the domain of your awareness. In the state of Unawareness you are likely to be at the effect of your circumstances. You get pushed and pulled by whatever current you find yourself in. You could say in a state of Unawareness you *are* your circumstances. You are flotsam and jetsam on the sea of life.

This is the domain of stimulus response, an automatic, mechanical reaction to life.

A stimulus comes your way and you automatically react. An example of this would be when you find yourself in an upset, perhaps in an argument or hot debate with someone and you are out of control. You are really hooked by something and you cannot get back to your center to even see or realize that you are so gripped.

Another example of Unawareness is when you identify yourself with a thought you have or an emotion you feel. This is tantamount to thinking you are the contents of your mind. You have a thought such as "I'm not athletic," and you cannot make the distinction between *having* that thought and *being* that thought. This thought that is not "the truth" but just a thought you have begins to shape your life. You might let the thought "I'm not athletic" determine whether you'll play in the company softball game or that thought could keep you from an uplifting practice of aerobic exercise or yoga. This is why we say in a state of Unawareness you *are* your circumstances. The circumstance is the thought that came passing through your consciousness like a bird flying past your window. Instead of watching it fly by you latched onto it and let it take you away with it.

Another instance of Unawareness is when you are so involved in trying to avoid something that you become the very thing you want to avoid. Remember, *we manifest what we are conscious of being*. Hence the adage, "what you resist persists." By putting so much attention and energy on a trait that you absolutely under no circumstances want to be identified with, you hold it in your being without realizing it. For example, you judge someone else for being uncompassionate and in doing so, the lack of compassion resides in you. This is the state of Unawareness.

The 1st Aspect of Knowing is the state from which sages and saints have admonished us to awaken. It surely is like a walking sleep. In Unawareness there is no agency in it. You are just an effect. In Unawareness there is no distinguishing going on so you cannot divorce your small self from your higher Self which is awareness itself. It may *seem* like you are choosing, it might even feel as if you are choosing but without awareness there is only reaction. The good news is that as soon as you become aware that you have been in Unawareness, you instantly spring into one of the other states.

~~~

The 2nd Aspect of Knowing is Conceptual. This is where we have something as a "good idea." We may even be committed to this idea. But it only exists as a concept, a mental construct. In the 2nd Aspect of Knowing we say, "Oh, yes, I understand that." This is where we see something as information. It is data. We know something, some *thing*. Therefore, this thing we know as information is separate from us. Conceptual Knowing is characteristic of the classical world view, the domain of knowing in an Either/Or world.

What we know in the domain of concept is evidence-based, believe it or not, true or false. It is based on circumstances that seem to be out of your control, external to you. You may still relate to yourself as a victim of circumstances only now you can be intellectually skillful in explaining *why* you are justified in being a victim of outside forces. Still, you try to control the circumstances through exerting force. In the 2nd Aspect of Knowing you attempt to manage the facts. You want all the information in front of you. You feel you have to know it all. This is the domain of analysis, breaking down the whole into constituent parts. You move the parts around. It's a make-it-fit world.

Conceptual Knowing is useful for planning because it shows you the limits of your mind right now. First, you outline everything you can see within the limit of what you are able to bring into your awareness. Once you acknowledge that limit, you can Allow for what else comes into your view that is not there at the outset of your planning. Conceptual Knowing also enables you to focus and exercise discipline in your actions.

Conceptual Knowing may give you focus but it is limited by linear logic, chronological time, and previous experience (aka "evidence"). When you know the world in this 2nd Aspect of Knowing, things show up like hard work. It is task orientation and pushing or pulling to reach the goals. There is nothing magical about the Conceptual domain.

You have no intimate connection to what you know this way; it is outside of you and separate. You are alienated from it. It is not a part of who you are. The Conceptual Aspect of Knowing lacks heart and circumvents soul. It is the domain of "should," "ought-to," and "must."

An example of this is when you have a particular goal you want to achieve. You construct a plan to achieve it. You lay out the actions step by step in linear fashion. And then you have to work hard at keeping up with your plan. If any outside circumstances come up to interfere with your plan, you lose control. You become frazzled. You have to force and push to get it done. You are not sure you can do it. You have a loss of confidence in terms of assurance of getting it done. You are constrained by the goal, rather than being inspired by the live possibility of it. The process becomes mechanical.

~~~

The 3rd Aspect of Knowing is Intuitive. Intuitive Knowing moves something beyond a mental construct and more into your *experience*. This is self-evident knowing related to you like a conviction you have, something you sense is "right."

You feel connected to what you know as something alive and pulsating, not as merely a dry concept. If it is a goal you have, you have a clear sense it is going to happen even if you cannot see *how* it will happen. In Intuitive Knowing you are open to the unexpected. You have transcended a linear, cause and effect, Either/Or world of fixed options and predictable futures and moved into the realm of Infinite Possibility.

You are aware that there are principles operating outside of your immediate view. You have stopped trying to figure things out. You are Allowing what occurs to present itself to you. You are "tuned in." Synchronicity and serendipity are present. You have given up trying to control every move. You have begun to glimpse the idea of your own being as a source of results even when you don't see obvious connections. You're consciously tapping into what that might mean. Life is much easier and more enjoyable. You are noticing the "magic" and you are open to it coming your way.

In Intuitive Knowing even though you are more deeply connected to what you know, it is still separate from you in the sense that it is "something out there" you are trying to tune into. There is still some separation.

Your days are full of "wows" and quantum occurrences. Great things happen unexplainable by ordinary logic. You have confidence when you are in Intuitive Knowing, however there still isn't certainty.

~~~

The 4th Aspect of Knowing is Participatory. Participatory Knowing means exactly that: You are participating in the creation of reality. In Participatory Knowing what you know is part of you; it *is* you. You know it *as your own being*. There is no separation. It is your participation that actually creates the experience you have of your reality. You are the seed, the blossom, and the fruit of your results. This is the aspect of the Observer-created Reality. You are the Observer and you are also that which you are observing. Both are aspects of the same whole even though there are distinctions just like the threads in a cloth. You can distinguish the threads; nonetheless the threads *are* the cloth.

Participatory Knowing is the domain of Intent. Participatory Knowing is altogether different from Unawareness in the sense that in Unawareness the circumstances are choosing *for* you, whereas in Participatory Knowing *you* are choosing with your Intent. In Participatory Knowing your relationship to "knowing" is *unshakable* and *undeniable*. It's happening and you know it's happening. It isn't even something you have to feel; you simply *know*.

Participatory Knowing is the domain of distinguishing. In the moment you are present to a new distinction it enters your awareness at the 4th Aspect of Knowing. When an idea as concept metamorphoses into a distinction, it is in your Participatory awareness and therefore, becomes part of you.

In Participatory Knowing you are operating in a high state of awareness. It is awakened awareness. You experience yourself as *one* with the source of creation. You are free from the outer circumstances from the standpoint that you are no longer a victim. Circumstances are just something to notice, to learn from and deal with from the source of your own power. You are co-participating in the creation of your world and you know yourself this way. In Participatory Knowing you are accountable for what shapes your world. *You* are the circumstance shaping the world instead of the circumstances shaping you. You are responsible for the results you create and for your own experience of life. You are aware of yourself as a generator of reality. You experience yourself this way. You know that what you resonate, you attract. In Participatory Knowing, life is an adventure. You are creating magic.

≈

What is the practical use of the 4 Aspects of Knowing? You can use this distinction to check yourself if you are not getting the results you want in life. Return to the goal you pictured when we began this distinction. Ask yourself: *Through which one of these Aspects of Knowing am I related to this result?* Since your state of being shaped by your Intent sets up the magnetic attraction for what shows up in your life, you can see that being aware of your state is of the utmost importance for creating the life you desire. When you notice that you are related in Unawareness or in Concept, it will be clear to you why the result isn't manifesting.

If you have been thinking "I don't know how I'm going to get this done" you have probably been in a state of Unawareness with the goal. If your goal isn't getting accomplished in the time frame you expected, you might be relating to it as a Concept. When you have a sense that it is going to be accomplished even though you aren't quite sure how it's going to happen, you are likely in Intuitive Knowing. When you are certain it's happening, regardless of the circumstances, you are in Participatory Knowing with your goal.

To change your current state is a quantum leap. In Unawareness there is one world available to you with all of its possibilities and limitations, and in another state a whole new world opens. In Conceptual Knowing you have a choice: you can realize you have no authentic connection to the goal and perhaps you're not even interested in pursuing it, or you can create an Intent to become more intimately related with it because you are truly devoted to accomplishing the goal. From Intuitive Knowing you can develop certainty by shifting to Participatory Knowing, aware of your oneness with the creation principle.

Are you starting to see yourself in relationship to these 4 Aspects? Since manifestation of results happens most easily in Participatory Knowing, you can use this distinction to shift your state. As we've been saying all along, it happens with awakened awareness and with conscious Intent. *The crucial factor is being able to notice and acknowledge your current state, without seeing it as a self-criticism in any way.* This is the value of seeing habits as Least-action Pathways.

The 4 Aspects of Knowing are not "the truth" nor are they true or false. They are created distinctions to give us access to manifesting what we desire. Awareness through these various Aspects does not necessarily happen in linear sequence. You could be in Unawareness and have a sudden awakening and be instantly in Participatory Knowing about your goal. When you have the 4 Aspects of Knowing as a distinction and you discern whether you "know" something in Unawareness, as Concept, Intuitively, or at the Participatory level you refine your power to create. When you become adept at shifting any "knowing" to Participatory Knowing … zzaaap! you're a master.

⌾ QuantumThink Recreation ⌾
Live the Wisdom of the 4 Aspects of Knowing

ONE» Think of a result you want in life that is currently eluding you. Identify how you are related to this result using the 4 Aspects of Knowing as your gauge: Unawareness, Conceptual, Intuitive, or Participatory. Just notice which Aspect you are in and see how that shifts the result for you.

TWO» As you go about your day today select something small, a result you want, and consciously shift it from a state of Unawareness or Concept into Participatory. The way to do this: Create the Intent that you are already in Participatory Knowing.

THREE» Advanced Recreation: Use the 4 Aspects of Knowing "in reverse" to shift an undesirable result. If you are in Participatory Knowing about a result you *don't* want, shift it to Concept and eventually have it fade into Unawareness, so it is no longer your experience. Example: If you are in fear about public speaking, you are holding it in your being. Shift your "knowing" to Conceptual by separating yourself from the fear and the thought by simply watching them. Then create a new Intent: *I enjoy public speaking.* Remember, this is not "positive thinking." This is realizing that reality is not "absolute" and that you are the Observer shaping your experience according to your created Intent.

~~~~~~~~~~

QuantumThink-Wave
What Is Your True Nature?

Who are you? How do you identify yourself? As the roles you play in the consensus society—as a father, daughter, homemaker, business person, teacher, musician, consultant, student? Do you identify yourself as your personality traits: convivial, saturnine, maverick, eccentric, conventional? Or perhaps you identify yourself politically, as a liberal, conservative, or libertarian?

Underlying the roles we play on the great stage of humanity is what is considered by wisdom teachings to be our "true" identity, our unchanging essence in a world of ceaseless change and flux. That essence is variously called the Self, Awareness, the Witness, Consciousness, the One Mind we share where there is no separation based on individual differences. There is no identity "crisis" and no case of mistaken identity. In that Self we experience our beauty, our magnificence, our peacefulness, our stillness, our unity, our joy, and our love. We are connected to All That Is. This is the deep longing we experience sometimes without even realizing it.

In "the perennial philosophy" a term used throughout the centuries to refer to universal wisdom common to all people, the nature of reality is both immanent and transcendent, within this world and beyond it, individual and universal, physical and nonphysical. From a new world view our identity is not an Either/Or but a Both/And. Perhaps due to the past conditioning of our culture to see physical and metaphysical as separate, our connection to the source, our ground of being, has been lost. Yet this experience of the Self is not far away. It is yours in an instant. In fact, you reside in your true nature whenever you remember to experience Being Centered.

~~~~~~~~~~

10 BEING CENTERED
The ultimate entertainment

A great meditation master and spiritual teacher named Yogananda[32] taught that we are very much like a radio, able to transmit and receive information and intelligence from anywhere in the cosmos—when our channels are clear, when there is no static interfering with the transmissions. One of the desires in life most of us have is to be in that state of clarity and focus, of Being Centered. People use this expression a lot, Being Centered. What does it mean to be centered? What are we centered in?

Generally when people say they want to "get centered" they mean they want to find a sense of peace or balance, harmony or focus. What we mean by Being Centered is being centered in present-moment Awareness. Then again, these are one and the same. We are in the state of peace when we are present. As in all of QuantumThink, the Intent of this distinction is that you experience Being Centered now as you read.

We want to distinguish present-moment Awareness as Awareness which is free of conditioning, free of judgments, and free of pre-conceived ideas or notions. We are making a distinction between Being Centered in this state of open Awareness as contrasted with being swept up by an ego state. What do we mean by an ego state? What we mean by "ego" is that part of us we could call our character part. If life were a movie the ego is our persona, our personality including our likes and dislikes and idiosyncrasies. The ego is like the role or character we play.

The ego often gets derided yet the ego is a necessity of worldly life defining our place in society, in our families, with our friends, and in the contributions we make through our work and creative expression. Some spiritual traditions suggest that the ego is an interference in attaining spiritual advancement. Consider that the ego is not a problem; it is only the identification with the ego's limiting beliefs that can keep you stuck. The ego makes life interesting. The ego is the vehicle through which we contribute our talents and gifts to one another. The ego fleshes out our assorted roles adding vibrance to the mosaic of humanity. The idea is not to try to get rid of your ego, but to love your ego without attachment to it.

‿‿

The sage says a being who has achieved Self-mastery sees the world as entertainment, like watching a movie. The Awareness is that aspect of us which can observe the ego aspect. In yoga this is called "the watcher." The Awareness is the aspect of ourselves able to make distinctions, when we are able to step outside of our ego persona and become the watcher. Being the watcher doesn't mean you are detached from life. On the contrary, becoming the watcher enables you to enjoy life even more because you aren't getting stuck or hooked by your ego's reactions. You are both the transcendent Awareness and the immanent personality simultaneously.

When you are Being Centered you are sensitive to what surrounds you. Rather than life blurring past you, you savor each moment. You are involved in your life and with the people you love and at the same time you are *free* to be fully with them.

When we say we experience Being Centered, isn't that what is really happening? We experience the present moment. We are alert. We have clarity. We are not being swayed or pulled by the circumstances or by our own reaction to things. We can be in perfect relationship with what is going on because we are clear and free and aware in that moment. We are present.

Can you recall moments like that? You know … those moments when everything slows down. Time stands still. You have an acute sense of awareness. You appreciate the beauty of nature. You are present to the experience of love. If you are engaged in your work or another activity, you are completely involved in the enjoyment and satisfaction of that activity. If you are not engaged in some activity, you find you are just able to be in the moment with no pull or need to do anything. There is a feeling of well being, serenity, calm—for no apparent reason. Isn't this what Being Centered is like? Consider that the place of Awareness is the same in all of us. It is the recognition of the cosmic spark. It is the experience of connection to the source of All That Is. Some call it the vibration of love. Others call it the unified field. You may have heard the experience of the watcher referred to as "the witness" or as "mindfulness." Any name for it never describes it completely because Awareness itself is unbounded and unlimited. The nature of such freedom is—bliss. The important thing is not what you label it or even how you describe it; *the important thing is your experience of it.*

We live in the postindustrial world. Life is busy. Technology is buzzing. We're not going to the mountaintop to sit there, unless we're on vacation or retreat. We can however create the mountaintop in our own mind, wherever we are. The rarefied air of the mountaintop—what does it symbolize? A place of serenity, of solitude, of communion with nature, of one-pointedness and union. From the mountaintop we see the big view, a panoramic vision of life with clarity. The iconic mountaintop evokes awe and inspiration, gratitude and optimism. Right now in this very moment you can know the one we call the watcher. Watch your own mind. Watch your own thoughts. Enjoy being the witness of your experience right now!

Like everything else Being Centered becomes easier and more natural once you have it *as a distinction.* QuantumThink isn't about telling you something you don't already know at some level of your being. What we are doing is generating distinctions that enable you to access your own power to create and be at your most effective in life. Once you become aware of this distinction, Being Centered in present moment awareness as distinct from being pulled and swayed by ego stuff, then more and more it becomes your natural way of being. You literally get lightened up.

Life becomes easier.

Decisions become easier.

Problems become just what is there to be solved—like a game to be played.

You begin to appreciate the ego personalities of both yourself and others. You don't have to take it so seriously. You can enjoy the quirks and idiosyncrasies of the people in your life like characters in a movie. You become like a masterful director. You can just enjoy the show, the wonderful play of life.

When we are Being Centered we call to our highest wisdom and mental acuity, attuned to the energy of what's appropriate in the moment. If you think about it, basically what we do in life all day long is make decisions. We're deciding: should I get out of bed now, what shall I wear, should I eat this food or that food, shall I lie down and rest or shall I read a book, should I walk over to the window and peer outside, shall I take a drink of water now, should I buy this item, shall I call my friend, which train shall I take to work. This goes on during all our waking hours. Now the question is what is driving your decisions all day?

You and I have an inner guidance system that enables us to tune into the vast wisdom and knowledge available to us through the nonlocal field of energy and intelligence. However, as a result of living in a mechanistic world view the mind flits from one object to another automatically. You bypass your wisdom channel when this is happening. To make better quality decisions it is wise to engage a regular practice of Being Centered. When you are Being Centered you can "watch" activity from a place of equanimity even as you are in action. Your decisions are grounded in Awareness and wisdom, focused and clear.

Just as your mind has parked itself in a habit of flitting sometimes aimlessly from one subject to another, from one thought to another, it is also possible for your mind to create a habit of steadiness. This takes conscious practice. Let's not make the erroneous assumption that it's just going to happen on its own. You don't have to think of it as "difficult" either. It simply takes conscious Intent and practice to develop new habits of mind. Steadiness of mind is tantamount to peacefulness of mind.

Being Centered can give you the experience of profound unity. Awareness is simply there nonverbally and preceding language itself. Modern science concurs that in some mysterious way we are all connected by virtue of a universal nonlocal mind, an underlying wave field that connects all matter, energy, and information and that the human mind has direct access to this field. When you watch the thoughts "you" are identified with this pure unbounded Awareness, the unified field of consciousness.

Perhaps what we call a "lost soul" is simply forgetting that underlying life's diversity is this state of unity and peace. There is a striking icon based in the Vedic scriptures of India called the Shiva Nataraj or "dancing lord." If you look at it superficially with limited ego judgments, you might ignore it because it is not part of your religion or culture or it doesn't make sense to you. Upon deeper study the Shiva Nataraj provides insightful knowledge about the mind. The ecstatic dancing Shiva visually symbolizes the actions of consciousness to create, sustain, and destroy and transform our creations. This dance of life happens in our thought process, in the cells of our bodies, and everywhere in the outer world with the continuous exchange of elements. The Nataraj figure also depicts concealment or "forgetful-ness" of our true nature underlying these dynamic processes, as well as illustrating grace we are granted that enables us to awaken to our creative force of Awareness again and again.

━ 〜〜

As you become masterful in The Art of Distinguishing you begin to get coached by everything in your immediate environment, not just from people but from situations and events, from nature. Life everywhere reflects itself back to itself. You can receive coaching from the loyalty of a dog, the freedom of a bird, the glee of a child, the contentedness of a senior. When you open yourself up to the signals in your environment, you receive important messages and you experience a partnership with the life force itself.

In this sense, Being Centered in present-moment Awareness is a foundation for coaching toward mastery. What enables a martial arts master or a tennis or basket-ball pro to know the exact move to make in any moment is a function of their Being Centered in present-moment Awareness. A fraction of a second off center can cost them the game. They are not acting from remembering something in that moment, though at some level either in their mental or bodily memory those learned skills are accessed. Present moment Awareness is what enables the appropriate move especially when something unexpected comes their way.

In the ordinary moments of daily life if you are in a conversation with someone and you are listening to them from a place of not-knowing, then whatever you would hear next would be "unexpected." And there are all those other things that happen all the time in life which show up like the unexpected. We call these emergencies or interferences or obstacles. It seems like they don't belong. However, in a new world view we are told by scientists that *the very nature of the universe is that it is unpredictable.* Anything can show up at any time. Technology develops so fast many companies are not even certain of what their core business will be in the immediate years to come. We personally experience change that happens so fast it alters the form and structure and direction of what was once familiar. If you know that the nature of reality has this quality of *unpredictability* then you can begin to interact with "the unpredictable" as ordinary. When you have this as your context, you can ask, *What allows for mastery given that life by its very nature is unpredictable?*

Being Centered allows us to become masterful in a world of unpredictability. If the martial arts master has to stop and review what to do next when the opponent is coming toward him, he isn't going to be able to be very effective. But if he has been well trained, he can rely on himself in that training. He doesn't have to think of what he knows. He just has to be consciously awake and aware and alert in that instant, Being Centered. The intelligence inherent in life will enable the best and right action.

〜〜

Being Centered is the opportunity to act from your highest wisdom and to master your mind. Every time you remember your Self with a capital "S" you awaken yourself, you enter that state of mind, if only for a moment. That moment is enough for you to choose—to drop a negative judgment, to notice a Least-action Pathway as just a habit and then move on, to choose an empowering Intent, to act from inherent wisdom. A moment of Being Centered in present-moment awareness is enough to awaken and shape the world freshly.

∞ QuantumThink Recreation ∞
Live the Wisdom of Being Centered

The Recreations for this distinction will give you a very real, heightened access to the super-conscious Awareness residing within you.

ONE»Practice Being Centered by becoming "the watcher." For at least a few minutes every day, become The Watcher. Watch your own thoughts. Watch your own reactions. Watch your own emotions. Watch the people in your life as the wonderful characters in your movie, and really *appreciate them* for being those unique characters. Enjoy being the watcher, as you would enjoy watching a movie.

Becoming the watcher means that without getting stuck in your judgments or your opinions or positions on situations and people, including your own self, you just notice. You watch. It is stepping back from your experience to notice your experience, without attachment to your internal commentary if it happens to be running.

When you become aware this way you put yourself instantaneously in the present moment. In this state you will find you are truly free to choose. In this state you will find you move from a world of Either/Or to the world of Both/And. In this state you experience Being Centered.

TWO»In any moment of Being Centered in present moment awareness, notice that you are able to shift your experience. When you are Being Centered you shift naturally, from an upset to being okay with whatever happened. For example, when you lapse into a Least-action Pathway like getting swept up in someone else's "trip," you can lose your Self in that moment. You relinquish your inner sanctum. However, when you remember Being Centered you quickly get back to your Self.

QuantumThink-Wave
Are You Tuning In?

Did you ever work yourself into a frenzy with continuous activity, or drive yourself in a high pitch momentum for days and weeks and months on end, relentlessly until your energy can't go any more? And then, oops! Your body takes a temporary leave of absence. You get a cold, a virus, or even injure yourself because you're just not paying attention to your body's intelligence. Your body is telling you, *Excuse me, my good friend, I'm tired. I need a rest.* Kindly and politely your body asks you, *Can we slow down a little? I need some fun time. Let's sit down for a few days and relax.*

Are you listening? Of course, in order to listen you have to tune in. This means consciously connecting to that silent place of knowing with the awareness you are doing so. Important messages await us not only in our email Inbox but in the silent intelligence that surrounds us. To listen, simply turn on your personal wisdom channel and tune in to Intuition and Nonlocality. You'll discover that listening this way is simply divine.

11 INTUITION AND NONLOCALITY
We hold these truths to be Self-evident

Sometimes we are drawn to do something and we're not quite sure why. You might be passing a bookshop you were not planning to go into and suddenly you feel a gentle yet insistent urge to walk through the door. Looking for what—you know not. A moment after you enter the store you place your hand on a book and it's exactly the topic you've been wondering about lately. You have just taken an Intuitive action. You were led to something you wanted that you didn't even realize you wanted until your "higher intelligence" guided you directly to it. Fortunately, you followed the promptings.

We don't always follow those promptings of inner guidance mainly because it's not a focus of learning in our typical upbringing. Throughout history men and women of considerable success and contribution have attributed their genius in part to their ability to use their Intuitive faculty, yet in our collective culture we haven't been taught to take our Intuition seriously. Intuition has been the intimate, "secret" companion of inventors, scientists, authors, and business moguls, yet we are not educated in the use of our Intuition as a natural and normal faculty of our human birthright.

We have said many times that in QuantumThink we are generating a new kind of knowing consistent with what's needed in our fast-moving, quick-changing quantum age. Intuition is a propitious access to a new kind of knowing. Intuition as a concept is in common usage and many of us feel we use it in some way or another, but now we want to explore the use of Intuition as a discipline. This means tuning in and using the faculty of Intuition in a consciously disciplined way, a part of your daily life.

The great thinker and revered teacher, J. Krishnamurti made an important distinction between discipline that constrains and discipline that sets you free.

Of the discipline that constrains, he said:

> "... it has been generally accepted that, in order to be efficient, you must be disciplined, either by a moral code, a political creed, or by being trained to work like a machine in a factory; but this very process is making the mind dull through conformity."[33]

Of the discipline that sets you free, he proposed:

> "And is it possible to be educated in the right way so that one's whole being is integrated, without contradiction, and therefore without the need of discipline? To be integrated implies a sense of freedom, and when this integration is taking place there is surely no need for discipline. Integration means being one thing totally on all levels at the same time. ... there would be no need for discipline

or compulsion because you would be doing something completely, freely, with your whole being."[34]

This is a very beautiful and coherent idea of discipline, that when your whole being is integrated, that is, without contradiction—there is no need of discipline because you are operating freely.

The sage says, *In order to command, you must first obey.* What does this mean? Before you can command a body of knowledge, a methodology or a technique, first you must learn its fundamentals by giving yourself over to what it offers. This is another way of speaking about the notion of discipline. You "obey" or "surrender" yourself to some form of knowledge and your openness to learning it results in setting you free to command your destiny using the acquired knowledge.

It is in this sense of being free to create that we "discipline ourselves" to QuantumThink. We use the principles from science not as scientific absolutes about the way things *are*, but as principles that open up the previously set boundaries of our thinking about what is possible and what is not. You open yourself to this new way of thinking, and you practice it, and in doing so, the discipline becomes integrated in your being so, as Krishnamurti said, eventually there is no discipline. The discipline vanishes and there is just freedom to be, freedom to create. You are not conflicted, there is no contradiction in your being, you are not conforming to anything. You are simply integrated within the "rightness" of your own being.

If Intuition is indeed a natural faculty of ours, doesn't it make sense that we elevate our relationship to it? Using Intuition in a disciplined way means you would be in a conscious practice of using it. As in any conscious practice, it begins with the Intent to expand your mastery by the full expression of your capabilities. You ingratiate yourself to your Intuition. You can generate that Intent in this very moment, to come into the good graces of your Intuition. As we delve deeper into Intuition and the scientific principles that underscore it, you will surely expand your relationship with the magnificence of your Intuition even before you finish reading this distinction.

～～

The word *"intuition"* derives from Latin roots meaning "to look at" or "watch over" and is defined as *"the obtaining of knowledge or truth without any external means to it; the instantaneous apprehending of information or knowledge without the conscious use of reasoning."*

Intuition expresses itself in many ways and in various forms. Intuition can come as an inner feeling like when we say "we have a gut feeling" about something. Intuition can come as an inner voice. Words or phrases will come into your mind. Intuition can come as a visualization. You may see a picture in your imagination. Intuition can express itself as remote viewing, "seeing" information about a place, person, or event that is at a physical distance from us. Intuition can come as a straight out "knowing." There is no feeling or voice or picture; there is simply an undeniable inner conviction.

Intuition can also come from "outside" of you. All of life is a web of interconnectedness. When you have an Intent to receive an answer to something using your Intuitive faculty, the signal of it may also come from the environment. You get a clear message, a clue, some specific guidance. A brief encounter with a person you may never meet again can influence the direction of your life forever with one penetrating statement or even one word. When you look and listen from the place of peace within, the wind will call to you, a lake will guide you, a tree in your yard that you pass by every day will whisper its wisdom.

Before you continue, pause here for a moment and consider: what would it be like for you to live more Intuitively—to approach situations and decisions, small daily decisions and major life-changing decisions, engaging the brilliance of your Intuition? What in your life would be made easier, more fun perhaps? What old concepts and beliefs would be released as no longer valid or useful? You can tune into your Intuition right now to elicit fruitful responses to those queries.

~~~

As a result of the old world view belief that only "matter" is real, it hasn't occurred to educators or even to most parents to teach young people about their Intuitive faculty, nor have so-called mainstream scientists been driven to investigate it. Perhaps this is because Intuition appears to look more like "magic." We think of magic as something like a childish fantasy, like something unreal. The irony is what most of us really *want* is a kind of magic in our lives.

What characterizes magic? Mystery. Wonderment. Enchantment. Something Wonderful. Awe. Ease. Free Spirit. Surprise. Serendipity. Delight. The Unexpected. Huge Results. Amazing Results. Outside the Limits of ordinary understanding, logic, and sense perception. We love the mystery and the wonder of magic! We want the certainty and at the same time we crave the surprise. We want to experience the shimmering stardust sprinkling serendipitous delight!

Contemplate the ordinary things of life that are truly magical. Childbirth, the Sun rising and setting, snowflakes and glaciers, mountain air, weather patterns, varieties of flowers, trillions of cells functioning in the body, dazzling gems embedded in the Earth's crust, falling in love, a starry night, a baby's hand reaching for you, human ingenuity, millions of galaxies spread over billions of miles, chemical reactions, Olympic performance, artistic creations. Is there anything about life that *isn't* magical? In the course of daily activity we don't necessarily take note that there is a magical quality to life *everywhere* and *in everything*. The fact of creation itself, that something exists rather than not, is the ultimate magic. Our very existence, our own individual self and the privilege that we are imbued with the ability to create. This is magic *extraordinaire*!

A magician does his performance and to us it looks like magic—like *wow, how did that happen?* There is a very important distinction about what we call "magic" and that is it only *looks like* magic to the spectator because the viewer lacks knowledge of how the "magic" works. The magician knows exactly how it was done. He knows his *system.* The magician has access to the way of the magic. You could think of the world of the invisible this way for us. There are forces and principles operating, but until a scientist discovers one of these operating principles and can replicate it through the currently accepted form of scientific experimentation we don't call it a "law" of the universe. We may not even consider it real even though it is.

～～

We have spoken of the scientific principle of Nonlocality which says there is an instantaneous exchange of information throughout the entire universe through the quantum field. Just that statement alone about the nature of our universe— *the instantaneous exchange of information throughout the field*—places the faculty of Intuition in an entirely new light. The fundamental "substance" of reality is not even physical matter as we perceive it in ordinary perception; it is more accurately understood as an "invisible" field of waves of possible information states.

Nonlocality comes from the fact that a quantum, defined as the tiniest sub-atomic substance, is at the foundation of our reality—and at this subatomic level *the quantum actually possesses no spatial dimension at all.* It is not an object as we know physical objects so it is not "located" anywhere. A quantum can exist as either a particle or a wave, and it does so both at the same time. What scientists found is that once two quantum particles, for example, of light, photons, were associated together sharing the same state, what they call *entanglement,* that any influence on one particle would also have the same effect on the other particle instantly, regardless of their physical distance apart. Since a quantum does not exist as a spatial object this makes sense. Again demonstrating an intricate order of interconnectedness and interrelatedness between everything in the universe.

What can all this mean for us? Remember, what we are focusing on here is not so much the scientific principles themselves; *what we are examining is how the discoveries of science shape the way we think.* Consider that we human beings are made up of the same stuff of reality as the stars and of everything else in the universe. We participate in the quantum relationship of Nonlocality. We can and do influence things and events at a distance from us. Our Intent, our emotional states, our feeling states affect reality. In QuantumThink we call these "quantum occurrences"—events and results in our everyday human affairs that happen non-linearly outside the realm of ordinary logic and rational understanding.

It is said that the universe is comprised of energy fluctuations informed by intelligence. Consider that there is only one unifying "substance" that underlies all of reality and existence and that this unified field is a field of intelligence. You could call this the *one universal mind* as a useful way to think about it. We experience the Nonlocal field effect whenever we exercise Intent and Allow for the connections to be made.

The corollary or counterpart to being able to influence things Nonlocally at a distance from us by way of our Intent is the fact that we can also tune in to things and events and knowledge that are at a distance from us using our Intuition. Just as the faculty of Intent is inherent in all human beings so is the faculty of Intuition. The use of our Intuition is our own access to Nonlocal mind, the universal field of intelligence.

The Bulgarian spiritual master Aïvanhov taught his students: *"The highest degree of sight is that of intuition which is both an understanding and a sensation of the divine world."* When you operate from Intuition it is an acknowledgment that you are connected to something more, something larger than what you have learned as "accumulated" information. Even what we might consider mundane activities contain the essence of this greater field of intelligence. Record-setting American basketball coach Phil Jackson, renowned for using mindful, holistic Zen influences to coach his teams to multiple NBA championships, said he "… discovered the game itself operated according to laws far more profound than anything that might be found in a coach's handbook." Living in a Holistic & Holographic universe where the whole is contained in every part deems it unequivocal that we ourselves are connected to the vast, Infinite Intelligence of the universe *if only we would tune in.*

~~~

Fortunately the frontier of physics is changing our old limited beliefs as quantum principles inspire researchers into areas previously overlooked. Institute for Noetic Sciences founder and Apollo 14 astronaut, Edgar Mitchell enthusiastically tells us of the "hallmark discovery" of the Quantum Hologram, the discovery that every object in this universe, large and small, continuously broadcasts the event history of that object nonlocally, and is received by and interacts with other matter through quantum information exchange.[35] Give yourself a moment to read that statement again. Now it starts to make sense: why, when you're thinking of your sister the phone rings and it's her saying hello, it begins to make sense what has Intent and Intuition work so well. We're not saying that scientists are rushing in to verify these suggestions, though some might. What we are saying is that explanations of mind capabilities that have eluded us until now appear to make sense in the context of quantum discoveries illuminating us.

Though it challenges old world view logic scientists are proving the fact of Nonlocality again and again in ways that astonish conventions of thinking. Research shows that the power of Intent can change already recorded events in the "past" and that the body can respond to events in the "future" that haven't yet occurred.

Nonlocality is an "a-causal" relationship to matter. It operates in a different domain than a stimulus-response, cause and effect, behavioristic, or mechanical relationship. Nonlocality is a quantum relationship unaffected by space and time, the instantaneous exchange of information through the resonance of the quantum field bypassing time and space parameters in ways that bewilder the classically trained mind.

Just as the magician knows the ways of his magic so are we beginning to decipher the dynamics of our natural faculties of mind and why they work. The scientific principles of Nonlocality, the Quantum Hologram, and Entanglement transform what once appeared like magic into pragmatic common sense. These proven principles open us to a more sophisticated and knowledgeable view of our Intuitive faculty.

When you are so entrenched in the habit of living with attention on the world of the five senses, mainly what you can see with your eyes, what you can hear with your ears and what you can touch or feel viscerally, you may not be so attentive to the world undetectable to our physical sensory apparatus. You may not attend to the world of the unseen and unheard, the realm of the invisible. *Yet it is apparent that communication takes place not so much from object to object or particle to particle, but rather as the possibility of instantaneous transmissions through a field of energy, information and consciousness, patterns of waves where everything is connected all the time.* As scientists have discovered it appears we've had all our attention on the objects in the field when we really need to put our attention on the nature of the field itself.

~~~

Intuition is a portal to Nonlocality because it is a conscious attunement to the field. Intuition gives us access to the magic of life. The more you become aware of and distinguish your quantum occurrences, particularly when you share them with friends, family and colleagues, you practice the *discipline* of seeing this kind of quantum magic that is at the very foundation of life. You realize that *you* are the one in the co-participatory dance with the forces of the universe. *You* are the one, through the use of your directed Intent and your reception of Intuition, generating the quantum occurrences in your life. You can still be overjoyed at the wonder of these occurrences, you can be delightfully surprised, yet you don't have to be in disbelief.

Now, external proof is fascinating and may be comforting; however, you don't need scientific evidence to convince you. You can experience the results of your Intuition directly. You can use your Intuition to tap into the dimension from which all life generates and create a powerful relationship with that aspect of yourself which is part of it. Most importantly you see that you can live with the ease of these quantum occurrences as your way of life. Virtually every one of us has the inborn ability to tune in. As with any faculty, whether we develop the effective use it or not is for each one of us to choose.

Why would you want to have Intuition become a natural way of life? Intuition expands your capabilities. Intuition allows you to "think" beyond limits of the conceptual mind. When you don't access your Intuition all you have available is your past conditioning and experience. In what ways can you benefit from the disciplined use of Intuition? Speed for one thing. Intuition enables you to access information beyond currently known or obvious options. Rather than having to logic out the possible options line by line, one by one, step by step, your Intuition can zoom right in to an opportunity that will serve you best. Your computer may be connected "online" all the time but the information you pick up depends upon what you decide to tune into. Intuition quickly shows you the appropriate action that will bring about a desired result. This requires no pushing or forcing.

Though Intuition may already be in play without our being aware of it, becoming masterful with it means consciously choosing to use it as a way of life. Tapping into Intuition requires Being Centered in a state of awakened awareness. In order to send and receive, to be a clear transmitter, you want to make sure there is no static on the radio. In the state of non-attachment, free of the pull of circumstances, you can be most effective with your Intuition. It is important to discern between ego cravings and genuine promptings of higher intelligence. As you continue to refine your mind through concentration, meditation, centering practices, and QuantumThinking, it becomes easier and more natural to use the faculties of our Nonlocal mind.

Important: When you make a decision using your Intuitive faculty, you cannot immediately see all of the possible results that will ensue from having made that decision. Allowing comes into play. This is new world view thinking. You know there is a greater whole within which your decision or action is taking place and the outcomes are always beyond the finite limits of what your mind can see in any given moment in space-time.

As knowledge of Intuition and Nonlocality becomes integrated in you, what was once ordinary living morphs into an amazing game of adventure and discovery. You experience the magic of life. Intuition and Nonlocality are portals to the genius in you waiting to be set free.

⟨ QUANTUMTHINK RECREATION ⟩

Live the Wisdom of Intuition and Nonlocality

ONE»Begin to practice using your Intuition and Nonlocality in a disciplined way so it becomes a useful everyday faculty for decision making and for accessing information not "local" to you.

(a) Be in awe of ordinary things, as much and as many as possible. Notice the magical in "common" things we take for granted.

(b) Consciously make at least three Intuitive decisions this week. Do this with awareness and the Intent to use your Intuition as your portal to Nonlocality. Remember to center yourself in pure Awareness to tap into this. Reality is multidimensional. Using your Intuition can also include using facts and ordinary logic. (Note: A "fact" is simply what happened, without any meaning or interpretation about it. Opinions, interpretations and meanings are not facts in and of themselves.)

TWO»Use your Intuition to tune in and consciously receive coaching from nature. Take note of the moon, a waterfall, a bird, a particular tree, your pet, a plant in your home. What message does it have for you? Life force messages are everywhere when you use your Intuition to tune in.

~~~~~~~~~~~~~~~

QuantumThink-Wave
It's About Time

Just in case you have had any doubt whatsoever that we are living in an Observer-created Reality where "what we bring is what we get" and there are no absolute realities, just reflect on Time for a moment.

We live in different Time zones so which one is the REAL Time? Even the Time Zones themselves change according to the minds of the "officials" in charge of changing such things. Even in the same area, some cities use "Daylight Savings Time" while others don't.

What about the year? How many cultures have their own calendar? When you study the history of time you discover the different calendars, even the one we currently adhere to in the West, have been ordained with the changing of rulers. There are different systems—lunar calendars, solar calendars, and at least thirty-three calendars depending on the culture, including the Western, the Chinese, the Hebrew, the Mayan, the Islamic and the Buddhist calendars, to name a few. Each one has their own rendition of when their "Time" began. Well, if you miss a New Year's celebration you can always find another one to hook up with.

What about the measurement of time? According to the National Physical Laboratory in England, the reason for the way chronological time is measured is to "keep man-made scales for recording time in step with the natural rhythms of the heavenly bodies." In the third millennium B.C. the sundial was used to measure time. In the fourteenth century A.D. the mechanical clock was invented, however it was the sundial that continued to be the master clock giving the ultimate reference of time, solar time. As the Earth rotated on its axis adjustments in time had to continually be made. Eventually scientists discovered that atoms are the best method for keeping accurate time, because atoms have natural vibrations that could provide the beat of a clock just like a swinging pendulum.

In 1967 scientists worldwide agreed to measure time using the atomic time. However they still have to make adjustments, adding or subtracting seconds to keep up with the Earth's natural rotation, since atomic time, the measurement they use, is not linked to the Earth's rotation. They call the new way of making these adjustments "Co-ordinated Universal Time," meaning they have to keep in touch with the natural rhythm rotation of Earth and *coordinate* their measurements to work out their time.

What does all this mean to us? There are rhythms and there are cycles. However, consider that whatever you imagine time to be may be a pure fabrication, though a useful one for our convenience. This is excellent news. If time is not absolute we don't have to be stuck with our notions about it. When we remember that all chronological time measurements are agreed upon inventions, we can use them without becoming victims of them. When we're not caught up in our concepts of time an amazing thing can happen: Time becomes a useful tool rather than an indomitable tyrant.

If you wish to live a life of mastery in the experience of unbounded awareness, doesn't this indicate living Beyond Time?

12 BEYOND TIME

From tyrant to tool

Did you ever wish you could stop Time, or at least slow it down a bit? What is your experience of Time? Perhaps challenging to answer since you probably have a totally different experience of Time depending on the circumstances you are in.

You have surely experienced those moments when time seems to stand still. You're in an exhilarating conversation and you look up at the clock. Hours have passed undetected. It felt like no time at all as if you entered a kind of twilight zone. In moments of merging, Being In One Conversation with whatever you are doing, deeply involved in your work, in meditation, watching a movie, or gazing at the stars, the distinction "you" and "it" disappears and so does time. What about those moments when you feel as if you are racing inside, revved up, and rushing as if time is running out. You're mentally exhausted and you haven't actually *done* anything. Your heartbeat quickens and unlike the presence you experience when "time stands still," in this state you experience a loss of presence. Anything that usurps your present state of awareness takes away a degree of mastery.

Our experience of Time varies and changes considerably yet we relate to Time as if it is "absolute." From a new world view we realize there are no such "absolutes." To think in a quantum world means going beyond limitations of physical space and chronological time. Whenever you create from Intent or use Intuition connecting to Nonlocality you experience going beyond the limits of ordinary space-time. Still it is obvious that time has become a ubiquitous aspect of daily life. The Oxford dictionary assessed that "time" is the most often used noun in the English language. We have taken a quantum leap into a new world view, into QuantumThinking, and what we want to do now is begin to notice to what extent we actually *experience* living in this new world view—or not—in terms of one of the fundamental aspects through which we are related to life—Time.

〜〜〜

The sage says, *Each of us lives in our own world according to our own concepts. According to your own concepts, you have created a world.*

Albert Einstein, who is best known for his revolutionary theories of relativity and special relativity basically proved (in the most simple way of saying it) that space and time are not fixed as people had previously believed; they are always relative to the speed at which one moved. Einstein said each person lives in his or her own created concept of space-time, the two now melded as one in science indicating that time and space are always interconnected.

Let's go deeper now into this notion of Time. Consider this very carefully: *The concepts of time you live in, to a great extent, give you your moment-by-moment experience of life—your emotional states, your sense of what you think can be accomplished, your relationships, your ability to be present, and your general feeling of well being.*

What do we mean by our "concepts" of time? "Beginning, middle, and end" are concepts of time. At the beginning of a project or new learning we are very jazzed and excited, and as we start to get the routine of it down in the middle of it our enthusiasm tends to wane; and then when we're near the end we start to get excited again, either about the result or about anticipating the process being over soon. What has our experience change from excitement to neutral and back again is shaped by our concept of time.

The concept of time overshadowing modern life is "scarcity," the idea that time is fixed and therefore there is never enough of it. *There aren't enough hours in the day to do everything I need to do.* Imagine the experiential feeling that concept gives you. You might feel harried, harassed, pressured, or frustrated. The concept of time called scarcity affects your actions with other people. *Hurry up, you're wasting time! I don't have time for this ... can you give me the bottom line?* Have you heard that before? How does it make you feel? Have you ever said that yourself? How present can you be with someone in the moment when your state is colored by "not enough time"? Since thoughts generate chemical reactions in your body, it has been suggested that thoughts of "running out of time" can even affect the aging process.[36]

The old world view has trained us to think that time is linear and moves in one direction in a straight line. Quantum science has long since dispelled that "concept" proving it to be inaccurate. In fact it is known that in the quantum world things can and do move backward and forward through time, transcending the limits of physical space and chronological time.

The question for us is: Do we live this way? Not really. We don't realize the extent to which we limit ourselves by our outdated concepts of space and time. Though you may thus far have had glimpses into another kind of reality, if you examine this closely you'll find that in the day-to-day we are "ruled" by the line of time. We decide what we're able to accomplish or not within a measured amount of time. We live in a linear, mechanistic, reductionistic reality reference. "Linear" gives us the concept of time moving in one direction. "Mechanistic" gives us the idea of things happening in a cause and effect mechanical action. "Reductionist" means that in terms of time we experience the world in a fixed box that reduces to units called hours and minutes and seconds.

When you base your "logic" on what you think is possible within a given period of clock time, your concepts of time shape your actions and limit what you will do or what you think you *can* do.

The old world view has indoctrinated us to see life as a series of separate events in fixed increments of time. We have "a window of time" and if that window appears to close we "missed the opportunity." We say, *I said I would do x, and it didn't happen.* From a cause and effect view you would only be able to see "we did *this* and it caused *that.*" But the "this" wasn't the "that" we said was going to happen, and *therefore, we did not do what we said we would do.* And so from this old world view of ordinary logic, that is, of "events" in one-way time, that would probably be the end of it. "It" didn't happen.

However, if you are living from a new world view—an interconnected, Holistic & Holographic universe of multidimensions, parallel universes, and Nonlocal mind able to see and have access into the past, present and future—you would see every event, every accomplishment, everything that occurs within a particular framework, not as a linear and isolated event, but as an integral element contributing to the whole of what is unfolding.

Take the example of former Vice President Al Gore. When he ran for president of the United States we could surmise that one of his Intents was to positively influence political, economic, and social will with regard to taking care of the Earth's ecology. When he did not become president we could have jumped to the conclusion that the opportunity was lost, looking from that narrow "window in time." It is obvious to us now that we would have been quite mistaken. From a new world view we could say that it was precisely because of the voting hoopla and the fact that he did *not* become president that he was led to play a major role in an Oscar winning documentary film where his Intent to get his message out and people in action on the environment was powerfully fulfilled.

When you view life from the whole you realize events are not isolated; they are related. Everything that happens belongs to the original Intent. Perhaps "x" didn't happen in the timeframe you envisioned; however, if you hold whatever did happen as related to your end result, you don't just give up. You use the opportunity of whatever happens to guide you to perhaps an even greater result when you are not locked into illusory time constraints.

When you think Beyond Time you realize that everything that is going to unfold is *already there.* Everything already exists in the possible world. You have access into the past, present, and future at any time. We know, at least we can conceive of this intellectually, that the past, present and future are all "there," all at once because linear time as we use it is an invented distinction that we lay over our world. "Past" and "future" are modern contrivances we use for convenience. Brain researchers have found that the *same* areas of the brain are activated whether you have thoughts of your personal past or thoughts about your future.

Time is not absolute though the reductionist classical-mechanical world view has conditioned us to live as though it is. Time is an invented construct we lay over our experience to order our lives. Dr. Fred Alan Wolf cleverly points out that even the "present moment" is illusory in the sense that you can never measure it because it is already vanished. In reality, what we refer to as the past, present and future exist simultaneously, Beyond Time. This is a possible explanation for the fact that when you effect a state change, a quantum leap in consciousness, you transform the past, the present and the future all at once. This happens as you alter your relationship with Time.

Let me go back a minute because your mind might resist saying, *Access to the past, present and future? That's impossible.* Why do we say it is impossible? Only because we are trying to figure out how we could do that using a limited linear, logical process. You can think of this like Einstein's man with the sealed watch. You know the watch is working even though your mind can't see or quite figure out *how* it's working. You know that the past, present, and future are here simultaneously even though you can't quite see or "understand" how. When a transformation occurs, the past, the present and the future shift in an instant. Such is the paradoxical and bizarre nature of quantum reality.

We are not throwing out a linear universe. Scientists tell us matter gets created at the point where space and time meet. Events do occur in our agreed-upon chronological time. As a methodology "cause and effect" may have its place. We are already adept in the ordinary logic and analytical process. Our Intent here is to become effective with quantum logic where things move backward and forward through time, and where quantum measurements don't make rational sense. Nobel Prize Laureate in Physics (1978) and former Head Scientist at Bell Labs, Arno Penzias said it this way: *"For real world problems, logic doesn't work anyway. That's why no one uses it."*

Concepts aren't absolutes. In an Observer-created Reality you realize that you are not stuck living with the concept that Time is scarce. An arbitrary concept of time means the concept is fabricated—made up; there is nothing "absolutely true" about it. We may think we "know" how much time it takes to complete a project. If we think there isn't enough time we begin to feel pressured and experience stress. The dilemma is that when you get yourself into the stressful state you take away your presence. *Anything that usurps your present state of awareness takes away a degree of mastery.* So the very thing you want, which is to finish the project quickly, is diminished by your less-than-present state. Now, when you recognize the concept of time *as just a concept* you naturally move beyond its limits and find yourself accomplishing more in less time without thinking about it. You attract resources and occurrences Nonlocally that bring about fulfillment of your Intent.

There is even greater reason to live both within time and Beyond Time and that is—so we feel comfortably at home in our fast-paced world.

~~~

Astrophysicists say the expansion of the universe is accelerating. Astrologers say the planet Uranus is speeding up evolution. Then how much faster can it get?

In his ingenious book, *Waking Up in Time*, contemporary British physicist, Peter Russell traces the time it has taken for evolution to reach the state we are in now, emphasizing the exponentially increasing speed with which change is occurring.

He states that most scientists now believe the Universe began between 10 and 20 billion years ago as an eleven-dimensional Universe of pure energy, and it took millions of more years for complex atoms to form. He tells us if you looked at this whole history of evolution as the height of one of the former twin towers in New York City, with the street level representing the formation of our planet 4.5 billion years ago, the Renaissance would fit into the top one-thousandth of an inch, less than a layer of paint. All of modern history would be the thickness of a microscopic bacterium, and the age of rock 'n' roll, microchips, and moonwalks would be too thin to measure.[37]

This gives you a very good picture of how things have sped up. And there is no indication that things are going to slow down.

So comes the question: What is the use of time in this new world view? How can we use time so that time is one of our *tools* rather than something we have to put up with or something that constrains us or stresses us out? We want to distinguish time as a *tool* rather than as a *frame of reference*. We want to transform time from a tyrannical frame of reference to a tool for our use. We will use an analogy that enables us to see this.

Mind is to Consciousness as Time is to Beyond Time

If your mind is your frame of reference then you are limited by whatever fills your mind in any given moment. If your *consciousness* is your frame of reference—the free and unbounded awareness with which you see your mind with all of its talents and workings—if you know that your mind is a tool inside of the frame of reference of consciousness, then you have a lot of power with your mind. We have been in the practice of using our mind and consciousness in this way in every QuantumThink distinction and Recreation. Yet, until you make this distinction, for most people the content filling your mind is your frame of reference, the background context from which you live.

When you can see your mind as a faculty in the context called "consciousness," the "no-thing" from which anything can come into existence, then the gift of the mind can be used as a tool inside of infinite intelligence, infinite potential, Infinite Possibility.

Consciousness is first and from consciousness comes the mind. The mind is a faculty we have available to us. Your consciousness is the awareness of what is going on in your mind. This consciousness or awareness is what enables us to distinguish the thoughts we have, and in distinguishing them, we have freedom to create outside of the thoughts that are already there. If all we had is mind, with no *watcher* of mind, no awareness or consciousness of mind then we would be limited by whatever the mind is doing at any particular moment, or limited by what the mind does as repetitive patterns of thought.

As an analogy with time, if chronological time is your frame of reference, then you are trapped by it because time has a very specific way that it works. It's linearly constructed and it's a measurement. It's a particular kind of box and you are boxed in by it.

On the other hand, if you could have as your frame of reference "outside of time" and then see that time is to outside of time (there is no word for it) as mind is to consciousness, then time becomes a powerful tool. It becomes a faculty. It becomes something we can *use* rather than something we are entrapped by.

The Intent here is for us to move beyond our ordinary concepts of time. Because in the new world we are in today things in terms of time are moving so rapidly that trying to fit them into linear concepts of time is not only erroneous; it is debilitating, it actually drains our energy. This is possibly the cause of stress, burnout, and the experience of overwhelm. Evolution is speeding up. It is frustrating and devitalizing to continue to live in fixed concepts of time in a world where systems are timeless and spaceless. The Internet is Beyond Time isn't it? We live in different time zones yet our communications and commerce know no boundaries.

~~~

If you are still wondering whether we really do influence our experience of reality according to our concepts of time, just think of what happens with each New Year. You refresh yourself, clear the slate, purify the field. The concept of a Happy New Year is a cultural Least-action Pathway that is a happy and gratifying one. Still, until you become aware of it as an arbitrary concept, your experience is culturally determined rather than consciously determined.

Masters refer to "being in the Now moment." Being in the Now means you are outside of time. When you are present you are outside of time. Yet we do have this faculty called time. People do not actually go beyond it because we don't make this distinction that we are making right now between time as the background reference of our culture and time as a powerful faculty you can use. *When you have the distinction Beyond Time you are able to wisely discern between when you are using time and when you are being used by time.*

One of the most useful assets of mastering our mind is the ability to just "drop it" and move on. Move on to the next Now. Drop the unpleasant thought, emotion, meaning, or experience and create the next moment as new, happy, and free. When you experience awareness Beyond Time you then have the capability to make that choice. If Time is relative to the speed you are moving, as Einstein proved, then think about this in your own experience. If you are "racing" inside, what is your experience of Time? You can literally slow things down when you shift your own state.

Exalted poet Walt Whitman wrote in *Leaves of Grass*: *"The clock indicates the moment—but what does eternity indicate?"* There may be a limited number of clock hours measured in a day from sunrise to sunrise, there may be a limited though unknown number of years in each lifetime, yet when you can summon the state Beyond Time you welcome and enjoy every moment fully present, fresh, and vibrant with life.

Maybe you can't stop time, however, you can create the experience of being Beyond Time. When you do you enter the sacred state. The camel driver in Paulo Coelho's *The Alchemist* tells the boy, *"If you concentrate always on the present, you'll be a happy man. ... Life will be a party for you, a grand festival, because life is the moment we're living right now."*

When you are present you are Beyond Time. You can experience this right now in this very moment. Follow your breath and become aware of your state. Allow any inner chatter to subside. When you are Beyond Time you are silent inside even while surrounded by motion and commotion. In this silent stillness you see with clarity and respond with alacrity.

The goal of wisdom "seekers" is *liberation*. Liberation from what? From whatever keeps you from your true blissful nature. To shape your destiny in every moment is to create an empowering relationship with time. Time, and Beyond Time, are marvelous, soulful dance partners.

☙ QUANTUMTHINK RECREATION ❧
Live the Wisdom of Beyond Time

The concepts of time you live in, to a great extent, give you your moment-to-moment experience of life, influencing and impacting your emotional states, your relationships, your sense of what you think can be accomplished, your ability to be present, and your general feeling of well being.

ONE»As you go about your day notice the various concepts of time that are giving you your experience in the moment.

TWO»Notice how your concepts of time direct and even dictate your decisions.

THREE»Notice that you experience a "state change," an instantaneous quantum leap in consciousness—when you are present to these arbitrary concepts. Important Note: This Recreation *can only be done in the present moment*, as you become aware of your experience and you note what concept of Time is creating that experience.

Examples of Outdated and/or Erroneous Concepts of Time

Limiting Concept #1: Scarcity.
There is not enough Time. Time is running out.

YOU SAY: Give me the bottom line. Can't talk now. Gotta' go.
              I don't have time for this.

AFFECTS: Relationship.

EXPERIENCE: Not present with the person; instead you are being with
              "gotta' go."
              Rushing, racing, squeezed, pressured.

Limiting Concept #2: Time-Space conflicts.

YOU SAY: I can't do *everything* because I can't be in three places at
              one time.

AFFECTS: Accomplishment, Creativity, Fulfillment.

EXPERIENCE: Resignation, Frustration. Sense of failure.

              You think you cannot do three things in the same time
              period.

              Cuts off thinking from Infinite Possibility and
              Living Fully Dimensionally, and limits Intent and
              Allowing.

Limiting Concept #3: Time is absolute.

YOU SAY: We're going to be late. I'll never get this done on time.
              You think something takes "x" amount of time as if you
              can predict or know this absolutely.

AFFECTS: Your state. Equanimity. Peace of mind. Actually getting it
              accomplished.

              You worry about what needs to be done and your guilt
              about it not happening in your arbitrarily conceived time
              frame slows the process and interferes with getting it
              accomplished or arriving someplace promptly. You are
              holding in your Participatory Knowing "I'm late!"

EXPERIENCE: Guilt. Fear. Pressure. Shoulds, coulds, musts.

Remember, you can live in a state Beyond Time and use time as your
tool. This is one of the most important aspects of living masterfully.

QuantumThink-Wave

Surprise, Surprise

I wonder why we still find it so surprising that scientific theories of "the way things are" always seem to change and are never absolute. Living in an Observer-created Reality of course it makes sense that certain seemingly "inalienable" facts turn out not to be the case when one looks further and changes the angle or aim of the inquiry.

Read the latest findings of cosmologists or quantum physicists and you'll find that while they may start with certain agreed upon fundamental assumptions, their theories take widely divergent routes as they attempt to explain concepts like time, the "big bang," evolution, the nature of matter and energy, or what the ultimate unifying principle might be. Even "constants" such as the speed of light are relative to certain physical conditions. If one can imagine parallel universes as some cosmologists do, then one can surmise that the laws of physics vary in other universes. As you read this you may be wondering who cares, and why should this matter to us?

We do enjoy and require some semblance of order and continuity in our lives and in the way we deal with natural laws. However, it behooves us to remember that *what we bring to our Observation shapes what we see.* In the way we attempt to define a human being scientifically or otherwise, it may be wise to remain open to surprise and to ask whether our starting point will take us in a fruitful direction that enhances life. Why start from the misbegotten assumption that we are strictly physical beings when it is more than evident that this is a Multidimensional Universe and we are Multidimensional Beings.

13 MULTIDIMENSIONAL UNIVERSE— MULTIDIMENSIONAL BEING
Why not take all of you?

So much about life is paradoxical. We say the absolute truth of existence can never be known ... yet we forever seek the truth. There is no beginning and no end we can glean ... yet we construct Time. We think mathematical equations are the only proof of scientific theories ... yet the very same things being proved existed that way before the equations. We went along with the idea that only matter is real ... yet the great scientists declare there is no such thing as "matter."

Perhaps the biggest cosmic joke we have ever played on ourselves by accepting the classical world view is that we have been led to approach life from one dimension, the physical dimension of "matter." Since it is so obvious to our ordinary five senses that "matter" matters, early scientists mistakenly concluded that matter was the *only* thing that mattered. Why should this matter?

Scientists don't always agree on the fundamental assumptions about the nature of reality and how it works however most concur that we live in a Multidimensional Universe. In addition to the three dimensions of space and the one dimension of time, they say there are six or seven more dimensions beyond our ability to perceive or imagine them in everyday terms. We are each individual whole systems comprised of the same elements and dynamics as the whole of the natural world. Even so, the classical scientific world view seems to have "overlooked" the fact of our Multidimensional *Being*.

Our interest here in QuantumThink is to examine how the widely divergent classical and quantum world views shape our predominant habits of thinking, so we can awaken our awareness, expand our possibilities. Verily, *context is everything*. In one dimension we see life one way. From another dimension we see something else entirely.

～～

There is a well known story of the blind man and the elephant that found its way across the world. Here is how it is told by the Feng Shui master, Dr. Lin Yun:

> "There are many ways to understand life and the universe: through superstition, religion, philosophy, science and so forth. While each approach has its own experts—scientists, priests, philosophers, doctors, poets—all are merely blind men receiving different impressions from touching the same elephant. A priest may feel its legs and say life is like a tree trunk; a scientist holding its tail may find that life is ropelike; a poet feeling an ear may proclaim life like a lotus leaf; a doctor holding its tusk may conclude that life is like a bone; a philosopher grasping its trunk

may pronounce life to be like a snake; and so on. From his own perspective, each expert's conclusion is knowledgeable and makes sense. Their theories, however, are merely parts of the whole picture."[38]

The sages say we each live in our own world according to our thoughts and ideas, yet don't we relate to *our* world as *the* world? In a subtle way you live as if the language you speak is *the* language, your religion is *the* religion, your country is *the* country. Each of us has the possibility of manifesting every human trait yet we'll relate to a person in one dimension of their personality. Every situation has an emotional, a mental, a spiritual, a soul component and we typically get ensnared by the limits of one dimension. Because of the power of our senses our focus tends to be on the physical aspect of our being.

Even though we may *understand* that reality is Multidimensional, the universe is Multidimensional, and human beings are Multidimensional, we don't live as if we are Multidimensional. We mostly operate in the world of the senses, of sensory data, what we can see and feel and hear, what we can smell and taste. Being conditioned to a one-dimensional view of reality has kept us superficial in the true sense of the word—on the surface, attending to what is "apparent rather than substantial." This has been a factor in prejudices created from seeing differences and separation, most notably in the color of skin, religious belief systems, and social status. Operating from perception alone can be quite unreliable hence the expression "optical illusion." The senses are easily fooled.

Contemplate this for only a moment and you realize it doesn't even make sense to hold that the physical is the only reality. Everything that has ever been created by humankind began in the unseen, imperceptible dimension of thought. The very life force itself that sustains all living creatures cannot be seen or measured (thus far) in physical terms. The *essentials* of life are outside the physical dimension of ordinary sense perception.

As we QuantumThink we have begun to attend to the importance of the role of the unseen or invisible world to the whole of life, because we have had our focus on it. With each distinction we focus a light, like shining a laser beam, on one aspect of the hologram. For us, the light we use is the light of our awareness. We could say the singular distinction we focus upon is where "we enter the hologram." You can ask yourself, where do you enter the hologram? What is your access point? What is your pathway in? You are never really "outside" of the hologram, so you could say that the entry point or path is the point of your Awareness. We are always speaking about the same thing over and over. The difference is in our access point—the place where we choose to place our attention and awareness. The primary Intent of QuantumThink is to heighten your awareness. It is to raise your level of awareness, moment by moment—because that, in essence, is the state in which Mastery is achieved. The extent to which you get hooked by any concept or idea or point of view or *access point*—the extent to which you get stuck there is the extent to which your Mastery is diminished.

The topic of where we "enter the hologram" of life is the focus of this distinction, Multidimensional Universe—Multidimensional Being.

〜〜

An area where a one-dimensional focus on the physical has limited us considerably is an area of the greatest importance to us, and that is our own well being. All of us are aware and people often say it: the number one most important thing in life is our health. When we think of our well being, or "wellness," as it is popular to say today, we tend to think of our physical body. However, in a Multidimensional Universe there are different energy systems and in a Multidimensional Being there are various types of bodies related to the physical yet distinct in their essence and function. Many different distinctions have been made with regard to the various bodies which in a Holistic & Holographic world are not only interrelated and interconnected; they interpenetrate one another.

In an Infinite Possibility universe there are any number of ways we might distinguish our Multidimensionality. The most popular distinction we hear is Body, Mind, and Spirit. Another example is to say we are comprised of a *gross physical body* which is the body of sense organs and chemicals, a *subtle energy body* which contains the mental and emotional emanations of ourselves, a *causal body* which is our dream state of imagination and Intent, and a *supracausal body* which describes the ultra-heightened super-aware state that transcends all attributes and actions.

We mention these various ways of distinguishing our nature to get us in touch with the fact of our Multidimensional Being. Whatever distinction you use, the main point is that we have existence in many dimensions and that all dimensions interpenetrate and impact one another and are wisely considered together.

It has become popular for people to say "we are spiritual beings having a human experience," a musing attributed to the French paleontologist and mystic, Teilhard de Chardin. We relate to such statements perhaps because they connect us to a kernel of truth—that the physical human body is a sheath or "space suit" appropriate to the conditions of planet Earth and implying there is much more to who we are. We are here to QuantumThink not to prove or convince; we are here to become aware of ourselves and to experience the distinctions of our emerging new world view in our own lives. How do you relate to your own being? How do you identify yourself? As your body? As your mind? Your spirit? What about your soul? Attempting a conclusion to be one "dimension" or another could certainly cause unnecessary and unnatural confusion.

If you have lived in the Western culture you are very familiar with Western or allopathic medicine that tends to focus on parts of the body, and tends to focus on fixing what's wrong. If you have lived in an Eastern culture you may be more used to dealing with the body as a whole system, a Holistic system, and the emphasis may be more on prevention of disease than on treating disease, although obviously they also have treatments. In the Western culture healing methods other than by conventional means came to be known as "alternative medicine." As doctors heighten their awareness and increase their knowledge they use new terms like "complementary medicine" and "integrative medicine" suggesting the wisdom of considering all systems together.

Why rule out any of it? All the assorted practices and expertise are available to us. The classical world view that proclaimed only the physical was real has so programmed our thinking as a culture that we can tend to stubbornly resist, ignore, or remain unaware of the latest findings of science as it relates to our well being. Why not be open to all of it? Einstein proved that what we call "matter" is in fact energy. Our body is energy. We are vibrating and emanating fields of energy. From a new world view shouldn't we address this fact when dealing with our well being? If we are Multidimensional Beings living in a Multidimensional Universe, why limit ourselves to considering only one dimension regarding something as precious as the state of our well being?

The old classical scientific view of the body as a purely physical organism has kept us trapped in limited ways of thinking about our well being despite overwhelming scientific evidence that confirms we are indeed more than the physical body. Advanced scientists and physicians regard the physical body and the mind together as one entity, the "bodymind," recognizing that the mind is present in every cell of the body and acknowledging their inseparability.

The Institute of HeartMath® research has proved that "energetic or electromagnetic interactions play an important role in the brain and nervous system's ability to communicate information." They have shown that "electromagnetic fields generated by the heart extend a number of feet outside the body, can be measured, and contain information modulated by one's emotional state;" that "a person's heart field can be detected by other people in proximity," and that "the interactions between people have been shown to produce physiological effects." They further hold that the spiritual body provides missing information—that "the individual spirit has a very real, dynamic and evolving structure, a kind of 'holographic blueprint' that maintains and evolves the pattern of physical structures."[39]

Though not every method or modality works for everyone in every case, the fact is there are energy-based healing modalities as well as those that include soul-based, prayer-based, and spirit-based approaches to maintaining the well being of our Multidimensional Being. Living the wisdom of our Multidimensional Being suggests that addressing our well being from a Multidimensional view may hold greater promise and opportunity, a literal quantum leap beyond the old chemical-molecular model alone. What we call "the body" is not limited to the physical. Consider that there is intelligence specific to each dimension, each one contributing to the whole of our state.

When you begin to see your well being from the point of view of your Multidimensional Being you can see much deeper into what is needed and wanted any time you experience an imbalance in any of your bodies. You are in a co-participatory dance with the healing factor (it may not be a person). We can take responsibility for our own well being rather than reacting automatically or leaving it solely in the hands of another. The more we learn about our Multidimensional Being the greater effectiveness we can summon to maintain a healthy state. We can research the latest known facts and logic and use our Intuitive Knowing to direct ourselves to the appropriate modalities and practitioners to restore balance.

Acupuncture practitioner and student of Chinese medicine, Jacob Barrocas, teaches us that in Chinese medicine every organ in our body has three aspects and functions: the physical aspect, the mental-emotional aspect, and the spiritual aspect. Take for example, the heart. The heart is the regulatory organ of blood flow and circulation in the physical realm. In the emotional realm, the heart is the center of love. In the spiritual realm, the heart is considered the seat or focus of the spiritual energy. In the Chinese system they consider all three systems together realizing the physical, mental-emotional, and spiritual all interpenetrate and impact one another. When you live from the perspective of your Multidimensional Being, you open yourself to the possibility of attending to your well being from any point in the Holographic body, from any and all "entry" points.

Can you recall a time when for no reason at all you simply felt wonderful? Of course you can. Our natural state is bliss and our natural state is well being. When you purify the mind—meaning un-attaching yourself from the automatic conditioned negative tendencies or programs of behaviors, consider that you can return yourself to this natural state of bliss and experience of well being.

It is said that those who achieve a state of Self-mastery develop a powerful nervous system. The nervous system is the connecting link between the physical and the subtle bodies. Our thoughts take place in the subtle body and our feelings are experienced in the physical body through the nervous system. The mental-emotional body is often considered as one because our thoughts are the basis from which our emotions are expressed. Because we are "meaning-makers" our emotions are in response to the meanings we give our thoughts.

The great meditation guru, Swami Muktananda told his students,

> "If you want to know how to get rid of your anger, I will tell you. Don't be angry."

In the West where we invest so much in the analysis of our emotions and the processing of them in various therapies, we don't want to hear such a simple answer. Our minds can react to that kind of a statement because we have so much entrusted in the meanings we ascribe to our emotional states. Nonetheless you may be able to see just from practicing the Recreations that when you become the watcher and notice you are in an angry reaction, and you want to get rid of your anger in that moment—when you can watch your anger from the place of Awareness you can actually choose to just let go and move on to another state.

We always loved that line, *"If you want to get rid of your anger, don't be angry."* It's funny. Yet we do have the power to choose to move out of it and on. The more we are in the practice of noticing and interrupting Least-action Pathways that don't serve us and our purposes, the easier it becomes to simply not be angry! Anyway, this shows why the mental-emotional body is considered as one. It is also considered part of the subtle body because its existence is at a different vibratory rate of energy than the physical body.

In many traditions there is a Divine energy which gives life to us and everything in the universe. In Japanese it is called *ki*. In Chinese it is called *chi*. In Sanskrit it is called *kundalini*. In Hebrew it is called *ruach*. In Mayan it is called *Ik*. In English it is called *spirit*. Nearly every culture has a word for it. The Hawaiian greeting "aloha" which means love is derived from "alo" meaning presence and "ha" meaning breath, hence; "the breath of life." This Divine energy is called the "life force" or the power of the Self or of Consciousness. It is said when this life force energy is flowing freely throughout all the bodies we experience a sense of well being.

As a Multidimensional Being you realize you can approach any situation in life from any and many access points in the hologram. Each dimension contains it own "strand" of wisdom augmenting your mastery moment by moment. *Guna* is a Sanskrit word meaning "strand" or "quality." Ancient Indian teachings distinguish other aspects of our Multidimensionality through three qualities called the "*gunas*." The three *gunas* are *sattva*, the quality of light and quiescence; *rajas*, the quality of passion and action; and *tamas*, the quality of darkness and inertia. This wisdom teaches that all things in nature and we are composed of a combination of these qualities and that attachment to any of the *gunas* could lessen the flow of vital energy or life force. You can imagine this. Too much quiescence, quiet inaction (too *sattvic*) and nothing much get accomplished. Too much high-pitched action (too *rajasic*) and you wear yourself down. Too much inertia, resistance to action (too *tamasic*) and you get lazy and contract into yourself. On the other hand, if you are aware of each of these qualities in yourself and use them in a balanced way you keep your life force invigorated.

What enhances life force? Purity, clarity, focus, and awareness. We can feed our Multidimensional Being with good food, with healthy emotion, with pure thought, with spiritual connection, and with *the breath*.

There is a connecting force between all the various bodies and that is the breath. Much has been studied, researched, and written about the breath. The yogi masters of India have made a science of the breath. The breath is the link between the physical and subtle bodies, and it is the bridge that can integrate spirituality into everyday life.

The word "spirit" means the animating or vital principle that gives life to physical organisms, which comes from the Latin "*spiritus*" meaning "breath." The very force that sustains life and keeps us alive is in the realm of the invisible. It is known we can live without food for a few weeks, we can live without water for a few days—but we cannot live more than a few minutes without air, without breath.

If you watch any athlete you will notice he or she takes a deep breath before a critical play or action. For people in the various speaking and singing professions, learning the art of breathing is essential to the use of their voice.

It is said that the practice of deep breathing with conscious awareness has a purifying effect. A contemporary teacher from the East, Sri Sri Ravi Shankar, developed a workshop based on the science of the breath. He says of the special breathing techniques he teaches: *"The practice produces renewal on all levels, spontaneous joy, and an increased feeling of well being over time."* Sri Sri advises, *"... health can be regained by attending to the source of the mind, pure consciousness."*[40]

Physicians and yogis note that great healing responses can take place in all of the bodies through techniques of deep breathing. It is said that negative emotions and toxins stored from the past can be released through the practice of concentrated deep breathing. A concentrated practice of conscious breathing can have you experience being more present. It centers you. It can create improvements in your experience of well being. The cells of the physical body are oxygenated. This happens too with physical exercise, with aerobic exercise known to increase the efficiency of the body's intake of oxygen.

When you are tired from the runaway meanderings of your mind, of your excessive thinking, you can find a place of rest in the breath. When you focus on the breath, you connect with the source, pure consciousness, the place of infinite potential, the place scientists affectionately call "the quantum vacuum."

~~~

Imagine yourself as a 21st century Alice or Alex in Wonderland. You look around you from a place of stillness and awe and suddenly you have an epiphany. You experience the entire phenomenal world as one moving mosaic—a beautiful painting in flux, colors swirling, energy whirling, the whole universe fluid and moving. In this painting, the air you breathe is filled in with color as well, so you can see there really are no separations, only distinctions. You can see the air that appears to be external to the physical body and the air that you are breathing in, are really one and the same. This connecting force—this force that links all the bodies—is from the identical source, just as the air inside the balloon and outside the balloon are one and the same. You pop the balloon and the air is rejoined with its source.

Scientists search for the Unified Force, the one force that is the connecting link, the one force that is at the source of everything. In human terms we can say this Unified Force for human beings is Love. Just as love is a connector of everything and everyone, the breath is a connector of our Multidimensional Universe—Multidimensional Being. We want always to focus on Love, but right now for our Recreation we want to focus on the breath.

☙ QUANTUMTHINK RECREATION ❧
Live the Wisdom of
Multidimensional Universe—Multidimensional Being

Practice Relaxation and Experience
The Multidimensionality of Your Being

ONE»Three different times today sit down for five minutes and consciously focus on your breathing. Take ten conscious breaths. Breathe in slowly and deeply. Notice whether you fill your lungs and/or your belly. Between the inhalation and the exhalation, gently hold for a few seconds. Then exhale slowly. Practice conscious breathing three times between today and tomorrow. Notice how you feel afterwards.

TWO»As you are breathing consciously, contemplate the following:

Your breath is your connection to life and the universe.
Your breath connects all the dimensions of your being.
Your breath has the power to maintain your sense of well being.
Relaxation is a conscious practice.

~~~~~~~~~~~

QuantumThink-Wave
When People Do Bad Stuff

Do people do things of ill will because they *want* to, because they are bad or mean spirits? A lot of folks might chime in a quick "yes" to that question. However, you should have already seen and experienced along the QuantumThink journey that much of the time people are not really at choice. (And yes, "people" includes you and me, too.) It may appear that they are at choice but consider that aggressive and violent actions are stimulus-response reactions of a person in a state of deep Unawareness. You can ask yourself: *Would an awakened soul willfully wreak havoc on another human being?* Not likely. Then why do "good" people do bad stuff?

In addition to our own individual brand of Least-action Pathways there are *cultural* Least-action Pathways and the pull of culturally conditioned fields, subtle yet oh-so-powerful force fields. Lacking awakened awareness a person is subject not only to their own automatic ways but also to the automatic ways of a largely conceptual classical-mechanical culture.

The Dalai Lama has said, *"Without compassion no politician and not even a magician can save the planet."* What would happen if instead of disdain and vengeance we put forth compassion for those of us who seem to be the "worst" dregs of humanity? Could we generate a shift in the underlying pattern of our human field? It is certainly worth giving it a go. There is no benefit in denigrating yourself or others for having been in a state of Unawareness. Instead, rejoice that you have become aware! Realize that anyone can awaken. The tendency to label a person as "good" or "bad" might simply be another limit of outdated and automatic cultural thinking. This becomes crystal clear when you move From Either/Or to Both/And.

~~~~~~~~~~~

14 FROM EITHER/OR TO BOTH/AND
There are more things than dreamed of in your philosophy

The well known 20th century design scientist, environmentalist, and philosopher, Buckminster Fuller once said, *"We are not going to be able to operate our space-ship earth successfully, nor for much longer, unless we see it as a whole spaceship and our fate as common. It has to be everybody or nobody."*

Why did he have to remind people of this and urge people to see it this way? Perhaps because as we have been saying all along, in the classical view of the world we see ourselves as separate—separate from one another and separate from the Earth. A humanity whose thinking has been focused in a one-dimensional physical reality, restricted to what is gleaned only with the ordinary five senses, might not immediately experience the world and ourselves as one whole living organism as we now know it to be. Bucky Fuller was one of the people who began to speak a new world view into existence in his own work, looking from the whole to determine how we can achieve efficacy especially with regard to our Earth's resources. He knew that to invent new systems that make more sense for *all* of us meant seeing beyond the Either/Or "your way or my way" reality. What do we mean by an Either/Or reality? Let's see …

Should you classically think or QuantumThink? Do you love Buddha or Jesus? Was Moses a prophet or was Mohammed? Are you a Conservative or a Liberal? Is it better to work for someone or own your own business? Do you prefer hot weather or cold weather? Either/Or options are ubiquitous in life, the list as endless as the sky. Either/Or thinking appears innocent yet this thinking mechanism can be one of the most limiting when it comes to creating new solutions and resolving issues which arise from its very mechanism. Like a pendulum swing it's back and forth, back and forth until the two options inevitably wind down to a full stop.

Either/Or thinking has been known to fray friendships, families, marriages, business partnerships, and national alliances. Fortunately we now have the opportunity to move our thinking and ourselves to the rich, infinitely bejeweled quantum world of Both/And. Let's don our jeweler's lens and examine the facts and facets of such a move, tantamount to a world-altering transformation.

∽∾∽

The classical world view is said to be a world of Either/Or. If you think about it, in a model of reality that scientists said could be examined, defined, and then predicted and controlled, it follows logically that things would have to be *Either* one way *Or* the other. For how could you predict unless you could say definitively that something is Either this way Or that?

Since the early 20th century scientists have made numerous discoveries that proved much of the classical-mechanical world view to be incorrect. For example,

222 Do You QuantumThink?

they discovered that energy is not just particles of matter; it has Both a particle-like existence And a wave-like existence, and that you could not see the whole picture unless you see Both. When scientists first discovered this wave-particle duality they assumed it would have to be Either one Or the other, wave or particle. There was much debate over this among physicists of that time until Niels Bohr put forth the Principle of Complementarity in which he essentially stated that in order to see the whole picture you have to consider Both the particle aspect And the wave aspect.

What can this mean to us in mapping this on to daily living? We are no longer stuck with Either/Or options. Where there are no absolute truths about the way things are, or about the way a person is, then what we have is a reality where seemingly contradictory events are Both true at the same time. That's the Both part. "And" means many more events can and do have an equally valid existence as well. Sounds good. However, despite the fact that our scientific understanding of reality decades ago moved From Either/Or to Both/And, the Either/Or thinking mechanism has continued to dominate our decision-making and has literally given shape to the everyday collective realities we take for granted—institutions that form our societies, the very systems and processes that govern direction and outcomes for us around the world.

An Either/Or reality fosters positionality. Doesn't it? If you live in an organizing principle of Either/Or then you are going to be driven by the vortex of opposition and agreement. You would have to take *Either* this position *Or* that one. You are driven by the forces of:

> agree–disagree
> right–wrong
> good–bad
> like–don't like
> better than–worse than
> this–not that
> my way–your way

One of the things you could see about this view is that it doesn't really allow for or acknowledge Infinite Possibility. You would generally come up with one of the obvious options that fit into the pull or sway of that system.

If you are looking from a new world view you are looking from a reality of "no absolutes." Then to try to impose an absolute where it isn't appropriate you are going to end up with some degree of vulnerability or lack of cohesiveness in that system. You can see this in the judicial systems of many countries. A person is Either guilty—Or not guilty. Something is "the truth" or it isn't. Isn't that the way the system is built, on that kind of Either/Or thinking? In this system there is no looking from the context or perspective of each person to see that there could be more than one so-called truth simultaneously, even when on the surface the two or more "truths" appear to be contradictory. You can see that this type of judicial system is constrained by the Either/Or system of thinking from which it was born. We're not saying there is anything wrong or right about this kind of system; we are simply looking at the connection between the judicial system and the world view from which it arose.

Another example of what springs forth from an Either/Or thinking system is the notion of a two-party political process. If you adhere to the letter and not the spirit of democracy you are likely to be confined by the two-party system because it forces you to look from the positions or the point of view of the "side" you are on. In an Either/Or world, the mind will edit out everything that is not one of those options. That is the trained response of that thinking system. The very context of an Either/Or reality pulls for that. It isn't even that you are intentionally doing that. Even when you don't fully agree with the platform or policies of the party or a particular candidate, the force field of an Either/Or thinking system pulls you to take sides, automatically.

A political process is not a hypothetical "example" to illustrate the mechanism of Either/Or thinking. We are speaking of a real structure of decisive importance that governs our lives. The question becomes: how does one reconcile a dualistic system inside of a new world view? Looking from a Holistic reality where everything and everyone is interrelated and interconnected, where there are distinctions yet no actual divisions—consider that moving from a world of Either/Or to a world of Both/And could be moving from a context of right/wrong or good/bad to a context of what works, or *efficacy*. "Efficacious" means *"that produces the desired effect."* What if you could simply look from a context of *efficacy—from a context of what will produce the desired result*?

Either/Or thinking relates to events and occurrences as isolated incidents rather than viewing them in light of a whole process that's continually unfolding. When you look from the whole process rather than from your mind fixating on one issue or one event or one interaction between people, you can see how any one event fits into the overall scheme and evolution of the process. You look from and for "what will produce the desired effect," what will work for everyone, knowing that this is possible in the face of a broad range of varying views and even apparent opposition. You can acknowledge the validity of Both/And all. When government representatives work in service to citizens, they are working for everyone, dealing with *Both* of the two main political parties, all variations of those parties, *And* also with citizens who do not align with any party. With regard to working within a two-party political process it means being able to come to it with an awareness of this Both/And reality and distinguish that this is the game you are playing. When you think from a more encompassing context of Both/And, a reality of "no absolutes," you can see that each party with all of its variations offers valid perspectives and is not wholesale right or wrong.

This isn't saying you are going to get some kind of ideal world. There are hurricanes and tornados and floods in nature. However, when you can include all of it, it gives you some room to see the value of any perspective, the gift in it, even when in any one point in time it doesn't seem to be working. Consider this for yourself whatever your native country is. If we could see the value that each party and all views offer by looking from the whole, the efficacy of any political system would shift instantaneously. Context is everything. You could look from embracing the values which are common and universal. You could acknowledge the beliefs even when they are not *your* beliefs. You could consider the possibility even when you don't agree with the possibility. Rather than have to eliminate or automatically reject one or the other you could use all views to further the creative dialogue.

In the culture of business and corporate organizations you can also see how Either/Or shapes the structure:

> management–labor
> hierarchical organization–flat organization
> people oriented–profit oriented
> old economy–new economy

and the list rolls on.

In academia you hear people speak about the necessity for us, especially as students, to develop "critical thinking," to reflect upon ideas and systems in a way that transcends bias, prejudice, and pre-conceptions. From a new world view "critical thinking" is not merely using reason to weigh the pros and cons of various positions. How can critical thinking be possible unless you can think from Both/And?

You might be thinking that this raises all kinds of *my way–your way* questions. You could be wondering: Is there no value in deeming something "good" or "bad"? The key is *discernment* in the context of efficacy. What will work now, what is best now for all concerned. The great advantage to moving to a Both/And perspective is when you can see the fixed positions and attachment to obvious options, you can discern from conscious choice what is "good or bad" and also move beyond them to a higher octave. Viable solutions arise from your Intent for efficacy.

~~~

All right, then what is the efficacy of Either/Or? The principle of duality is evidenced throughout nature: hot and cold, dark and light, young and old, day and night. From an old world view we might see these complementary opposites as separate. From a new world view we realize they are one and the same in different states, opposite ends of the same spectrum. To know one is to know the other, its complement: duality and unity, heaven and earth, dry and moist, abundance and dearth. If you know black you can know white. In Chinese philosophy these dual principles are known as *yin* and *yang*, the masculine and feminine principles. In the symbol for *yin* and *yang*, ☯ a circle divided by a curved line forming identical complementary shapes, one side is black and the other side is white, representing the duality of nature. There is a small white dot within the black side and a black dot in the white signifying the presence of one in the other. The circle that forms the perimeter represents the unifying principle which encompasses them both. The quantum view tells us ours is a relational universe, that everything is accomplished through patterns of relationship. It is said that polarity kept in balance evolves and progresses us. It is when the resistance to one or the other polarity becomes out of balance that problems can ensue. Most important is the *relationship* between the dual principles. Viewed in this light Either/Or transforms from antagonism to rapport.

What does it mean to quantum leap to a world shaped by Both/And given that complementary forces are a fundamental essence of life? How do we reconcile the forces of Either/Or in the larger, more encompassing perspective of a world of Both/And? Other instances of where the Either/Or model shows itself can shed light on this for us.

Either/Or is the basis of most competitive sports. *Either* I win *Or* you do. And the competitor who is able to train well and demonstrate the highest level of excellence—the one who masters his sport best in the moment of competition, wins. At the same time the striving for excellence conditions the totality of the sport in such a way that future athletes entering that sport begin at a higher measure of excellence.

British biologist Rupert Sheldrake proposes a theory of *morphic resonance* that can explain this. Morphic resonance suggests that all similar structures from atoms to galaxies and everything in between including plants, animals, minerals and humans are interconnected through morphic fields (morphic means form), which accounts for their similarity and evolutionary effect on one another. In a collective and cumulative memory characteristic of morphic fields, the greater the similarity in form, the more each member of that field influences the field and is also affected by the field. In sports, for example, once a higher standard of measured performance has been achieved it becomes easier for future athletes in that sport to reach that performance level and go beyond it. Once Englishman Roger Bannister in 1954 broke the record and ran the first sub-four-minute mile in history, six weeks later Australian John Landy followed and broke Bannister's record. At one time running a mile in under four minutes was thought to be impossible. Now it's the standard for professional middle distance runners and has been lowered by almost seventeen seconds in the last fifty years. Such is the power of a field.

In nature organisms continually strengthen themselves in the face of elements that challenge them. So you end up with more highly evolved, developed species. As a graduate student in economics, Zack Lynch coined the term *co-ompetition*[41] to illustrate how both competition and co-operation are going on in nature's processes all the time. In fact, the presence and interaction of both of these forces is what makes evolution possible and what makes new products of nature emerge. What he is saying is that *only when you look at* Both *of these processes together—cooperation* And *competition—can we really understand how systems work*. From the point of view of natural systems we see again that an Either/Or approach does not accurately depict reality.

～～

What about for you and me? Either/Or thinking makes its appearance regularly in the personal decisions we make, in business directions we take, in collective views we mistake for "absolute truths." The automatic tendency toward Either/Or often leads to contradictions that defy common sense. Company leaders proclaim "people as their most important resource" than rush to cut the training and development budget first to reduce expenses, forgetting that the more personally and professionally developed people are, the greater the probability of profitability. In marriages, two people deeply in love split up over seemingly irreconcilable Either/Or issues. Could thinking from Both/And reduce the divorce rate?

We desire to be "in the moment." Yet if we stay isolated in the moment without attending to the big picture of life's continuum, we would certainly be disconnected from our purpose in the whole of life. In Chinese Taoist philosophy it is maintained that the individual should seek to be in harmony with the underlying pattern of the universe, the Tao, or "the way." According to Taoist philosophy, the Tao can neither be described in words nor conceived in thought. One has to do nothing strained, artificial, or unnatural. Through spontaneous compliance with the impulses of one's own essential nature, one achieves unity with the Tao and derives from it a mystical power.

To live in Both/And is to live in accordance with your essential nature. Yet in everyday life, how often do you feel you must make an Either/Or choice between two options? If you are making a career change and two opportunities are presented to you and you want to do both of them, what do you decide? Do you even consider it possible to arrange your life to do Both/And have everything you want rather than compromise?

People around the world are eager to know ... When will we achieve peace ... is it possible to achieve peace ... how can we achieve peace? Does peace begin within you or does its achievement lie in the hands of governments and political powers? ...

Consider the move to Both/And. When we limit ourselves to Either/Or we can miss the crucial point that it is *Both* our own inner state *And* the outer world between nation states that can bring peace.

From antiquity to modern times we witness Either/Or in private interest groups vying for their position. Endless debates over issues like climate change—is it caused by humans or a natural cycle? When you become educated about Sun-Earth cycles and you also research the scientific facts about the effect of our manufacturing and consumption practices on the Earth's atmosphere, you're clear it is a Both/And answer. Does it even matter who is "right" when you look from efficacy, from what will work now to take care of Earth, from *what will produce the desired effect*?

The value of Both/And thinking is boundless. We are at home with paradox: *We are powerful when our mind is quiet. Our mind is our life and we are not our mind. We are the watcher and the actor simultaneously.* Asking Either/Or questions precludes our capacity to think from Infinite Possibility. The move From Either/Or to Both/And is a leap to a new evolutionary cycle. In a Both/And reality you are creating solutions as distinct from merely solving problems. Solutions for healthy and harmonious and sustainable living spring forth from the Both/And world of Infinite Possibility.

Thinking from a Both/And world opens all manner of opportunity to redesign our institutions and societal systems in ways more congruent with the nature of reality as we know it in the 21st century. When you begin to view life from this perspective, you can include everything. *It doesn't mean you agree with everything;* it means you can *be* with everything for exactly what it is, part of the process. You can use whatever happens, you can use the differences and what appear to be problems; you begin to deal with them as clues in the game of Mastery.

Irish novelist James Joyce wrote:

> *A man of genius makes no mistakes. His errors are volitional*
> *and are the portals of discovery.*

As we allow in options that don't appear to "fit" our own views we are expanded by them. We have authentic compassion for other people's ideas, situations, dilemmas, and reactions to life. Both/And enables us to live in wisdom.

⌒ QuantumThink Recreation ⌒
Live the Wisdom of Either/Or to Both/And

Move from a world of Either/Or to a world of Both/And.

ONE»As you go about your day notice when the Either/Or mechanism shows up within yourself and between you and the people in your personal and professional life. In the moment you notice it, shift to a Both/And perspective. Watch what unfolds in the outcome when you do this.

TWO»Become aware of all the ways the Either/Or thought pattern shapes discussions, debates, news, media talk shows. Allow yourself to just be with it from a transcendent state of being the watcher.

QUANTUMTHINK-WAVE
Fashioning the Drama

What does it mean to live in an Observer-created Reality? It means reality is not just "out there" separate from us waiting to be described by some super-human one who "knows" the correct description. We are not separate, discrete objects who happened to be dropped on the surface of Earth to stand by and watch the show; we *are* the play. We actively participate in what shows up in our world. We have roles. We are the actors, as Shakespeare eloquently wrote, on this great stage. We are the protagonists, the leading ladies and gents. We are the ones fashioning the drama.

In an Observer-created Reality we are the ones *generating the learning*. We are not sitting back waiting for the knowledge to be infused into our memory banks. We bring about learning through our own ability to call forth our awareness of something in a fresh and novel way. This is becoming adept at A New World View of Learning—The Art of Distinguishing.

15 THE ART OF DISTINGUISHING: A NEW WORLD VIEW OF LEARNING
Realities are created

As the story goes ...

It is said that the Supreme Being or Divine Intelligence that many call God was all-encompassing and all powerful and all intelligent—and alone. So what God decided to do was to differentiate the Oneness into the many in order to realize himself, to make himself known. God differentiates from the One into the many in order to *experience* his very own Self.

As human beings endowed with the grace of creation, we too enact this process of differentiating so we can experience the richness of this abundant universe. To differentiate means to make specialized or distinct. To do this consciously with awareness is to practice what we call in QuantumThink *The Art of Distinguishing*. When we "Distinguish" we bring something into our awareness, from non-existence into existence, from the possible world into actuality. To Distinguish is to create realities.

Contemplate the many ways great thinkers and seers, saints, sages and scientists have characterized the way we bring reality into existence. It is said we *dream* reality. It is said we are *meaning makers*. It is said we are *shape shifters*. It is said we are *reality generators*.

What does it really mean to say "we create our reality"? Can you and I create a rose, a kangaroo, or a sunset? Not likely! That remains the dominion of the Divine creation principle, the ultimate mystery. However, we *can* create language that enables us to Distinguish a rose or anything else. We *can* generate awareness of any object or idea. We *can* direct Intent and attention and activate energy and resonant fields. It is in this sense we create meaning and our experience of a rose, its beauty and sublime fragrance—to become what we call *our reality*. Just as Michelangelo carved out his classic sculpture of *David* as he said because it already existed in the block of Carrara marble as possibility waiting to be actualized in form, we invisibly carve out possibilities from the infinity of creation.

There is a vast difference between imaginings that are figments of fantasy, and Distinguishing realities that are coherent with life. Coherent distinctions stem from presence of being. As QuantumThinkers you realize that purity in the atmosphere of your own being is essential.

~~~~~

You bring something into your awareness ... so where does this "something" come from? Where else than from the source of all creation, Infinite Intelligence. Leading edge science tells us we live in a nonlocal field of intelligence and energy. Spiritual sages say the world exists on the screen of our own consciousness. By now you know this from your own experience of working with the field consciously. When you Distinguish, you literally bring something into existence from the nonlocal field—from the possible world into the actual world. You choose a possibility. If you continue to hold that possibility you make it more established and thus you make it more real. It shapes your experience. If others join you in holding that same reality, it becomes even more entrenched and so begins to shape other peoples' experience as well. This happens not mysteriously at all; it happens all the time in simple, ordinary ways.

You have a friend who is an investment banker. One day this investment banker becomes keenly interested in spiritual literature and spiritual practices. He begins to Distinguish himself in his own speaking as a spiritual aspirant and later as a spiritual teacher. He enrolls in a doctoral program in the study of spirituality. Once attired only in designer suits and ties he now dons flowing unstructured pants and loose fitting shirts. His demeanor is calm and relaxed. Former clients, friends, and family who once related to him as an investment banker now come to him, not for financial advice, but for spiritual dialogue. He has shaped a different reality for himself and for those who know him. This is one typical way we create realities through Distinguishing—a process of transformation within the world of already established familiar options.

More pivotal to The Art of Distinguishing and our focus here is that we can literally bring something into existence for the first time. We can create something that wasn't in a person's awareness, and thus not even remotely a part of their reality until it was Distinguished for them.

Before we *Distinguished* QuantumThink as "a new system of thinking" the fact that you think in one *system* or another may not have been in your reality. In QuantumThink we ask a fundamental question: *If thinking creates our reality, then what creates our thinking?* We Distinguish that our mind and habits of thinking function within the parameters of beliefs and ideas we have "accepted" about the nature of reality called our "world view." When we Distinguish "thinking conditioned by a classical-mechanical world view" from "thinking conditioned by a quantum view" you experience that thinking is not "free" and independent; it is shaped by the world view in our awareness. The QuantumThink premise Distinguishes that since we have all been entrenched in the classical-mechanical Industrial Age world view, a limited, one-dimension view of reality as material, reductionistic, and mechanical—that our thinking has thus been conditioned in limited ways, often automatic ("mechanical") in our beliefs and in our ideas about what constitutes the nature of reality and how it works.

The Art of Distinguishing provides entrée to different realities. As soon as you Distinguish automatic conditioned patterns and habits of thinking, you go beyond them. The moment you Distinguish that the classical "old" world view is based in assumptions that have been proven to be mostly mistaken, you open yourself to discovering the more accurate and up-to-date principles. Thus,

Distinguishing awakens us to living in an expanded reality in sync with the world as it is today, attuned to what leading edge thinkers refer to as the *new world view*. Until you make these vital distinctions you have no way of accessing the full magnitude of what each thinking system makes possible in your life.

Distinguishing gives you visibility. When you Distinguish the old world view principles and the new world view principles in your own thinking in the moment they occur you give yourself a moment of pause … in which to choose consciously what you want to make real and energize in that moment.

Every day you wake up in one mood or another. When you Distinguish that any unappealing thought you have passing through is just a Least-action Pathway, a vestige of old mechanical habits—in that moment you are free to choose. You realize that a thought is connected to the entire experience for that day. Do you want to energize and thus sustain the reality of being in the doldrums, or will you "shape shift" and create a context of happiness for today? Unless you can Distinguish what's present, how can you create anything new? This is the extraordinary gift of The Art of Distinguishing; you have *immediate* access to generating realities. Distinguishing constitutes a method of Self-awakening. You bring yourself "present" because you can only Distinguish when you are consciously aware in the moment. This gives you creative command over your experience, your choices, your life, and your world.

Distinguishing integrates knowledge as part of you so you can access it anytime. Have you ever had an occasion when you're with someone you know well and on that particular day you both experience a deeper connection than you've ever felt before? The communication is fabulous, exhilarating, satisfying, profound. Afterwards you wonder how to get that kind of connection back again. The experience lives in your memory as something special yet you can't quite figure out how to re-create it. This is where Distinguishing is powerful. If you can Distinguish what had that connection happen you can generate that quality of relationship anytime with anyone. You might Distinguish, for example, that it was Listening From Not-knowing that made it possible. Rather than chalk this up to serendipity or that the stars looked favorably upon you that day, you engage The Art of Distinguishing. This is a subtle yet poignant difference in living consciously.

~~~

Contemplate:

When you Distinguish what you *do*, what you do becomes knowledge.

When you Distinguish what you *know*, what you know becomes wisdom.

When you Distinguish your *wisdom* you are living it.

~~~

Note that when we Distinguish we are not defining or analyzing nor are we prescribing how-to steps or any moral code of action. In an Observer-created Reality we realize there is no fixed way that something *is*. Therefore, when we Distinguish we are not attempting to describe any fixed attributes of reality. There is no need to define that which by its nature defies definition. Distinctions in this sense are not definitions; they do not describe a fixed state or detail "the way it is." Distinguishing is open-ended. Distinctions continue to evolve as we keep looking. You consciously observe something in a way that opens portals of possibility. When you can Distinguish between the *conditioned mind* and the *awakened mind*, you fling open the doorway to conscious choice.

Like having your own Hubble Telescope, Distinguishing lights through the dust clouds camouflaging your access to Infinite Possibility. You continue to see more and more of what's directly in front of you. When we Distinguish we bring something into our awareness in the present moment in a way that creates a reality, gives us an experience, opens a possibility, transforms our relationship to life.

When people hear about QuantumThink, itself a system of distinctions they ask: *What is a distinction?* A definition gives us a concept or a way to identify something whereas a distinction gives us the *experience* of it, important since it is through experience that we gain wisdom.

Imagine you are watching the news on TV or on the Internet. You can't help but notice that the emphasis or "spin" of most news stories is negative in tone. You step back from your own experience in the moment of watching and become aware of the "gloom and doom" effect on the state of your mind and heart. Lacking access to The Art of Distinguishing you can easily fall victim to the reportage. You might react (in the 1st Aspect of Knowing—Unawareness) by criticizing the news media or journalists. Perhaps you resolve indignantly never to watch the news again. What *experience* are you generating for yourself? Resistance, frustration, disappointment. Again, that is the automatic, reactive mode. What else is possible? You can practice The Art of Distinguishing and give yourself a totally different experience from the same set of circumstances, watching the news.

There are plenty of possibilities. You could Distinguish the pattern of negative slant news reporting as a cultural Least-action Pathway, an automatic and mechanical habit that news executives, producers, and reporters as well as viewers around the world have become accustomed to, fixed on the idea that on TV "grim spin" generates financial win. You could Distinguish this media habit as a product of old world view conditioning of focusing on "what's wrong." You could Distinguish the Least-action Pathway belief that in storytelling conflict is essential for making a story sassy. Whatever possible reality you choose, the point is with awakened awareness you can *Distinguish* the very same circumstances in a way that transforms your experience of a common everyday occurrence. You take yourself from a reactive state of irritation and frustration to a state of equanimity, clarity, and compassion. You don't have to get caught up in the circumstances. You generate a different kind of reality, a more desirable experience for yourself and others.

A critical point to glean here is that the reality we create this way *is not necessarily based in evidence*. Why is this so important?

Most of us would like to create a better world reality, a more evolved state of affairs than the one we have known throughout the history of civilization—a world without war where poverty and hunger are nonexistent, where people are productive and successful and happy, nourished in every way. If you base the possibility of such a wonderful world in common past-based evidence you might find it challenging if not deem it altogether impossible. Our minds are conditioned to "believe" that what already exists is the "hard truth" about life. You can laugh when you think about it: everybody wants a better world but very few want to believe it's possible. How often do you hear people say, *"Well, that's just the way it is."* How much do you use that expression yourself? That is the nature of a material-based world view. Old world view thinking tends to assess what's possible based on what we already "see" or believe. The more evidence we can find to justify that "it's always been that way," the more solidified is the belief. Toss in a few scientific experiments or a public opinion poll and now you are convinced, *"There is no way that can happen. There is simply too much evidence to the contrary!"*

Fortunately, the quantum world view overthrows the premise that the primacy of life is material. What we perceive as solid matter is actually nonmaterial at its source. Even so, the pull of sense objects (i.e., existing circumstances) is strong. If you are serious about wanting to create a peaceful world where all people are nourished and productive and happy, then this is where you go beyond even the deep impressions and encrusted beliefs of traditional culture and your own conditioned mind. We are speaking about global issues however this is just as applicable to any new reality you wish to create for yourself personally. If you base your dreams on current circumstances you surely plant yourself forever in the cliché box.

Many people argue for their limitation using brain science: *But my brain is wired that way; it's ancestral, it's given by our genes, our brains are set up that way. We're wired for war.* The paradox is that despite the most embedded "conclusive" evidence about "the way things are" the plasticity of the brain is a fact. We have the ability to interrupt neural patterns and create new connections. We can and do alter the neural circuits when we consciously Distinguish something novel. We have the capacity and the awareness to create entirely different realities. Isn't that what visionaries and pioneers, entrepreneurs and inventors have done throughout history?

We call The Art of Distinguishing "A New World View of Learning." Why do we need *A New World View of Learning*? What is "learning"?

There is a present-moment experience. Then there is something we call "learning." Learning in the way we ordinarily speak about it is a reflective act. We reflect back to the experience and we Distinguish something we gleaned from the experience. When we Distinguish what we do (i.e., our original experience), what we do becomes knowledge in the form of information. We can apply this information ourselves and/or we can pass along the learning to others.

Learning originally took place by oral tradition. Knowledge and wisdom were passed down by word of mouth in conversation. Eventually human ingenuity invented ways to give permanence and consistency to the knowledge. We devised symbols and words and ways of recording them in writing, printing processes, and digital storage. Knowledge banks have been accumulating exponentially ever since.

Traditional education has been focused on the acquisition of knowledge. We would gather information, organize it into text books, and teach students to memorize it so they could later apply whatever they could recall. Yet in our Information Age where data is infinitely increasing you can see the unworkability of even conceiving to learn by memorization. The most one could hope for is to specialize, to take one small area of this gargantuan, growing knowledge bank, assimilate it and attempt to keep up with it. This type of learning is obviously necessary. However, in our day-to-day lives, in our ordinary activities, to live in a world where the very essence of life is in continuous flux and change, isn't it incumbent upon us to expand our way of learning?

With the advent of computers and the Internet we no longer need to "memorize" information the way we once did. You and I are living in a universe of networks, a reality of never-ending webs and connections from the electrical circuits of our brains to the light circuits of our telecommunications. The entire collective mind of humanity is instantly accessible and amazingly so with a click. What kind of learning is appropriate in our new world? In this networked quantum age the ability to *connect* to information is as paramount as the ability to *collect* information.

Socrates used to tell his students he knew nothing. This was a curious thing to say for someone who is considered one of the great philosopher-teachers of all time. Socrates taught by asking the students questions and having them inquire until they arrived at the answers for themselves. The underlying assumption here again is that all knowledge is available to all of us; all we need do is connect to it. Since we are all a part of the Infinite Intelligence of the universe, if you are willing to expand your understanding of what this means, you could say that *real learning is simply a matter of becoming consciously aware of an aspect of your own being.*

—◦◦—

We can consider *Generating* the 5th Aspect of Knowing. We create distinctions all the time but until you "Distinguish" that this is what you are doing, the power of Distinguishing as a creative force can elude you. When you know yourself as a *generator* of distinctions and therefore of realities, you are in the 5th Aspect of Knowing, Generating. You are the one generating, discerning what something can be, and what it makes possible.

You become like a scientist. Scientists model realities from cosmic patterns and Distinguish them as natural laws so we can benefit from their insight. Quantum physicist David Bohm spoke of an underlying order of reality where everything is one interconnected substance. He *Distinguished* a "holomovement" of the universe, a movement of things unfolding into the ordinary reality we glean with our five senses and enfolding back into the hidden aspect of the possible world—continuing in this back and forth *holomovement*. Through Bohm's distinction we better grasp how we are interconnected as "one."

Distinguishing as *A New World View of Learning* illumines information. If you study the world's religions from an information standpoint you typically learn the beliefs, traditions, and rituals. However, when you Distinguish the world's religions you generate learning beyond the obvious facts. You create the *wisdom* of the information. You may become aware of the perennial questions people have asked since the beginning of time that led to the emergence of religion. Perhaps you see the common threads and the interconnections among all religions. You Distinguish the difference between the cultural understanding and the dogma and rituals of a religion. The Art of Distinguishing enables you to view religion as one expression of spirituality rather than identifying spirituality solely *as* religion.

Distinctions that seem "right" to us have coherence; they have consistency with life. The nature of life is to keep unfolding into ever-evolving knowledge and higher awareness, with the essential nature of our very own mind shaping new realities all the time. We are in a momentous time of revising, revamping, and re-creating our existing institutions and systems and the way we see and live in this world. As a generator of distinctions you can create distinctions that are coherent with the nature of life as it is for us today in our current state of evolution. To participate in A New World View of Learning is to connect to information and intelligence and through The Art of Distinguishing to integrate it and live the wisdom of it naturally. After all, what is the purpose of knowledge if not to live it, to make it practical and workable in our lives?

When you Distinguish you also create an access for others. A software company executive said when he shared the distinction From Either/Or to Both/And with his staff, *"I saw the power in that once people got the distinction, there was nothing I had to do. They started speaking in those terms, using 'intent' in speaking about their vision. I smiled to myself because I realized that once the distinctions were there, the right actions would follow naturally. I didn't have to force anything."*

In this world of increasing options and marketplace clutter the ability not just to describe but to Distinguish your business or your profession is invaluable. If you *describe* what your business does you provide information. If you *Distinguish* what your business makes possible for the customer or client you establish connection. Connection indicates clarity. When you are present to what makes your business unique, you also bring that presence to your customer. You are in effect setting up a field that attracts customers and clients who resonate with what makes you or your business distinctive.

Younger generations practice The Art of Distinguishing perhaps without realizing it. A teenager has an inspired vision that sees possibilities beyond the form of the current culture. Yet because there is little if any context created for young people to be able to see how their Distinguishing fits in to an overall picture of evolving society, their thinking tends to be limited by Either/Or thinking that compels them to find fault with the status quo—making their own view *right* and the previous view *wrong*.

Parents love to tell you how much they learn from watching their babies and what they learn from watching their 3-year-old or 5-year-old. But what happens later on when the kid grows up? What happens when that same baby becomes 10 or 15 or 21 years old? If you are a parent are you still watching to see what you learn from this person who is younger than you—your child? And if you are the younger child, do you have some thought that you know "better" than your parent, who you think is "out of it"?

Whether you are the mother or the child, manager or associate, teacher or student, husband or wife, government leader or citizen, now you realize that true learning is collaborative. You bring singular characteristics and perspective to the learning process. You generate the learning *together* from the quantum field, because that is your Intent.

Imagine that as we begin to learn through practicing The Art of Distinguishing, we speed our learning. We can be more effective. We would work in a context of collaboration to evolve the status quo. By mastering The Art of Distinguishing we can create our systems and structures anew and appropriate to the current era. We could create more workable realities rapidly. We could be and would be a compassionate society.

~~~

The shaman-sage, Hunbatz Men, Mayan elder and Keeper of the Knowledge, summons us: *It is time for all of you to become shamans.* Shamans are people who live in wisdom, he explains. What enables you to live in wisdom? You guessed it: practicing The Art of Distinguishing. In moments when wisdom flows through you and you articulate what you see to another, you know the joy and contribution of offering your wisdom in service.

Listen to this ancient sacred hymn from the *Rig Veda* call to us:

> "Oh heroic one, move forward with resolve
> to make this sacred offering of yourself to life.
> May you plant the banner of victory
> in the service of humankind."

Toltec wisdom points out that there are structures in nature to direct the otherwise free-flowing energy into form. Distinguishing can also be thought of as a "structure" directing the free flowing life energy into form so we can experience it fully. Distinguishing brings form that generates realities. Perhaps most significantly *Distinguishing integrates the knowledge as living wisdom—wisdom that is alive in you.*

Contemplate once more:

> When you Distinguish what you do, what you do becomes knowledge.
>
> When you Distinguish what you know, what you know becomes wisdom.
>
> When you Distinguish your wisdom you are living it.

You might be wondering, "What can *I* generate as a distinction?" You can begin with your own brand of wisdom. You have wisdom that is unique to you and that flows through you. Yes, you do. Have you ever just *known* something without understanding how you know it? Have you ever noticed that your particular vantage of an issue or situation or solution is different than anyone else's view on the same matter? It is as if you are the chosen vehicle for that knowledge.

Artist Peter Max calls himself the middleman for the painting. Spiritual teacher Punditji says in the clear state of presence you just sit and what needs to reveal itself will reveal itself like a song flowing through you. Dhyan Yogi whispers we should know ourselves as a hollow flute through which the wind blows and makes music. Wisdom is distinct from opinions or perceptions. It's the difference between living in the world of the senses and living in the world of deeper awareness.

To paraphrase Maximus, the hero in the movie *Gladiator: Who you are echoes into eternity.* Your wisdom matters. Your wisdom is needed now in this cooperative evolutionary process. When you know yourself as a generator of reality, when you Distinguish this for yourself, then being a catalyst in evolution won't puff up your ego—it will just be matter-of-fact. This is the 5th Aspect of Knowing: knowing yourself as a generator of distinctions, knowing yourself as a dreamer of reality, knowing yourself as maker of meaning. We can master this wondrous, divine capability by practicing The Art of Distinguishing.

QuantumThink Recreation
Live the Wisdom of The Art of Distinguishing:
A New World View of Learning

Know yourself as a generator of reality through practicing The Art of Distinguishing.

ONE»Three times today notice the difference between a description and a distinction.

TWO»Distinguish one "song of wisdom" that flows through you and write it down.

THREE»Practice The Art of Distinguishing together with another person while in a conversation, something specific that creates a new reality for both of you.

QuantumThink-Wave
You Are Happiness

Spiritual masters teach that our natural state is bliss. However, you can know this yourself from your direct experience. Did you ever just sit outside somewhere by a lake or stream or on a mountain, or even in your own living room, and you notice you are just blissful—for no reason? This is your natural state. You may have forgotten but this is the natural state of pure Awareness. You may call this "being in a good mood." Yet, this is your natural state.

What if everything was just fine the way it is? Whatever is going on in your life right now, whatever your circumstances, whatever is occurring in the world around you—all of it being just what it is—you are fine. This is your experience. You are happy, content, satisfied with yourself and your life, moment by moment. Isn't this what we all want, really?

Do you think it's too daunting to experience that all is well when circumstances appear otherwise? Remember that in an Observer-created Reality there are circumstances and there is the matter of how you are related to those circumstances. It is in that relationship of yourself to your circumstances where your power lies. Even though as it is said everything we do is for the sake of happiness, still it is not the circumstance itself that is the source of happiness. If you are in a relationship or a marriage and that marriage ends—if you have made that relationship the source of your happiness, you render yourself as rudderless on the sea of life, tossed about by the shifting tides. If your happiness is dependent on circumstances and you take the circumstances away, the situation, the job, the money, the girlfriend, the chocolate chip cookie, what happens to your happiness?

No matter what your external circumstances are, if the window of your mind is "cloudy" then even the most beautiful, sublime circumstances will not matter. Conversely, when you know yourself as the state of happiness—happiness as the natural context from which you live—then no matter what circumstances may arise, you remain happy.

Pure consciousness is blissful and free. Consider that you don't have to work on achieving bliss; you already have that. We only need to clear the meanings we give the thoughts getting in the way of us experiencing our natural state. It is like a window that gets cloudy and dirty. You don't have to get a new window to see out; you just have to clean the window. Then you can see again. Then you realize your natural state is happiness.

This world is called in Sanskrit the *lila* of Brahman, the play of consciousness of the Force behind all manifest existence. You have that power. Knowing yourself as the Observer in an Observer-created Reality, you can hold that your natural state is happiness. This is not positive thinking. This is tuning in to the great, formidable Power of your own Mind. Then you don't have to worry about what happens because you know yourself as happy, no matter what. If you lose your job, you can say you are happy and you lost your job. Perhaps you're not thrilled at first that you lost your job. You may be feeling down, you may be experiencing loss; however, your state of happiness is impermeable. Such is the power of your very own mind. Know that you *are* happiness. You can live in the experience that everything is always just fine and you are just enjoying the play.

Look at the sky. It's the color of love.—SADE

16 Emotions and The Power of Mind: Transcend, Transmute, Transform
Love from the inside out

A man was driving down a country road one day in a great mood. All of a sudden he felt a bump, and then a thump and he realized he had a flat tire. He got out of his car, looked around and saw no one. (These were the days before cell phones and tracking systems in cars.) There were no houses or stores and he wondered, "what am I going to do?" He searched in his trunk for a jack to change the tire himself and he realized he had no jack. Then he remembered—his friend, Fred, lived about a mile away. It was a nice day. He would walk over to Fred's house and borrow his jack, and come back and change the tire.

On his way to Fred's he began thinking. What if Fred wasn't home? ... No, it was Saturday, and surely Fred would be there, puttering around in his garden. Then he remembered, the last time he saw Fred, he didn't act that friendly. His mind continued on ... Now that he thought about it, Fred was kind of funny about his possessions. What if he didn't like the idea of loaning the jack? He kept walking, starting to feel anxiety now. Okay, maybe Fred would loan him the jack, but he wouldn't be happy about it. He would feel like he owed Fred something if he borrowed it. The man started to feel very uncomfortable, getting hot under the collar. Plus the fact, he thought, if anything happened to the jack, like he brought it back in worse condition than when Fred loaned it to him, Fred would *really* go crazy.

He saw Fred's house now a few steps away. And then he thought, either way, he would be made to feel like he was indebted to Fred for this small favor. He walked up to the house and knocked hard on the door. Fred opened it. Before Fred could say a word, the man looked as his friend and shouted, *"You can keep your stupid old jack!"*

This is an old story told by the TV actor-comedian famous in the 50s, Danny Thomas. Think of it as "the Danny Thomas and the Jack story." It illustrates something about The Power of Mind with regard to Emotions. This is a joke, but don't we do this all the time?

Emotions are powerful. But there is something even more powerful and that is the power of our very own Mind. In this distinction, we want to explore the relationship between Emotions and our own awareness from the perspective of a new world view, of course, to see what we can distinguish for ourselves toward enjoying a great life.

Lacking mastery, our minds are said to be like a drunken monkey, incessantly chattering away our judgments and opinions and interpretations. There is nothing wrong with this in and of itself. The only point is that it erodes our present-moment awareness. Mastery of the mind is not "mind control" in the sense of behavioral conditioning, the stimulus-response mechanism born of a cause-and-effect world. We are speaking of mastery that gives you choice, not a programmed conditioning that takes it away.

In mastery of the mind, we can bring the great power of our emotions into our own hands and use it to our advantage. Some people may not like this idea, that you can master the power of your own emotions. They might prefer to think of emotional life as "free" and spontaneous. But let's go further. Let's remain open to what might unfold in the dialogue.

To master the mind you would need to know something about the workings of the mind. One asks, what is the mind?

> Some people think the mind is the brain.
> Some people think the mind is its psychology or the intellect.
> Some people think the mind is consciousness.
> Some people think this kind of conversation is too deep—why should I have to know my mind? Of course, if you are engaging in QuantumThink, you are probably not in that last group.

However you define the mind everyone would agree the mind is the great instrument of our human life. In Eastern traditions the mind contracts to become what we experience as our individualized form of consciousness, and therefore contains all the attributes of consciousness. Consciousness is free and blissful and aware. In QuantumThink we consider the mind that way. Where cutting edge science and spirituality are drawing closer is on the idea that it is consciousness which creates the manifest physical reality, and not the other way around. Consciousness is the primacy of life.

Consciousness takes on the attributes of whatever you are aware of. The mind takes on whatever you fill it with; hence, *as you think, so you become.* To know the mind it behooves us to notice what habitually fills our mind. What there is to master is the activity of our very own mind. A powerful aspect of our mind is our emotional response to life.

"Emotions" is an emotional topic. Did you smile inside at that silly pun? It does demonstrate something about emotions right here at the start: that emotions are *a response to meaning.* And since we are living in an Observer-created Reality, we are the ones ascribing the meaning.

There are many new so-called disorders being invented all the time. "Attention deficit disorder." Did you ever notice that once a new disease or disorder has been labeled the incidence of that disorder rapidly increases? This is the dynamic of an Observer-created Reality. *You **will** find what you are looking for.* What you focus on expands. The more you go looking for a "disease" the more incidence of it you will find. This is the universal principle—the Observer effect. Your own consciousness in the form of your individual mind is creating the reality. Even when we distinguish ourselves as QuantumThinkers, our old world classical conditioning may resist this. We may not want to accept that what we hold in our consciousness has *that much* effect in the outer reality. Yet, it does.

There is something called "body dys-morphing disorder" where people think there is something wrong with their body when there really isn't. Their thoughts are so strong, and they have no mastery over their own mind, so they might see marks on their face when there really aren't any.

All these disorders are being labeled where a person's mind seems to go out of control. Then the scientists in their laboratories study the physiology of these people and they say, oh, there is a hormonal imbalance or there is a faulty brain connection. Of course now that the person's thoughts are driven to this Emotional state, the scientist is likely to find the electro-chemical correlates of that state. But they may have the cause of the imbalance backwards.

The Dalai Lama tells the story of when he visited with a group of physicians at a university medical school. They were talking about the brain and stated that thoughts and feelings were the result of different chemical reactions and changes in the brain. The Dalai Lama asked them: is it possible to conceive the reverse sequence, where the thought gives rise to the sequence of chemical events rather than the other way around? He was surprised to find a scientist answer that they start from the premise that all thoughts are products or functions of chemical reactions in the brain. What he noted was their rigidity not to challenge their own thinking.[42]

We are not saying that if a person has such a disorder that they shouldn't be treated with some type of medicine that can balance the chemicals. This would be foolish, indeed. What we are saying is that if we can get greater insight into the way our Mind works to create the Emotional responses we have, we can interrupt those mechanical Emotional patterns that do not serve us, and we can connect to a higher aspect of our Emotional selves.

~~~

Emotions can be said to be the "charge" or power, like an electrical charge powering the Intent. "Emotion" means *energy in motion*. Emotions are a response to the thoughts we have and the meanings we give to those thoughts.

Emotions are experienced in the body as kinesthetic feelings. Emotions have electro-chemical physiological correlates that we experience, and that can be measured with scientific instrumentation. Distinguished holistic research physician and neurosurgeon, Dr. Norman Shealy, tells us, *"Emotions are physical feelings ... they are physical reactions to mental attitudes and beliefs."*[43]

Emotions give us information. They speak to us. If you want something, and at the same time you are thinking you cannot have it, in your emotion you feel "doubt" because these two thoughts—*I want it. I can't have it.*—are out of harmony, not flowing in the same direction. In this sense your emotions inform you. They let you know when you are out of sync with what you desire. Experts tell us emotions are reflected in our posture and our spinal alignment. At the instinctual level, emotions help us avoid danger or harm and can even save our life. So emotions are an important communication system, a Personal Central Intelligence Agency of our being.

Emotions have energetic emanations in the subtle energy body. This is the energy we feel from another person. If we have a thought and we give that thought no meaning *in the sense of being attached to that meaning,* then our emotional response is a lot different from those cases where we attach a stronger meaning to it, one where we are personally invested.

You can see it in this matter of emotions that even if what the mind thinks is not real in the physical manifest sense, still we will stimulate an emotional response. This is what happens every time you watch a movie. In the movie *Jaws* the writers and the producers and directors and actors and lighting and sound and set designers take you on an emotional roller coaster ride. Don't they? When you leave the theatre you know this did not happen in your life. It was a movie. Yet, the emotional power may have been just as strong.

There is a story that many spiritual masters tell: You see something on the ground, and it looks like a snake. The fear response shoots through your body. You may freeze on your spot. Then you muster enough nerve to get closer to it, and you discover it is just a piece of twisted rope. This is The Power of Mind. The Power of Mind is formidable.

~~~

We live in an energetic universe, and we are energetic beings, moving energy into and through the physical body and outward. Dr. Shealy says it this way:

> "We are a walking crystal. A crystal is piezoelectric material. This means it converts physical pressure into electricity. You can feel the vibration of people speaking.
>
> "Every bone in your body is vibrating. Every tendon is piezoelectric. Our body is a walking crystal. We store electro-magnetic energy. We can receive, we can transmit and we can store electro-magnetic energy."[44]

From a perspective of a new world view, that everything in the universe and we are energy in flux, an aspect of mastery is to learn to work with our own energy. Because energy is convertible, we can also transform energy. Since the emotions are powerful energy, we can learn to work with this energy.

We can say that emotion is electrically charged energy. We even use the expression, "an emotionally charged" experience. The nature of energy is that it is in flux. Emotional energy trapped in the body is known as stress or tension. To remain in a healthy state, energy needs to flow. Since emotion is energy, it is important for our well being to keep our emotions moving and conscious. Neuroscientist Candace

Pert, renowned for discovering the opiate receptor, the bonding site for endorphins in the brain, and for demonstrating that the mind is in every part of the body, states: *"I believe that emotion is not fully expressed until it reaches consciousness."*

In QuantumThink we say that we are in a time of an evolutionary shift unlike any we have witnessed before in the history of humankind. And that the nature of this evolution is in the evolution of consciousness itself. Looking at Emotions in this context we can say that from a perspective of an old world view, the classical-mechanical world view where we see things and each other as separate—we could say that Emotions experienced as automatic reactions to circumstances are in a lower evolved, mechanical-like state. This means you have a stimulus-response type reaction to an external circumstance. You are not willfully generating this type of emotional response. It is happening as a result of past conditioning or association with that stimulus.

Consider that in a lower evolved state the emotions are a reaction to circumstances. Even positive emotions react in a stimulus-response fashion. They are so quick. The meaning associated with the emotional response may not be spelled out in a sentence. It can occur all at once like a gestalt, *a meaning field,* a holistic configuration where the parts cannot be separated out from the whole at all. To see this is to experience this in your own being. You will have an opportunity to do this in the Recreation.

You can see that in a lower evolved state, emotions are consistent with seeing the world as a world of parts where we are separate from one another and from everything else. Jealously, for example, can only exist if there is another to be jealous of. The sages say, where there is "another," there is fear. Otherwise fear cannot arise. So the sense of separation is the cause of the arising of many negative states associated with emotions.

〜〜

Since the universe is Holographic, evolution itself can be seen in any aspect of life. Emotions can evolve as well. We can take just the following examples.

In a higher evolved state:

Sympathy becomes Compassion.
Sentimentality becomes Empathy.
Lust becomes Passion.
Thanks becomes Gratitude.
Likes and dislikes become Appreciation.

There was a great saint of old, Bhagawan Nityandanda, for whom it was said people came from miles to be in his presence, even though he rarely spoke to them. Nityananda said: *"The heart is the hub of all sacred places. Go there and roam."* The higher Emotions are not simply passing fancies; they are the core of our being.

What there is to master is your very own Mind. This does not mean you don't feel. It means you feel even more deeply because you are conscious of what you are feeling rather than being knocked out by it. You can allow the energy of the emotion to flow rather than resisting it or restricting it. Then the energy is not stuck. Energy stagnant or stuck creates toxicity. You can see this with stagnant water.

Emotions are responses to the meaning we give our thoughts. You can generate a new meaning for the very same thought and give yourself a new emotional experience. You have a jittery feeling about an upcoming event, you call it "anxiety." You become aware of this and you make up a new meaning and you refer to the jitters as "excitement." You've transformed the energy of your Emotions from a negative state to a positive state. It is known in brain science that when you do this you change the neural connections in your brain and the chemicals in your body follow suit. This is The Power of Mind.

—~~

When you fully experience your emotional responses to life you are not trying to control them in the sense of forcing them one way or another. You are simply watching them. In this state you are not identifying with the emotion; you are centered in the state of Awareness.

The state of awareness is said to be the place of the Highest Emotions—the place of Love, Compassion, Kindness, Joy. According to research done on the heart-brain connection and the importance of what is now known as "Emotional Intelligence," when we become focused in the heart—in the loving, caring emotions, the brain and heart become entrained in a coherent state of focus. This coherence shows up in the electrical brain and heart wave recordings.

As we QuantumThink, centered in *conscious awareness* we find ourselves naturally in the state of Love and Compassion and Kindness and Joy, because these higher emotions are considered the attributes of the Self, that is, of pure Consciousness itself.

People tend to think of emotions as "positive emotions" or "negative emotions." Joy is good, anger is bad; anxiety is bad, love is good. From a new world view there is no absolute reality "out there." Reality is Context-dependent. Therefore, anger in and of itself is not negative. Anxiety in and of itself is not negative. Rather than classify emotions in and of themselves as positive or negative we can make a distinction between the emotion itself and the *effect* of the emotion on our state. We can begin to see emotions *as affecting our state* negatively or positively. And this has everything to do with the *meaning* we give to our thoughts.

For example:

When you have an Intent for excellence in sports in order to get to the next level, anger can be good; you can use it.

The emotion of love can become negative if it becomes obsessive love.

The emotion of anxiety can become positive when you are excited and energized watching your favorite athlete or team win.

People sometimes enjoy great pleasure in feeling sadness or melancholy deeply in their being. You can experience this when listening to some great classical music or listening to jazz or blues. You can become sad watching a touching movie or witnessing an act of compassion. We may not consider sadness bad or negative in these instances. Even jealousy can become positive when a context is created for it. Just watch one of the classic Italian romantic comedy films with Sophia Loren and Marcello Mastroianni.

In this time of Conscious Evolution, the indication is we are moving toward consciously living in this sacred state of the heart. *In the event, we aren't there yet, let's see what we can do.*

What keeps us from living in that state of the Self, the state of the Higher Emotions?

YOU KNOW HOW IT IS . . .

You sit around and read a lot of philosophy and inspirational things, and you're thinking, gee, that sounds good. And then you hear the phone ringing, and you're being called into an emergency meeting; you get a text from your girlfriend saying "it's over," and you're thinking about the client you just returned from seeing who made it perfectly clear about his dissatisfaction with something you're sure you have no control over. But you're sitting here reading *Do You QuantumThink?* and we're telling you if you can live in new distinctions—embrace a new world view—this is all going to work out. So what happens now that you've worked up these Emotional states?

We have distinguished Intent as the active dynamic of creation, and Allowing as the passive dynamic. We have another power and that is the power of Attention. If Intent creates, then Attention energizes. What we put our Attention on expands. We add mass to wherever we focus our Attention. In QuantumThink we have our attention on becoming more aware and awake, more consciously aware. Yet, *conscious awareness alone is not mastery.* Mastery is a practice, a moment-by-moment proposition.

We are energy beings. An aspect of mastery is becoming masterful with using energy, with converting energy states in the moment it is appropriate to do so. Emotion is energy. Since energy is convertible, when we are consciously aware we can use this Emotional power to our advantage. The sage says, *Use everything to your advantage.* Whatever happens, we can use it. You cannot get rid of energy. And of course, we do not want to suppress it or dam it up in any way. We want to keep the energy moving. If the energy is not in the form most conducive to a great life, what can we do? We can convert it.

WE CAN CONVERT THE TENSION.

Many people today are being taught to meditate to reduce tension and alleviate stress. When we connected to our Multidimensionality we practiced a deep breathing technique which also has the effect of inducing relaxation. Meditation is a great practice. Maybe you can't always sit down and meditate, but you can always become aware of what you have your attention on and shift it. *You can bring about a state change anytime, anywhere.*

We can ask ourselves, how can we use our tension? Since everything is energy, then tension is energy. The nature of energy is that it is convertible. It can be converted or transformed into another state of energy. Just as food is energy which we can take the nourishment from and release the unusable part, tension is psychic energy that can be used as nourishment and the unusable part released. We can transmute the energy. Transmute means you take something from a lower, base state into a higher state.

Tensions kept in their lower state become static on the radio of our being. We affect others with our energy. We radiate according to what we have our attention on. One of the most powerful energies we emit and transmit to others is our Emotional energy, including our tension, without realizing the extent to which we affect the people around us.

There was a spiritual teacher in New York known as Rudi. He called tension "energy under pressure." He told his students, *"If you are talking to the tensions of somebody, you stop relating. You are feeding your energy into the tension and the tension will grow. The minute you identify with it, you are feeding it. You become one with the tension. But if you can detach, what you are consciously doing is not allowing the tension to connect with you. You are denying that connection because you wish for a deeper connection."*[45]

If you can detach yourself from the tension, then you don't identify yourself with it. You do not have to feed the *tension* with your *attention*. When you notice it in this way, you can release it. You can release it if you do not identify with it. When you do not identify with it, you can use the power of it. You can refine the energy of tension; you can convert it. You can *transmute this energy.*

The alchemists took the baser metals and turned them into gold. If a tension arises you can use the intense power of it to take yourself to the next level of awareness. You can use it as a portal, as a clue. You can ask yourself, *What is it I am supposed to be seeing here? What is the purpose of this particular tension?* Remember, Emotion gives us information. You can ask yourself what the message of this tension is to you, whether it is your own tension or someone else's. You can use it to bring yourself consciously awake. Then you can put your attention on (that is, *energize*) what you want rather than what you don't want. What you focus on expands.

Once you transform that energy you can literally take a deep breath and release the unusable part of the tension. In this way, you convert the energy of a "tension" into an energizing "attention." The sage says, *Use everything to your advantage.* A champion tennis player or golfer finds a way to win even if they are playing on an "off" day.

There is the legendary story put forward as "true" yet discovered to be modern fable. People are so inspired by it they continue to tell it anyway. The story is of the night the virtuoso violinist, Itzhak Perlman, played a concert in Lincoln Center with only three strings on his violin instead of four, when one string broke after he got on the stage. The writer who chronicled this "occasion" says he closed his eyes, breathed in, and then went on to play the most sacred and divine music ever. Later when questioned about it, Itzhak Perlman said, *"You know, sometimes it is the artist's task to find out how much music you can still make with what you have left."* This is the essence of mastery. Emotion is energy. Mind gives you choice. Emotions and The Power of Mind. Use everything to your advantage.

⊚ QuantumThink Recreation ⊚
Live the Wisdom of Emotions and The Power of Mind: Transcend, Transmute, Transform

ONE»Today, practice tuning in to every Emotional experience you have. As you go about your day, and have all the varying experiences and activities that comprise your day, tune in to your Emotional states as they are occurring.

If you have a conversation with someone, notice what happens in your body, and become aware of the Emotion in your experience.

If you are watching a movie or TV, become aware of your changing Emotions as you respond to what is on the screen or to what is being said.

If you are practicing a sport, or walking in nature, or singing or dancing or whatever you do, notice your Emotional state. Feel the experience of it in your body.

If you are thinking about something, and your mind gets wrapped up in it and taken away by it, notice your Emotional state and feel what this feels like in your body.

TWO»At least one time, Transmute your Emotional energy. Especially in a situation where you are hooked by a negative emotion—either your own or someone else's—when you notice yourself stuck in a Least-action Pathway Emotion or stressed by anything, Transmute the energy to create a state change. In the moment, ask yourself how you can use Emotions and The Power of Mind to your advantage. Be guided by your own higher Intelligence.

THREE»Consciously generate an Intent to develop further one of the following:

Emotional Attributes of the Self

Of these Higher Emotional states associated with the heart, notice which one you are least attuned to. Then, if you wish, generate a conscious Intent to develop one of these deeper in yourself. Note: There is nothing to "do" here—except self inquiry, and conscious creation of an Intent—to Allow to unfold for the rest of your life, *if* you so choose.

Love
> This does not mean falling in love, like romance.
> This is Love for humankind and all of creation.

Kindness
> This does not mean being nice to someone.
> This is Kindhearted as a way of being.

Compassion
> This does not mean feeling sorry for someone.
> This is Compassion for the human being trying
> to make sense of existence and their life.

Joy
> This does not mean being happy with your circumstances.
> This means knowing yourself as the state of Joy,
> regardless of the circumstances.

Have fun with all of these and really allow yourself to be immersed in the conscious experience of your Emotions and The Power of the Mind.

QuantumThink-Wave
Revolutions of Evolution

Evolution happens all the time. Think about it. You have evolved through so many cycles in this one lifetime alone. In your physical body, of course, that's obvious. What about in your emotional life, in your emotional body. The way you think about things, the tastes and preferences you have now compared to what they were five years ago, ten years ago. Perhaps you have become more worldly, more sophisticated. Once you shunned classical music, now you are a patron of the philharmonic in your city, or the opera or ballet. As a teenager you only wanted sex and rock and roll. Now you're older and you still want sex and rock and roll. Just kidding. Now you want a meaningful relationship with someone who shares your values. Evolution takes its course through so many different areas of life.

You know two people and they are both the same age. Their chronological age is 50 years. One is like a 20-year-old in the way he dresses, his social life, his interests in the world, his activity level. The other is like a 70-year-old. He sees himself heading toward the latter stages of his life. He dresses in an "elderly" fashion. His interest in worldly affairs is waning. He stimulates few if any new interests for himself, resigned to be in waiting mode as the wind-down occurs. The other 20-year-old in spirit is thinking about starting a new business. He has a vigorous exercise program. His friends are twenty years his junior. Two people the identical age and they are as different as they could be. Still another way that "thinking creates reality" in our Observer-created world. The quality of our thoughts, the habitual ways we think about ourselves and our life express themselves in our spirit, in our activities, in the lines on our face, in what we attract into our resonant field. What creates evolution for us as people? An expansion in our awareness. We can choose this, *consciously.* Think about it.

17 CONSCIOUS EVOLUTION
Wake up on your own or by an alarm—you choose

What is life?
How did it get this way?
Who are we?
What is our purpose?

We can imagine that since humankind could reflect we have attempted to figure out the nature of reality. All these questions have been around forever in the background of everything we do. Ultimately, life is a mystery. It may be forever a mystery. Perhaps this is God's cosmic joke. It's a good joke, though, because it leaves us to explore forever into infinity.

How we got here and why, we don't know, though we attempt to find out. We do this through scientific exploration and discovery; we do this through religion, we do this through personal inquiry and through direct experiences that we call "mystical." There is one thing we can say and that is, there is evolution. Here we are speaking about evolution very specifically in the context of a process present everywhere in life.

What is evolution? Evolution is a process of unfolding, defined as "the unfolding from its original state to its current state." Evolution is development to what we would consider a better state. We could say that evolution appears to be the natural order of things at a very fundamental level. At least this is the word we use to describe this continual unfolding of every aspect of life from the beginning of time.

Over the millennia spiritual masters have admonished us, *Wake Up!* The notion is that we have been in the stage of evolution that has rendered us in many ways mechanical, living as sleepwalkers in a hazy dream of existence—rather than in the experience of an awakened state of consciousness.

Until now in QuantumThink, we've presented the reason for our mechanical ways as a result of being conditioned to think from a mechanistic world view, known as the classical-mechanical world view. We have said that the old world view that began in the 17th century trained us to see life in that picture of reality, as a material universe of parts that fit together in a mechanical, machine-like manner. We have also said we now have a new version of reality based on more accurate and modern knowledge, the quantum view. And we can condition ourselves to think in sync with this expanded and very different reality known in the quantum age.

Now we have a different twist on this.

～～

Did the old world view just show up? Where did it come from? In an earlier QuantumThink distinction we heard the Kabir quote, *"Most know the drop is in the ocean, but most do not know the ocean is also in the drop."* This says what a Holographic universe is all about. The whole is present in every aspect of itself. As human beings we contain the whole of the world and we also reflect the whole of ourselves in the greater whole, into the external world that appears before us. *We project ourselves in the world through our creations, and then we condition our own minds again according to how we view the world through those very creations.* World views are like evolutionary feedback loops of thought, energy, and information. Everything in a Holographic universe exists in some form in everything else. If we can invent Evolution, Evolution must be "there" in us as a possibility to be invented.

Consider this:

If we, as a human culture, were evolved to the point of our mechanical-rational aspect of ourselves, then in the context of a Holographic universe it makes sense that we would project that mechanicalness onto the world outside of us through our ideas and inventions and artifacts—and as our world view.

We could imagine that it is we ourselves who projected the model of a universe as a machine, based on the fact that we ourselves were at the level of evolution that functioned in a mechanistic, machine-like manner. Since the drop is in the ocean and the ocean is in the drop: *We could imagine that we projected a mechanical view of the world into our society, and in turn, that the industrial age view produced by that view conditioned our thinking inside its machine-like perspective.*

~~~

If nothing is separate from anything in the universe, then you can say that everything we create, our inventions and our artifacts, are extensions of ourselves. The car is an extension of our legs. The computer is an extension of our brain, the Internet is an extension of our "One Mind." Plays and movies are extensions of the roles and personas we play in life. We could say that even the fiber optics we invented to transport information using light—is an extension of our DNA, those strands only a 50 trillionth of an inch wide that carry all the information of who we uniquely are. In a very real sense, what we create are reflective externalized extensions of ourselves. A man and woman marry and have a child. The child is an extension of the parents' bodies, the ova and sperm. The child develops in many dimensions and eventually reflects back to the parents by teaching them what he or she has learned.

Swami Muktananda said, *The world is a palace of mirrors.*

Consider that the mechanical world view was just an extension of the level of Evolution humankind had reached for the most part at that point. Life needed to be analyzed, organized, and categorized in order for us to survive. We externalized ourselves in the world by creating orderly systems, analytical models, and machines that were based on our own collective level of consciousness. We were mechanical as a whole and this is what the intelligence of humankind was able to distinguish at the time, the magic and genius of the classical-mechanical age that influenced all our societal and scientific disciplines.

Our psychology was based on that, from Freudian analysis to the behaviorism model of stimulus-response. Our art and music were based on that, with the severity that the Neo-classical art movement was known for, and the clean and clear, precise music of the classical composers. Our education was based on that, as it was divided into various disciplines and subject matter. Our science was based on that, by dissecting critters and isolating chemicals. Our government was based on that, including the separation between church and state. Our medical profession was based on that, by seeing the body as a machine with its various parts that you could fix, one at a time.

~~~

You can see how the world view shapes the world you and I live in daily. On a personal level, we would see each other as separate, our determinations as black or white, our options as limited to what we ourselves had jurisdiction over and could control. So this idea that our results and what we think we are capable of is shaped and limited by our world view is not a dry theory; you can see this present and alive all around you.

Now, if we are coming to a new state in the evolution of ourselves—in a new world view reality—then we can begin to see the development of a scientific model and society that is based in an Observer-created reality. Our technology and our artifacts have already been thrust out ahead of us to teach us. Perhaps this is how we wake ourselves up.

This is why everyone continues to quote Einstein when he said the level of thinking which gave us what we have is insufficient to dealing with it. Our technology and our artifacts and inventions, our extensions of ourselves, the offspring of our current culture and state of evolution, are thrown out into the world so we can see who we have become.

We invented the Internet. It is an extension of our nonlocal consciousness. Now the Internet reflects back to us, and we learn that the nature of reality is spaceless and timeless, chaotic and self-organizing webs and networks, continuously in flux, and requires the use of all the dimensions of our being, including our Intuition and logic combined, to effectively deal with it. The Internet shows us that we live in a universe of Infinite Possibility, continuously expanding. It teaches us that the accumulation of information in our "local" mind is no longer feasible nor is it necessary.

We have distinguished "our new twist"—that we externalize a world view according to our stage of evolution. Let's take this a step further. You could say that the machinery that emerged as extensions of ourselves is what enabled the *next* level of evolution. Because of machinery we became physically freer. As we became freer on a physical level we were able to go to the next evolution of our intellect and spirit. We advanced to the higher quantum mind that could now invent computing, fiber optics, deep space travel, and the Internet.

The days of repetitive functions for human beings are coming to an end. Smart, computerized machinery can handle it. Rote learning—learning something so you can repeat it back later—is over for students, irrelevant for young people living in the global Internet information society.

Look to your own mind. That is what we are doing here. Breaking free of and releasing the mechanical habits that are no longer relevant. We're breaking free of the conceptual reality so we can re-connect to the heart. We are freeing our energy for increased and higher functions of Mind, Emotions, and Awareness. The classical-mechanical world view brought us a great, organized, mechanized life, and now it is time to expand.

If, as we are suggesting, that all we can "know" is that there is evolution—in our personal lives this translates as the continual learning and development for our own evolution, a perennial flowering and blossoming of our own selves.

There are many different kinds of evolution. We tend to think of physical evolution which happens over long stretches of time. Various theories of biological evolution focus on an organism's ability to *adapt* to its environment. Now we are in a time of evolution that has to do with an evolution in consciousness itself. We can make an important distinction between *adaptive* evolution and *Conscious* Evolution. What we are saying in QuantumThink is that to attempt to *adapt* to our new world view is possible but it may not be very effective. It would be something like watching a film where the sound track is one frame behind the visual film. It is out of sync. The picture of new reality is always one step ahead.

Conscious Evolution can be instantaneous. What can move faster than the speed of light? Anything that is nonmaterial. Our consciousness is nonmaterial and can be considered to move *superluminally,* faster than the speed of light. Or perhaps more accurately stated, consciousness doesn't actually "move" in the sense that we ordinarily think of movement in space, time, and matter. Consciousness shifts. Consciousness changes states. Consciousness connects. The effects are immediate.

Can we evolve our own biology consciously? Perhaps. There are studies being done on the effect of consciousness on DNA. Whether or not the completion of the human genome sequence is a factor in the speeding up of biological evolution, and whether or not this is a cogent idea, remains to be seen.

For our own practical purposes though, for you and me in our everyday lives the one thing that we happily have jurisdiction over is our own consciousness, our own mind. We *can* evolve our own consciousness. We can awaken to clearer states. *As you think, so you become.* As you evolve your own mind and awareness you unfold a sublime destiny of what you can become. The irony of an evolution of consciousness is that it must be consciously chosen. Then what exactly are we choosing?

In this Multidimensional universe of Infinite Possibility there are many ways we could distinguish Evolution. For simplicity and focus let's use the following four ways to distinguish it.

We could say there is in the largest sense, Cosmic Evolution.

Cosmic Evolution relates to the entire natural universe, of which we and all the rest of the hundreds of billions of stars in this galaxy and billions of other galaxies are all a part of. We are made of the same stuff as the stars.

We could say there is Universal Evolution.

Universal Evolution is the evolution of humanity at large, as a whole. In the distinguishing of a new world view and learning to QuantumThink, we are working in the context of Universal Evolution.

In this time of a leap in consciousness for humanity we will continue to see the movement from isolationism to the brotherhood of humanity coming together. Technology has played an important role in having us experience our interconnectedness and now it is up to us to realize the sanctity of our connection.

We could say there is Worldly Evolution.

Worldly Evolution relates to us as individuals in terms of the roles we play in the world, the specific and unique gifts you have been granted, that is, born with, that you are here to offer and give to the rest of the planet through your expression.

We could say there is Individual Evolution.

Individual Evolution refers to your personal growth—the lessons you are personally here to learn. Some people consider this their soul's journey.

〜〜

Why do we bring up this distinction between Cosmic, Universal, Worldly and Individual Evolution? There is an essential factor in the process of awakening awareness towards self-mastery, especially with regard to your Worldly and Individual Evolution. That factor is the factor of *your own choice.* The irony of Conscious Evolution is that it must be chosen, *consciously.*

You have the opportunity here and now, regardless of when and where you are reading these words. You and I have the choice to evolve our own selves, by creating that Intent, by continuously welcoming the surprises of our own unfolding, and by noticing and enjoying the lessons we are here to learn. In choosing Conscious Evolution your life lessons become easier because you are looking for them so you can work with them. You know there is synchronicity and Intent at play and that the circumstances coming your way are for that reason—so you can have your lessons and evolve. Like moving around the gameboard of life, as you learn, you advance.

Your goal achievements become easier because you are working inside of a much larger context. When you choose Conscious Evolution you put yourself in tune with your purpose and providence is offering up everything you need to live your purpose. Consider that in order for the planet and humanity to evolve now, it is going to take each one of us following our dreams. This is not merely lofty language or idealistic prose. When you follow your dreams, you are doing something that is an expression of your purpose. In Sanskrit the word *dharma* is used to express this. Dharma in this context means "right duty."

Consider that your dharma, your right duty now, is to live your purpose. Your purpose doesn't have to be a grand feat or "cause." Living your purpose is expressing what is uniquely you. This is what is needed and wanted on the planet right now in order for us to make this quantum leap into the next octave of awareness for the whole of humanity, if, as Einstein indicated, we are to go to a level of thinking appropriate for dealing with the world of today.

To QuantumThink is to live consciously, to deliberately and willingly choose Conscious Evolution, to create and hold the Intent for an evolution of our own consciousness. What does this mean?

At the end of the 19th century Richard Maurice Bucke, psychiatrist and contemporary of the great American poet Walt Whitman, in his book *Cosmic Consciousness* distinguished three levels of consciousness: Simple Consciousness which he said animals possessed, Self Consciousness that most ordinary humans possessed, and Cosmic Consciousness that only "some" extraordinary people had reached. In humans, Simple Consciousness is a kind of instinctual consciousness similar to what animals have, an awareness of the body in space though lacking the ability to reflect on one's existence. Self Consciousness is the ability to reflect on your existence and think about your own thoughts. Cosmic Consciousness is the state where you experience unity consciousness "a consciousness of the life and order of the universe" and of your oneness with all. Bucke outlined characteristics of Cosmic Consciousness that basically depict an enlightened fully Self-realized being in an elevated state of joy, sensitivity, and morality, who has a direct experience and consciousness of life as eternal. He then proceeded to give examples of people who had reached Cosmic Consciousness, including familiar figures such as Walt Whitman, Jesus, Buddha, Dante, Mohammed, Moses, Lao-Tse, Shakespeare, and Pascal. This was one way of distinguishing levels of consciousness that still resonates with people who read his book today.

We are now in a decidedly different era. We are in a time of evolution when Cosmic Consciousness is no longer the sanctuary of only an elite few. *We are in a time of evolution when each one of us can live in the fullness of an illumined consciousness. All we have to do is choose it.*

Many great thinkers are distinguishing ways we can consciously evolve our world for the better. Futurist Barbara Marx Hubbard created "conscious evolution" as a worldview of social evolution, taking the state of the world and society into our own hands. Pioneer in evolutionary spirituality, Craig Hamilton established an Internet network of "spiritual evolutionaries" to show the importance of individual transformation and collective consciousness working together. Expert on societal change, Don Beck revitalized the original work of Clare Graves known as Spiral Dynamics. His model is a system of societal value "memes," a kind of collective DNA that distinguishes an eight stage development of evolutionary cycles applied to cultures and individuals ranging from "instinctive" and "magical" through "purposeful" and "achievist" and upwards to "integrative" and "holistic." Science writer Janine Benyus advocates Biomimicry—that by observing nature's evolutionary design our science and technology can consciously mimic the genius of natural systems to minimize environmental impact while producing prodigiously. Cell biologist Bruce Lipton declares we have an evolutionary mandate to end violence through "survival of the most loving" consciously cooperating together as cells of the body do, not just to survive but to thrive.

In QuantumThink, Conscious Evolution means consciously choosing to evolve your own consciousness. Whatever realm of Conscious Evolution you examine, every one of them fundamentally *requires* our own individual Evolution of consciousness. Though many "believe" it takes a crisis of sorts to spur evolution on, this simply is not "the truth." We don't require a crisis to evolve. We can choose it. Evolution is the nature of life. We can choose to become a culture of Wake-ups.

At the time of this writing in the early 21st century it is said by modern and ancient soothsayers alike that it is the time of "The Great Shift." The *sine qua non* of this shift is a quantum leap in consciousness. What we are distinguishing here is Conscious Evolution that is specifically and precisely the evolution of consciousness itself—chosen consciously with the awareness that one is so choosing. The Great Shift is not only a matter of going to your next level of awareness; it is a profound knowing that you are living in a time that renders *you* an essential factor in this monumental leap for humanity. It is to know yourself as an integral aspect of the living cosmos. It is to transcend limited beliefs and conditioning that would have you imagine yourself as anything less.

This unprecedented season for humanity has also been called The Great *Awakening*. Conscious Evolution is tantamount to conscious awakening. Awakening must be a consistent practice. We are conditioned by classical-mechanical thinking to see things in isolated increments, as stop and start, stop and start events. Yet, in our quantum world, energy is always in flux. It moves as bursts and it never stops. There is consistency.

What does it mean to choose Conscious Evolution? It means you are choosing to evolve your own mind and state of awareness. It means you are choosing to participate in the co-creation of a higher octave for humanity. It means you are choosing to have life be great. It means you are not waiting for The Great Shift to happen. The wait is over. It means you are choosing this now.

Barbara Brennan, former NASA physicist and expert in human energy fields, tells us that creativity begins in a state of pleasure, that the movement of energy originates from a state of pleasure. Pharmacologist Candace Pert says the opiate receptor distribution patterns in our brains indicate we are really here to enjoy ourselves, "hard wired for bliss." When you begin to imagine the pleasurable journey your life can take, why not take the conscious steps to stay in that pleasurable field?

~~~

When you choose Conscious Evolution does it contribute to others? Of course it does. We exist in fields. Once elementary particles have shared the same quantum state what affects one instantaneously affects the other. This is the principle of Nonlocality. Even in being brought together in modern times through rapid advancement in technology and communications in what author Thomas Friedman says has created a Flat World, even with collective knowledge and the ability to collaborate like never before in the history of humankind, we still have to attend to getting along with one another.

We can choose Conscious Evolution *not* as an alternative to the fear of humanity destroying itself. We can choose Conscious Evolution because in doing so we joyfully continue to unfold the ultimate divine mystery adventure of existence in the highest, most inspired nature of which we are capable.

This act of choosing Conscious Evolution is a Grand Intent generating a probability field of actions and events that lead you to awaken, even in the midst of automatic reactions. This is the possibility of Conscious Evolution—mastery of your own mind and the opportunity to enjoy life and well being at a level unsurpassed in the history of human experience.

☜ QUANTUMTHINK RECREATION ☞
Live the Wisdom of Conscious Evolution

ONE»Contemplate what is it to choose Conscious Evolution, and consciously choose it, or consciously decide not to choose it. It is fine to not choose it. If you elect to not choose it, write down the reason why you made this choice.

TWO»If you chose Conscious Evolution, then jot down a few notes on what each of the following mean to you in your life:

Individual Evolution: What lesson are you here to learn?

Worldly Evolution: What expression of your purpose are you here to accomplish?

Social Evolution: What role might you play in the evolution of our social systems and structures and processes?

Universal Evolution: What is your vision for the next evolution of humanity at large?

Cosmic Evolution: What do you see about the evolution of the universe?

QuantumThink-Wave
A True Treasure Story

Once upon a time some seafaring friends invited people to their home on the water to use their boats for a real live treasure hunt. We went out hunting in seven small groups. The captain of each group was given the key to open the coveted treasure chest. Each group assiduously deciphered and followed written clues and cryptic symbols on the map. It was a great afternoon adventure.

Finally, my group reached the tiny island where the awaited treasure was to be unearthed. We saw the other groups gaining ground, in close proximity. Time was of the essence. We all arrived within minutes of one another, each with the key we had been given by our host. Eager to reap the reward and exhausted from the subtropical heat, we rushed to the spot marked "X." The competition was fierce but friendly.

Together members of all the groups lifted the heavy treasure chest onto the flat land. When the lock was at last in clear view everyone burst out laughing! The lock had seven keys. It would take each one and all of us to reveal the precious treasure.

18 The Holomovement of Purpose
You really do belong here

What if frogs became extinct? Would it matter? Aside from making an adorable storybook character for children, does a frog have a purpose? If you look into this matter you might be surprised to discover that according to their specific species frogs are sensitive environmental indicators, provide sources of medicine, and serve as natural pesticides and food for other animals such as birds. It seems that everything on this planet has a purpose. You and I have a purpose here. Whether you are in the experience of it or not, you have purpose. You belong here. Yes, you do.

Life is perfect. Have you ever noticed how one person is passionate to become a nurse while another lives only to sing? One finds satisfaction chasing storms of nature and another, fascinated with food, becomes a chef. What has one person attract to astrophysics, another to architecture, and still another to anthropology? Count to infinity to delineate each area of creativity and service to the world. Someone or many of us are drawn to do whatever is needed. Perhaps these choices are not based in ordinary logic alone. In this seeming chaos there is elegance, an inherent order to worldly life that springs forth all the goods and services and ideas and professions needed to support life on Earth. Consider that it is not simply that we are born and when we are old enough we look at a list of job options available and pick what sounds good. We are drawn toward what resonates within the core of our being.

The destiny and free will debate has intrigued philosophers for centuries. Do we have a certain destiny or are we choosing freely what happens to us? The answer, if we can humbly venture one, is surely a mysterious Both/And. You can always check your own experience. What do *you* think? Is there purpose to life? To *your* life? We do like to think so. Yet there is paradox here. What about our Observer-created Reality? Does purpose exist independent of our ascribing the meaning of it? If there are no absolute realities, then how can we have a decisive purpose? Are we the ones making up meaning and purpose or is there something inherent in life, in each of us, to be gleaned and distinguished? All good questions for QuantumThinkers.

Whether or not we live through many lifetimes or just one, the fact is we have this one now. We are here. This is it. What you choose to think about your life and your purpose from this moment on is entirely up to you.

∽∽

From the dimension of the Divine we might say that our purpose is to become *fully realized* as expressions of what we think of as divinity itself, All That Is. Certainly the great wisdom teachers have passed along this message: Our purpose is to reach Nirvana, Samadhi, Heaven, Universal Truth, Enlightenment. Referred to as the *perennial wisdom* because those who have sought the path of enlightenment from diverse traditions and widespread eras reached the same conclusion: We are here for this purpose, to become fully Self-realized in the awakened experience of our highest nature. However you wish to characterize it or whatever beliefs you have surrounding it, it is the ultimate state of transcendent awareness, fully awakened consciousness, liberation of the soul, free of suffering and pain, a walking embodiment of compassion and love.

And yes, this is one dimension underlying the purpose of QuantumThink itself. However in this distinction, The Holomovement of Purpose, our focus is your *worldly* "Purpose." What you bring to Earth. Distinguishing your worldly Purpose is one of the most powerful and profound ways you merge in the field of Infinite Intelligence. Though the "ultimate truth" can never be limited by any description, we do use words to point to it and we play our part in this world to express it. Your Purpose is simply divine.

Listen to the common theme resounding among teachers present and past as they speak of purpose eloquently. Author and minister, Catherine Ponder wrote: *"A loving Father can only do for you what He can do through you."* American author and life coach, Debbie Ford muses: *"Our life is a brief, precious journey, and our mandate is the expression of our unique gifts."* Danish theologian-philosopher Søren Kierkegaarde proclaimed: *"God has given each of us our 'marching orders.' Our purpose here on Earth is to find those orders and carry them out."* Indian poet, Rabindranath Tagore's exquisite verse suggests: *"Man discovers his own wealth when God comes to ask gifts of him."* Brazilian novelist, Paulo Coelho wrote that your *"Personal Legend … is your mission on earth"* and when you know what it is, *"everything is clear and everything is possible."*

You read these glowing messages and you are inspired. Then what next? What has us not only uncover our Purpose; what can have us *experience* living the wisdom of our Purpose? Distinguishing The Holomovement of Purpose, naturally! Are you ready?

When you come into the world, the first thing you do is breathe in. When you leave this world, the final thing you do is breathe out. The entire universe appears to be in this continuous movement of the in breath and out breath, the ebb and the flow of a tide, the rising and setting of the sun, the popping in and out of existence of an electron, the 1 and the 0 of computer language, the coming and going of a thought. Nature is rhythmic. These movements are not separate; they are aspects of the same whole. Our lives have different rhythms yet all belong to the same whole.

We have been saying that the idea that we live in a Holistic & Holographic universe means our reality is fundamentally comprised of wholes rather than parts as was previously believed, and we've begun to see the many ways this affects us. From a classical world view which analyzes things into parts, we don't experience the people and things in our lives—not even ourselves really, as "wholes." We see parts, pieces, a fragmented reality. We've been conditioned to focus on incremental incidents, on content, the "stuff," rather than on context, the bigger picture. We relate to what is in our immediate view.

The great quantum physicist, David Bohm, explained the reason for this. He said we don't see the "wholes" because the deeper underlying level of reality where everything is one whole connected substance is *hidden from our ordinary view*.

Bohm described the totality of existence as one universal field, dynamic and flowing, an unbroken whole in constant flow where everything is connected though we cannot see how because of this hidden aspect to reality which he said was "enfolded." He called this underlying order to reality the *implicate order,* hidden or implied, *enfolded*. It is folded into the background, into the possible world that is not in our immediate view. Bohm called the ordinary world that we *do* see and interact with the *explicate* order, the *unfolded* aspect of reality, and said there is this continuous movement of the unfolding and the enfolding which he named the *Holomovement* of the universe.

In this continual movement between these two orders of reality, what we don't see—*the enfolded*—becomes manifest in our ordinary reality, it *unfolds* into what we do see, and then it enfolds back again hidden from our view. Everything inter-penetrates everything else in this continual enfolding and unfolding he called the Holomovement of the universe.

You can see this graphically if you think of the Sun rising. The Sun is coming up and we say it is day in one part of the world while the rest of Earth is darkened. The rest of Earth is there, but light is being cast upon one aspect, making it visible. Our lives are also like this.

~~~

Imagine your life is one whole story. In a well-written novel or screenplay everything that is written is a part of the whole; there is no non sequitur. There is nothing in the story that does not belong. Every minute detail plays an integral role. So you are always connected to the whole of your story, to the whole of your life's Purpose—even if most of it is *enfolded*, hidden from your view. In an episode of the classic TV comedy series *Seinfeld* they ran the story backwards and we understand it perfectly. We always have access to the whole of the story. At any given moment in time, you see only abstracted aspects of your own story, wherever the spotlight shines, yet you know the parts you see are connected to a larger whole, actually as one unified whole, the continuous enfolding and unfolding we say is The Holo-movement of your Purpose.

In QuantumThink we say a vision is a *living possibility*. What does this mean? Physicists have made a very important distinction: the distinction between the *actual* world and the *possible* world. What they're saying is both of these worlds have existence: the *actual* world which we think of as the world we perceive with our ordinary five senses, and the *possible* world, the world of Infinite Possibility, the aspect of the world that exists outside of the realm of our ordinary physical senses. This world of possibility has existence also. We generally don't think of what we don't see as having existence, do we? We think of it as "not existing" or we don't even think of it at all. Yet our visions live in the possible world. Our visions have existence. A vision isn't something that happens someday in some vague chronological future. A vision is a living possibility, a force field, an energy. A vision is a force in the world the moment you create it. A vision has existence.

We bring this up now because Purpose is very much like vision in the sense that Purpose, in and of itself, exists in the *possible world*. If you look with your ordinary senses where do you see Purpose? You can see *expressions* of Purpose, *manifestations* of Purpose, yet Purpose in and of itself exists in the possible world.

You hear a lot of people saying today, *I want to live my purpose*, or *I'm not living my purpose*. Or when we see someone who is really down and out spiritually or physically, we say *that person is lacking a sense of purpose*.

We all want to feel we have some Purpose on this planet in this life. Without meaning to sound trite, we want to feel as though we make some difference somewhere. And we don't want to know this just conceptually; we want this to penetrate. We want to have our Purpose known and experienced as undeniably and irresistibly who we are. You may not be here to save the world. (That should bring you a sigh of relief!) You may not be associated with a huge global mission. You may not feel morally obligated to accomplish something specific during your lifetime. Yet there is something deeply fulfilling about knowing what you are here to express.

～～～

We tend to think of our Purpose as finding the THING we are supposed to be doing. Yet, Purpose is not a thing. Purpose is more a natural unfolding, a Holomovement. Observe nature all around you. What is nature's Purpose? You may think this sounds like a ludicrous question. Because Mother Nature has many expressions, infinite expression. We tend to look at our career or our life in different stages or our job progression as isolated parts. And often we are looking or waiting for the right part—THE one. Remember, reality is Multidimensional. We live in a world of Infinite Possibility. Yet we tend to live in a diminutive way and limit ourselves and our joy because we are looking for THE right expression.

Consider that these jobs, this career progression, career change or new business, achievement of mega or mogul success, or whatever you are doing at any time or stage of your life, is just one of many expressions of your Purpose. The Holomovement of Purpose reveals itself in your family relationships, with your friends, in your recreational interests, in everything you do.

The seed contains the potential of the fully grown plant and of every orchid blossom within it. Producing results from a new world view, living from Purpose is an exquisite unfolding, like a flower blossoming. Rather than having to pry the petals open, you plant the seed, you provide nourishment and light, and you allow it to interact with the environment. You Allow the blossoms to unfold.

~~~

Mindfulness author, Jon Kabat Zinn, suggested we ask ourselves over and over again, *"What is my Job on the planet with a capital J?"*[46]

Purpose is like your Job on the planet with a capital J. It is as though you were given a gift, something that is unique to you, something that is distinctively YOU, and now your Job is to give it.

The Judaic scripture, *The Torah*, says,

> *Deeds of giving are the very foundation of the world.*

In the Gnostic Gospels, Jesus is quoted to have said,

> *If you do bring forth what is within you, what you bring forth will save you.*
> *If you do not bring forth what is within you, what you do not bring forth will destroy you.*

In the great literary and philosophical writings of the 19th and early 20th centuries there was an underlying theme of alienation of the individual. We could ask, what was the cause of such feelings of aloneness, apartness, discontentedness that often led to loneliness, anxiety, and despair? Perhaps it was as simple as this fragmentation, a disconnectedness from one's own Purpose, a chasm in seeing and feeling one's personal connection with the whole of the planet and the whole of life.

If you could distinguish for yourself what you are here to do, what you are here to share with the world, what your role is—your Job on the planet with a capital "J"—you would be living in a whole new reality because you would be on a life adventure of the myriad expressions your Purpose can have. You wouldn't have to limit yourself to any one particular expression, unless you are at conscious choice with that one expression. Just as nature doesn't make one type of flower, or paint one picture of a sunset or express one land terrain or weather pattern, you don't have one expression of your Purpose. It is expressed and can be expressed in any number of ways as you travel through spacetime and as the world around you changes.

Illustrious abstract expressionist artist Jackson Pollock said, *"The painting has a life of its own. I try to let it come through."* You could look at your Purpose this way. Your Purpose has a life of its own. You can just allow it to come through you.

When you begin to live your life from your Purpose, from the Holographic vision for your life, something very interesting happens ... *Nothing is wrong ... and nothing is wasted.* You begin to see everything and anything that happens as part of the unfolding; you see it as a lesson, learning, or clue to the whole of what you are here for. You begin to see the value in everything, the *genius* in everything. This gives you great power in your life. Even in those circumstances you consider to be the "worst" or "negative" circumstances, you can see how that led you or will lead you to the next expression of your Purpose. You'll even see the value in your Least-action Pathways. Your Least-action Pathway authentically acknowledged can be a life altering Zen moment for someone else.

In The Holomovement of Purpose you see your life from one totality, from the perspective of the whole. You see how every aspect of it, every point in time, the people who were predominant in your life, what you were doing, where you were living—have all played an integral role in where you are right now and where you are going.

Consider that nothing is wasted, nothing is wrong, *nothing went wrong*. Your first three wives or husbands or girlfriends or schools or jobs were not a mistake! That "terrible" thing that happened to you, whatever it was, is an aspect of the totality. When you can see whatever occurs in this context, you experience life as "perfect." It doesn't mean everything that happens is preferred or pleasant; perfect means it all fits together. You can make sense of it and take action with prudence and wisdom. This is mastery in action.

The Holomovement of Purpose illumines misunderstood or questioned occurrences in your life. Suppose you are an actress. An obvious pattern in your life that has been of great concern to you is throughout your life many people want to confide in you and discuss their deepest feelings. Whether it is a friend or family member phoning you or whether it is a "stranger" you meet as you are out and about, people seem to just start pouring their heart out to you. This has been troubling to you because you feel that people are pulling on your energy and you want stay focused on your art form, acting.

When you distinguish this pattern in the context of The Holomovement of Purpose and make the connection to the whole of your life story, you have a big *aha!* Universal intelligence has been training you to be a great actress by presenting you with the gamut of intimate human emotions expressed through all those individuals who come to you to openly share their feelings. Now you appreciate how these assorted stories have been a real-life study that enables you to portray the depth and range of human emotions.

〜〜

New world view scientists tell us *life exists as patterns of relationships*. It isn't that the patterns are necessarily exact, identical, or even symmetrical. In nature there are patterns scientists call "fractals," geometric patterns that are not identical but self-similar at smaller and smaller scales, such as a the branching of a tree and its root systems, the familiar fern leaf, and mathematical formulas that produce digital art graphics. What appears chaotic is perfectly orchestrated Intelligence. Even though it seems as if things have been happening throughout your life "accidentally" or incidentally, when you notice the similarities and synchronicities a pattern appears and you realize the patterning is significant.

Some of us, no matter where we are, in a store or a park, a party, or a meeting will tend to meet people in the financial industries. Others of us, no matter where we are, on vacation on the other side of the world, will always draw to ourselves people in the media. We attract to us what is consistent with our resonant field, the blueprint of who we are. What is so easy and natural for you that you don't even think of it as anything special yet other people marvel at it? These are all clues to your Purpose.

You can begin to distinguish The Holomovement of your Purpose by catching the patterns in your life. When you see the rhythms that *unfold and enfold* throughout your life you see the underlying unity crystallize. It's an Observer-created Reality after all. When you look for them, the patterns emerge. Ask yourself:

What kinds of things come your way, repeatedly through your life?

What tends to attract to you? What types of people? What interests, activities?

What kinds of relationships do you draw to yourself?

What industries, talents, topics enter into the field of your attention?

Contemplate this example of how "the clues" connect. You are now 35 and you're masterful at business networking for joint venture projects. When you look back over your life you recall that when you were eight, nine, ten years old you were the kid on your block who gathered all the other kids together to play games. When you were a teenager you were the one who organized your friends to create parties and raise money for charities at the same time. Throughout your life you have always brought your family together to celebrate special occasions with artful ambience. Now that you think about it, there is another feature to this for you: in all these instances you are the one who adds the lighthearted fun to the occasion. This is an essential ingredient for you. Then you realize that in your current work putting together business deals you tend to set up meetings that include some form of recreation. As you look further you will see even more instances of the way you add lightness to every activity. Perhaps you have a deep appreciation for art and music, so the deals you put together are in that arena. Your Purpose could be: *Evoking harmony and prosperity and fun bringing together people in business and in the arts.* Once you begin this level of distinguishing you'll find you are able to keep refining it because you opened a context for noticing the nuances. The Holomovement of Purpose evolves as you consciously evolve yourself. Purpose isn't static; it is a richly colored, fluid mosaic full of dazzling surprise. Most important in distinguishing a statement of your Purpose is that it deeply resonates with you.

~~~

Whatever your age or stature in life you can distinguish your Purpose. If you are young and still in school or just beginning your career journey, being aware of your Purpose gives you inner guidance and direction. This makes life awesome. When you're present to your uniqueness, jealousy vanishes. There is no need to compare your own journey to another's. Saying you're "unique" is not just a nice platitude designed to make you feel "special." As an expression of the Universal Intelligence you realize each of us is a channel of wisdom we are here to offer. When you distinguish your talents, gifts, idiosyncrasies and proclivities, your contribution is natural, matter-of-fact. If you encounter hurdles or seeming obstacles, trials, or "down" moments and you can see them from The Holomovement of Purpose, you find solace.

When you distinguish your Purpose in your 40s, 50s, 60s or 90s you delight in seeing the connections in everything you've ever done. You have a fresh appreciation for every passage of your journey. Worry about the past and anxiety about the future fade. The timing of your personal unfolding is wholly your own. You realize that even in "retirement" your life is ever-new because you unflinchingly offer your gifts and talents wherever you are.

Realizing what you are here for, whatever "that" is, you step forward with renewed strength and confidence in what you bring to any situation. When you relate through the lens of your Purpose you are living an enchanted, exuberant, enthusiastic existence. You live your life adventure knowing you cannot *not* be "a contribution" because you are part of the totality of life. This is so freeing. It takes the weight of the world off your shoulders.

Looking from the whole of your life, looking from your Purpose, you can see everything that occurs as clues to the mystery adventure called your life. Even the minute seemingly petty details, looking from the whole of your life, have value and appear to have a larger Purpose. You know, the word "quantum" refers to an amount. And quantum science deals with the very small. Yet, you can see in quantum technology this science of the small is extraordinarily powerful. So these very small things, these minute occurrences become powerful forces in your life. You are making new discoveries along the way and in an intuitive way because you are taking note of everything that is in front of you, using everything as a clue to what's next. In living from Purpose we are literally tapped into higher knowledge, the all-encompassing intelligent source. It's a collaboration. You are generating your Intent, you are Allowing what unfolds to show itself, you're watching for it expectantly, and you are following the guidance it gives you. When you distinguish your Purpose all of sudden everything looks different. It feels different. You're at home in your own life.

To live your Purpose you give yourself over to it. You are ushered to and presented with all the experiences you need to fulfill on your Purpose. You have been born into the right family, in the right country. Look closely. You'll see that the gifts and talents you were born with are exactly the talents you need to deliver on your Purpose. These talents are clues to your Purpose. That's the destiny part. The free will aspect is whether you act on the intuitive pulses and whether you choose to develop what you've been given. Your choices direct your destiny.

You not only have talents—you have spiritual and energetic and soulful qualities that render your relationship to the world and your channel of wisdom different than mine or anyone's. We are here to invoke our own wisdom and to evoke each other's wisdom. We are turned on when we're expressing our wisdom. That is when we experience our connection to Divine Intelligence. We call it *passion.*

⌒⌒

Old world view thinking has conditioned us as a culture to wait for "the leader." We imagine "they" are going to do it. A new world view calls upon every one of us to express our leadership in whatever we bring to the game. The Holomovement of Purpose can be distinguished for a country, a company, for an organization, a community, for a family, for an individual. When your brand is in sync with the deeper underlying Purpose of your company, you strengthen your resolve and your results. Bringing conscious awareness of the distinctive Purpose of any entity grants focus and verve to a common endeavor.

You are a connecting point, an access point into Infinite Intelligence. You are integral to the whole.

Grande dame of modern dance, Martha Graham, described it well, *"There is a vitality, a life force, a quickening that is translated through you into action, and because there is only one of you in all time, this expression is unique … It is not your business to determine how good it is, not how it compares with other expressions. It is your business to keep it yours clearly and directly, to keep the channel open … You have to keep open and aware directly to the urges that motivate you."*

Once again, when you realize *I am necessary,* simply because you are here, there is no ego tripping about it. When you relate to life through the lens of your Purpose you are living an enchanted, exuberant, enthusiastic existence.

In a TV interview Italian fashion designer Giorgio Armani was asked if he had fun doing his work. He replied, *"I do not do this for fun. This is my work … and I derive great pleasure from my work."*

Isn't that what all of us want—to derive *great pleasure* from our work? Whether or not you are paid for the work you do, when you are doing *your* work you derive great pleasure from it. We are suggesting of course that your Purpose is Your Work. Your Work is a lifetime activity, your privileged wisdom expressed outwardly. It is the gift you were given when you came here; it is your gift to contribute as your Job on the planet with a capital J. It follows that when you are clear about your Purpose, when you distinguish it and you can really see it unfolding in every aspect of your life, you will derive so much pleasure from Your Work.

How marvelous for all of us to know that we are here for a purpose, that each of us is a unique wisdom channel on the cosmic broadcast network, that we make a contribution, and yes, we *really do belong* here.

⟨ QUANTUMTHINK RECREATION ⟩
Live the Wisdom of The Holomovement of Purpose

ONE»Take quiet time for yourself to sit down and reflect upon the patterns that have shown themselves throughout your life. Contemplate and jot down notes:

1. What do people come to you for regardless of whether you were 5 years old, 15, 25, or 85? What is the nature of the requests they make of you?

2. What is the nature of the conversations you tend to have?

3. What kinds of things draw you in and attract your attention?

4. What do you find yourself continuously doing, in terms of the nature of activity you find yourself in regardless of who you're with or what the setting?

5. What do you do with effortless ease, grace, and passion?

6. If you had a microphone to the world and every person on Earth was listening intently to you, and you knew the message would penetrate, what is the one message you would want everyone to have?

The idea here is you are looking for the patterns. You are looking for the self-inherent order in the seeming chaos. You are discovering your Purpose in the Holomovement that is your life.

As you inquire into this for yourself, see your Purpose from the whole of life and the whole of the world. We are traveling through spacetime. Consider the time you are in. You are not separate and isolated from the world and the era and state of evolution around you. What is going on in the world now? What are the trends? What are the indicators? What are the implications? You are interconnected with all of it.

TWO»Discuss the questions from Recreation ONE with a family member, good friend, or business associate. In the unfolding of the dialogue, the answers will become more specific and you will have increased clarity. Use these recreations as clues to seeing all the nuances of your Purpose, what is distinctively and uniquely yours and yours to give.

QuantumThink-Wave
Hide and Seek

Sometimes you might feel as if you want to "hide" things about yourself from others. Yet when you realize that even people without *new world view* distinctions per se are sensitive enough to pick up your Energy emanations, you start to laugh at the idea that you are hiding from others. When you become sensitive to fields and people around you deeper than at the purely physical level, how can anyone hide?

Don't let this scare you. There is tremendous freedom in allowing others to know you exactly as you "are." When people feel they have to put up a façade or social mask it places great stress on a person. The freedom *to be you* is truly a divine state. When you are surrounded by Wake-ups, there is nothing to fear in being yourself. You are bathed in compassion and light. You can generate this for yourself. You can create and hold the Intent that regardless of who you are, what you do, and what you have, you are appreciated, loved and respected. Live in that Participatory Knowing.

Then what is there to hide? The Least-action Pathways? The "shadow" darker aspects of you? In the child's game, Hide and Go Seek, one child hides and the other children are supposed to find him or her. Of course the child hiding has to be in a place where he or she can be found; otherwise there is no game. What happens when the children hiding are found? They are jubilant! They're laughing and excited that someone discovered them!

19 ENERGY IN FLUX
Fields of dreams

$E=mc^2$. The rock star of scientific equations. Have you thought about it? It changed your life. It made possible satellites for your worldwide television viewing and space shuttles for your moon travel; lasers for your CDs, and global positioning systems that measure polar ice movements and talk to you in your car telling you how to get to your desired destination. The discovery behind the most famous equation in modern times monumentally changed our view of the nature of reality. $E=mc^2$. Energy equals mass times the speed of light squared. What was the great scientist telling us?

Energy and mass are convertible; they are virtually one and the same. In the earlier view of physics, the classical view, scientists used to think objects *have* energy; and then Einstein showed that objects *are* energy. Energy, matter and light; they are all related.

Why do we say "we don't know how to think for this world"? Because we have been taught to think in terms of materiality—a world of solid objects—when in fact there is no such thing as a "solid object." Yes, of course we *perceive* outer world everyday objects as if they are solid and fixed; our senses are designed to relate to the ordinary world that way. Yet we are energy beings living in a universe of what we can call "Energy In Flux." What we call "matter" is essentially energy in a slow, dense state of vibration, a fluctuation so minute as to be virtually imperceptible. Quantum physicist David Bohm called matter "frozen light." Max Planck, a founding father of quantum physics, famously wraps it up in his declaration, *"There is no matter as such."*

A challenging aspect of thinking from a new world view, isn't it—that reality is continuously and dynamically moving Energy In Flux, when it *so* appears otherwise? We are *comfortable* relating to objects through our ordinary senses which tell us objects are solid and fixed ... even though they're not. We are accustomed to seeing events in intervals, as start-stop, stop-start though in reality nothing stands still. "Matter" *seems* all too real and subtle energy doesn't.

Quantum physicist Fred Alan Wolf states unequivocally *"Life is transformation of energy."* You and I are energy transformers. If life is essentially a continuous transformation of energy, shouldn't "Energy In Flux" be a main topic of study in standard education? What do you know about energy? Are you familiar with it? Do you sense it? Are you attentive to energy? Since our old world view conditioning has been based on what we can see, hear, touch, taste or smell and generally speaking, energy is "invisible," most of us haven't taken the opportunity to develop a conscious relationship with energy. Now we are ready.

To distinguish Energy In Flux is to be aware of energy as a fundamental aspect of life, to interact with energy *consciously*, to know life as dynamic, to know subtle energy that surrounds us and moves through us. A most superb way to awaken our thinking and enhance our mastery is by keenly attuning ourselves to energy we feel and sense. Without attempting to become scientists, without delving into the metaphysical, we want to create a conscious relationship with "everyday" energy we can tune into.

～～～

What is energy anyway? There is no "energy in general." Energy comes in countless definitions, forms, measurements, dimensions, orders of magnitude—from the natural elements that we think of as the forces of wind and water to the physical mechanical, electric, magnetic and gravitational forces. Kinetic and inert, particles and waves, radiant and dark, dense and rarefied, Energy In Flux expresses itself from the gross to the subtle.

Scientists work with energy. They learn to harness it, manipulate it, and transform energy states for invaluable use such as electricity and ingenious use such as space travel. Physicians work with energy or at least "read" it through modern technologies like lasers and electromagnetic resonances and ultrasound used to accelerate the body's own restorative processes. Advanced healers work with energy in another dimension known as *subtle* energy, aware that healing energy doesn't come from them but moves through them to their client.

You don't have to know science or be a healer to know energy. The greatest scientists used the simplest everyday objects and thought experiments to discover life altering insights. We can start with what is ordinary.

When you think of energy what do you think of? A vital force that makes you feel alive and fresh and invigorated. It seems elusive. Yet we know we want energy; we crave it. We desire the feeling of being energized so we tend to become aware of our energy when it is "off" in some way. We feel depleted without it. When our energy is "on" we call it *vitalized*, meaning "to endow with life." We're ready for anything! When we're tired we say we need energy, we have "low energy." We want more of it or a higher quality of it.

Where will more energy come from? Based on our old world view conditioning we typically look to the physical. We think we need more sleep, more food, more relaxation, and *then* we'll have more energy. All of that may be true; however, when you become aware of *subtle* energy you ask different kinds of questions that lead you to greater mastery of your own energy states.

～～～

What can the fact that everything and everyone is Energy In Flux mean for us in the workaday world? A lot. Much more than we've been aware of. Energy is informed with intelligence. Energy In Flux has messages for us. As you attune yourself to Energy In Flux, you become familiar with energy *systems* at a subtle level. You start to notice what happens to your energy when you eat a certain food or combinations of foods, when you drink a particular beverage or too much of one, a lot of water or not enough. You become sensitive to your environment.

Have you ever entered a room and felt like you couldn't wait to get out of there but you weren't quite sure why? Nothing on the surface appeared irregular yet you felt uncomfortable there, uneasy. Consider that you were experiencing the subtle energy of the room—perhaps the people in the room, the cleanliness or lack of it. Even though it didn't look messy or dirty to the eye, you experienced an inharmonious energy. Similarly, when a room or a closet in your home hasn't been cleaned or dusted in a while you can feel the denseness or the stagnation of air flow or life force. Suppose you're at home or at work in a clear and peaceful state. A noise or other disturbance enters and shakes up the field so you now experience it and yourself as fragmented, scattered. Then there are the times you feel positively drawn into a room or crowd of people, perhaps at a party, and you feel as if you could stay in that place all night. These are energy fields you are relating to.

Where are you right now as you read this? Become aware of the room or surrounding area. Can you sense the energy there? How is the lighting and the air flow affecting your energy? Is the energy high or low, aggressive or gentle, dense or refined, chaotic or balanced, fragmented or coherent, congested or clear? This may sound mundane to you at first however when you awaken your relationship with subtle energy you literally lift your consciousness because you can make choices that energize rather than enervate.

Everything—people, places, and things—have their own energy signature, a distinctive energy we sense beyond the purely physical. We are always in an energy exchange with other people and with our environments. Enter a cathedral, a synagogue, a mosque, a meditation hall, a concert hall. The energy field is distinct, it is unmistakable. It envelops you. You're affected by subtle energy that's been accumulating there for years. All the prayer and meditation and chanting and singing and connection to love have conditioned the space. A basketball court, a music recording studio, a special room in your home—each acquire a characteristic energy that affects us.

Meditation masters recommend you sit in the same spot when you meditate, and if you use a mat or a meditation shawl, to use always the same one during your practice. It is said the place where you sit for meditation gets filled with life force, *chi* or *shakti*, expressed as the energy frequency of your meditative state. Then whenever you come to sit there for meditation, you fall into a deeper state of meditation easily because the energy of that place, that mat, that shawl, connects with you. Think of those whom we consider the "Great Beings." Maybe it is not so much a "religion" as it is an *Energy* that we attune with when we think of them.

We are talking about subtle Energy In Flux.

~

Subtle energy is somewhat of a catch-all phrase for the range of energy outside the current focus of physics. Some think of subtle energy as low frequency electromagnetic energy and others think of it in a different category beyond the frequency range of classical space, time, and matter. While modern science is fully engaged in the study of physical energy systems the same cannot be said for the study of subtle energy. Research the topic of subtle energy and you'll find controversy. This is largely due to the lack of general knowledge about it and paucity of scientific instrumentation to measure it. Does this mean subtle energy doesn't exist or isn't a viable field of investigation, simply because we as yet cannot extensively measure it? Only limited thinking would have one say so.

Just as Eastern cultures as well as indigenous peoples from around the world have been more engaged in the study of consciousness itself than our Westernized scientists have been, they have also been more attuned to the whole range of Energy In Flux. Lacking insight on such aspects of reality, we've tended to classify energy adept people as "alternative" labeling them "mystics" even though their sciences of subtle energy systems have sustained thousands of years of experience and scrutiny. Subtle energy systems have been distinguished in precise and practical ways. Well known examples are Acupuncture, Feng Shui, and Chakra Energy Healing.

Acupuncture is an ancient healing modality that balances the flow of chi (subtle energy/vital force) in a person by stimulating specific points along the course of the fourteen major energy channels of the human body called *meridians*. It is thought that when chi flows smoothly and harmoniously through the meridians that all systems work together maintaining good health.

Originating several thousand years ago in China the art known as Feng Shui (literally "wind and water") has been used to direct the flow of energy or chi (life force energy) through architectural design and placement of physical and decorative objects. The purpose of Feng Shui is to achieve harmony and balance in home and office environments for maximum well being, creativity, and prosperity. It is said a person or a place can have too much energy flowing to one area or too little. You've probably experienced this yourself when you've had furniture that blocked a passageway in your home. You "knew" subtly that the energy was blocked. You move the furniture and you feel better in that room. We are connected to our environments. The flow of energy in physical spaces affects us.

The *chakra* system introduced to us by the ancient Indian culture distinguishes a system of subtle energy centers corresponding to and interpenetrating the physical body at the areas of major glands. Chakra, meaning "wheel" in Sanskrit, refers to the fact that the energy of chakras can be sensed and/or seen as spinning vortices of energy. These centers of subtle energy are said to be connection points where we take in and send out energy vibrations as information. The vast body of chakra literature describe their Multidimensional meanings and functions, each chakra with its own color, sound, gemstone, planet, and mental-emotional-spiritual qualities, one of the most important being a system representing levels of consciousness. In her enlightening book, *Wheels of Life*, Anodea Judith depicts the chakras as gateways between the physical and spiritual dimensions.

〜〜

For some people chakras, energy fields, and meridians are as typical as breakfast, lunch, and dinner. Perhaps you are one of them. Or maybe you've never known a meridian from a chakra. Well, you do now!

In fact there is increasing use of acupuncture by Western trained practitioners as scientific and anecdotal evidence for its benefits accumulate, and as we open our collective mind to the economic and emotional advantages of nonintrusive energy healing. Modern corporations and typical homeowners alike engage architects and interior designers who employ Feng Shui principles.

On the other hand, there are TV shows and books dedicated to the attempt to debunk anything to do with subtle energy, their authors relentless self-appointed crusaders for the "cause." That is how strong the old world view conditioning is, even though ample evidence for subtle energy fields and the intentional effects of mind on matter and of mind-to-mind communications are statistically undeniable. If you have been listening to the old world view thinkers on this, wondering how acupuncture can possibly work (is energy healing "for real" and what's up with psychic surgery anyway?), now could be a good time to "get over it."

We laugh at the droll comment of comic Stephen Colbert, host of TV's spoof opinion show *The Colbert Report*, "I can't prove it, but I can say it." Any one of us can "say anything" without regard to whether it has validity or not; we witness this daily in news and entertainment media the world round. We do want to rely on scientific evidence—and we also rely on direct personal experience. It serves us well to keep in mind, however, *in an Observer-created Reality we're likely to find what we are looking for*. Be it a scientist, debunker wannabe, or any one of us, consider that we can and do tilt the outcome of any "study" depending upon the conclusion we're out to "prove." Reality is Context-dependent. The power of Intent is formidable.

A true story: A woman who loved to play golf had a severely swollen wrist for several days. Her son took her to an acupuncturist for treatment. In forty-five minutes her wrist was back to normal and she thanked the acupuncturist profusely for bringing her great relief. Even after experiencing these visible results later she insisted she "didn't believe in acupuncture." This is how deeply embedded the old world model is.

Of course if you have come this far in QuantumThinking you are most assuredly moving beyond the "only matter is real" limits. However … just in case you're not "there" yet … As you continue now with this distinction, if you find yourself stuck or limited by talk of Energy In Flux that doesn't match your scientific or personal notion, this is a wonderful opportunity for you to notice where you place stops on your own thinking.

Wherever you are now on this subject, let's continue to explore together.

As always we are here to awaken our own awareness to embody the wisdom of thinking consistent with the most advanced scientific knowledge. We can take an informed leap now and begin to relate to subtle energy intelligently. This is crucial to a life of mastery since in many ways subtle energy precedes physical manifestation.

~~~

The subtle energy surrounding the human body that appears as a radiant emanation is often referred to as the "aura," a general and possibly outdated term that can undermine the science that more aptly refers to it as a biofield or bioenergy field. The aura is nothing spooky or woo-woo. You sense it yourself. Did you ever encounter a friend you haven't seen in a while and remark, *"You look radiant!"*? When energy is free and flowing we sense this kind of radiance around a person. Energy flowing and balanced is the healthful condition of our body. When energy becomes stagnant we become dull and experts say such blockages in subtle energy can eventually lead to physical ailments.

What else do the subtle energy experts tell us? Leading authority in energy healing and master of human energy fields, former NASA astrophysicist Barbara Ann Brennan states that since all physical problems show in the human energy field before they precipitate down into the physical body, it is possible for people to be healed before they get an ailment. Master healer, spiritual teacher and intuitive, Starr Fuentes stresses the importance of getting to "know" our subtle energy selves. She says, *"The subtle bodies get weak before you get weak; the subtle bodies get strong before you get strong. We must learn and experience our light bodies so we can surpass the limitations imposed upon us by dwelling in the heavy senses."*

The emanation of radiant energy is being measured with modern technology by visionary research scientists. UCLA Professor Emeritus, Dr. Valerie Hunt is one of the first scientists to record human energy fields. From her extensive recording of the bioenergy fields of healers and their clients Dr. Hunt clarifies that though we tend to think of subtle fields in layers, or as surrounding the body, the bioenergy fields are actually inside and out and that they blend and fuse together in organized patterns that can be altered. She advises: if you *correct the disturbance in the field* the symptoms disappear. But if you treat symptoms directly then when the stressful situation appears and aggravates the energy the ailment returns. She says, *"Healing is an active process. We do not 'react' to a healing modality; we 'transact' with it. This indicates your field has intelligence."*

Let us be very clear: in *no* way are we offering medical advice here. We mention these things to become aware, to think in a new way about our Multidimensional Being from the context of an energy field-based reality. Traditionally we're not taught as young children, *Here is your bodymind. Now it is up to you to learn about it, tune into its innate intelligence, and take care of it.* No, we're taught, *Here is a doctor, here is a nurse. When you're not well, see one of them.* Imagine the possibilities when we as a culture embrace and become knowledgeable about subtle

Energy and can consciously and knowledgably "transact" in partnership with our doctors and nurses.

Russian physicist Dr. Konstantin Korotkov uses a breakthrough technique called Gas Discharge Visualization (GDV) that allows direct real time viewing of the human aura. Using a special camera that translates the physical, emotional, mental and spiritual energy emanating to and from an individual into a computerized model, researcher and client can together see the imbalances affecting the person's well being so they can be addressed specifically. According to these experts the auric fields organize themselves in response to their environment and it's possible to restructure the auric field, recharge it and balance it.

$\sim\!\sim$

A simple way for us to relate to subtle energy is to think of it as *life force*. The basic Recreation for distinguishing Energy In Flux is oh, so simple. What increases life force? What diminishes life force? What invigorates you? What depletes you? Just staying in these questions naturally brings you heightened sensitivity.

When energy is blocked, unbalanced, or thwarted, whether in a place or within one's self, effectiveness, creativity, and joy are lessened. Conversely, when Energy In Flux is increased, improved, enlivened, stimulated, balanced, we enjoy an atmosphere of enthusiasm and positive feelings of growth and well being. We all know from personal experience that "happiness energy" is good for you. Life force flows. Life force grows.

You can begin to become aware of what feels good or "right" to you Energetically, and what does not? As you become more aware of subtle Energy In Flux your intuitive intelligence beckons you—where to go, what to buy, what to do, even how to arrange your home and office.

You might find it quite satisfying to discover, for example, how the chakras fit in to our ordinary daily life. To give us a sense of this let's take a moment now to touch the essence of what each of the chakra centers signify.

Most agree there are seven major chakras. The first chakra located at the base of the spine is the center of survival and grounding; the second chakra at the lower abdomen the center of reproduction, sensuality, and security; the third chakra at the solar plexus the center of power and will and sensitivity; the fourth chakra at the heart the center of love and connection; the fifth chakra located at the throat the center of communication and self expression; the sixth chakra located at the forehead between the brows and often called the "third eye" is the center of intuition, vision, and wisdom; and the seventh chakra at the top of the head, the culmination center of consciousness where we are united with All or what we call Divine Intelligence. It is said the upper chakra centers pull in refined, spiritual energy and the lower chakras pull in grounding energy from the Earth. The heart chakra is the center, the integration point. Again these are to give us a *very* simplified "briefing" so we can begin to become aware of the multitude of distinctions of subtle energy centers.

All right then, how does this play out for us? Suppose a person's attention (not *yours* of course!) is focused on power by forcing, by demanding, by a tyrannical nature, by pushing. We easily recognize this type of third chakra energy in political leaders who demand by force rather than command by connection. This Energy can occur also in our business leaders and at home in our family relationships.

The heart chakra is all about *connecting* beyond self-centered interest through spirit, love, kindness, and compassion—transcending the ego states involved with the "lower" chakra centers of survival, gratification, and self-centered power. If you keep your consciousness focused in the lower chakras, how will you be open to receive the wisdom of the heart? Of course from a new world view of Both/ And we realize that the first, second, and third chakra energy centers can also be expressed in their more useful and *evolved* states—as being grounded, able to enjoy life through our senses, and to feel, be sensitive, and express oneself powerfully for the good of all. Why is it so important to know the world of Energy In Flux? When you are aware of yourself at an energetic level, you have choice; you can shift your energy focus.

Spiritual Master Aïvanhov likens the aura of the body to the atmosphere of Earth, in the sense that it both protects us and also detects and receives information. We are in continuous exchange with the energy systems of the objects, people, places and living creatures surrounding us. Realizing this you can be attentive to what energy you are sending out and what energy you are taking in. Imagine how well versed younger generations would be if we included the chakra system as routine in education.

Thought creates reality. Do we require more explanation? Perhaps. Is a thought consciousness, energy, nothing? No one can say for certain. As scientists point out we cannot (yet) measure a thought directly; we can only measure the brain activity of a person who is having a thought. Energy comes as a result of a thought. We can surmise then ... what directs energy? Our very own mind. With every thought you have you alter the energy of your body. How does thought become reality? Does subtle energy in some way coalesce to become manifest?

Let's contemplate once again the amalgam of science, experience, and wisdom of Nobel Laureate physicist, Max Planck, in context:

> "As a man who has devoted his whole life to the most clear-headed science, to the study of matter, I can tell you as the result of my research about the atoms, this much: There is no matter as such! All matter originates and exists only by virtue of a force which brings the particles of an atom to vibration and holds this most minute solar system of the atom together. ... We must

assume behind this force the existence of a conscious and intelligent mind. This mind is the matrix of all matter."

How do we receive information from the nonlocal quantum field? It's not hocus-pocus. Quantum science tells us there is an underlying interconnectedness between everything and everyone. Recall that the principle of Nonlocality means there is instantaneous connection without any apparent exchange of energy or force. Intent may not be energy in and of itself yet Intent *affects* energy. Scientific studies conducted on the effect of human intention on subtle energy fields by William Tiller, physics Professor Emeritus of Stanford University, showed him that "a person can direct the flow of his energy in a chosen direction." Intent activates energy. If consciousness gives rise to all that is, then consciousness affects energy. We could say it this way: *consciousness moves energy.*

How can we "work" with subtle energy? You and I can direct energy with our Intent. Master Aïvanhov points out if you try to use your thought directly on matter, it may be challenging.

Consider, then, we can use our thought and Intent with greater flair on subtle Energy In Flux. Please don't accept this as something for you to "believe" or not. Experience this yourself by practicing it. Try it when you find yourself in a noisy restaurant or at a chaotic family dinner table. Waves spread out as they travel. Create the Intent for "calm" and watch the wave action.

In the same way that we cannot speak of Time without Space, consider that we cannot speak of Energy without Intelligence. It is known that every "body" radiates and absorbs energy infused with intelligence. Quantum holography tells us that every "body" radiates the whole event history of that "body" and exchanges information with others. This discovery of modern science is consistent with ancient Shamanic wisdom that says each of us is bathed in a luminous light body. Alberto Villoldo, modern day shamanic healer and teacher of energy medicine describes the luminous light body this way, *"The Luminous Energy Field contains an archive of all our personal and ancestral memories ... "* and that *"These records or imprints are stored in full color and intensity of emotion."* If so much information is available to us subtly, surely we can begin to learn to tune into energy intelligence.

The great paradox of living in an Observer-created Reality: do we *tune in* to the energy or do we *generate* the energy? Once again it is a Both/And answer. We condition the energy field and it in turn conditions us and our behavior. Energy comes before physical matter and at the same time physical matter emanates energy. It's a continuous dance. Alter the energy and you change matter; change matter and you shift the energy. However because of its subtle nature it is much easier to work with energy in many areas of life.

When we don't understand something we say, "I'm too *dense* for that." Physical matter is denser energy. When a physician looks at your arm he may not see much. He looks at it in a more subtle energy realm of an x-ray and sees more, and in an MRI more still. As we develop instruments that enable us to see ever more refined energy states we might also have greater access to transforming them energetically. While we await the arrival of such technologies, we have another avenue available to us: *we can refine our own capacities.*

What is the quality of your energy field? Whatever state you are in, you can relax and be happy about it because your Energy is also In Flux. You always have the power to refine your energy, to clear it, balance it, purify it.

One important way you can *balance* your energy is simply by not dissipating it. We can squander energy just as we can squander money or sex (both of them are energy as well). Unnecessary arguments, worries, doubts, and fears can squander your energy. You can also dissipate energy through pushing and forcing, third chakra style. Are you going too far with a desire for power, or can you jump to a more refined state and appreciate your power from a place of equanimity, sixth chakra wisdom-style?

When you refine your vision, when you refine your hearing through becoming intimate with Energy In Flux you can extend the spectrum of visible and auditory reception. Most of us have seen the waves rising from road pavement on a hot summer's day known as thermals, a phenomenon that happens when heated air meets cooler air. Ordinary people can be trained to see auric fields. What we are able to sense may simply be a matter of tuning in to a frequency range where subtle energy emanations become available to us, just as when we tune a radio dial to a particular frequency range we can hear what's being broadcast on that station. When a TV station wants to reach more people the broadcaster increases the signal.

〜〜

From his research on the effect of thought on water molecules Dr. Masaru Emoto [*Messages From Water*] noted that the *purity* of the energy determines the *efficiency* of the energy. When the fuel line in your car becomes clogged your car doesn't run as well. If it becomes too clogged it can even stop altogether. A murky stream doesn't move. Sea creatures cannot live in it. Emotions running wild like unruly children, hijack clarity.

We can have dense *thought* energy—a "belief" you are stuck with, a Least-action Pathway emotional pattern you allow to run its loop rather than interrupting it, or a thought you are attached to. When a person is "down" we say there is a dark cloud hanging over them. Like a thick fog, doubt and fear energy prevent the light of intelligence from reaching you. Negative or guilty or judgmental thoughts can muck up your energy field. Ideas that fixate as dogma obscure the light of awareness. Being "incomplete" does, too. These are dense energies. Once you become aware of these inefficiencies, you can clear them.

Clogged physical environments clog energy including our own. We're affected by the surrounding space. How do you feel after you thoroughly clean out a room or a closet during Spring cleaning? *You* experience a clearing like a delightful breath of fresh air. Remember, life is Holographic. Charles Schulz's *Peanuts* cartoon character, Pigpen, traveled through life with a cloud of dirt over his head. Though Pigpen was said to be "happily dusty," most of us prefer to be free and clear and *pure*!

You can *purify* your energy through any of the dimensions. What you eat, what you think, what you hold in your emotional body, your connection to spiritual energy, cosmic energy, and divine energy—all these comprise the energy systems of a human being. You can check your energy field in any dimension.

Balancing, clearing, and purifying energy, like everything else begins with Intent. With Intent, anything is possible. One moment your energy feels heavy, thick, sludge, like you can barely move. The next moment a friend or family member phones you and that one delicate expression of love alone lifts the fog. They bring you light. We're always in an energy exchange. When an atom in its ground state absorbs a photon, a particle of light, the atom is raised to a higher energy state. Imagine as metaphor, as we add light we raise our energy state. The lighter you become in the atmosphere of your own being … well, *do you see the light?*

~

Today there are many practical tools for balancing and raising energy frequencies: mats, magnets, and medallions designed to interact with energy fields. We mention them here simply to expand our awareness. Whether any tool or system works well or not is up to you, based in your direct personal experience of them and based on your Intent. Ours is not a one-size-fits-all world. An aspect of mastery is Intuitive Knowing what is right *for you.*

Ancient Holistic energy exercises like T'ai Chi, practiced daily by over ten million people in China alone, and Qigong, "working with the life energy" continue to grow in popularity. There are also modern groundbreaking advanced healing systems applied to the human energy field. Body Talk System is an integrative energy healing technique where the practitioner relies on the body's inherent knowledge of itself to locate weakened energy circuits, stimulate repair, and store the corrected energy patterns in the body's cellular memory. Founder, Dr. John Veltheim says his system enables the body to re-synchronize itself so communications between "systems, cells, and atoms … can operate as nature intended."[47] Dr. Donald Epstein, developer of Network Spinal Analysis says his technique demonstrates that subtle energy can move the skeletal structure and have the body restructure itself … allowing a person to "access the tension and restrained energy as fuel for spinal transformation" and "allows the person to perceive more subtle energy cues of their body."

Emotional Freedom Techniques (EFT) founder, Gary Craig, asserts that negative emotions are a result of disturbances in the body's subtle energy field and that a technique of tapping to stimulate the nervous system can resolve emotional issues.

It seems clear: we can develop our relationship with ourselves as energy systems and use our learning to our advantage.

We are living in a "live substance" universe. Scientists at the University of Bonn have a device that can hear plants "scream" when they're stressed. When you realize everything is Energy In Flux infused with more or less life force, you begin to treat things around you a lot differently. Instead of relating to things as merely inert objects, you increase your sensitivity to the energy fields of your computer, your car, your clothes, your environments, your plants, your animals, your food. Rather than shop for fresh oranges absent-mindedly you become aware of the life force in them. You're aware of your influence and exchange of energy with the people and things around you, and of their effect on you.

~~~

Ancient Vedic wisdom teaches that as you refine your consciousness and purify your energy state you naturally acquire *siddhis*—various "powers" of higher states of mind like clairvoyance. Spiritual seekers are always cautioned not to get hung up in the "powers," to always stay focused on the goal—*awakening*—Self-realization for the benefit of all. As we shift from the old world view of ourselves as physical "machines" to the new world view of ourselves as spiritually based energy systems with the power of thought and conscious Intent, we relate to everything we do in a graceful, sacred way.

Energy In Flux indicates more than just *things* in fluctuation. There are cyclical changes. You can sense the energy of the time. What is the energy of the time we are living in now? This is a time of monumental leaps in consciousness, in awareness, and of a grand opening of humanity's heart chakra.

We are here in QuantumThink to think in a new way, not just have some clever ideas or different approaches; we are here to think from a new system, an expanded and more accurate and up-to-date view of the nature of reality. We are living in a time of evolution unlike any we have witnessed or known. It is a time when all the systems we have enjoyed that are now outmoded are being invented newly. $E=mc^2$. If all matter is energy, if all life is transformation of energy, then to think in a new way about the colossal changes we need to make in the world—to have our standards and practices in economics, ecology, and education achieve efficiency and excellence that work for everyone—*it is essential to relate to the systems of energy that comprise our existence.*

Have we discovered all the forces of nature? Highly unlikely. 19th century physicist, Lord Kelvin, whose crowning achievements include inventing the scale of absolute zero and advancing the development of electricity, is nevertheless remembered for his infamous miscalculation: *"There is nothing new to be discovered in physics now"* said in the year 1900. Think of it: that is just five years before Einstein's world-altering discovery. Such a statement epitomizes the type of conclusion derived from old world view thinking confined to what's currently "visible" or presently known.

Things that once appeared fantastic and imaginary become the normal course of events. Science fiction writers often predate real life anticipating in their stories technological developments that actually occur later on. Gene Roddenberry's classic TV series *Star Trek* inspired the inventors of the cell phone and the home computer, and a developer of jet propulsion.

Already there are other forces and forms of energy being brought to light. In the healing domain, Dr. Valerie Hunt has detected another type of subtle energy in the human body organized differently than electromagnetism, a "standing energy" she calls a *bioscalar wave*. She says the bioscalar energy is the "phenomenon of all healing procedures" and that each of us can generate it; we can bring it into our body with our consciousness and the "body establishes new energy field patterns that are self healing."

Nassim Haramein of The Resonance Project points out that everything is not only energy; everything in nature *spins,* from the largest galaxy to the tiniest electron. From asking the question *"What is the origin of spin?"* he postulates that whatever this force is could be the fundamental force unifying all forces, sciences, and ancient philosophies. Nassim suggests that what scientists call "dark matter" may be nothing more mysterious than simply the uncalculated and as yet unidentified force responsible for generating the spin that energizes everything in the universe.

Would we not render ourselves at least arrogant if not foolhardy to conclude there are no new solutions outside of our current beliefs, technology, and information— to our quests for renewable and perhaps unlimited self-generating energy sources, for efficient and affordable healthcare, and for untold other discoveries that could newly shape our fate?

People from around the world resonate powerfully with "The Force" in *Star Wars* described by Jedi Master Obi-Wan Kenobi as "an energy field created by all living things." Energy In Flux, a vast subject, subtle yet oh so profound. *May the Force be with you,* and, *May you be with the Force!*

❧ QUANTUMTHINK RECREATION ❧
Live the Wisdom of Energy In Flux

ONE»Check your energy atmosphere three times today. Is it dense or clear? Notice where your energy is focused. Are you in your "force" mode? Sensuality mode? Heart mode? You don't have to "do" anything with it; just become aware of it.

TWO»Relate to everything in your personal surroundings today as Energy In Flux. Your computer, your food, the trees, the sun, your furniture, your rooms. Treat every entity as infused with life force. Notice any changes in their energy field when you infuse them with your attention, light, and love.

THREE»Determine where you need and/or want to purify your Energy In Flux. Look at the physical, from your own body to the environments you inhabit, your home, your office and work space, your car, the places you frequent, etc. Look at your thoughts, your emotions, your spirit, your soul, your connection to Divine source. You can now intervene and generate your Intent to purify your energy fields and lighten up.

~~~~~~~
✑ QUANTUMTHINK-WAVE ✑
Time for A New Science

If *"there is no matter as such"* as father of quantum mechanics Max Planck declared, then what does physics actually study? The behavior of things, not the things themselves.

Who has investigated the science of consciousness? Not "consciousness studies" but the scientific discipline that explores the nature of consciousness and what it is capable of—just as we study biology or chemistry.

People ask, (at least scientists do), what is matter? What is it made of? How did it begin? How did it get here? How did it get to end up in the state it is in? People ask, (at least some people do, and more scientists should be asking), what is consciousness?

Consider that these may not be "Being In The Right Question" in the sense that if there is no "is" or way that something "is"—if it's all a moving mosaic of endless possibilities that we guide and refine, narrow into probabilities, and eventually manifest into actualities, then we can ask different kinds of questions. We experience life through what we call consciousness or mind, including the mind we experience through the heart or feeling. Now we might ask, what is consciousness capable of? How can we best use or work with consciousness? These questions which acknowledge the dynamic quality of consciousness/mind will lead us in much different directions than attempting to define what seems to be essentially indefinable. "Consciousness" is not a fixed "thing." The conscious generating of Intent defies a fixed state. Still, we can work with it. We can delve further into its dynamics.

If consciousness is fundamental to all the Multidimensions of reality, then who is studying it? If the current scientific method is directed and designed for the study of the physical-material dimension of reality only, then perhaps we need a new branch of science. If our current instrumentation and scientific protocols are not able to study the nature of consciousness, then maybe we need a new method of measurement.

Most astute scientists would concur (as non-scientists do also) with Einstein's statement that we cannot solve our current problems with the same level of thinking that created the current problems. Then it follows strictly as a matter of ordinary logic: we cannot explore consciousness—which is nonmaterial—with a scientific method developed specifically for studying the material aspect of reality. Perhaps it's time for a new science *and* a new method ... that would give us insight into how anything manifests. Until then, we can explore Resonance.

~~~~~~~

20 RESONANCE—THE ZING OF STRING
Magical, musical codes of intelligence

We are here to QuantumThink for one reason—to create a magnificent life. What creates our reality and what is our masterful access to it—that's our topic, isn't it. We're not here just for a new idea, or a hope, a prayer, and a dream of a magnificent life for ourselves and the world—we are here to *manifest* it. *Intent expressed as thought experienced as feeling and inner knowing creates reality.* How does it happen? The distinction Resonance offers all the clues.

As you know, QuantumThink is not about science; it *is* about how the discoveries of science shape the way we think. We take delight in realizing that modern scientific insights are merging with universal spiritual wisdom. To QuantumThink is to embody practical wisdom that syncs with what we know at the edge of knowledge today. Thus far we've been focused on all the ways the quantum world is paradoxical and simply doesn't follow the rules of ordinary logic. Now we're in a new octave of awareness. If you have been reading and contemplating and practicing these distinctions you've taken the leap. Now that we're thinking from new world view principles, logic-lovers out there, you will be happy to hear it's time for us to call upon ordinary logic and put it all together. Are you ready? Let's go then …

We feel life. That's how we experience. How is it possible to experience the moonlit sky or the song of a bird or the majesty of a distant mountain range? Feeling isn't just emotion or physical sensation. What we experience extends well beyond our body. We feel life with our whole being. Wisdom teacher Seth used the phrase *feeling tone* to denote what he called the deep musical chords of our being. It is as though our body is a big sensing device and beyond the physical in the invisible aspect of life we feel still more in our heart, soul, and mind.

I dig your vibe. An expression popularized by early jazz musicians. Maybe they were far out however they weren't far off. Particle physicists today say that everything in the universe is fundamentally constituted not of particles as we once thought but of tinier than tiny strings and that these strings *vibrate* as if infinitesimally small violins are playing the music of life. Creation is vibration. Vibration is creation. Vibrations generate sound waves that pattern themselves into what we call reality. People have been trying to tell us this for a long time. *Have we been listening?*

"In the beginning was the Word and the Word was with God and the Word was God" reads John 1:1 in the Bible. Vedic, Buddhist, and Jain traditions proclaim the world comes into being with the sacred sound of *Om*, the primordial hum that includes all sounds and embodies the essence of the universe. The vibrating sounds of the twenty-two letters of the Hebrew alphabet are considered the energy pulsing building blocks of creation. For Mayans the first humans are given life by the sole power of the word. Their symbols of O and L sounded together as *ol* mean "awakened consciousness in the form of vibration."

You and I, the stars in the sky, the chair you're sitting in, the crowd noise we call din, all are vibration. The only difference is the frequency or rate at which we vibrate. Think of it though … nothing vibrates in isolation. Vibrations reach out and connect and activate each other. When "sympathetic oscillations" meet one another in similar frequency range we call this "*Resonance*." They don't just meet— they influence one another and the entire resonant field. We feel ourselves and one another because of Resonance. We influence one another with what we resonate. Technicalities aside, one of the highest accolades we confer on a person, an idea, a work of art is, *"I really resonate with that."*

How does one connect with Resonance? It's quite simple. Just notice what and who you resonate with. When you hear the sound of a gurgling brook, the whishing of a waterfall, the gentle slapping of waves caressing the shore, the wind rustling leaves on the trees, the birds chirping playfully to their flock, what do you feel? When you hear people shouting at each other, even in a "civilized" setting such as a TV news opinion show, what do you experience in the feeling tone of your being? We may not be able to pin it down exactly and in any descriptive way yet each of us knows of what we speak now. Resonance is like the silent heartthrob of life, vibration that oftentimes cannot be heard within the range of human hearing yet we can feel it.

We may have been trying to "connect the dots" to understand life. Even so, spiritual wisdom and at least one modern theory of science, "string theory," agree there are no actual dots out here to be connected. There are just vibrating strings playing off one another. In English *resonance* is one of the few words the dictionary defines by reference back to itself, as *resonant quality* or *condition*, perhaps because Resonance is fundamental to existence. Resonance, "The Zing of String," turns out to be the *sine qua non* of creation, the essential condition.

I

Resonance is vibration, vibration is sound, and *the power of sound is awesome*. The mere tone of someone's voice can make you feel misery or make you feel ecstasy. As newborns nestled in mother's bosom we entrain to the beat of her heart and it positively affects our brain development. Native drum beats can synchronize our brains and adjust imbalances in our mind-body-spirit. Because of Resonance, classical music stimulates plant growth and a lullaby soothes a baby to sleep. Because of Resonance, chanting evokes a centered calm and Beethoven's chorals invoke Divine presence.

Sound creates realities. Cosmic radiation that showed up as excess noise in a radio receiver gave rise to the Big Bang theory that cosmologists use to explain how the universe began. Ultrasound creates an image of a fetus and promotes cellular regeneration.

Sound moves matter. An opera diva's voice can shatter glass and scientists experiment with the ability of sound to move matter and build objects so astronauts might someday use sound to build things in space.

Why should we care? We generate sound, too. We resound. Consider that what you and I resound, what you and I vibrate can also shape matter. Remember that nothing vibrates in isolation. Yes, indeed, habits of thinking, or more precisely said, our *system* of thinking does shape reality and our experience of it. At this point in our QuantumThink journey it may be easy to accept that we create the reality of our *experience*, yet perhaps even for seasoned QuantumThinkers it may still be challenging to imagine that our consciousness directed by Intent in some way *manifests* or even *arranges* physical reality "out there."

Swiss scientist, Hans Jenny (1904–1972) developed a science he named Cymatics to study the effects sound waves have on matter. He placed sand on a metal plate and used sound to vibrate the plate. Depending upon the various vibrational frequencies the sand formed different distinct geometric patterns. Some looked similar to mandalas, the circular designs used in meditation, others looked like cells. Jenny found that the higher the frequencies, the more complex the shapes. *Sound generates form.* You can see this for yourself on YouTube.com: Just search Cymatics. This is sound made visible.

From the furthermost galaxies to the cells of our bodies everything is vibration with detectable sound. Even so, Resonance is more than meets the ear. Resonance indicates *you attract what you vibrate.* You experience this in the most ordinary ways, like on those days when you find yourself in a bad mood having the proverbial "bad hair day." What typically happens? Situation after situation tends to get botched. On another day you find yourself in a *most* agreeable mood. Everything goes well. It seems magical. Quantum occurrence after quantum occurrence bestow their benevolent grace upon you. It's not coincidence; it's Resonance.

What if you were granted an extraordinary gift that was so powerful it could influence other people, influence the results and circumstances in your own life, influence collective consciousness, influence our shared world? In fact you are in possession of just such a gift: Resonance. Everyone born on this planet comes with the sacred power chip inside. Spiritual teachers say things that penetrate deeply. Master Omraam Aïvanhov taught, *"The thoughts, emotions and acts of human beings, their aspiration and impulses, their plan and prayers, all escape from their author and his vicinity and spread out in every direction."* What about the teaching of meditation master Gurumayi Chidvilasananda: *"Every time you experience your own love you are supporting thousands of lives."* Our strong and habituated thoughts generate Resonance, the noble as well as the ignoble ones.

The popular DVD and book *The Secret* inspired millions of people across the world with the idea of "creating your reality" through "the law of attraction" and infuriated others who scoffed at the prospect. The "law of attraction" is not actually a scientific law per se and *The Secret* may not have satisfied our scientific standards of proof. Nonetheless, millions of people resonated with the kernel message: essentially, that you attract what you vibrate.

What makes people get so upset when they hear about the realities of mind-to-mind and mind-to-matter principles? We already know the answer. In the history of traditional education we have not been taught to QuantumThink. Remember that the classical world view oriented us around "reality" as *matter*, as *physical*, as a conglomerate of solid objects, as an "I'll believe it when I *see* it" mentality. Perhaps people's upset is simply due to a clutching attachment to those old, outdated ideas about the nature of reality—coupled with an absence of facts at the edge of scientific knowledge, especially about the physics of mind.

What is "real" in one generation is invalidated in another; what is "unreal" in one generation is substantiated in another. What would a man or woman who lived seven hundred years ago think if we showed them video images on a computer screen? Would they insist it's not real? This is not to get preachy but simply to open our thinking to possibilities that from our current perspective seem like hogwash, insanity, chicanery, or in the very least impossible. What we detect with modern instrumentation certainly sheds new light on "out of the box" thinking. Scientists have already begun to prove that our Intent conditions the field surrounding us, that our beliefs affect the readout of our DNA and therefore its behavior, and that our thoughts not only affect matter—in some real way our thoughts are actually "one with it."

If we truly want to expand our thinking and the richness of life it is always a good idea to take note of how often and how vehemently we will argue for limiting and even *inaccurate* beliefs. Certainly it is more satisfying to discover there are specific ways that all this works rather than either blindly believing or blindly rejecting or parroting a general phrase or two about it.

Contemplate this definition of *nonlocality* from Apollo 14 astronaut Edgar Mitchell who founded the Institute of Noetic Sciences as an organization dedicated to the scientific research of the powers and potentials of consciousness:

> Nonlocality: "The omnipresent and omnidirectional transfer of influence (including thought, emotion, intention) at the quantum level instantly, simultaneously, and ubiquitously, through wave-like or field-like resonance wherein spatial and temporal factors are inconsequential."

Dr. Mitchell states it so clearly: Our thoughts have a *"transfer of influence"* beyond spacetime factors.

To label the undeniable discovery and realization of the connectedness and influence of mind-to-mind and mind-to-matter as a "new thought movement" or to place this in any other limited box or label is to trivialize the scientific evidence and the spiritual wisdom as well as your own directly verifiable personal experience.

Thought creates reality. How does it happen?

We love to say we are spiritual beings having a human experience. What is the *human* part of this? Form. Human experience is possible because spirit takes form.

An estimated one billion people in audiences and viewers around the world watched, rapt and spellbound the unsurpassed artistry of the opening and closing ceremonies of the 2008 Olympics in Beijing, "One World One Dream." Respected Chinese film director Zhang Yimou used drums and bells, flying dancers and modern technology to create a spectacular patterning of human ingenuity and form in motion. What has us experience such intense delight in seeing patterns and symmetry? Perhaps because we recognize patterns as the nature of life itself, visual harmonies witnessed everywhere throughout this universe, and we long for them.

Could any of us not be totally awed and blown away by the resplendent harmony and geometry in nature? Look beyond the surface deeply into any phenomenon and the patterns do amaze. At the micro scale spilled milk is not something to cry about but to watch with wonder as microscopic photography of ordinary spilled milk droplets perform a perfectly patterned dance as their molecules bounce off the kitchen floor. At the macro scale our solar system's planetary orbits "draw" nearly perfect geometric shapes as they circle and meet one another's cycles, illustrated on page after page of John Martineau's small book with a big message, *A Little Book of Coincidence.* The paths of Jupiter and Saturn form a hexagram every twenty years. The orbits of Jupiter and Earth outline the shape of a six-pointed star, often called the Star of David, a pattern Martineau tells us is also seen "lurking in every crystal."

Is the universe just *randomly* Energy In Flux? Hardly. This universe is mathematical, this universe is geometric, this universe is rhythmic, it is cyclic; it is a universe of pattern and form. Pattern and form, when you think about it, are encoded in us, literally in our DNA. The early Greek philosopher Plato said that Ideas or Forms were universal and changeless truths known to the soul, *inherent* in human beings. In his dialogue *Timaeus* he alludes to the manifest world being an impermanent *copy* of the original unmanifest "Forms." In the modern world we know that RNA is a temporary *copy* of the DNA code that manifests in the form of our own bodymind. Lo and behold, the idea of an intelligent blueprint underlying everything in our ordinary everyday world has been around quite a while.

What do we make of all this for ourselves? The dynamic self-organizing patterning of nature provides another clue that makes sense of our capability to create. This universe is mathematical, this universe is rhythmic and cyclic; this universe is geometric; ours is a universe of pattern and form. And *form follows rules.*

The logic is simple:

Everything is vibration.

Vibration is sound.

Sound creates resonance.

Resonance moves matter.

Matter takes form.

Form organizes in patterns.

Patterns adjust according to resonance.

It follows that physical matter responds to resonance.

Continue the logic:

We are vibration.

We resound.

We generate Resonance.

It follows that our personal Resonance affects the world around us.

In a very real sense, not as hype or motivational build-up of our egos, we have no idea how powerful we are, without *doing* anything. Old world view thinking has us imagine that our thoughts and feelings about another person are separate from them—so whatever you say to a friend or associate or family member about the "other guy," your judgments and opinions and diatribes, *you mistakenly believe* don't reach him. We gossip or verbally jab someone: "Don't say anything to Joe—I'm just telling *you* this in confidence." You "believe" your statements said with passion and perhaps indignation have no effect. We can re-think that now. We feel life. That's how we experience. What you experience you resonate, and your vibration reaches out to the world.

When you glean Resonance as a distinction you experience your profound relationship to all of life because we do in fact exist in fields—fields of intelligence, of information, energy, awareness, Resonance.

Among the strongest fields are our family fields. Have you ever considered that you have a real and instantaneous effect on the individuals in your family and in your family as a whole by what you hold in your resonant field about them? The principle of Nonlocality indicates we can influence one another's well being outside of space and time limitations. As you think of your mother or your father, you hold the reality of them in you; what you feel for them, what you believe about them.

The distinction Resonance is unlimited in its practical applications. If you were once married and are divorced, how do you think about your former husband or wife? Many people hold a negative Resonance toward their so-called "ex" and then wonder why their relationship isn't harmonious. It is so easy to restore coherence to a relationship that began with love (remember?) when you are aware that fundamental to a quantum world, despite a stack of evidence in your mind about a person, there is no absolute way that he *is*, she *is*, they *are*, it *is*, or you *are*. You can shift your resonant field with regard to any person in an instant, back to a coherent state of love, even when you have gone your separate ways.

Let's make this practical. Suppose your mother is not yet computer literate even though you really would like her to be. If you have convinced yourself that your mother won't be open to new technology, if this is what you are resonating about your mother, then it should come as no surprise at all if she resists the idea when you suggest it! To takeoff on political strategist James Carville's famous phrase coined during the 1992 Clinton campaign, "It's the *economy*, stupid!" think of it this way: "It's the *field, silly!*" It isn't that we're "slow to learn" (definition of "stupid"); it's that we can sometimes "forget the wisdom" (definition of "silly") of *fields*. When you get a result you didn't want or you don't get a result you want and you find yourself wondering, *How did this happen?*—or—*Why isn't this happening?*—whether the result is personal or in the general culture, check out the Resonance, smile, and remind yourself: no wonder it's happening this way, *"It's the field, silly!"*

Can you and I alter the resonant field? Of course we can. You can hold the Intent your family is healthy and happy and you are likely to find it works. You can create the Intent that your relationship with your former spouse is supportive and harmonious. It's an Observer-created Reality after all.

～～

Like everything else, Resonance is either generated consciously or it automatically follows the existing tune of the circumstances. There are Least-action Pathway *resonances* that we can interrupt just as we can with any Least-action Pathway. The way is quite simple. Resonance is frequency and frequency can be felt.

Feelings are clues to what we are vibrating, and therefore, to what we are generating and attracting. Rather than believe you are stuck with your feelings you can use them as clues. A Least-action Pathway of our human culture has been that we have no "control" over what we feel. You hear people say, *I can't help it. That's just how I feel about it.* Yet, in quite ordinary ways we do attempt to have a crying child shift to a happy state or a friend move from frustration to optimism.

Tapping into our *feeling intelligence* consciously with Intent is one of the most powerful ways we can work with our ability to manifest results. It is important to keep in mind that what we call "feeling" is vibratory in nature; feeling is the Resonance of our being. And vibration has a significant relationship with and a real effect on what we call matter. Consider that Resonance is the liaison between mind and matter.

You emanate what you Resonate. What you feel "within" reflects itself in the "outer" world. As you heighten your awareness you shift your frequency. The more expansive the thought, the more refined, the less dense, and the easier it is to move things and flow. Expansive thoughts are thoughts of love, joy, compassion, genius. In contrast, judgmental or angry resonances have dense energy and such thoughts tend to contract. Just as light can pass through anything and transform it, the light of human awareness has inherent power to transform.

II

Great thinkers in antiquity were dialed in to what modern scientists are discovering. The ancient Greek philosopher Hermes Trismegistus, a real or legendary figure also identified with the Egyptian god of wisdom, Thoth, put forth one of the earliest renditions of our universe as Holographic in the adage, *"as above, so below"* known as *the law of correspondences,* one of the Seven Hermetic Laws. You can interpret the meaning spiritually—that what is in the Divinity "above" also exists in humans "below" and you can also interpret it scientifically—that the principles in the macrocosm "above" also operate in the microcosm "below."

As above, so below. Resonant fields occur at every level of organization in nature from our cells to our brain to our evolutionary biology, from the physical to the energetic to the magnetic, from the subtle to the nonmaterial realms of intelligence outside of spacetime. The distinction Resonance is not a philosophy; Resonance is a dynamic of manifest reality in play all the time.

Quantum physicist David Bohm and neuroscientist, Karl Pribram are often spoken of together because independently they both arrived at the Holographic nature of life—Bohm of the holomovement of the universe and Pribram of the holographic nature of the brain. Recall for a moment the *implicate order* that David Bohm distinguished, the field of Infinite Possibility, the aspect of reality that is hidden from view until we focus on it and bring it into actuality. Karl Pribram described this in terms of the brain. Pribram tells us that our brain acts as an analyzer of waveform frequencies, meaning that the brain responds to patterns and those patterns evoke a hologram or picture of reality. He said *"our perceptions look, feel, and sound the way they do because of the ability of our brains to take patterns from the implicate order [the field of all possibility] and bring them into focus."* Using Bohm's metaphor of a camera he says, *"When a camera lens is out of focus all you see is a blur, but when you focus the lens you see a picture."*[48] In other words, all the umpteen possible "pictures" of reality are always present—yet they are "blur" in the background of our experience until we focus the lens of our awareness on one and slide a picture into focus.

Brain cells resonate to the specific frequencies of what the environment presents and resonate with those forms. Pribram points out the brain responds not in a cause and effect manner, but as a whole field when what he refers to as a "challenge" to the system is presented, that is, something novel. *"If you get back into the potential— implicate order—then the fluctuations have a chance to reorganize. … The whole [brain] system can reorganize on the basis of this challenge … "*[49] Very exciting, isn't it, to realize that we can change our entire brain field, and set up different connections simply by introducing something novel into our lives.

Interestingly yet not surprisingly, this whole-system change in organization quantum leap-style also happens to the sand on the plate used in sound-on-sand Cymatics experiments we mentioned earlier. When a different sound frequency is introduced to the sand, Cymatics proponent, Jeff Volk says a new sand figure doesn't emerge gradually, it happens all of a sudden. In a given moment it transforms into a new structure. He says first there is a pattern of constancy, then chaos, then the quantum leap to the new form.

~~~

From the brain to the sand plate and *back to us in everyday life* … It follows that when you "challenge" your mind with a new thinking system, QuantumThink, it's logical that the shift in Resonance generates a literal quantum leap in consciousness. So if you are feeling a little chaotic along the way, not to worry! When we introduce something new, it doesn't change just one part, the whole system shifts. Why, naturally it does, because *it's the field, silly!* This is why it is so important to create a new Intent, to generate a different blueprint and reorganize the field.

Author and authority on the connection of brain, mind, and biology, Dr. Joe Dispenza gives us another prudent biological reason for thinking in a new way. He says thinking the same thoughts over and over again can eventually lead to overusing a cell's DNA causing the DNA to "make cheaper proteins," to malfunction, thus weakening the body.[50] As QuantumThinkers we realize we can always interrupt our Least-action Pathway thoughts and create anew and keep those healthy proteins going!

We are establishing a conscious practice of noticing automatic and mechanical patterns and habits, Least-action Pathways that do not lead to our heartfelt desired results. To transform the resonant field we introduce something *novel*, a newly stated Intent. At the same time we are also introducing something new from an all-encompassing view, a new *system* of thinking. We are "challenging the system" of mind both from the whole of it as well as from a specific Intent. Thus, in quantum manner the whole way we relate to life reorganizes itself, not as cause and effect, but as a resonant field effect.

How important are resonant fields? Perhaps more significant than we have imagined. The heart, the brain, our cells, are all resonant fields, transmitting and receiving information and intelligence both within space and time and beyond.

Institute of HeartMath® researchers have found that the electromagnetic field of the heart transmits information between people and that one person's brain waves can synchronize to another person's heart. They suggest that the heart "plays a role in intuition by accessing an information field outside the bounds of spacetime." And how about this amazing "proof" of things moving backward and forward through time in the quantum world: HeartMath® notes there is "compelling evidence" that both the heart and the brain receive and respond to information about a future event *before the event actually happens.*[51]

Though none of this should really "surprise" us at this point in our journey, it is always exciting to be reminded of the quirky magic of quantum reality.

Resonance also plays a role in developmental biology. Biologist Rupert Sheldrake's theory of *morphic resonance* suggests that biological forms influence each other across time and space through morphic fields of pattern, order and structure that hold and communicate the collective memory of a species. Sheldrake tells us: *"By morphic resonance the form of a system including its characteristic internal structure and vibrational frequencies, becomes present to a subsequent system with a similar form."* Resonance connects form with form.

At the cellular level Intent and Resonance are dynamically in play shaping the physical reality of our biology. Cell biologist Bruce Lipton teaches us that each cell is intelligent and independently capable of adjusting its genes; that our cells read the environmental cues and communicate it to the biology. In his charming sharp-witted style he says that even though we've been *"told that the machine is running by itself,"* that *"our beliefs select our genes. ... When I made my intent known to the system, the system adjusted me to conform to the intent. The cells will adjust to what you told them to do."*

~~~

You might be wondering, why all the technicalities to distinguish Resonance? We're here to become Wake-ups. We are here to think from a new world view, up-to-date with the nature of reality as we know it at the edge of discovery. Though not (yet) in general public awareness, these scientific findings are significant aspects of our emerging *new world view*.

Let's review the facts. We have a "transfer of influence" across all fields. Biological forms communicate with one another as vibrational patterns of three-dimensional nonphysical form; information exchanges outside of physical and energetic mediums; our hearts and brains radiate and transmit intelligence through nonlocal fields. Our minds are "one with" the implicate order, the field of all possibility where we can choose with our power of Observation (when we're aware and awake enough to choose, that is) to "lock on" to the coordinates that form images, ideas, and relationships that eventually become 3D realities. The logic is undeniably clear: Resonance is a powerful friend, a guiding force of creation for human beings that we have access to by virtue of our birthright.

Flick through the hundreds of channels on cable or satellite TV or click on the mega millions of topics on the Internet and you see that the different realities we live in are legion. Each of them is a resonant field. All these vibrational frequency patterns create the infinite diversity of our world. We can think of them as "reality currents." Your consciousness holds reality currents in place. It really is all about what "vibes" we connect to, what we resonate with.

What happens when we "un-consciously" hold onto reality currents? You hear people say they're *struggling*, struggling with money, struggling with relationships, struggling with schoolwork, struggling with health, struggling to get ahead, struggling with excessive substance use, struggling with stress, struggling with "inner demons," struggling to survive. Now, how do you feel—right now in this very moment—after reading that? It pulls you down just "hearing" it. Read it again. Is that what you want to experience? Hardly. What a great gift we have to be able to tune into Resonance so when we're in a reality current that doesn't serve us well, we can change the station and tune into one that does. This does of course require awareness in the moment. In distinguishing Resonance we get this message profoundly: *When you master your mind, you master your life.*

The masters teach that you become what you focus on, so therefore focus on the highest. It is said if you focus on a great being you absorb the qualities of that being. Similarly if you focus on a scoundrel you pick up the vibrational essence of the scoundrel. Focusing on what you want displaces what is undesired. In an Observer-created Reality what you focus on expands. $E=mc^2$. In everyday human terms, increase Energy and you increase mass. Have you ever noticed that when a relatively unknown individual receives skyrocketing media attention and focus from millions of people that the person seems to become "larger"? "Hair and makeup" notwithstanding, consider that their radiant field is *energized* by the amount of attention directed and it literally transforms their appearance.

When you are consciously generating Resonance are all the circumstances going to line up in your direction? Maybe not. However, you can become masterful with regard to your relationship with circumstances. In distinguishing Observer-created Reality—it is in that relationship, of ourselves to our circumstances, where our power resides. Intent sets up and generates a resonant field. Resonance attracts.

When you begin to create from conscious Intent and the result you desire isn't forthcoming, you might wonder, *why isn't my Intent working?* Consider that Intent cannot *not* work. This is the nature of inherent universal principles. They are working whether we believe in their validity or not, whether we're aware of them or not, whether we like them or not. It is wise to establish a highly useful new habit of asking yourself, *What am I resonating?* If you want to manifest a specific result it makes sense that your Resonance would need to be in a sympathetic frequency range of that result. You want to be *vibrationally simpatico.*

Some resonances are harmonic and some are not. The glass shatters when an opera singer reaches a high pitch beyond the resonance range of the glass. What happens to you, to your spirit, when someone screeches at you and shatters the resonance of your peaceful state? A break in affinity. Incoherence ensues. You can generate harmonic Resonance *consciously* when you take note of the quality of the field.

Conscious fields are powerful, that is, fields where the people who comprise them are consciously aware of the field *as* a field. Most of the fields we pass through, in shopping malls, grocery stores, office buildings are not particularly *conscious* fields and are therefore experienced as a bit chaotic or as having a lack of coherence. However, you and I can generate *conscious* fields with the awareness that we are doing so. When you come together with others to generate a *conscious* field, the field is focused and guided by a deliberate, created Intent. In science "coherence" means waves that are in phase with each other. You can generate conscious fields within your company or with your own family. We need only use ordinary logic to realize that when we're vibrating in sync with one another we can produce amazing results together and more rapidly.

~~~

Just as our individual Resonance affects our immediate family, our collective Resonance can collectively affect our human family *when we focus together*. There are already scientific proofs of this.

The Global Consciousness Project started at Princeton University is an international collaborative study of the effect of global events on collective consciousness using random event generators. Their findings, which the researchers say are subtle yet significant with odds against chance of a million to one, show that collective consciousness becomes orderly and causes coherence *when focused* on a major event—such as the response to the attacks of September 11, or the memorial of Princess Diana, or the World Cup championship, or the day Barack Obama was elected the 44th President of the United States of America by an overwhelming majority—"demonstrating that human consciousness interacts with random event generators, apparently 'causing' them to produce non-random patterns."[52] A key point the researchers make is that the collective field is beyond the physical and the electromagnetic.

Mind is primary and mind is powerful.

Just imagine what would be possible in the world if, for example, the United States Congress operated as a *conscious* resonant field. Just imagine them realizing the power of themselves as a coherent field as distinct from a chaotic field. Not because they "have" to because of a crisis, but because they *want* to, as consciously aware leaders of our destiny. Just imagine members asking themselves together, *What is our Intent in this situation?* They could ask themselves, *Are we Being In the Right Question*, a question that will naturally bring about the desired results—or are we in a question taking us in an irrelevant or even damaging direction? Can you imagine the United States Congress becoming aware of whether or not they are *Being In One Conversation, listening with their whole being* to one another? You may or may not be a member of Congress, however you can always apply this in your own life in any and all the resonant fields you participate in.

III

Spiritual teacher Master Omraam Aïvanhov said if you meditate on something for a long while, even on an idea such as compassion, that eventually you will see it as a geometric shape. The Mayans described Absolute Being, what they call *Hunab K'u*, not as a personality but as the Giver of Movement and Measure, symbolized in geometric form as a square within a circle.[53] Platonic solids are said to be the five fundamental geometric forms at the base of every single form in nature—the tetrahedron, cube, octahedron, dodecahedron, and icosahedron. Underlying all physical manifestation is geometry, form, the nonphysical blueprint for the physical. Think about it … if energy and vibration were just free flowing scattering to the wind, then life would be just that—scattered and chaotic. However, the nature of Nature is that she provides containers, structures to "hold" the energy. Geometry is the underpinning of reality.

Visualize the *Star Trek* crew members standing underneath their mode of travel, the transporter that instantly "beams" their molecules through space to another physical location quantum-style with no apparent traveling in between. Their pattern of information that maintains their physical form is what gets "transported." Science fiction maybe, however it does give us a picture of what we are speaking about when we say *creation is vibration*.

How powerful are patterns and blueprints? Consider DNA, the blueprint of uniqueness. Experts say if a DNA strand was unwound it would stretch more than five feet but be only 50 trillionths of an inch wide, and yet encode all the information necessary for building and maintaining life. We scrape our knee and the body repairs itself for the most part back to its original form, magnificently. Russian researchers have found that DNA does not just build proteins: DNA stores information. And further, DNA doesn't merely store information; it is a transmitter chip. Scientists say DNA strands can be converted into fiber-optic cables that guide light along their length and may soon lead to optical computers using light instead of electricity for their calculations.[54] How powerful are nature's magical codes? It is estimated that DNA can maintain its integrity for fifty thousand years and more.

We live in a Multidimensional Universe. In one fundamental dimension the universe is consciousness, in another it is energy, in another it is physical, and in yet another dimension the universe is *mathematical*. Mathematics is a science of relationships of quantities, structure and order and includes geometry, the science of the relationship of surfaces and the size, shape, and properties of space—in other words, *form*.

Thought creates reality. How does it happen? It appears that every pattern of vibration is sound that becomes form, a blueprint in the invisible realm that eventually becomes physical. That we are spiritual beings having a human experience means we participate in the creation of forms. Consider that when we hold any picture habitually, the Resonance generates a pattern, a blueprint that eventually manifests energetically, emotionally, spiritually and physically.

What can we glean from this for ourselves in our Intent for a most enjoyable life? If you attempt to change only the physical and it doesn't sustain itself it may be because it is necessary to change the underlying pattern of Resonance. More effective though is to generate a new pattern, which as you strengthen it, will displace the old pattern.

While you are dreaming of earning millions of dollars you might at the same time be un-consciously in Participatory Knowing that "it can never happen." Intent as a principle is not the culprit. Distinguishing your own Resonance becomes invaluable. When you realize you are holding a pattern of Resonance for "it can't happen" you can just notice that. You realize *that* pattern of Resonance is not "the absolute truth." Then you can generate a new pattern. Using this example, you could create the Intent, *It is possible for me to earn millions.* Just that tiny shift can alter your resonant field and the results that attract from your new possibility.

In the distinction Transformation As Distinct From Change we realized it is easier and more effective to generate a new pattern rather than attempt to change the old one because in order to change something you have to keep it around. Trying to change something keeps in place the very thing you don't want! People say they want to "think outside the box." This typically means they want to think more creatively, have ideas outside what's ordinary and common, in order to accomplish something different, new, exciting, innovative. It might be more accurate and expedient to generate a new "box," not a box to be entrapped by, but a fresh and fertile geometric Resonance.

Thought may not be Energy yet it activates it. Thought may not be matter yet it shapes it. Thought may not "be" Resonance yet it generates it. Thought may not be Energy or matter but simply a connection, a direction, a force of its own unique brand. Perhaps thought simply tunes us in to one set of coordinates or another. What we are doing here is expanding our thinking another octave to see thought and Intent as generating patterns that are not linear, rather the patterns are geometric. Our most focused Intents take form. Remember how enthusiastically movie goers loved the movie, *The Matrix.* Something in the geometry Resonates deeply.

~~~

Why do we love a good mystery? Perhaps because it reminds us of the Ultimate Mystery—the very fact of existence. If we have any inkling whatsoever of curiosity and questioning, we look for the Clues to Solve the Great Riddles of Life. Everywhere in nature and in the recordings of humankind we find the most astounding and elegant pieces of the puzzle. One such "mystery" clue is known as *sacred geometry*, the idea that there are certain universal forms observable everywhere in nature, foundational building blocks of reality, and that the Resonance of these fundamental forms can activate higher states of consciousness. This is illustrated in the architecture of cathedrals and temples throughout our lands.

You may or may not have heard of sacred geometry. This is because the topic has been taught in what are known as the "mystery schools." We could ask why should methods for awakening consciousness be kept a "mystery"? One reasonable explanation put forth is that a person needed to have reached a certain level of responsible maturity and spiritual advancement to learn about such things because when the higher states are reached, (as we have pointed out), it is said one acquires the use of certain "powers" of creation and the holders of the knowledge wanted to make sure people used the knowledge wisely. Now we can consider that we're in an era when such ideas can be discarded simply as old ways of thinking. If we continue to lock in place the idea that enlightened minds or awakened thinking is only for a special few "spiritual elite" how can we ever expect to live the wisdom?

It is said we only require a critical mass of Wake-ups for humanity as a whole to make the jump to awakened consciousness. When you see all the rubble and trouble surrounding you, you can understand why rap artist Talib Kweli sings *"Life is a beautiful struggle"* as the amazing Mary J. Blige joins him in the chorus with the lyrics, *"I try, you know I try."* We are in a time of learning to QuantumThink so we can be agents not of "trying to change" but to be agents of *conscious creation*. Would Divine Intelligence have given us the capability otherwise?

Recognizing patterns can serve to awaken us. As an example, evolving from its early mystical beginnings, the Enneagram, pictorially a nine-pointed star symbolizing the nine faces of human personality types, is being used today in business, education, and in personal consulting as a system that distinguishes the *automatic* behaviors and patterning of each personality type. The purpose is not to identify them as fixed traits; rather the purpose is to transcend the habitual to attain a higher conscious state.[55]

You can tune into geometric vibration in ordinary experience to heighten your awareness and make conscious adjustments. What do you feel from meeting at a round table as compared to sitting at a rectangular table? What do you experience in a trapezoid-shaped room as compared with a square room? It isn't that one geometric shape is "better" than another; it just gives you the opportunity of a different experience. You may not have ever thought about it this way, yet geometry has a definite mystique about it.

We are distinguishing Resonance, The Zing of String. The songwriter intuited that romantic love begins with vibration: *"Dear when you smiled at me, I heard a melody ... Something inside of me started a symphony. Zing! Went the strings of my heart."*[56] Mayan elder Hunbatz Men teaches us: *"Early Mayan sages defined language as y'ak, which when inverted, as is a characteristic dynamic of the Zuyua Mayan language, reads k'ay, meaning 'song.'"* The song called "My Grandfather's Clock" written in 1876 by Henry Clay Work has resonated with people since then, with many renditions sung through the ages, even with a rendition by Boyz II Men in 2004.

The song is based on a legend about a longcase clock that stood in the lobby of a hotel owned by two brothers. The clock kept perfect time until one brother passed away and the clock began to lose time at an increasing rate despite attempts by clockmakers to fix it. When the other brother passed on, the clock stopped forever. Was it chance … or was it Resonance? Musical clues to the mystery of life show up everywhere, even on a decorative postage stamp that arrived in the mail: "*Life is a song. Sing it.*"

IV

Astronomers tell us the lowest note in the universe is the sound of a black hole singing in a B flat, fifty-seven octaves lower than middle C. The "notes" appear as pressure waves rolling and spreading from a supermassive black hole with a period of oscillation of 10 million years. The deepest, lowest notes a human can hear has a period of oscillation about one-twentieth of a second.[57] The magnetic fields along the Sun's outer regions called the corona carry magnetic sound waves in a similar manner to musical instruments like guitars and organs. *As above, so below.* Whether 10 million years or one-twentieth of a second, the same principles of vibration and sound, waves and oscillations, mathematics and music are prevalent throughout nature. Is it any surprise that Earth's fundamental resonance mode known as the *Schumann resonance* and our own human resonance are in a similar frequency range, currently about 7.8 Hz. This universe is mathematical and this universe is musical. Because of mathematical patterns, cycles, and rhythms and sounds, we have music.

Pythagoras, early Greek philosopher, astronomer, mystic, and mathematician every schoolchild learns about in geometry class, discovered the ratios of numerical relationships in what we know as the musical scale. He considered the pattern of seven notes each a whole tone apart and repeated again in every octave as corresponding to the vibrations of nature. Pythagoras used the phrase "music of the spheres" to indicate divine harmony in the celestial spheres, the musical vibration of the planets according to their mathematical proportions of revolutions and distance from Earth. In modern times theoretical physicist and a founder of superstring theory, Michio Kaku proposes that the universe is a symphony, explaining, "*When these little strings vibrate, they create notes and we believe these notes are in fact the subatomic particles that we see around us. The melodies that these notes can play out is called 'matter' and when these melodies create symphonies, that's called the 'universe.'*"

The Sun sings, the planets sing, a black hole sings, the universe sings. We sing. We are musical beings. How does this relate to our thinking?

~~~

Imagine you are a one-thousand stringed musical instrument. You have an Intent to connect with "the one," the beloved partner to share your life with. Nine hundred fifty of your strings are harmonious with that Intent. But what about the other 50? There are strings that are not harmonic with your Intent. Fears, doubts, stray wonderings. You may have doubts that you'll ever meet a suitable person. You have recurring thoughts that you really don't want to get that close or intimate with someone. You have judgments about relationships in general; that they don't really "work." All those thought-strings are not playing in harmonic Resonance with your desired Intent.

However, there *are* still those other wonderful, optimistic, dream fulfilling 950 strings harmonically resonating. So of course one day it happens. You meet someone you are really attracted to on many levels and it's as if there is a little thought bubble over your head that says, *Hi, I would really love to be in a relationship with you but I know it will never work out.* How do you think *that tune* is going to play out? Even if this example of a loving relationship is not specifically relevant for you, there are other areas where you may find your habits of thinking are not congruent with your heartfelt Intent.

To be in Participatory Knowing is to have the instrument of your being harmonious. The great news is you can tune the strings of your instrument *consciously* just as the concertmaster violinist does to lead his fellow musicians. When you become attentive to your *feeling tone*, you can adjust the harmonics of your being to attract and maintain what you seek.

Why are harmonics so important? There are certain root harmonies that are considered to be the fundamentals of all music. They sound pleasant and we enjoy hearing them. When we hear them we feel good. Acoustics and sacred music experts say the octave and other musical relationships appeal to us because they mirror the way the universe works, thus touching something deep within.

A wise and knowledgeable author suggests, *"It is the mathematical resonance within the sacred geometry symbolism which touches our soul."*[58] The musical fifth is a harmonic sound produced when two tones are in a specific relationship to each other, one tone vibrating one and a half times as fast as the other; in musical terms C and G are played together.[59] In his booklet, *The Harmonic Lyre*, Stephen Ian McIntosh suggests the musical fifth "is an archetypal expression of harmony that demonstrates the 'fitting together' of microcosm and macrocosm in an inseparable whole." Renowned harpist and singer and pioneer of women's sacred music, Ani Williams points out that the proportions of the architecture of sacred spaces and the intervals of sacred music both feature the musical fifth. As regards the octave, the seven chakras correspond to the seven tones of the musical scale as do the seven colors of the visual spectrum. There seems to be a close connection with the divine Resonance and with our own Resonance. Otherwise why do we chant mantras, sing hymns, intone scriptural texts? When we hear great music we say *it's got soul.*

～～～

If you have any vestige of skepticism about the perfection pervading natural phenomena of which you and I are part and parcel of, stay with the logic here because this becomes fascinating. The correspondences of universal patterns are nothing short of magnificent. The desirable harmonic of the musical fifth shows itself visually in another fundamental pattern of sacred geometry variously known as "the golden mean," "the golden section," the "golden ratio" or phi, numerically 1.618 to 1. In his book, *The Golden Section: Nature's Greatest Secret,* Scott Olsen ingeniously outlines all the ways this golden ratio is expressed referring to it as an elegant mathematical ratio and proportion relating and uniting parts to the whole, consciousness with creator, suggesting that consciousness may reside in the geometry.[60]

The golden ratio is the division of a line into two segments such that the ratio of the whole line to the larger segment equals the ratio of the larger segment to the smaller one. Notice the similarity in a single string of a musical instrument: when you divide the string at the two-thirds point and you pluck each segment, the two parts sound the same as each other only one octave apart, and the division gives rise to a third tone of the combination of the two tones. And one more refrain ... the Fibonacci series, a series of numbers starting with 1 such that each succeeding number is the sum of its two predecessors. Thus we have 0, 1, 2, 3, 5, 8, etc. This is said to be the way nature reproduces herself.

The golden section has been observed in every form of nature from a cell to the human body, from leaves on a tree to the fruits that nourish us, in the spirals of DNA and of snails, and as well is found in human endeavors of art and architecture, music, and science. Most famously, Leonardo da Vinci used the golden section as the perfect proportion of the human body.

We mention these spectacular correspondences to highlight once again the over-whelming elegance of mathematical relationships, geometric blueprints, and musi-cal proportions that underlie all of material form and appear to be the link between spirit and matter. *Thought creates reality.* We see how it can happen. The logic is compelling.

To create and manifest results is to tune into the source of all creation, the Infinite Intelligence we like to call Divine.

As musical beings we can lighten up and have some fun making music. The musi-cal theme of a movie sets the tone for the story. What is the musical theme you're playing? We can think of the elements of any aspect of our lives as musical notes and ask ourselves how they play together as music. We can look at the qualities of how we might think of ourselves personally, as confident, secure, safe—or as unsure and insecure. How about the notes of the "reality currents" you are traveling in? There could be many ... A spiritual awakening? A sincere hope for moral fortitude so you can get to a proposed place called heaven? A stable place of simply enjoying your life? A monetary or career climb? A once in a lifetime chance of connecting with your soul mate? A contribution to the whole of humanity now and in decades to come? A YouTube phenom? How do they play out? Which qualities are harmonic with one another?

Old world view thinkers wanted to divide and attack and control nature yet from a new world view perhaps it is time to simply be in harmony with the way nature actually works.

What happens when songs are out of tune? When you are not present to Earth as the host of your life we can see what happens. For example, we take our oceans for granted, dumping everything from toxic waste to gasoline to giant "trashed" submarines and loading it with background sounds of military sonar and commercial shipping. What are we doing to the resonant field? How is it affecting marine life, the fish we eat and thus, ultimately ourselves! Bioacoustics scientists say that the unnatural man-made noises beneath our oceans are throwing our marine life out of sorts. Hearing is their primary sense, used for communication and navigation. When they can't hear they can't see, and this affects feeding, breeding and other crucial activities. Acoustics researcher Brandon Southall, sums it up squarely: *"People are inherently tied to the ocean for food, for cures to diseases, for weather … things are more interconnected than we ever could have originally envisioned."*[61]

The distinction Resonance affects everything from family to fish to our own fulfillment. When you wish to discover another level of mastery in your ability to manifest desired and desirable results, you can ask yourself, What am I broadcasting? What am I Resonating?

A most important and perhaps innocently overlooked aspect of personal Resonance in daily life is our voice. Voice is signature. Dolphins and whales are considered to be among the most intelligent creatures on Earth. A pod of bottlenose Dolphins saved the life of a California surfer under shark attack by encircling him, providing enough protection for him to surf to shore. When you go to swim with dolphins, experts train you how to relate so *we* don't infringe upon *them*, so we are kind and we respect and honor them. You learn that their sound is their signature, how they identify themselves. Their Resonance is overwhelmingly joyous.

Voice can reveal your age, your emotional state, your confidence, your disposition, your attitude, language, ethnicity, nationality and your energy level and vitality. Sharry Edwards, sound healing expert advises, *"The frequencies contained in the vocal pattern provide a holographic representation of the body and its energy patterns."*

What is in your own voice? Listen to your own voice as you speak. Listen to a recording of your voice. Watch the wave actions in your musical instrument. Ask yourself what you are broadcasting. Are you putting out cacophony or harmony and symphony? What does your voice manifest in your personal world? Now that you have Resonance as a distinction you can take note. Is your sound of old, outdated "recordings"? Vocal coaches propose exercises to set your voice free. Many of us have voices that are "locked up." They say when you free your voice you undergo a transformation. Sometimes it is as simple as taking in enough oxygen when we're speaking to alter the power of Resonance transmitted vocally.

Listen to the tone of your own voice. Is it meek and fearful, boastful and aggressive, authoritative and pushing, compassionate and loving, sweet and inviting, locked up and apprehensive or open and clear? What is the attractive force field of what you resonate? Are you attracting abundance, optimism, opportunities? Do you resonate good health and well being? Do you attract love and kindness your way? Do you attract inspiring, exciting, creative people? Check the strings of the instrument that is *you*. Are there any out of harmony with your Intent? If so, you can re-attune.

We have spoken about conscious listening. *There is also conscious speaking.* Conscious speaking is creative Resonance. What we say vibrates, extending out as waves. Masters of sound and harmonics, musician Steven Halpern and chant master Jonathan Goldman remind us that sound waves carry consciousness. Consider that your state of consciousness is infused and carried in your speaking. Just as we have automatic habits of thinking and listening we also have Least-action Pathways of our intonation as we speak. Imagine: you can transform your experience of your own confidence level *by consciously altering the tone of your voice.*

In music, pauses are as important as the notes being played. This is also the case in speaking. Silence allows the waves of what was just said to linger and settle in and penetrate. Pauses are important because they enable Intent to hover in the space between you. Then you don't "step on each other's lines" as actors say in moviemaking. Watch a well directed film and you'll notice. An actor pauses for a "beat" … and the moment is that much more poignant.

There is silence in Resonance. It is said the sages are silent even while speaking. Silence is a state of being, a feeling tone from which speech arises. The paradox of being attuned to Resonance is that you need to be silent to hear it. If your mind is noisy, what can you hear? When your mind is busy, what can you feel? When you are speaking and you are silent your words are heard powerfully. Silence creates space. People connect with you because there is room to hear you.

V

We said in this distinction we would be putting it all together. It has been an extended chapter, a kind of symphony with five distinct yet related movements all with the self-familiar theme of Resonance as the manifesting dynamic of creation. As you distinguish Resonance you glean how thought expressed with Intent and experienced as feeling tone, becomes form. This is because of mathematical and geometric patterns that respond to sound and vibration, and are fundamental to existence. Resonance is your state. Your state is a field. Your state is your Participatory Knowing. Your state is a field of attraction. Your state is variable and fluctuating according to your Intent. Your state can be conditioned consciously. Your resonant field is your subtle energy patterning.

Resonance is harmonics. We have multiple resonant tones in our own being just as in Tuva, south Siberian Russia there are "throat singers" who have a singing technique of producing two distinct tones simultaneously, a low toned fundamental pitch and a series of flutelike harmonics.[62] In this Both/And world Resonance occurs at the deep level as the "feeling tone" of your being, the essence that is "you"; and Resonance occurs as your shifting states, from moment to moment, day by day, and through different phases of life. *Resonance brings everything together. Resonance is the heart of unity and wholeness that characterizes All That Is.*

Consider that a patterning dynamic occurs in your health, your relationships, your money, and in our collective interests, as humanity. From the perspective of a resonant field, just as cells can leave the healthy harmonic of our body so can the harmonic of the planetary body go awry.

The idea is to interrupt the unhealthy patterning resulting in dissonance like increased storms, severe draughts, and excessive fires and earthquakes that in turn affect the well being of our cities, our homes, our bodies, our financial systems, and our personal security. Every time we manufacture food that makes us ill we throw off the harmonics. Every time we distort an integrated life process or cut ourselves off from nature we throw the Resonance off-key.

Now we can practice Being In The Right Question and ask: *what are the proper harmonics of Earth?* Then we can do what's necessary to bring about healthy rhythms and symphonic sound. With awakened awareness we see the totality of systems and their interconnection, we live from that Intent, and Allow for the actions that naturally spring forth from that direction. Then being "green" becomes much more than just following a trend for fear of irrevocable damage. You realize that cutting off supply of any resource is not truly a solution to conservation, but simply a Least-action Pathway of old world view thinking of resources as "fixed" and in finite supply. You can think Holistically & Holographically about the universal pattern of birth, life, and renewal and realize that every natural resource can be kept in continuous supply, in growth and renewal, in balance and plentiful. Life is dynamic connectivity. Physicist Fritjof Capra said it well: *"The cosmic web is alive; it moves and grows and changes continually."* It is complex yet simple. Indigenous cultures knew it. Now it is about *living it.*

$\sim\sim\sim$

Mastery is a business of subtlety. How can you become masterful in your creation unless you are aware of what you resonate? It may be an orderly, exquisitely and majestically patterning universe however it is *not* a deterministic one. The great news is like everything else in life we can become conscious of our own Resonance and shift it. We are imbued with will, with the ability to create, with the possibility of choosing, with the manifesting dynamic of Resonance—*and with the ability to shift our Resonance.* We can sing a different tune.

Today sound is already being used as a healing force, a medicine. When you view sound or vibration as the fundamental movement and essence of the manifest world, sound as a healing factor makes perfect sense. Consider healing with sound is possible because we can determine the frequencies required for healthy cell conditions and using the resonant frequency stimulate those cells into their healthful range.

Sound is used to cure and allure, to motivate, to meditate and to concentrate. When you are focused on a project, a signature Resonance is created around it. The project develops a vibratory life of its own. Everything vibrates. Words vibrate. Prayers are powerful. Mantras are powerful. Chanting is powerful. Devotional chanting sung in groups with musical instruments and sometimes dancing is called *kirtan* from the Sanskrit. Contemporary kirtan artists Sri Michael and Uma Nanda Saraswati known as the band Lokah produce kirtan music that can be played in any dance club across the globe yet the Intent is for universal peace and love, or in the translated words of the "Lokah" song lyric, *"May all beings everywhere be happy and free."*[63] While you're dancing and listening to angelic singing harmonies you're drinking in the sublime divine Resonance.

Since reality is fundamentally energy vibrating at varying frequencies, suppose we truly begin to live in this reality of Energy In Flux as our natural way, and we begin to have distinctions for various frequencies in our everyday world—attuned to the energy of ourselves, of a physical environment or space, of the food we eat or the medicines we take, of the people we are with. What would that make possible in terms of creating and living "happy and free"?

Suppose we could actually tune into what the particular frequencies are that create different states, like good health, for example. Suppose scientists committed to mapping frequencies of dis-ease just as they have done with the human genome. Can we elevate our Resonance beyond succumbing to bacteria, toxins, ill willed people, pain or sorrow? Suppose you and I could learn to consciously adjust our own frequency to a range where disease cannot exist—simply becoming an unsuitable, unlivable environment for it.

If someone is out of your frequency range you might not even hear them even though they are speaking because there is no connection made. You and I are tuning forks. Whatever resonates with your frequency will attract. Consider we could make ourselves "invisible" and inaccessible to lower vibrational frequencies by maintaining the highest state ourselves, the highest frequency. Change the underlying pattern and everything changes with it. We're not stating this as an absolute truth or as something else for you to believe in. Just see whether you resonate with it.

~~~

Access to what creates is our topic. However, our task is *mastery*. Mastery of the mind. In QuantumThink we say *"When you master your mind, you master your life."* Is this a statement of fact? Is it just a promotional statement on a website? Either way the idea is worth pondering. Promoting awakened thinking for mastery of the mind could turn out to be a very good idea, indeed.

The distinction Resonance is all about manifesting realities *consciously*. Whenever you let yourself indulge in lower evolved emotional Least-action Pathways like anger, resentment, or guilt, or desires like greed or stinginess masquerading as ambition and frugality, you can ask yourself, where does that feeling of anger go? Where does the vibration of greediness reside? Consider the Resonant field that is you.

We have said that in a Holistic & Holographic world of Infinite Possibility that we are the potential of any human trait. Why bother to fool ourselves into thinking we are irresistible bundles of kindness and gentility if we are not manifesting that? The trait we manifest is what we resonate and what we resonate eventually emerges in form of one sort or another. When the anger or frustration becomes a habitual resonant frequency, we render ourselves out of sync with the fundamental harmonics of life—compassion and love. When we go out of harmony with love, what can we expect? It's not that we are ever "not-love." Rather *we lose our connection to the experience* of love; we go off-line with love. However, we can get our connection back any time, any place, in an instant. This is why we say, *When you master your mind, you master your life.*

The revered meditation master Swami Muktananda used to tell a story about a man sitting under a tree with nothing to eat so he began cooking up a meal for himself in his mind. He put too many chili peppers into his meal so he began screaming aloud *it's too hot, it's too hot!* Another man sitting nearby asked him what was wrong and the man cooking in his mind explained he had put too many mental chili peppers in his meal. The man asked him *if you were only cooking in your own mind why didn't you make it the way you like it?*[64]

Mastering your own mind is now *de rigueur*. Mastery of the mind is in vogue. Mastery of the mind is an idea whose time has come. Until you achieve some mastery with your mind and the thoughts that generate your resonant field then "knowing" the principles is of minor assistance. Remember, mastery of the mind is not mind control; it is not the push or pull of old world view cause and effect dynamics. Mastery of the mind means you establish the habit of awakening your awareness and presence of mind in the moment. Mastering the mind enables you to break free of automatic conditioned reactions that don't work and choose beyond cultural habits that no longer fit. Mastery of the mind means you know the principles of creation for human beings at the edge of knowledge in your era. To be a walking-talking embodiment of universal wisdom—this is no longer a "mystery" at all.

Resonance. The pièce de résistance of creation for human beings. Resonance is the essential element that enables us to make sense of the dynamic of creation and the inextricable role we play within it. Fundamentally and ultimately, what we create we resonate and we resonate what we create. We resonate according to our Intent whether consciously generated with awareness or whether our Resonance occurs in the automatic drift of circumstances. How we recognize this awesome fact, the extent to which we learn how it works, the deftness with which we develop ourselves to use it—this is our great task of mastery. From that deepest Resonance, a place of the silent beat of life, comes all of creation and everything that manifests on Earth. Creation is vibration. Vibration is creation.

Science has become a kind of well respected "god" in modern culture and rightly so as science works extraordinarily well to discover the basis of the way things work in this wondrous universe, to formulize and make results repeatable, and to ingeniously put their discoveries to practical use for the good of humanity, Mother Earth, and all creatures. To prove something in science includes the ability to repeat the result under specified conditions. Even so, there are many significant outcomes that have been repeated even though science has not yet found a way to prove them using existing methods.

The state of enlightenment has been achieved by many persons throughout recorded time though we don't yet have a standard scientific method for "proving" the state of an enlightened being. Nonetheless the experience is irrefutable. We may not yet have our arms in a snug and secure embrace around the idea that our thoughts manifest our reality because of Resonance. However in continuing to distinguish Resonance we can look deeper at the way this works and experience it rather than just parrot a phrase or blindly "believe" it.

The important thing is to look in your own experience. Confucius said, *"Knowledge without practice is useless. Practice without knowledge is dangerous."*

As a continual practice for awakening, notice what you're vibrating. Consciously generate your own Resonance. Life is a song. Sing it.

⨎ QUANTUMTHINK RECREATION ⨎
Live the Wisdom of Resonance

ONE» Speak consciously. Take a musical pause.
Today three times with three different people, pause before you speak. Become aware of the "song you are singing." After you speak, pause and allow the vibration of meaning and message to resonate in the space before proceeding with the conversation.

TWO» Generate a new resonant field for an area of your life.
Select a result you desire now. Spend a day noticing the Resonance you are vibrating with regard to this desired outcome. What you are resonating expresses as thoughts and meanings and feeling tones. If your Resonance does not match the Resonance of the desired outcome, just notice that. When you entrap yourself in a limiting thought form nothing can get in and nothing can get out. Free yourself from inharmonic or incoherent thought forms and thought patterns you have been living as "truths." Then, generate a new resonant field with your Intent. What would you be saying to yourself if this new field was in place? What would you be experiencing? What would you be feeling?

THREE» Tune in to voice.
Listen to voices, the tones and quality of other people's voices. What does it tell you about them, emotionally, mentally, spiritually? Notice what voice qualities you resonate with and those you don't. **Listen to your own voice at various times throughout the day.** Notice the tonality and any Least-action Pathways of voice you express. Awaken your self-expression by becoming aware of your voice quality in the moment.

For more fun ...

Sound. Have a conversation with someone you are close with, using sounds only, not words and nothing decipherable like words. Using non-verbal but audible sounds, communicate the following: sadness, anger, enthusiasm, joy, irritation, love, peace, compassion, kindness. Notice the Resonance of each of those states and how powerfully they "communicate" even without words.

Sing. Find a song that resonates deeply with you. Listen to it beyond the meaning of the lyrics. SING, sing it. Notice what singing it does to your state of Resonance.

Listen. Listen to recordings of different sounds, chants, bells, hymns, and speaking. Notice what it does to your own Resonance.

QUANTUMTHINK-WAVE
Consider the Source

You drink a glass of water. Was it pure? Was it beneficial to you? What was its source? A natural spring? An artesian spring where the water was fully matured and came up from the ground naturally? Aahhh, ... so good. The *quality of the source* has everything to do with the effect of the water in your body.

When someone gives you their "opinion" do you consider the source? Did the person relaying it have an agenda or spin coloring it? When you read a newspaper or watch the evening news on TV, do you consider the source of that story or editorial? You hear a bit of information and you might question it. Where did this information come from? Was the source of it reliable, credible? You consider the source.

Consider that the quality of whatever knowledge, information or counsel you receive from another individual or organization is directly related to the maturity of that person's or group's evolution. Ability for open mindedness, to think beyond automatic conditioned beliefs and conclusions. In this case we are speaking about evolution in terms of wisdom and ability to *live that wisdom*, as distinct from merely espousing or speaking it.

The source shapes and gives rise to the rest. Clarity from someone's communication will be consonant with the source, meaning the clarity of that person. This is just ordinary logic. How can someone generate something from themselves that they are not?

Conversely, what *you* give is also a function of the level to which you have developed yourself, and to what degree of mastery you have personally achieved. Whatever you partake of, be it food, beverage, the company of people or knowledge, it's always wise to consider the source. It's beneficial to contemplate this.

You may think of someone as mature or immature, a novice or a master, informed or uninformed, opinionated or pundit. In any of these examples, what they give forth is going to be consistent with their own development.

What characterizes a wise person? The degree of their connection to source. Ultimate source. You can give to the extent that you yourself have mastered something. When you master your own state, your own field, people receive your level.

This book is for the purpose of waking up. What are we awakening? What happens when we awaken? What gives us the power to awaken?

Perhaps we are awakening to that very power itself. We call it Divine. Where does it exist? Where does it reside? If it is not physical then it is truly as the ancient scriptures say, formless. Without form but residing within form as form. It is Source. In a sense it is the beginning and mathematically we call the beginning zero (0). Zero seems to indicate nothing. Yet if you think of "no-thing" as empty you'll find you're seriously mistaken. There is great power in the Zero-Point State—when you awaken to it.

21 ZERO-POINT STATE:
THE POWER IN NOTHING
Creation starts here

Just for a moment, now ... after you read this paragraph, close your eyes and observe your own mind. See if you are able to sit with an empty mind free of all thoughts, even for a minute or two. If thoughts come in (as they are likely to) just let them float away gently as a leaf in the wind. Sit for a moment in the inner stillness.

Now you are back. From this state of peaceful equanimity, consider: *Stillness is empty—however, it is not nothing.*

Since time immemorial spiritual masters have summoned us to "go within" to the place of stillness. Perhaps you thought of this as metaphor or a poetic way of speaking. Yet, it is literal. By turning the attention "within" we connect to the most fundamental dimension of reality. When we connect this way on a regular basis it has increasingly positive effects on us. This inward focus is called in our culture *meditation*. Meditation is the staple of every mastery tradition, the core practice. What makes meditation so important? We say that QuantumThink is a *walking-talking-living meditation*. The truth is you cannot actually QuantumThink unless you are in a meditative state, aware of your own Awareness. There are many different types of meditation yet at least one goal of meditation appears to be common to all and that is to still the mind. What happens in this state? Nothing. Zero. Yet, in this state that we are distinguishing as the Zero-Point State we discover The Power in Nothing.

～～～

Even in science "zero" is not really nothing. In physics the zero-point refers to the state when all motion ceases and energy fluctuations come to a rest which occurs at a temperature of absolute zero.[65] However, scientists tell us, Heisenberg's quantum Uncertainty Principle requires that there be a small amount of residual motion even at absolute zero. Nothing is ever completely at rest. There is always some fluctuation. And when all the residual "invisible" energy fluctuations are added together in typical quantum paradoxical fashion the state of "absolute zero" contains enormously powerful energy. It turns out that the zero-point is indeed quite something. In fact, renowned Quantum physicist John Hagelin states, *"At the deepest level of nature's dynamics, the characteristic energy is so enormous that the energy density in a single cubic centimeter of empty space exceeds the entire mass energy of the visible universe."*[66] That's worth repeating. There is more potential energy in one cubic centimeter of empty space (i.e., "nothing") than in the mass energy of the entire visible universe!

We have said that the new science has proven much of what we used to think we knew about the nature of reality to be inaccurate. Not so astonishing given the collection of well-intentioned inaccuracies put forth by scientists throughout the ages—the flat Earth, the Earth-centered galaxy, matter as solid, the inability of brain cells to regenerate—to name a mere few, have been proven wrong. Another example of a scientific assumption shown to be inaccurate is the idea of a vacuum. What science once thought to be empty space, or "nothing," based in the knowledge of zero-point energy turns out instead to be a plenum, full. What was once called a vacuum is called a plenum because it is replete with energy. There is more to empty space than meets the eye.

To remind ourselves once again, QuantumThink is not about science; it *is* about how the discoveries of science shape the way we think. It is worth exploring this reversal of knowledge to see how we can use it, at least metaphorically if not literally, to shape our thinking for a life of mastery.

~~~

How can there be so much powerful energy in what appears to be "nothing"? Let's contemplate the facts together. Zero-point energy is defined as "the *field of quantum fluctuations* that exists at a temperature of absolute zero." However, according to physicists, there is never a state where there are absolutely no fluctuations. There is always some hint of activity. This fact is key to understanding the enormous potential energy. Astrophysicist, Bernard Haisch, a leading authority in the zero-point field, explains it so well that even if you are not scientifically minded it will make perfect sense to you. He says, *"If you add up all these ceaseless fluctuations, what you get is a background sea of light whose total energy is enormous: the electromagnetic zero-point field."* He explains that because the zero-point field is the lowest energy state it is unobservable, and since we see things by way of contrast (dark and light) and because of the fact that everything is filled with the light of the zero-point field with no contrast, we don't see it. *"Since it is everywhere, inside and outside of us, permeating every atom in our bodies, we are effectively blind to it. It blinds us to its presence. The world of light that we do see is all the rest of the light that is over and above the zero-point field."* Most interestingly Dr. Haisch proposes that *"It [the zero-point field] may represent an unlimited source of energy available everywhere."*[67]

We can look at these facts on their own and think, okay, that's nice, but how does this relate to me? The natural laws operating throughout the universe are also functioning in you and me. We can consider that for human beings there may be great potential power, "invisible" power, and perhaps the source of all our power in what appears to be nothing, empty space. The identical principles that exist and operate throughout nature at the edge of infinity also operate in us and in all smaller aspects of reality down to the sub-atomic levels, down to the quantum domain. We can learn about the nature of the universe by looking at ourselves, and we can learn about ourselves by looking at the nature of the universe.

It is worthy of mention in this time of nations seeking energy independence and of our planet's ecology guardians seeking to reduce the effects of fossil fuels that investment and research into utilization of this unlimited energy source seems to be an idea whose time *should* come![68]

You have to be in a state of calm to be able to create anything. It's that simple. Why? Because "we" don't create in a vacuum, by ourselves, isolated. We create by virtue of being an expression of ultimate being, in tandem with the underlying sea of light, consciousness, Infinite Intelligence. The place of silence where all great beings know themselves as one is the state from which all masterful accomplishment derives. We are calling this the Zero-Point State.

Zero-point energy is the state of rest for matter. The Zero-Point State is the state of rest for mind. As illogical as it sounds the Zero-Point State—The Power in Nothing could be the most important thing we can distinguish to *access* our power to create.

At the very beginning of our QuantumThink journey we said this is an adventure into your own mind. We noted that in the general culture, due to the old world view premise that "only matter is real," we've never learned the relationship of our own mind to others' minds and of our own mind to matter. Yet this knowledge is at the heart of what creates.

What they didn't teach you in school are the 5 Natural Faculties of your very own mind, each of which we have distinguished along the way. Now as still another access point of entry in the hologram we can consider this "distinction within a distinction," the 5 Natural Faculties of Mind and each one's central dynamic. Contemplate each faculty of mind and the totality of them and reflect on all the ways you have been exercising these faculties as you QuantumThink.

5 Natural Faculties of Mind

Faculty of Mind	*Associated Dynamic*
Power of Observation	Intent
Power of Nonlocation	Intuition
Power of Transmutation	Energy
Power of Meditation	Awareness
Power of Manifestation	Resonance

Let's contemplate together. The power of Observation means your ability to hold anything in your awareness in such a way that you make it a reality. The dynamic of Intent means what you bring to your Observation activates the field of intelligence. The power of Nonlocation means the ability of mind which is "not located" in the sense of having a spatial or temporal quality, to "go" anywhere. The dynamic of Intuition is our access into Nonlocality becoming attuned to specific information or messages we are receiving or sending. The power of Transmutation means the ability to use Energy in one form and transmute it into another form, a higher or more evolved form, to convert our experience and feeling of life. The power of Meditation is the ability to still the mind and center ourselves in pure Awareness so we may rest or choose or create. The power of Manifestation is the ability to bring things from idea into form either experientially or as a practical external result using Resonance.

The point we wish to emphasize is that the dynamic of Awareness is essential to all the rest of our mind's faculties. To exercise your Intent you must be *aware of your Observation*, what you hold in your consciousness at a given moment in spacetime. To tune into your Intuition is to be *aware of your power to connect to intelligence* and information in the field Nonlocally. To transmute Energy you have to be *aware first of the quality of the Energy* that is present. To consciously and proactively utilize your power of Manifesting outcomes means being *aware of the Resonance you emanate*. To fully embrace the fruits of the power of Meditation is to engage in the practice of becoming *aware of Awareness itself*.

The Recreation for the distinction Zero-Point State is Meditation. You may be familiar with Meditation as a practice or with the idea of it at least, though you might not have considered Meditation as a natural faculty of mind, *your* faculty.

~~~

Spiritual teachers often say we all go looking for happiness outside of us yet the true peace and happiness is found not in outer sense pleasures but within ourselves. Swami Muktananda wrote that we strive for accomplishments and attainments and relationships all day long and then at night we are exhausted and all we want is sleep. He says during sleep you don't want to accomplish anything, you don't desire to relate with anyone, you simply want rest. When you awaken you feel refreshed and energized. He compares this to the process of Meditation.

You might be wondering, if QuantumThink is a *walking-talking-living meditation* then why establish a formal practice of Meditation? It's a Both/And phenomenon. An athlete with natural talent and honed skills in a particular sport adds body conditioning to their overall repertoire so they are better able to use those talents and skills specific to their sport. Just because you can win a tennis match from time to time doesn't mean you've mastered it. It takes conditioning. Tennis coaching and match competition fine tune the distinctions of tennis while daily physical conditioning enhances the *ability to utilize* those talents and honed skills. Similarly, as you learn the QuantumThink distinctions and you condition your ability to be in the Zero-Point State of calm, you master QuantumThinking ever more easily and effortlessly.

There are many different methods and types of meditation. Active meditation. Mindful meditation. Empty mind meditation. Guided meditation. Object meditation. Devotional meditation. A book by Jonathan Sear describes ten major traditions of meditation.[69] Dr. Fred Travis, Director of Center for Brain, Consciousness and Cognition at the Maharishi University of Management points out that brain states are distinctly different during various practices of meditation. He compares Tibetan Buddhist meditation with its focus on unconditional loving-kindness and

318 Do You QuantumThink?

compassion, Mindfulness Meditation which focuses on watching the mind, and Transcendental Meditation® referred to as "effortless transcending."[70]

We're not here to recommend or promote or discuss any specific form of meditation. You can discover for yourself which one(s), if any, you resonate with. Our Intent as QuantumThinkers is to distinguish in our direct personal experience what we could call "the meditative state of all meditative states," the Zero-Point State. Consider that to distinguish the Zero-Point State in your experience is to connect with the inexhaustible source of creation. "Connect" is a word with limits as it implies "two" separate entities. It may be more accurate to say we are part and parcel of Infinite Mind.

Whatever your preferred idea of the ultimate mystery, the cosmic creative source of all creation (you know ... the One with the great sense of humor) ... be it God, grace, the Void, Universal Spirit, Jesus, Krishna, Allah, Hashem, Hunab K'u, Divine Being, or Infinite Intelligence—whatever belief or archetypal image you personally relate to as a reference to this awesome, ineffable source of all of creation—in this distinction we can use a simple word with profound meaning, *Source*.

The field of all fields, the unified field of consciousness is described by ancient philosophers and modern scientists alike. The most classic of Chinese literature known as the *Tao Te Ching*, a treatise on creation and enlightenment said to be written around the 6th century B.C. by the sage Lao-Tse, contains poetic verses that have been translated in many ways and have been meditated upon for centuries and millennia. The "Tao" generally translated as "the way" refers to the eternal, changeless and nameless, formless presence from which all creation is born. The Tao is "one," unchanging and infinite. In Chapter 5 of the *Tao Te Ching* the Tao is said to be "empty yet inexhaustible, giving birth to infinite worlds." Certainly this syncs with leading scientific insight.

Scientists have long searched for the nature of a unified field that would have us understand the nature of reality at its most fundamental unity. John Hagelin makes a penetrating declaration: *"I have spent the last quarter century conducting cutting edge research in unified quantum field theories, and have led an international scientific investigation into the nature and origin of human consciousness. The conclusion of these 25 years of research is that human consciousness, at its deepest level, and the unified field which underlies the whole of Nature, are one and the same."*[71] He states unequivocally: *"The unified field is consciousness, universal consciousness. Consciousness is the unified field."*[72]

~~~

The Zero-Point State as we are using it can be said to be the state when the mind is at rest. When the fluctuations of mental thoughts and rampant emotions simmer, when they go from high intensity oscillations and subside into a state of quietude and tranquility, we connect in the Zero-Point State. A resting state of mind, a mind aware of itself in the Zero-Point State is merged in the Source of consciousness, the ocean of consciousness of which each of us is a precious drop. We cannot force or push ourselves there; there is an Allowing to it. In the Zero-Point State we are free of automatic conditioning and thus, we are able to choose freely and freely create.

You can try this experiment at home. Please do. Give yourself a "bad" thought, totally fabricated of course … for example, how about, *I'm not good enough,* a popular favorite. Hold that thought for a few seconds, and then visualize that thought disintegrating into thin air like a thought bubble popping out of existence. Now remember that you can create a new thought, for example, *I am part and parcel of Infinite Intelligence, the Great Self.* Create the new thought. Now you can express silent gratitude for the grace that enables you to enact that five-fold action of consciousness, represented by the ancient icon we have discussed, the dancing Shiva Nataraj. This ecstatic dance symbolizes the five-fold nature of consciousness and of creation itself. We bring something into existence by naming it. We sustain it by holding it in our consciousness. We "destroy" it or it goes out of existence when we take our focus off of it. These are three of the actions. The fourth action is that this process has become hidden, concealed through "forgetfulness." We forget that we have access to the awareness that enables us to choose new thoughts. Then through the fifth action called "grace" we remember it again. In other words if we forget the *Source* of creation in our own awareness, we tend to get lost in the changing creations themselves. However, due to grace we remember that we can connect with source and create something new, something more empowering. Perhaps this is what is meant when reality is spoken of as an "illusion" in the literature of consciousness. Our thought creations are real, however they have a transitory and ever-changing nature, coming into and going out of existence, just as energy particles leap in and out of existence in the world of scientists.

It is said that because of grace we are able to remember and become aware. We are not simply the changing thoughts that pass through our minds; we are that which witnesses the thoughts. In Meditation we get to consciously experience that five-fold action of mind. We watch the thoughts come and go. We become the witnessing Self remembering that we are the Awareness doing the watching, and we realize we can bring something else into being as duly appointed co-creators of the ecstatic dance of life. Meditation is a remembrance of who we are beyond the roles we play and the karmas we have created. Meditation is an access to remembrance of our Source.

Remembrance of our connection to our Source does not mean throwing out our worldly individuality. A lot of people love to ego-bash. They feel compelled to blame "the ego" for all their problems and for all their suffering. *I couldn't help it—it was the ego! Oh, that nasty fellow, that dratted ego, if only I could get rid of my ego.* Consider that this is just another vestige of Either/Or thinking. Things in and of themselves are not "the enemy." Fire can warm you or scorch you. Earth can smother you or support you. Water can drown you or cleanse you. Air can poison you or keep you alive. It's all about how you relate to each element. It's all about how we *relate* to the ego. People criticize the mind blaming it for their woes and troubles, yet sages say it is the *tendencies* of the mind, not the mind itself that brings difficulties.

The ego is not the problem. We need the ego to continue the play of life. Without the ego there would be no differentiation, no idiosyncrasies, no individual callings and purposes, no spice in life. Our egos are the actors that live out soul's purpose and spirit's calling. Our egos express passion that propels us to create new ideas and improved structures for living cooperatively. Ego makes life exciting, interesting, fascinating, diverse. The ego colors our genius in art and science and philosophy. It is not the ego in and of itself that presents life's rocky roads; rather it is the *attachment to* or *identification with ego states* that produces our dilemmas. The myth of choice is relevant here. If a person was awakened enough to be at choice, would he *choose* the ego states of greediness, arrogance, or mean-spiritedness? Recall the wisdom of Jesus: *Forgive them for they know not what they do.*

Distinguishing questionable habits of behavior or mechanical thinking as Least-action Pathways is not to condone or make excuses for those habits, nor is it to condemn them. Let's not confuse "forgiveness" with "acceptance." The significance of remembering the myth of choice is twofold. If it is your own Least-action Pathway you can interrupt it, give it no meaning, and consciously generate a desirable Intent. If it is another person's Least-action Pathway of their ego state you can stand in compassion and bring your light to them. From a QuantumThink perspective of "one," forgiveness is truly for one's self, for harboring judgment rather than compassion. If there is only "one" who is there to forgive? Some people may not like this idea. We love to be right about how wrong "they" are, don't we? Yet to truly live the wisdom is to actually live the wisdom. No that was not a typo you just read. The *tao* of living the wisdom is authentically looking at one's own habits and choosing the highest virtues.

Perhaps you've read stories told by sages of renunciation, the separation between the material and the spiritual. A king gives up his throne and his worldly possessions in his fervent quest for spiritual enlightenment that will bring him peace. He goes on foot into the wilds of the forest with no material trappings expecting enlightenment as reward for his sacrifices. And yet as he sits alone in the wilderness, spiritual liberation and peace of mind elude him. The king's idea of renunciation is based in the fallacy of an Either/Or system, i.e., Either "material" Or "spiritual" and a clouded understanding of renunciation which caused him to selfishly abandon his worldly responsibilities as king.

Ego without Source is ineffectual; Source without ego is abstract. Infinite Intelligence cannot stay abstract or there would be no world. The idea is to be non-attached to your ego personality. Bestselling bard of all time, Shakespeare wrote, *"All the world's a stage, and all the men and women merely players: they have their exits and their entrances; and one man in his time plays many parts ... "* Between the entrances and the exits of the many parts we play, behind the scenes in the backstage of our soul is the watcher, the Self—meaning Awareness itself as the Zero-Point State. As we practiced in Being Centered, we enjoy the quirks and idiosyncrasies of the characters in our movie because of the ego. If we are here to evolve ourselves then the ego assists us in doing this. How do you feel about your own ego? The sage says *use everything to your advantage.* Love your ego, love your Self.

~~~

So ... what is Meditation?

A young woman was attending a transformational seminar being led by a gentleman whom she knew had been the translator for many years for a great meditation master. If anyone could teach her what is meditation surely this man could, she thought. During the break she ran to catch him as he was walking out of the room. Wait, just a moment may I ask you, please, can you tell me about meditation? He stopped walking, stood silent for a moment and looked nonplussed into her eyes. He asked, *"Do you meditate?"* *"Yes, I do,"* she replied. *"Then you know more about meditation than I do."*

How can you explain to someone your personal experience of Meditation? That would be Conceptual Knowing at best. There is only one way to know the benefits of Meditation and that is to practice Meditation. We'll have that opportunity in the Recreation.

Meditation is the mother of all 5 Natural Faculties of Mind because the dynamic of Meditation is Awareness. Every time you remember your Awareness, your Self with a capital "S", you awaken to the Zero-Point State, stillness, if only for a moment. That moment is enough for you to choose—a different Intent, long enough to tune into Energy you can transmute, long enough for you to Allow an unfolding. In doing so, you *consciously* shape the world. To live in the Zero-Point State is not to become inactive; it is to be fully enlivened. We imagine we're powerful when our mind is busy yet paradoxically we are most powerful when our mind is at rest.

You watch some TV sitcoms or movies and inevitably you'll come across a scene of meditators chanting the sound of all sounds, OM. Invariably the scene spoofs meditation and "OM-ing." In the "real" world cynics snap, *We can't just sit around and chant OM all day.* Obviously we need to take wise and intelligent actions in this world; then again since the sounding of OM connects us to Source, it seems a wise place to start. Context is everything. Context is space. In the wisdom of the *Tao Te Ching,* "Shape clay into a vessel; It is the space within that makes it useful."[73]

Facts and experience alike indicate that there are highly practical benefits to meditative states, documented time and again in clinical studies conducted at leading universities and scientific institutions across the lands. Meditation has been shown to enhance focus, clarity, and mental acuity.

In a growing number of schools students are being taught to meditate. In some schools they are also being offered hatha yoga classes, a form of meditation that uses body postures called *asanas* for maintaining focus and enhancing mind-body-spirit harmony and balance. Yoga is said to clear the mind and increase the experience of well being. The effects of meditation reduce stress and produce calm, improve scholasticism and increase self-confidence.

Wouldn't you imagine that parents would be elated that their children are training themselves to maintain steady, clear minds and balanced bodies? Most parents are. Yet in Aspen, Colorado and in Massena, New York, and in Alabama parents demanded that these classes be taken out of the school, citing a conflict in religion and state.[74] Though some forms of meditation have roots in ancient civilizations in the Eastern part of our shared world, the fact is that meditation and yoga are not considered to be religious. Why do parents fear their children having meditation and yoga classes when it is scientifically proven to be so beneficial, when it has been proven to reduce violence in schools, increase test scores, and improve self-esteem and handle stress better?[75] It can be a simple "reason" of unfruitful culturally conditioned Least-action Pathways kicking in.

We all seek peace. Everyone wants peace. People seek solutions to eliminate violence among youth. A ten-year study called "Report Card on School Violence Prevention" found that the $10 billion spent on security guards, metal detectors, and zero-tolerance punishments did little to improve the quality of a day in the life of the average student. This indicates that the traditional "outside-in" approach that school and law enforcement officials have used to reduce violence in the wake of Columbine simply hasn't worked.[76]

We want peace in our schools and we want our children to be at peace within themselves. Meditation equalizes emotions and quells violence. Children who meditate say they are happier, calmer, and doing better in school. Yet when people are not thinking from an awakened state, when the mind is so conditioned to misconceived beliefs and fears—then even when a viable, scientifically validated and subjectively confirmed solution is presented and *is working*, people force out of existence the very solution they desire! Meditation brings peace to children and yet parents will force it out of the schools. The Least-action Pathways are strong. Due to a lack of awareness in "grown-ups" of the distinction between "religion" and "yoga" parents and clergy cut off what is beneficial for their children. You can see why a society of Wake-ups is *essential* if we are ever to *genuinely* embody the wisdom of spiritual teachings at the heart of all religions.

Consider that this is not dissimilar to the puzzlement of why the United States Congress would not vote to allocate a trifle two percent of the U.S. annual defense budget to establish a cabinet level Department of Peace?[77] St. Francis of Assisi advised, *"While you are proclaiming peace with your lips, be careful to have it even more fully in your heart."* A concept of peace is not enough to have peace be our established reality. Reality is Context-dependent. Create a context of peace in your government and peace is likely to follow. Create a context of peace within a child and peace in the school hallways is likely to follow. Avant garde musical composer and pianist John Cage once said, *"I can't understand why people are frightened of new ideas. I'm frightened of old ones."*

~~~

We are here on Earth to evoke one another's wisdom, to learn from each other, and to create collaboratively from the place of inherent genius, the fertile stillness of the Zero-Point State. Just as each of us has a unique Purpose to give to the world, each culture also has its unique Purpose and gifts to offer as a culture. The West has traditionally been associated with pioneering and with advancements in technology and science which in turn develop the world society as a whole. Generally speaking, Eastern cultures are associated with spiritual wisdom and holistic practices for the mind. Now it is time for fusion—for the world to come together, neither in conformity nor in uniformity, but in collaboration and integration of our specialized gifts for the benefit of others and all. To paraphrase the keen wit and wisdom of Sri Sri Ravi Shankar, yogi master and spiritual head of The Art of Living Foundation, *We accept the foods of all cultures; why shouldn't we also enjoy the wisdom of all cultures?*

Meditation is a discipline that yields positive results. One literally cannot meditate unless there is a true interest in meditating. *Consider that authentic discipline can only come from within each of us of our own choosing.* Otherwise it is an external law imposed on us and laws as we know can be easily broken. People do not enjoy being told what to do. Have you noticed? How do *you* respond when someone tells you what to do or how you should be? Children are people, too. Old world view thinking has "trained" parents and educators to attempt to discipline children with old world view methods, telling them what to do, how to be, and threatening consequences if the children don't conform to their standards and rules. Beloved Lebanese-American poet and theologian Kahlil Gibran wrote in *The Prophet*, *"Your Children are not Your Children, they are the sons and daughters of life's longing for itself. They come through you but not from you ... You may give them your love but not your thoughts for they have their own thoughts. You may house their bodies but not their souls."*

What would be possible in our world if we pointed the way for children to tap their own wisdom, develop discipline themselves, and give them sensible explanations and compelling experiences that would have them naturally initiating their own discipline?

We are stewards of reality. By virtue of our birthright and the gift of grace we each express the creation principle; this is our essence. To be in true harmony and integrity with ourselves is to be free to create. The wisdom informs us that the true teachers realize that the way to have their students become masterful is to allow them to discover the answers for themselves, the wisdom within themselves. Self-generated self-discipline begins like a covenant with one's Self and evolves into an integral way of being, vivifying the virtues of temperance, compassion, kindness and love. In the Zero-Point State we access the Source of all wisdom.

Swami Vivekananda, a spiritual teacher from the East who lived in the latter part of the 19th century said, *"Science and Religion both seek the truth; there's no reason they shouldn't converse."* Vivekananda voiced that 100 years ago. Okay, it took some time; nonetheless this is finally happening. One of the most significant things going on in our new era, in this new time of evolution for humanity, is the re-converging of science and spirituality. It's happening as scientists begin to realize that pure consciousness could very well be the source of all material reality. Many scientists today are studying the Vedic literature of India, considered the most ancient teachings on the science of consciousness. Others are studying Kabala, Sufism, and the Christian mystics; the traditional cultures of the Aborigines, Druids, ancient Mayans, Incas, Hopi, and others known to have direct personal knowledge of consciousness.

Why are scientists studying these ancient teachings about the nature of consciousness? We are at a turning point of Conscious Evolution, of becoming cognizant with the nature of reality proven in scientific realms and experienced in spiritual realms, and realizing that these realms are not separate; they originate from the identical Source. The divine brought us to science and science is bringing us again to the divine.

~~~

The Zero-Point State can come upon you spontaneously. When you enter a place of sanctuary, a church, synagogue, mosque, great hall, a sacred site or a beautiful surrounding in nature you go immediately into a restful state. The Resonance of the place silences the chatter of your mind. The Zero-Point State can have the power to alter your life forever. Apollo 14 astronaut Edgar Mitchell holds audiences spellbound as he recounts when he traveled to the Moon and on the way back home to Earth when he looked out the window of the spacecraft and could see simultaneously the Earth, Moon, and the Sun he experienced that everything in the universe was alive with consciousness and that this quantum moment changed his life forever. You might not be taking a trip to the Moon anytime soon, however *you can always access the Zero-Point State as a conscious choice.*

Whether brought about serendipitously by unforeseen circumstances or by consciously generating it, the Zero-Point State is the ultimate state of lucidity. The Zero-Point State is replete with gifts. The gift of serenity, the gift of creation, the gift of choice. There is another gift that comes from the Zero-Point State, a gift for the soul. Sri Sri Ravi Shankar speaks about various types of restlessness saying it is fortunate to experience the restlessness of the soul because in that restlessness is a longing for connection to Source. The great gift of the Zero-Point State is that it's our *natural* connection to Source.

Zero-point energy is the state of rest for matter. The Zero-Point State is the state of rest for mind. Even so, some say they find it uncomfortable or even difficult to be with themselves in quietude, just "being" without "doing" anything else. They admit they need diversion, an activity of some kind to distract them from the meanderings of their own mind.

Where do people go for refuge from the incessant activity of the world and chatter of the mind attempting to make sense of the mundane merry-go-round? Some turn to drinking, drugs, sex, sleep, power; some unfortunately regress to violence either verbally or even physically. What about you? Are you able to just sit and be with yourself in stillness without any other stimulation or diversion? Do you command your own mind, or does it take you over? How is the state of your own mind? Your mind can take you places you don't even want to go. We all experience this. As you QuantumThink and heighten your awareness you become even more acutely aware of those moments when your mind seems to run away with itself. This keen awareness is good. A thought visits you—and the stream of relative thoughts follow along in formation like a flock of pelicans with no prompting necessary from you.

Some say they actually try to reach a state of calm yet it eludes them, perhaps because they try to aggressively grab onto it. The classical-mechanical world view has trained us to "push and pull" to get something to happen. Rather than clutching at stillness like a hungry wolf … you can simply *Allow* this state to come to you. Hold the Intent for it. You don't have to work so hard. Let stillness embrace you.

Meditation master Gurumayi says her own guru would tell them as children that even to be able to sit still quietly for a few moments—this is an achievement. What can we do to achieve a steady mind? What can we do to condition ourselves and develop our ability to live in the Zero-Point State? Now it is so simple: You meditate.

Think of it. … Just as we plug in our cell phones and handhelds to recharge them, we can plug in to the ultimate power charging station. When you meditate you plug in to the Zero-Point State and recharge and renew yourself. You replenish yourself at the Source of all power. At night we recharge our bodies in sleep; in daylight we recharge our minds by connecting to the Zero-Point State.

～～

What distinguishes the Zero-Point State? Clarity, purity and peace. All beings long for peace. Peace of mind, peace of spirit, peace among nations. Yes, we seek peace in the outer world yet as we know from a new world view there are distinctions between "inner" and "outer" yet no actual separation. Mahatma Gandhi, whose life literally was his message, counseled that we must *become the change we wish to see in the world.* Our collective state is projected in the outer world as the circumstances we live with. If we want to see coherence and cooperation and harmony among people, creatures, natural resources, and elements of nature, it behooves us

326 Do You QuantumThink?

to establish the state of coherence and cooperation and harmony within ourselves. How do we achieve this? Meditate. The masters say happiness lies within you. Like the Cracker Jack box you look within and you find the prize, happiness within yourself. You locate the priceless pearl.

Science and spirituality took separate forks in the road yet they were never actually separate. Along the development of human affairs we *distinguished* them and then we forgot that we did that. The oneness of the systems which constitute life has been here forever. There is a popular theme in so-called conscious cultures to drop thinking and the intellect (sometimes referred to as "mind") in favor of the heart. Famous poets and masters have also spoken in those terms. If science and spirituality are remembering to converse then shouldn't the heart and the intellect converse also? To QuantumThink is to Live Fully Dimensionally integrated and embracing all our faculties. Isn't it possible that you can think from your heart? Holistic & Holographic means one is contained within the other and they are interconnected. Masters say the heart is the center of the mind and the mind is located in the heart. If we conclude that we cannot think and act from the heart simultaneously we put false human limits on Infinite Intelligence.

How does this pan out in life? That's easy, a no-brainer, as we say in the vernacular. A vivid example: Achieving peace on Earth through the vehicle of war hasn't worked ... ever. The mind of the heart tells you not to kill people. The reaction of fear has you kill people. The intellect tells you these two instructions don't mesh. If you are truly in your "right mind," your heart of hearts, how could deliberately strategized mass killing known as "war" ever be a solution for peace?

Awakened thinking is heart-based thinking. Imagine your thinking and your intellect as heart-based. Yes, we can hold that reality. It's an Observer-created Reality after all. It's time now.

⌇⌐

Your mind is your life and you are not your mind. Your mind is your life because where your mind goes is your reality and gives you your experience in any moment. You are not your mind because you are the Awareness that can command your mind. In the Zero-Point State we experience that we don't have to match our identity to any of the changing thoughts that happen to pass through our mind. If the thoughts come, *I can't do that* or *I'm not good enough* or if you question whether you deserve love, money, a gratifying relationship or anything else of a "wretched-self syndrome" nature, as you watch the five-fold action you realize you are not those thoughts. Obsessions with what might go wrong with your health or someone close to you, unfounded fantasies about what might go wrong with an event in your life—these are simply passing waves.

In the Zero-Point State we realize our genius. This is the state where we *access* our power to create. This is the state where we have full use of our miraculous minds. This is the state when we can instantaneously respond most appropriately. The Zero-Point State is the state of *spontaneous mastery-in-action.*

Mastery begins with awareness and takes place *in action.* You cannot rely on a formula for mastery, because it is expressed only in the present moment. In her book, *Self-Powerment,* Faye Mandell emphasizes that thoughts about the future or the past usurp presence. A nanosecond of distraction on a critical play and you hit the ball out of bounds. Mastery is not remembering; it is *remembrance* of your invincible connection to all-knowing Source. Masterful action is not remembering from the past nor is it anticipating from the future. In the clarity, in the stillness, in the *silence,* you connect with the aspect of intelligence perfect for that situation in that precise moment. This is spontaneous wisdom in action. This is living wisdom. Remembrance is your rendezvous with the great Self.

A vital key to mastery is the willingness to self-inquire, a desire to examine your actions and your habits. Not what you *imagine* you say and do, not how you *would like* to think about what you say and do; self-inquiry is being honest with yourself about what you *actually* say and do. When you grok the distinction Least-action Pathway simply as "the way the thought goes because it has been that route before"—if you see such automatic thoughts and behaviors as outcomes of old world view conditioning, you aren't compelled to add to it any self-deprecating meanings. The distinguishing of mechanical, unaware habits as Least-action Pathways is invaluable assistance for candid self-inquiry. You notice the habit, knowing you can interrupt it when you see it, and you create a new Intent. The Zero-Point State makes self-inquiry possible. In the Zero-Point State you are present to yourself. Vietnamese Buddhist monk, peace activist and spiritual teacher, Thich Nhat Hanh elucidates you can only love if you are "there," if you are present. He adds, *"True presence relieves suffering and sorrow ... There is someone else who needs your true presence—yourself."*

〜〜〜

When you generate from Intent you are tapping into the origination of everything manifest. Some people call this Source consciousness, others call it God. Many call it Love. It is also called Light.

A movie director begins shooting the scene shouting, *"Lights—sound—camera—action."* Everyone knows the biblical imperative, "Let there be *light*." It appears that everything begins with light. We invent photography, movies, and holograms, pictorial representations of reality all made by manipulating light. A skillful photographer knows how to control the amount and quality of light falling on the photo sensitive material that records the picture. A hologram takes highly focused laser light to both make and see the image. There is no picture without light.

It also appears there is no reality without light. Light is in some way *fundamental* to existence. Light certainly plays the starring role. Light expresses itself in every dimension. Our existence depends upon versatile light.

Fundamentally and ultimately we live on light. Plants use light from the Sun to manufacture carbohydrates and to transform water and carbon dioxide into oxygen—required for our physical sustenance. The amount and quality of light we get (or not) affects our emotional state and our energy. All colors of the spectrum combined become white light. It has been shown that we require full spectrum light coming into our eyes to maintain balance. You can use colored light to change your brain wave connections, your state, and the quality of your eyesight. Full spectrum lighting has been shown to improve job performance, have a calming effect on students' behavior, and can positively affect food and food production.[78] Authority in the field of light, color therapy and restorative vision, Jacob Liberman prophesies light as the medicine of the future: *"Invasive medical approaches to treatment will become outdated as we enter the light age. Scalpels will be replaced by lasers, chemotherapy by phototherapy, prescription drugs by prescription colors, acupuncture needles by needles of light, eyeglasses by healthy eyes. Health and longevity will be the norm. ..."*[79]

Light seems to be infinite in its abilities. Light is used for communicating everything from body clock cues to road signals. Tiny strands of glass known as fiber optics that carry light rather than electrical energy are preferred because of the ability of light to carry large amounts of data without electromagnetic noise that can interfere with for example, phone line transmissions. Light is a carrier of information and intelligence, perhaps *the* carrier.

Light plays a prominent role in our language in the sense of intellectual or spiritual clarification. Throw some *light* on the matter. The *light* bulb went on. I see the *light*. There is *light* at the end of the tunnel. Metaphorically "light" is something we want and aspire toward. An en*light*ened being (knowing), *light*en up (ease), I feel better because I feel *lighter* (free). There are people around the world who refer to themselves as "*light*workers," people dedicated to carrying the light of conscious living.

Light sustains us in so many ways. In fact, according to astrophysicist Bernard Haisch, the light of the zero-point field is what sustains the material universe we call home. Haisch and his colleagues have twice proven scientifically why matter only appears to be solid and stable, though in fact it isn't. We have noted all along that one of the eye-opening discoveries of modern science is that objects only appear solid and fixed; however, the microscopic domain shows them to be Energy In Flux and mostly empty space. Of course we now know that "empty space" isn't empty and it's not material either. Bernard Haisch says the inertia of matter can be traced back to the zero-point field of light: *"To put it in somewhat metaphysical terms, there exists a background sea of quantum light filling the universe, and that light generates a force that opposes acceleration when you push on any material object. The action of that quantum light is what makes matter the seemingly solid, stable stuff of which we and our world are made of."*[80]

Well, it does seem clear that the subject of light is important to us. The question is what does it mean in "light" of the distinction Zero-Point State? It seems the cosmic sense of humor always returns us, scientists and laypersons alike, to ask what is the fundamental "medium" from which all life derives. The joke is on us as it appears that the "medium" is not a medium at all, at least not in the sense of it being "stuff" of some kind. And as we've suggested earlier, if there "is" no "is" then what can we *distinguish* in this Observer-created Reality? What can we bring to our most fundamental Observation? And more importantly, why should we care? In what way will distinguishing what is most fundamental contribute to the quality of our daily lives and the sustaining of that quality for generations to come? Where do science and spirituality merge? Light is our biggest clue.

~~~

The universe is light. There are two kinds of light, inner light and outer light. As QuantumThinkers we realize they are connected. Both kinds of light enable us to see, one with our physical eyes, the other with our spiritual eye. Visible outer light that enables us to see and diffract into colors is electromagnetic energy. Inner light that enables us to see into our consciousness is the light of awareness. In QuantumThink we say, *"The most powerful force in this world is the light of your own awareness."* It is a statement to remind us that for ordinary people in daily human life our own awareness is key in everything we experience and discern and create. When we connect to the most fundamental state, the Zero-Point State, the State that transcends attachments and Least-action Pathways; the State that takes us beyond compulsive, thoughtless actions and beyond obsessive, divisive beliefs; the State free of fixed, arbitrary conclusions about "the way things are"—in this pure conscious State we experience a quantum moment, a "clear light" experience, *the light of awareness.*

Great scientists and sages agree that light is special. Physicist Fred Alan Wolf says light is mysterious because it is the only wavelike "energy" that doesn't need a medium to travel through. He astutely reminds us: *"The nature of light has been at the core of nearly every revolution in thinking about the universe."* Physicist Peter Russell says light occupies a very special place in the cosmic scheme more fundamental than time, space, and matter, which he says he *"later discovered was [also] true of the inner light of consciousness."*

Consider that the Zero-Point State connects our inner and outer worlds. If the light of consciousness is what enables us to see then the better we condition ourselves to that state, the clearer we are, the purer are our human creations, the more effective we become as individuals and as the family of humanity.

Metaphor, metaphysics, and materiality. Lots of questions and lots of diverse answers. Is the zero-point field of science the same as the Zero-Point State of consciousness? Some say yes, some say no. On the surface they appear to be saying different things though maybe they actually concur. Read on and consider.

Astrophysicist Bernard Haisch tells us our universe is pervaded by an underlying sea of light however he also suggests with impeccable logic that the zero-point field cannot be the same as the principle or force preceding it that created it. Physicist Peter Russell wraps it up elegantly: *"Physical light has no mass, and is not part of the material world; the same is true of consciousness. Light seems in some way fundamental to the universe, its values are absolute, universal constants. The light of consciousness is likewise fundamental; without it there would be no experience."*[81]

Astronaut Edgar Mitchell declares: *"To be aware of the zero-point is tantamount to being aware of only awareness itself."* Theorist, Ervin Laszlo presents the scientific basis for the A-field, an all cosmic information field he modernized after *Akasha*, the Sanskrit term for the most fundamental field which *"underlies all the manifest phenomena of the cosmos;* and *"becomes all the manifest phenomena."* Laszlo distinguishes further: *"The zero-point field of the quantum vacuum is not only a superdense energy field; it is also a super-rich information field—the holographic memory of the universe."* Physicist-inventor, Mark Comings suggests that our core assumptions have to be questioned, especially the one that says we live in a universe of scarce energy resources, that energy scarcity is a misconception and that *"We are one with the quantum plenum."*

Spiritual teacher Master Aïvanhov speaks of light as a living spirit, *"The physical world around us is nothing but a condensation of primordial light. God, the active principle, projected light and used this light as His basic material for creating the universe."* Spiritual teacher Swami Muktananda proclaimed: *"If through meditation we saw God's light sparkling within, the veil would be drawn aside, and we would be able to see creation as it really is. As we meditate more and more, the divine conscious light comes into our eyes. Our eyes see the same light outside us, and we know the universe to be nothing but that light."*[82]

It appears we cannot *equate* the fundamental unified field of consciousness with the electromagnetic zero-point field, that is, the visible light we see with our eyes. However, it does seem that at the most fundamental ground of being we *can* distinguish a luminous field that is a state of rest for matter and a state of rest for mind. Through a kind of seamless yet timeless morphing process light becomes thought becomes energy becomes physical manifest reality.

We could debate this for a very long while, however perhaps the most valid answer for you and me lies … yes, you guessed it … within ourselves. The most powerful force in this world is the light of *your own* awareness.

～～

We have come full circle in our QuantumThink adventure to discover that All Paths of No-Paths lead to the Self—the Awareness that is aware of life, aware of differentiation, aware of distinctions and aware of the oneness of itself. We began with the distinction of the universe and everything in it as Holistic & Holographic. We suggested that when we go beyond the *concept* of unity to the *experience* of it that this quite literally transforms the whole way we relate to one another, to Earth, and to the entire cosmos. We place ourselves in that state where we can watch ourselves and at the same time participate in our destiny. We are distinguishing this as the Zero-Point State. We free ourselves from the constraints of industrial age mechanicality and separation and automatic habits of mind that have kept us separated, bound, and limited. We create in tandem with Infinite Intelligence, with "Source of All." In the Zero-Point State you are in the *experience* of the source of all creation and thus you experience oneness and unity with All That Is.

Our topic is what creates and our task is mastery of mind. Then what is our access to achieving mastery with our own mind? Distinguishing the Zero-Point State in daily life not as a separate "spiritual practice," rather as a way of life.

Author of the classic, *Autobiography of a Yogi*, the revered Paramahansa Yogananda said, *"It is not so much your passing inspirations or brilliant ideas so much as your everyday mental habits that control your life."* As we realize the Zero-Point State as our connection to the fundamental creative state we know we can be a living embodiment of that wisdom. We can exercise our ability and *privilege* to choose consciously. *This* is mastery of the mind. However, it takes practice.

It may sound odd to say we need to practice being in the state of *nothing*. Comedian Jerry Seinfeld expresses his inimitable logic on the practice of nothing this way, *"I am so busy doing nothing ... that the idea of doing anything, which as you know, always leads to something, cuts into the nothing and then forces me to have to drop everything."* Meditate on that a while! It's funny yet it's not unlike our attempts at reaching the "nothing" of inner experience.

The great gift of practice is that the new state becomes established as your "regular" state. Automatic chattering and incoherence are displaced by the powerful state of freedom. There is coherence. Coherence means waves coming together in focus. From the Zero-Point State we discover The Power in Nothing. The Zero-Point State is the place of inner stillness where all great beings converge. This is the state from which all masterful performance derives and where creativity thrives. There is clarity. There is strength. There is peace.

Zero-point energy is the state of rest for matter. The Zero-Point State is the resting point for mind, and a mind at rest is mind at its best.

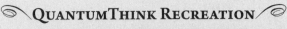

QuantumThink Recreation

Live the Wisdom of the Zero-Point State:
The Power in Nothing

ONE»Meditate. Find your preferred way of meditation and practice it daily, even if only for five minutes.

If you do not have a meditation method you can use this one:

Sit in a chair with your back elongated and straight.

Place your feet on the floor or rest them on a pillow so they are comfortable and flat.

Close your eyes and take a few deep slow breaths.

Notice any tightness in your muscles and allow each one to relax, consciously.

Allow your eyes to remain closed as light as feathers.

Notice any thoughts that visit you and instead of hanging on to them ...

Let the thoughts come and go like birds flying by.

Allow the activity of the mind to subside into the Zero-Point State.

Continue to become aware of your own Awareness.

Just allow the thoughts to fly out easily.

Sit for a few minutes each day and increase your time up to 20 minutes.

Notice how refreshed and centered you feel at the end of your meditation.

Experience Meditation as a powerful faculty of mind.

TWO»Zero-Point State in-Action. During active moments *while* you are in action rest your mind in the Zero-Point State and reflect on The Power in Nothing. Enjoy!

~~~~~~~~~~~

QuantumThink-Wave
The Highest Dharma

Why choose a life of mastery? Would you choose any less for yourself? When you connect to your own power you are fine in any circumstance. When you connect to your own power you are in a state for great and grand achievements that contribute to your enjoyment and those around you. A striving for whatever the meaning of divinity represents is a striving for mastery. Is it inborn in us?

There is a Sanskrit word, *dharma* that translates as *right duty* or *righteous duty*. What is our dharma? Like everything in this universe, dharma resides in Multidimensions. First doing the right thing for yourself to take care of the precious life you've been granted by grace. Then doing right toward your family who hold you in their graces, who let you snuggle safely in their retreat, who take care of you and consider you their own. Then to do right for others, those close to your heart and those you walk a similar path with, those you encounter daily seemingly by chance, and those with whom destiny arranges a meeting. The *Bhagavad-Gita* states, *"When a person responds to the joys and sorrows of others as if they were his own, he has attained the highest state of spiritual union."*[83]

Masters say the highest dharma is to know the truth of your own Self. Can there be anything higher than realizing one's Self as a spark of the Divine flame, the source and substance of all creation?

Joseph Campbell advised us all: follow your bliss. There is the dharma of doing what you have come to offer this world, to do your job, to be the fully expressed realization of who you are, to be aware of your talents, traits, and tendencies, embrace your special idiosyncrasies. It is to develop your yearnings to reach for the highest expression of who you are and making that sacred—offering the sacrament of your self expression to the world. When you create an Intent for mastery everything shifts from that moment on. You have created a sublime context for living. Dharma is being that which you cannot help but be.

~~~~~~~~~~~

22 LIVING FULLY DIMENSIONALLY
Your money and your life

Everything in your life depends upon the depth with which you take it in—the awareness you awaken yourself to around that experience, that person, that book, that teaching, that topic. For example, have you ever heard what many people automatically say about books? "You don't learn about life from books," a non-thoughtful commentary at best. If you think deeper on this you realize a book contains a lifetime of the wisdom of the person authoring it, a wealth of experience, extensive research, thinking, creativity. Depending on the dimension with which you absorb it, you can literally transform your life from a single book.

What about the comment, "It's just words"? *Just* words? Words give us our relationship to life. According to the famous story of Helen Keller, she said there was no "world" for her until she was given her first word, water. The Bible reads, *In the beginning was the Word*. What can you relate to if not through a word? Even if you say "the void," the silence, the ineffable, just speaking these ideas is also done, guess what, with *words*. As this is a Both/And world and an Observer-created Reality we are wise to acknowledge that we can make "less" or "more" of words since *what we bring is what we get*, and sometimes it is best to minimize the effect of words in terms of the meanings we ascribe or take in from them. Even so, we relate to life through language. And we realize that *Intent* reigns supreme behind all words. Intent is "the word behind the words"—the subtext as they say in screenwriting. *I love you.* Three simple words, a most powerful phrase. What is your Intent when you say it?

Everything in this world exists in multiple dimensions simultaneously. The richness of our experience and the effectiveness of our ability to create are both indelibly linked to the Multidimensions we acknowledge. In QuantumThink we call this Living Fully Dimensionally. Let's face the fact … you can't really QuantumThink unless you are Living Fully Dimensionally. This means living the wisdom of knowledge at the edge of discovery in sync with inner knowing that is universal beyond culture or credo.

Today as a result of modern science we know so much more about the many dimensions of reality and of the human being than our standard industrial age education had previously acknowledged as "real."

What we thought of as solid matter is really Energy In Flux.

What we thought of as objects are mostly empty space.

What we thought of as absolute, fixed and static actually isn't.

What we thought we could predict with absolute certainty, we cannot.

What we thought was "nothing" because it is invisible to the eye
comprises more than 90% of the entire universe and contains enormously
powerful energy.

What we thought had nothing to do with "reality," that is, *mind,* turns out to have quite a lot to do with reality.

At the time of this writing physicists say we live in an eleven-dimensional universe, but who knows how many dimensions are yet to be uncovered or how many different ways we can distinguish what we are uncovering?

To keep things simple and organized, in QuantumThink we distinguish seven dimensions. Every aspect of life participates in each of these seven dimensions, each one distinguished by their characteristic form of intelligence and all of which are unified, integrated and interconnected:

the Physical dimension of ordinary matter and the physical body;

the Energetic dimension of the subtle fields that comprise and emanate from all form;

the Virtual dimension of mind and all extensions of mind and awareness;

the Spiritual dimension of heart where we experience the interconnectedness of all;

the Cosmic dimension of natural law, operating principles functioning throughout the universe and within you and me;

the Esoteric dimension of soul, stories of evolution and prophecy;

the Divine dimension that encompasses and is responsible for all of creation, the dimension that transcends dimensionality, forever the ultimate mystery.

Whatever you personally consider "Divine source" to be, consider: Divine source differentiates as soul, becomes enlivened as spirit, guides through natural law, becomes defined in thought, activated in energy, and manifests in matter. We live in an intelligent universe and you and I are connecting hubs of that intelligence. Thought infused with meaning vibrates out and eventually takes form in experience, all of it following universal wisdom according to cosmic purpose and given by grace. Our soul intelligence yearns. Our mind intelligence dreams. Our emotional intelligence responds. Our spiritual intelligence connects. We are alive because we are connected to spirit, light, and love. The more you are cut off from spirit, the less aliveness you experience and the less others experience the life force in you. The gift of grace is that we can tune into that life force in an instant, whenever we choose, in a moment immeasurably Beyond Time.

Why are we wrapping up our QuantumThink journey by distinguishing what it is to be Living Fully Dimensionally? When you are Living Fully Dimensionally you expand your vision and your mastery as you become aware of how everything in life has existence in each one and all of these seven dimensions. Religious scriptures, for example. You can read the stories as literal historical accounts, as allegory with special messages, and as metaphor for the distinctions of Conscious Evolution. That Moses led people on an Exodus so they could free themselves from slavery in Egypt and settle in a land of milk and honey—could be read as the ability of mind to free itself from the enslavement of ego habits and become liberated as a Self-realized Being experiencing the bliss of existence. Everything in life depends upon the depth with which you take it in.

You must have noticed (wink) this chapter is subtitled, "Your money *and* your life" playing on the classic stick 'em up Western movie scene, "Your money *or* your life." We have arrived in the closing chapter of this episode of QuantumThink and we haven't yet delved into the subject of money. Yet money is something that touches each of us deeply, intensely, whether or not we like to admit it. That we may not like to admit its importance in itself is "telling" regarding the topic of money. It seems obvious that in a monetary-based society people, institutions, business entities and government organizations require money. Even beggars require money. Everyone wants money yet many of us are reticent to say so. In our monetary based society it makes sense to have your money *and* your life integrated, harmonious, and complementary. What does Living Fully Dimensionally have to do with "your money and your life"? We are here to explore and discover. Let's start at the beginning.

～～

At the beginning of QuantumThink we ask the question: *What do people really want? What do we all want?* And we answer by saying fundamentally we want to know that we have the power and the wherewithal to create what we truly desire in our lives—for ourselves and our families, our companies and our nations, for humanity and our world at large. We proceed to discover and get access to what it is that creates anything at all. We realize upon examination that our predominant habits of thinking are generating our reality. We update our knowledge with the facts of mind-to-mind and mind-to-matter connections and we condition ourselves to think from the system that distinguishes those principles. We experience that Intent is the active dynamic of creation and that Allowing is the passive dynamic, the faculty of mind we use to relate to what is as yet invisible and unknowable to us when forming our Intent.

Now, after imbibing the QuantumThink system we can ask once again: What do people really want? And we can respond in still another way. Consider that what we want is *freedom*—freedom to create, freedom to express, freedom to be. Please note that *freedom* does not mean behaving any way we "feel like it." Freedom is *not* unrestrained license in a bubble of selfishness and desires gone out of control. In fact, to the extent that *anything* dominates us, including our own mechanical desires, we are not truly free anyway because freedom implies *choice*.

Clamoring for freedom, people have toppled empires and staged uprisings and revolutions to become sovereign nations and for the right to express freedom of religion, freedom of commerce, freedom of choice. Countries have declared independence from controlling dictators and dominating imperialists. Wars have been fought for the right to be free. Although these destructive methods may not be the way to real freedom, *sustainable* freedom, the evidence shows that people long to be free. The United States government funded a World Values Survey questioning 350,000 people in 52 countries and found that the most important element for happiness within one's country is the degree to which people have free choice in the way they live their lives.[84]

Freedom from oppression and tyranny is as relevant in a corporation as it is in a nation-state as it is in a person. We all want freedom in our spirit that we call self-expression. Adolescents rebel against uncompassionate teachers, power-abusing authorities, non-listening parents, and an ineffectual status quo, for the freedom to express their ideas and individuality.

The mastery traditions distinguish the very nature of consciousness as existent, blissful, and free—the essential meaning of *sat-chit-ananda* in the ancient Sanskrit. *Freedom is our essence.* Is it any wonder that we would yearn for the experience that we are supremely free? We desire freedom in all dimensions—freedom in our bodies to experience fluidity and flexibility, freedom in our minds to create from our unlimited source; freedom in our hearts to love and establish intimacy; freedom in our souls to know the joy of meaning and purpose; freedom in the sacredness of life to simply be at home and *at peace.*

~~~

What is the one area where "freedom to be" might literally alter the world? Money. Look in our society. What is a person or nation or company more *attached* to than money? What happens in your relationships when money gets involved? What happens in what could be an otherwise "friendly divorce" when money comes into the picture? What happens in you when your money resources are being threatened in any way, real or imagined? How many meanings we all have around money. Money is often associated with power or the lack of it. Money slides easily into Either/Ors and grips itself there: Scarcity or abundance, high or low social status, voice or no voice in society.

Money. There is so much around this word. Just saying it, just hearing it. What does it evoke for you? Money. What comes to your mind? What comes to you emotionally? What do you feel in your body? In your soul? What are you Resonating with regard to money? The important question is, as always, how does this relate to you personally? What is your relationship with money? Is it a conscious relationship, deliberately chosen, or is it culturally conditioned?

There are so many mixed messages in the culture. Notice the phrases emblazoned from our societies to our psyches regarding money. Least-action Pathways around money are historic. Consider the following as to why we are so emotionally entangled with regard to money. The haves and the have-nots. Money makes the world go round. Money is the root of all evil. If you're so smart why ain't you rich? Never pay retail. Can't buy me love, sang the Beatles. Jesus proclaimed, it is easier for a camel to go through the eye of a needle than for a rich man to enter the kingdom of God. Perhaps if we understood biblical language of that time we might have a completely different meaning to Jesus' declaration than in our modern interpretation.

Because of these emotionally charged Least-action Pathways surrounding money and because we have not yet examined the phenomenon of money by Living Fully Dimensionally in our relationship with it, we could speculate that most people are confused with regard to their relationship with money.

A case in point: You are QuantumThinking and you are doing quite well. Now we come to money and all of a sudden your ability to QuantumThink stops short. The cultural and familial messages around money are having a bonanza with your mind. All of a sudden you are back in the limitation of the physical dimension of solid matter that the classical world view had declared as the only thing that was "real." Now we are thinking money is scarce, money is hard to come by and even if you do manage to accumulate it, money is difficult to hold on to. Then you reach the conclusions that come from those Least-action Pathway thoughts about money. If money is so difficult to come by then you can just make up that money isn't important after all, so I am not going to concern myself with it. Or that you better watch out for all the people "out there" that are trying to get it away from you, the "tax man" being a popular favorite. You convince yourself that money isn't worth all that attention because if you do succeed in garnering it, you might not be able to hold on to it because the government will take it or the economy will take a downturn. Of course, since what you focus on expands, if you begin to shy away from money the principle of Resonance indicates money will shy away from you, too. Aha! You've proved it to yourself … all those thoughts you had *must* have been "true." It comes full "vicious circle" as it is said in the vernacular. So you see you can make yourself breathless just thinking about all the cultural Least-action Pathways surrounding you with regard to money.

If money is that important in our culture and our global society (which it is), then doesn't it behoove us to establish a *conscious* relationship, an empowering relationship, a *Fully Dimensional* relationship with money? After all, if we cannot develop a healthy relationship with money, how can we expect to rid our planet of a scarcity mindset ricocheting as poverty and crime, greed and power mongering, desperation and inequalities, when what we truly desire is a world where all people live happy and healthy and productive lives, living their passion and their purpose.

The great question becomes, how can we begin to achieve freedom with regard to our relationship with money? Naturally it begins with an Intent to achieve such freedom of relationship with money. As with everything else in this quantum world, money and its meanings are not absolute. We can either live in reaction to society's default meanings surrounding money, or we can create a conscious relationship with money. Distinguishing money through the 7 dimensions can quantum leap us to freedom in our relationship with money.

~~~

Here are a few of the symbols for currencies in various countries: € £ ¥ ₱ SR $. What happens when you see the one that belongs to your country? What happens when you see the symbol for another country's currency? You also experience this difference when you visit another country. Perhaps the paper bills seem like Monopoly money, like play money. This demonstrates the meaning we ascribe to money. The meaning is not there in the money itself; the meaning is within our own consciousness.

Some say love makes the world go around; others say that money does. Perhaps the statements aren't as disparate as they seem at first glimpse. *Money makes the world go 'round*. We may not like that expression. It sounds too crass, too superficial. It's not God-like. On the face of it money seems to be the least spiritual, the least God-like, the least soulful. When you distinguish money through the dimensions you are likely to find how mistaken those thoughts have been. *Money can't buy me love*. We like that better, even though we've seen some "evidence" that it might not be true! Philanthropist, fundraiser, and global activist, Lynne Twist wrote a precious, important book, *The Soul of Money*. You may wonder how we can even *think* about "soul" and "money" in the same sentence. Yet as Lynne points out, brushing up against the *"hard realities of life can be the place where we develop a kind of spiritual practice in which we use the money that comes to us as an instrument of our intention and integrity."* [85]

The great sages and saints taught that the true nature of the Self is consciousness and consciousness is supremely free. What does it mean that consciousness is free? If you think of water as a metaphor, it has no shape until something contains it. A container in the shape of a river bed, an ocean floor, a bottle, or a cup. Like water, whatever contains our consciousness is the shape it takes. The water will be limited by the container. Our own consciousness will be limited by our thinking. Our experience of money will be limited by the beliefs, conclusions, and ideas we habitually hold about money. We don't have to despise money nor do we have to worship it. We can simply appreciate it and all that it represents and makes possible.

Factually, money is a means of exchange and everything after that is a matter of how we are related to money and the meanings it holds for us personally and collectively. We are living in the realization that *context is everything*; that we are shaped either by a created context (consciously chosen) or by the default context (unaware, already there). We can create a conscious relationship with money. We can generate a context for money that is life-enhancing. This is where Living Fully Dimensionally becomes paramount.

In the Physical dimension money as currency is representational, that is, it represents the value of goods and services. Though money has a physical presence in the form of what we call currency, paper bills and coins, and that which backs it up, (in previous eras the gold standard), in modern society we relate to it mostly in the Virtual dimension. Electronic transfers, ATM, debit and credit cards, computer transactions networked beyond time and space are the way of our world. In the Virtual dimension money is an *idea*. In the Energetic dimension money is a flow of energy throughout the system of exchange. Money as energy follows universal laws. Writers of prosperity books speak about money being magnetic due to its energetic properties. Think of it. Consider that you can energize your money according to your conscious Intent. Money is an exchange of energy. In relationships we give out love and support and friendship and kindness and we receive something in exchange. When the energy exchange is out of balance the relationship gets thwarted in some way. This is also the case with money exchanges. When a monetary exchange is not necessarily "equal" but *energetically* in balance and equitable, it feels "right."

We abhor poverty. Why? Ultimately, it is a poverty of spirit, of life force, a dissipated low energy that manifests for us in the physical. We see in the outer world conditions of people who are limited by physical lack; it affects their spirit. Which came first? Consider Resonance. When you infuse spirit into your being, you begin to flow the energy and the physical circumstances can transform right before your eyes.

Money in the Spiritual dimension connects us to the vital life force and our creative essence including our interconnection with others. The Spiritual dimension is the dimension of heart. In the body the heart is the hub of what feeds the cells of our bodies, an exchange of fluids carrying nutrients and oxygen are going out and coming back in to be revitalized. Connecting to the Spiritual dimension connects you to unlimited, replenishing Source—the source of all intelligence, all life, the source of all creativity, innovation, tranquility, joy and the long sought after peace. When this is truly understood you appreciate money in a whole new way.

In the distinction Conscious Evolution we distinguished that what is "within" us subjectively we extend into the objective reality we call the external world. We could call it the teleology of technology. Money is at its heart an extension of us into the world. Look in a window of your favorite shop. What do you see? Creations. So much creativity. So much imagination, spirit, energy, discipline, work. In the physical dimension we see a dress. The creative spirit of the person who dreamed the dress design, the ingenuity of the textile designer of the cloth, of the engineers who make the machines work, of the manufacturers, dye makers who produce the colors, the stylists' arrangement of it in the shop window, the ideas in the minds of the advertising and marketing people who make us aware of it, the packers, the shippers, the distribution networks, the communications that have it happen, the supportive *fashionista* who assists you in finding the perfect shoes and right accessories, the sales person who rings it up and hands it to you. Countless thousands of people have participated in your feeling glamorous and fabulous when you don this dress for that special occasion or just on an ordinary day. This is true of every product and service and idea ever created.

For everything in our physical world, this list goes on and on with increasing complexity. Just contemplating this we can experience the interconnectedness of all of us. And there are ancestral and archetypal contributors as well, the origins of dressing. To *appreciate* is to value something or to increase the value of it. The masters say a heart full of gratitude begets abundance.

The great Russian painter, Wassily Kandinsky said, *That is beautiful which is produced by the inner need which springs from the soul.* Every day in the physical world that we share and live in we play out our roles, as whatever profession, as mothers, fathers, daughters and sons. Yet, at another aspect of our being, there is a different kind of wisdom that somehow we *know*, something deeper that goes beyond the ordinary every day. We can call it the wisdom of our soul. You don't have to be religious or believe in God to know the wisdom of the soul. It's just a way to name it. You don't need someone to tell you what the soul is. You just know it. Looking from the Esoteric dimension of Purpose, money is the representation of what you are expressing creatively from your soul, from your life's purpose. Can you imagine that every time you exchange money, you are connecting with the soul of other people, and of yourself who earned it? Consider that the "invisible" realms of the energetic, spiritual, and soulful dimensions are as powerful as our life of form in the physical.

The physical by definition is limited by spacetime whereas the spiritual is not. Examine your personal relationship with what or whom you consider to be Divine, God, or Truth. Whether you relate to Jesus, Buddha, or Confucius; Krishna, Allah or Hashem or any other symbol of ultimate reality, the question to pose to yourself is: in what dimension am I relating to Ultimate Being? Clearly it is not in the physical realm. For example, suppose you have a relationship with Jesus. You cannot connect to Jesus in the physical dimension because to our knowledge Jesus does not currently inhabit the Earth as an incarnate being. Even so, your connection to him may be the strongest connection you have to anyone in your life. If you ever needed further verification that the physical dimension is not the ultimate, there you have it. Period. Full stop.

～～

The Divine is the dimension of the *sacred*. Just the sound of that word, sacred, makes one feel something in the depth of one's being. What's it all about, Alfie? What if it's all about knowing one's Self as the divine aspect. We're not speaking of an Either/Or reality of choosing the spiritual over the material. On the contrary. When you are Living Fully Dimensionally you realize that beyond all appearances of separation of outer from inner life, money represents our connection to the source of all creation and of all abundance. Consider this insightful money logic from the authors of *Inner Security and Infinite Wealth*: if we have no limits on the "inside" in our capacity for love, joy and inner peace, then we also have no limits on the "outside" both in how much money we can have and how much pleasure we can derive from all the material aspects of life.[86]

Is money sacred? Not in and of itself, but rather as the representation of our divinely bestowed talents and gifts, resources and abundance, as representing our soul's yearnings and our spiritual connection. Prosperity author and minister Catherine Ponder calls this a universe of "lavish abundance." Australian writer, Peter Erbe wrote in his profound book, *God I Am*, "my Being is my sustenance" to indicate that fundamentally and ultimately, all abundance is sourced in the Divine dimension that encompasses and is responsible for all dimensions. And this source is unlimited.

Returning to the beginning of this adventure in awareness when we asked what we really know for sure about life ... we said *we know for sure there is creation*. Money represents creation in all of its dimensions. From this perspective we could actually see money as a way of exchanging our divinely bestowed talents and our power and ability to create.

At its foundation money represents a person's creative ability given by virtue of divine birthright. We produce something, we use it, and then we have excess of it, so we trade it. The trade becomes complex so we represent it with currency, beads, gold, coins, paper, and now with electronic transactions and plastic cards. Underneath it all are the individuals' gifts, their contribution to society, their ingenuity, their productivity, their service, their divinely given gift to give.

How would Living Fully Dimensionally transform your experience of *your money and your life*? When you sit down to pay your taxes to your government, you could be thinking, *WOW, thank you so much for those beautiful, efficient roads I drive on that get me places quickly, thank you for those magnificent parks where I take my family to boat on the lake and run in the fields.* When we pay our bills we can become aware and appreciative of all the people providing us with services, electricity, water, our homes. The masters say a heart full of gratitude begets abundance.

What are you focused on when you send out the energy exchange called money? Fret not, friends. This doesn't indicate you are an unworthy person. Remember in QuantumThink we realize that our conditioning up to this point in evolution has been largely mechanical, automatic and one-dimensional. We have been living mostly conceptually, swimming in the Least-action Pathways of the collective culture. When you see your bill paying as separate from the dimensions that infuse the value you are receiving for this energy exchange, the commodities, the goods, the services, the experiences—you can understand how you may be missing the joy that comes from exchanges of money energy and spirit.

Now we can open our minds and our hearts to so much more regarding the everyday matters of commerce and to see how it adds to our experience. The vital point is *you have the opportunity to create a conscious relationship with money*. Intent as the active dynamic of creation is the most formidable force available to us as people. Imagine that when you begin to consciously create your Intent as you exchange money, whether earning, saving, investing or spending it, you transform your relationship with money and widen your experience of freedom. You can't really begin to create yours or the world reality with mastery until you begin to Live Fully Dimensionally in every area of life, and especially in an area as fundamental to our very existence from the mundane to the spiritual—money.

~~~

What makes Living Fully Dimensionally so important? Every aspect of our ordinary lives, from our money to our relationships to our well being to our creativity, has expression in every one of these seven dimensions. Living Fully Dimensionally means we are aware of our interconnectedness and interdependence. It means we are adept with the natural laws of mind-to-mind and mind-to-matter connections. It means we hold life as sacred, not just in our intellects but in every fiber of our being. It means we look deeply into every aspect of our experience to appreciate the profundity of being granted existence.

Consider that unless we are Living Fully Dimensionally, life on Earth is likely to continue predictably as it has. Without having to look too far, when you examine the *state* of the world, it hasn't changed all that much—save for the technology, costuming, and styles. We used to hang people; now we give them lethal injections. We used to kill each other with muskets and bayonets and cannons; now we use machine guns and smart bombs and ballistic missiles. The economics driving war and weaponry and killing and the politics that ordain such matters haven't gone away; they have merely become more sophisticated.

The awakening of consciousness is the most important thing we can do on this planet. We are in a time of evolution unlike any we have witnessed or known. Conscious awakening is essential for everything from your mind's tranquility to the planet's sustainability to the economy's stability. All the money in the world won't change it. It never has, it likely never will. However, the higher our collective conscious awareness, the more the world will change for the better.

We are in a time when every institution as we've known it is up for rethinking, redesign, and restructuring. The fabric of life on this precious Earth will be new, and perhaps as unrecognizable as our IM, iPhone, and Tweet culture would be even to ourselves a few decades ago. What if we could QuantumThink our economics, health, education; QuantumThink our politics, government, media, our entertainment, our money? How will we achieve it? Many people on the planet might believe that if we have enough money we will solve all our problems. Consider this statement again carefully: *All the money in the world will not bring about the changes we wish to see, however, a quantum leap in consciousness most assuredly will.*

☜ QUANTUMTHINK RECREATION ☞
Live the Wisdom of Living Fully Dimensionally

ONE»Notice your relationship to money in all its varying forms as you go about your typical day. Ask yourself and take note of:

1. What is automatic and mechanical about the way you relate to money?

2. What specifically has been conditioned by the Least-action Pathways of the culture you live in regarding the messages and assumptions around money?

3. What is conscious about your relationship with money?

4. In the context of Living Fully Dimensionally, in which of the 7 dimensions are you in relationship to the topic of money in your routine daily activities?

5. Create a statement of Intent to establish a conscious relationship with money.

TWO»Notice in which of the 7 dimensions you are predominantly related to the following areas of life.

Relationship (Significant other "romantic" relationship)
Whether or not you are currently in a relationship with someone, you can still take note in which dimensions you predominantly relate with other people.

Well Being
When you feel something emotionally, physically, or spiritually, are you also relating what you are experiencing to any of the other dimensions in Living Fully Dimensionally?

Creativity
Whether it's with your own creativity or another person's creative expression, how many dimensions are you relating to as you create or enjoy another's creative expression?

You can choose to begin Living Fully Dimensionally in any and every area of life. When you commit yourself to Living Fully Dimensionally you live life at its fullest as the unlimited being that each of us are. Live the wisdom of this; live it in you, *as* you.

QUANTUMTHINK-WAVE
Blessings Everyone

A lot of friends sign their email messages, "Blessings." It always evokes a warm feeling and deep connection.

I remember being at a holiday service where Rabbi Loring Frank was presiding. He looked around at the audience and said with sincerest humility that all the wisdom had already been said, and everything had been given already to all of us. So he asked himself in a meditation, what could he possibly give? What could he bestow on us that we didn't already have? And he realized the one thing he could offer is blessings. He could confer blessings on this congregation as a Rabbi, yes, but I realized in his modest way he meant also, as one person to another. He could bless. What does it mean to bless?

A Siddha Yoga monk, Swami Anantananda, wrote that he practiced this silently—sending other people blessings. He would notice people, anywhere, it didn't matter whether he knew them or not, and he would just appreciate them, in whatever activity they were in. People working, walking, whatever they were doing. And doing this put him in touch with a sense of the sacred.

The meaning of *blessing* is something that contributes happiness and well being. It is to invoke this consciously, as a regular practice. After all, we already send people our silent thoughts about them. Why not send people our blessings?

Going Forward

"'Would you tell me, please, which way I ought to go from here?' 'That depends a good deal on where you want to get to,' said the Cat. 'I don't much care where—' said Alice. 'Then it doesn't matter which way you go,' said the Cat."

—LEWIS CARROLL, *Alice's Adventures in Wonderland*

The truth is Alice really *did* care where she was going, even if in a moment of distress about being lost she said she didn't. The truth is we all care. Every single person on this planet cares where he or she goes. When each one of us awakens to the truth of our unity we care also about where *all* of us go. We care about the rest of the people in the world, about the infinite species of plants, minerals, animals, oceanic and planetary systems. We care about our creations and structures and about future generations and the rest of the universe, too.

In QuantumThink our focus is on creating a wonderful life, consciously with awareness, an awakened awareness in the moment and with knowledge of the universal principles we have the use of for creating realities. As we go forward it is worthwhile to consider what we are moving forward into. To say it more appropriately to an Observer-created world—we ought to consider *what we bring to reality* as we go forward.

To live without reverence for the fact of creation itself could be the ultimate asleep state. We have a word in human culture: hypocrisy. It means "the practice of professing beliefs, feelings or virtues that one does not possess; falseness"[87] and carries a great weight of judgment behind it. Hypocrisy means you imagine yourself to be one way (kind, compassionate, gentle, merciful), and then you act out something inconsistent with it. You judge negatively, blame people, snap anger at people, attack people, kill mercilessly and justify the atrocities by calling them "casualties of war." Then we call ourselves "God-fearing people," the highest statement of reverence for the might of God.

QuantumThink is about *living* the wisdom, not merely knowing it. Consider there is no way we can live the highest virtues, there is no way we are living the wisdom, as long as war continues on this planet. It is not a question of pie in the sky, unrealistic optimism in a "dangerous world" where countries and people have to defend themselves against the enemy. It is a question of Intent. To accomplish the elimination of war, poverty, crime or any other unnecessary injustice we start as we do with any creation; it begins with the Intent for it to happen. The power of collective Intent has been scientifically proven to quell violence. All the money in the world has not and will not bring about the changes we want in the world however, a quantum leap in consciousness most assuredly will. The irony of an evolution in consciousness is that *it must be chosen, consciously*. It is still our choice:

crisis awakening or conscious awakening? In the event you haven't yet chosen this for yourself you always have another opportunity to choose to consciously evolve. Right now as you read these words is a perfect time.

~~~

Without mastery of the mind nothing works well. People used to say practice makes perfect. Today we can say practice *is* perfect. The paradox of mastery is that it is a *practice*, a moment-by-moment proposition. In fact, the most important message of QuantumThink is this: if you want to master your life you have to master your mind. We have said it in many ways: your mind is your life and in the same breath, you are not your mind. Your mind is your life because whatever you experience is a result of what you hold in your mind. Paradoxically, you are not your mind since you are that Awareness that can watch what you hold in your mind and be free of any mental conditioning. Because of that freedom we have the power to create and we have the inborn genius and capability to master our own mind. Mind is the friend of differentiation, the play of consciousness as the masters call it, the exquisite, elegant dance of distinctions that we call our reality.

From a QuantumThink perspective we have seen that what binds us most are the beliefs and conclusions we have made about life. An aspect of mastery is discerning between your *preferences* and your conclusions lived as "absolutes" that bind you and limit you. You could establish a tremendous freedom for yourself in distinguishing that.

By now you have experienced the power of your own Intent in manifesting a reality field not only for yourself but for others around you. When we look at this on a larger scale, you can now not only imagine but *know* at a Participatory Aspect of Knowing that you can and do influence the field of the world around you. On this deeper level we know we have come into this life for something more. We know perhaps that we have come to evolve ourselves to a higher awareness, to a more noble way of being, to bring a unique gift to the world in these changing times. The companies who can integrate the distinctive features of the Internet and TV and cell phones—and connect those to the mind, the heart, and the soul—will be the most successful companies of the immediate future. At this deeper soul knowing, we realize that the people in our lives including those unknown to us personally whom we serve through commerce are not happenstance; they are somehow intertwined with our personal destiny.

The Mystery of ALL Mysteries cannot ever be imagined in its entirety for it is limitless, infinite and ever-changing, expanding and evolving, ever designing itself anew in ingenious and magical ways. What place do you and I have here in this vast array of gases and explosions into matter that becomes coherent? We are not separate from creation. The cosmic smile is that we think of ourselves that way, that perhaps we can figure it all out. Of course the cosmic paradox is that we can ... because we are simply divine.

Albert Einstein declared, *"Humanity is going to need a substantially new way of thinking if it is to survive!"* Many great and thoughtful leaders have sung that tune in unison, that we need to think in a new way. We have that new way now. This is not the author ego-tripping. I didn't choose QuantumThink—it chose me—as the vehicle through which it would express itself. QuantumThink is an access point, a tool of expanded thinking made for this era, new thinking to use to awaken ourselves from the slumber of hypocrisy, finally, one and all, for once and for all. When we give up the pretense and stop pretending we've mastered living the wisdom, *then* we have the opportunity to live the wisdom, to be a culture of Wake-ups.

Throughout the twenty-one plus one distinctions of the QuantumThink system we acknowledge and use the inextricable relationship of mind to matter, the power of conscious Intent to activate an energy, a resonant field that draws to it the eventual manifest results—whether in fitness of body, emotional equanimity, clarity in decisions or in the ways to invent our systems and structures anew, ways not rigidly stuck in the way we thought about them 400 years ago or even 50 or 5 years ago.

Mastery is looking from the context of *what will work best now for all and everyone.* How can Earth's resources be continually replenished in harmony with their usage? How can we have productive, purposeful, abundant lives for all peoples that eschew forever the worn-out and inaccurate concept of scarcity? How can we honor our diverse cultures without getting lost in ancestral bigotry and hatred? This is what it means to QuantumThink, to live consciously awakened—and instead of being a mere grown-up, to be a Wake-up.

～～～

Let's discuss *living the wisdom.* This is where we began the QuantumThink expedition into new thinking. This is where we've been going all along and this is where we continue. Quite frankly, knowing the wisdom is of little or no practical value. The history of humankind proves that over and over again. *Knowing* the wisdom may be titillating to your intellect or your ego, knowing the wisdom may inspire you and give you "hope"; nonetheless, only *living* the wisdom matters. What does it mean to live the wisdom? It means you are the walking-talking embodiment of the great virtues. You emanate it. You exude happiness, compassion, kindness, love. His Holiness, The Dalai Lama said it well, *"We need a little more compassion, and if we cannot have it, then no politician or even a magician can save the planet."*

Living the wisdom means you think from the whole and for the whole, from the context of *how can we have this work for everyone.* Living the wisdom means you are Living Fully Dimensionally. Living the wisdom matters to your heart, to your spirit, to your soul, to your mind, to your daily life, to your moment-to-moment experience of yourself. Living the wisdom matters to the people you engage with, to the people and planet you serve; it matters to the evolution and sustainability of life. Living the wisdom means you are fearless and fervent in your fortitude for effecting this transformation so needed at this time. It means you courageously express your Intent regardless of prevailing circumstances.

Can you imagine where we might be now if in the mid-16th century Nicolas Copernicus had been afraid to expose his beliefs that the Sun was the center of the galaxy and that the planets revolved around it because these ideas would seem heretical to church canon? Can you imagine Galileo, known for inventing the high-powered telescope, being fearful to put forth his inventions and ideas despite the fact that he was forced to publicly renounce his view that the planets revolved around the Sun? Yet, his discovery led to Kepler's laws of planetary motion.

These ideas which turned out to be fact challenged the "authority of the day" however the Vatican did not officially take Copernicus' book off the "banned" book list until 1835 and did not officially recognize the validity of Galileo's work until 1993. This is not at all intended to criticize the Vatican but rather to point to the necessity of awakening ourselves beyond old "knowledge" to be open to an entirely new way of thinking about the nature of reality, how it works, and our pivotal role in it at this critical juncture for life on Earth. Courage is a virtue. Today we are living in the midst of a wide range of human beliefs which are as outdated and factually incorrect as these notorious historical examples. To go forward now and finally take the literal quantum leap in consciousness that has us *authentically* living the wisdom; this is our most sacred privilege.

The good news is that you don't have to give anything up because the quantum world view includes the old world view. The old world view is not really "old" and the new world view is not really "new." The old world view is simply a view that limits our experience of life and the new world view is one that expands it.

The aim and Intent of this book and our connection is to put it all together—the history of the behavior of humankind, the knowledge and wisdom of the spiritual, the scientific discoveries and most current facts and research about the nature of reality and how it works—to see the big picture, to update ourselves. If you long for peace, if you desire sustainable and healthy life, it is incumbent upon you and all of us to begin now. Live this. Update your facts. Be discerning in the research. Keep opening your mind. Experience the fruits of knowledge directly in your own awareness free of automatic and conditioned judgments and conclusions. People speak of a critical mass necessary for the leap. Who will be the catalyst for such a leap? Will it be you? Will you be a light that ignites others? For a photon, a particle of light, there is no time and there is no space either. Consider that *we are seeds of light*. And as light seeds we can go anywhere in the universe with our Intent. This is what all the great teachings of old have taught. And this is what our science is proving today. Consciousness as light becomes matter. Intent alone traverses the world instantly. (Could Einstein's C, the speed of light in his famous equation, in another context mean *consciousness*?) As people we have the inherent power to direct light through our Intent in the form of thought expressed through language.

This book is not a one-time read. It is meant to be used, to be read again and again, contemplated, and practiced. A shift in context shifts the entire resonant field and that means the way you relate to everything in your entire life and the world we collectively share. This book is meant to be a companion, a resource and friend for conditioning ourselves to truly think in a new way, not just to intellectualize it but to embody it. It is my Intent that at some time in the not-so-distant-future this book will no longer be necessary because humankind will be living the wisdom.

We're creating the world anew. How are we going to achieve it? In this age of transformation it is going to take each and every one of us. The institutions aren't going to do it. Don't rely on the government, the stock market, the corporation, any of the "theys" or the "thems" to do it for you. Institutions are comprised of us. There is no "it" out there. Every awakened mind is needed and wanted. Reggae legend, considered one of the great lyricists of all time, Bob Marley sang: *"Open your eyes, look within. Are you satisfied with the life you're living?"* If you live in a ghetto stop waiting for the landlord to clean it up. Clean up your own little place. If you live in Dubai think about what you can use your wealth for in addition to building super-sized luxury. Being an activist even with the best of intentions may be obsolete now. If you consider yourself an activist you can generate transformation from a place of *including others* rather than convincing others.

This is the time we're in. This is the era your soul chose to participate in (if you believe such things). The time that will enable us to create a new reality, not by one thought at a time but by a Whole System Jump.

The late, great quantum physicist, David Bohm, said, *"In some sense, we have to have enough faith in our world view to work from it, but not that much faith that we think it's the final answer."* And this is a good thing to keep in mind, that no single world view is going to be the final answer or the absolute truth, because the nature of reality is infinite, expanding and evolving. We are going to continually discover new operating principles. But as Bohm says, we can have enough faith in our world view to work from it, to see what it makes possible for us.

Think about it. You can live according to the push and pull of the circumstances or you can live according to your consciously generated Intent. This is the gift of awakened awareness. You can choose. You can condition the fields that you travel in with your own Intent. You can include others and generate something magnificent for all.

To QuantumThink is to be in the question, *what will have us be not just effective, but masterful in this dramatic evolutionary leap for humanity?* We looked at what we are really mastering, and we suggested that we are mastering The Art of Distinguishing. Now we can go into another dimension of mastery. Looking from the context that our predominant habits of mind shape our destiny, then we can say again: what there really is to master is our very own mind.

So today a new world view is coming into our awareness. We call it the *new* world view, but the new world view has really been here all along. It's just that it hasn't been in our conscious awareness. We had not been distinguishing it. Again, the paradox is that we have to *consciously bring it* into our awareness. We're doing that now.

Many questions have arisen in our day in the field of science among which many scientists have found disagreement. Whether or not there is an objective reality "out there" whether anyone is observing it or not, whether or not our thoughts literally manufacture reality, whether or not there is a divinity named God, whether or not reality is causal and determined or noncausal and probabilistic—these are questions still being debated among scientists, theologians and interested laypersons. *The point in QuantumThink is to examine the way such discoveries shape the way we think.*

We are in a time of evolution unlike any we have known, read about, heard about or witnessed. What must evolve now is our own human consciousness. The new world view is emerging around us and paradoxically we are the ones bringing it into existence.

~~~

The big buzz word now is "green." During the week of Earth Day 2009 on the HBO late night series *Real Time*, host Bill Maher raised the question, how did taking care of Earth's environment become a *partisan*, political issue? The absurdity is sadly laughable.

Imagine a context of evolution of consciousness, a world of Wake-ups. Everything we do could be shaped by its capability of awakening consciousness—our architectural design, transportation, our lighting systems, entertainment, sound systems, color schemes, school and medical environments, from punitive to restorative, from consequences to creative. Spaces can lift consciousness, colors can lift consciousness, sound can lift consciousness. *We* can lift consciousness.

A lot has changed in our world since I started formulating QuantumThink into a book. That is to be expected as we realize that the pace of change is accelerating faster and faster. As the economy undergoes a transformation people are drawn to re-examine their values and what is important, to determine what is excessive and what is sufficient, to think about what is ineffective and what is efficient, to understand what is endangering and what is sustaining. What used to be scoffed at as "tree hugging" has become the sexiest buzz word, Green. Green this, green that, go green, be green. Institutional advertising prides itself on their green messaging. This is a positive direction and something to be happy about. Still we need to stay awake and take this further. We don't want to end up in a pendulum swing of denying the privilege of abundant living and enjoying the use of natural resources, nor do we want to make the grave mistake of demonizing open systems like capitalism and democracy.

It is crucial to be discerning and to *make a clear distinction between the systems themselves and the people who are implementing the systems.* Resources are meant to be utilized and continually replenished through maintaining harmony with nature's renewal cycles. We can take the cues from nature and cease manufacturing products that cannot be transmuted, cease producing energy plants like nuclear power and offshore oil that are dangers waiting to happen. We can eliminate selling foods that make us ill and chemicals that pollute. Isn't this simply a matter of awakening to the unity and interconnected and interdependence of all systems? As long as automatic and mechanical ways and limited conceptual thinking habits are kept in place, it is challenging for *any* system to work at its highest effectiveness. In this time of optimism for the future, a time of energies that are guiding us toward restructuring our systems and institutions, with awakened thinking we can have our systems and structures work—for everyone. We can Be In The Right Questions. We can slough off the crust of old ways that are no longer workable or relevant and allow for fresh ideas to emerge.

It's interesting that Green is the buzzword. Once again we can look to our host who keeps us alive, Mother Earth, Gaia, to show us the way. Green in the physical realm means new growth of natural organic life. Green light in the energetic realm is healing energy. Green in the spiritual realm is the color of the heart chakra. Green is associated with money and money symbolizes our creative ability, our soulful yearnings, our spirit of life force, our connection to the Source of all. The clues abound around us.

There are the old stories of the end times, dark and gloomy and dreary—and there are the new stories of "The Great Shift," a transformation in consciousness that takes us to an elevated and noble state. Now dear friend, it is an Observer-created Reality. You are the Observer with the choice of how you view things. You are the one with the emanating Resonance based on which reality current you choose to hold in your awareness. Would you rather hold a doomsday scenario or would you rather hold an exalted one? It truly does come down to you and me and what we choose. We have been graced with the divinely given ability to shift and change and shape and transform our world free of old habits, free of automatic conditioning, free of what no longer works, and even free of the contingency based on standard scientific method. Now we can go deeper to discover what each of us is here to contribute, what we are here to evolve to, to free ourselves and to finally know ourselves as true love.

Can we ever put an end to war, crime, bigotry, poverty? Of course we can. Doomsday prophecies and predictions notwithstanding by now you realize in a quantum world nothing is fixed. Everything is in continual flux. Everything is malleable. Our meanings and prophesies can change. We can change the future. We can even change history. And we do.

As you know now that you are QuantumThinking, the invisible aspect of our living systems are much more significant than our 18th century scientific method can reveal. Maybe we need to develop some new methods for proving the validity of propositions and theories. Before the time of the age of reason, how did anyone prove anything? How did they know what to do? What did they use as their point of reference for making the "right" or appropriate decisions? What is *your* point of reference for making the "right" decisions? It's time to move forward from the context of *what will work and what is best now?* We can leap from hope to belief to proof ... *to Intent.*

Since we know information does "travel" through the collective mind field, not like physical movement but by exchange and connection of information, then perhaps we need another method in addition to the one we have now. In the meantime we can use our inborn instruments of knowing: intuition and nonlocality.

The double blind method is considered an important part of the scientific process. It is intended to prevent research outcomes from being influenced by observer bias. It's pretty interesting to look at the definition of the double blind method from the perspective of an Observer-created Reality. Can there ever really be a study that is not "influenced" in some way—by the person conducting the experiment, by the person(s) who initiated the idea for the experiment, by the people who agree to fund the experiment? If consciousness/mind plays such an essential role in the manifesting and shaping of reality, perhaps it's time to evolve our scientific method. Carl Sagan said, *"Science is a way of thinking much more than it is a body of facts."*

Robin Hood, the legendary archer-outlaw-hero of England's Sherwood Forest who stole from the rich to help the poor is a good story yet not necessarily an effective methodology for abundant living. The Beatles sang "money can't buy me love." A straightforward message. Until humankind lifts their consciousness, awakens their soul, ignites their heart field, what can happen in the right direction so all people live in abundance?

If the great beings have achieved the ultimate state, then so can we achieve it. This was their message to us. When there is a leap in consciousness people begin thinking not only for themselves but for all of humanity. The highest virtues kick in and reign, not mere lip service and proclamation of being virtuous as we have seen until now, but actually living the wisdom. In this state, clear, innovative thinking is natural. Everyone is taken care of. We eliminate poverty, hunger, crime, war, terrorism, disease, suffering. Now that is an awesome proposition. "Redistribute" the consciousness, and the money representing the exchange of creativity, service, soul, and divinity—the money is "a given."

~~~

It isn't a full circle we've come to; it's a spiraling outward, onward, and upward in the metaphysical sense of what we feel and imagine when we say "something higher." In this way as we come to the end of this book the direction is to return to the thinking system, the principles, the distinctions, the practices. Because as the profound statement from Gurumayi in the very first chapter indicates, our conversation here was never intended as stimulus for "a useless debate"; our conversation was intended as a seed that germinates in us something higher.

I haven't told you anything you don't know at some level of your being and deepest knowing. I have put something in words so together we can finally condition ourselves to live the wisdom. It is a matter of consciously connecting to it.

So my dear friend, how is your QuantumThinking going? How have you changed since you've been reading this book? Are you expressing yourself as a co-creator on Earth? Is your awareness heightened? Is your focus sharpened? Is your vision clearer? *Is your experience of joy more present?*

Wherever you are now, remember: everyone evolves at their own rate. As you develop yourself you alter your destiny.

Years ago when my husband and I first started being together, we would discuss what we thought about relationships and our relationship specifically. I candidly told him that to me a relationship was for the purpose of attaining the highest state of evolution together, with the relationship a powerful vehicle through which to develop. He looked at me with puzzled eyes and said, "I have no idea what you're talking about." When I heard him say *that* my heart sunk, my mind gasped and I thought, *uh-oh ... oh no!* This was a point in time when we were considering a lifetime commitment to one another in marriage. But then a nanosecond later my mind said, *It's okay, everyone evolves at their own rate.* There was nothing for me to be concerned about and nothing for me to do to "fix" the situation by trying to explain or convince him to see it my way. Every person has his or her own destiny and I can't be in charge of anyone else's—not even someone I dearly love. I can only attend to my own. He would manage himself according to his own destiny and choice. Now, imagine all of that happening in the same moment: Both the "uh-oh" and the "it's okay," and all the thoughts that come with it. That's how quick the mind is. Transformation is instantaneous; it happens in literally no time at all. Anyway, the point is ... I am sure you get the point! It was a great lesson for me that I have realized on numerous occasions. I realize I cannot push or pull anyone else's evolution. I can only express the Holomovement of my Purpose with the Intent that in some way my path imparts a contribution of value to others on the way.

$\sim\!\!\sim$

As the world changes and as what has been known and familiar to us evolves and transforms, there are at least three ways we can be related to what is happening: we can remain unaware that anything different is happening, and just react as it comes toward us; we can be aware that things are changing and try to prepare ourselves to adapt to the changing environment; or, we can be aware of what is happening and be a force ourselves in the way things go, an indispensable factor in the way things change and evolve.

To QuantumThink means to be aware of all the distinctive dimensions that comprise our reality and to engage in the profundity of what each dimension offers. When you're Living Fully Dimensionally you go beyond a life of superficiality. You experience the deeper meaning. You appreciate the magnificence of every part of this amazing world. You enjoy the elixir of simply being alive. You are inspired and on your spiritual knees in gratitude for all you have been granted. To be a walking-talking embodiment of what it means to be an awakened soul—this is our privilege and this is our choice.

◈ QUANTUMTHINK-WAVE ◈
Mind Over Matter

Old world view–circumstance rules.
New world view–Intent rules.

ENDNOTES

PART I—WAKE UP

1 Gurumayi Chidvilasananda, *My Lord Loves a Pure Heart: The Yoga of Divine Virtues* (South Fallsburg, New York: SYDA Foundation, 1994), 80.

2 I am deeply grateful to friend and mentor, quantum physicist and author, Fred Alan Wolf, Ph.D. for our many stimulating discussions over the years. Dr. Wolf once explained to me how the discoveries of science come into our language. After thinking much about that fact, I had the insight that we actually think in whole systems based on the discoveries of various scientific models, also whole systems.

   I realized that our thinking and therefore, without even realizing it, all of our results are shaped by the *whole* of the prevailing world view including its discoveries, beliefs and conclusions. When these discoveries are uprooted by more accurate discoveries, when the beliefs no longer hold true, when the conclusions do not serve us well, we can update our thinking to be in sync with more accurate and effective views. This is the purpose of the QuantumThink® system of thinking: to make a literal quantum leap in the basis from which we think, as a whole system.

3 Neale Donald Walsch, *Conversations with God: An Uncommon Dialogue, Book 1* (Charlottesville, VA: Hampton Roads Publishing Company, Inc., 1995) 62.

4 Geoffrey Shugen Arnold, "Mind is Buddha," *Buddhadharma: The Practitioner's Quarterly*, online article http://www.thebuddhadharma.com/issues/2005/spring/shugen.html.

5 Philip Cohen, "Mental Gymnastics Increase Bicep Strength," *New Scientist.com*, online article 21 November 2001, http://www.newscientist.com/news.

6 John Hagelin, Ph.D., Research on Creating Permanent Peace, http://hagelin.org/about.html.

7 Masaru Emoto, *The Hidden Messages in Water* (Hillsboro: Beyond Words Publishing, 2004).

8 The term "nonlocal mind" may have originated with physician, Dr. Larry Dossey, though it is used by other new world view thinkers. It is based on the principle from physics known as "nonlocality" which in essence describes the interconnectedness of all, outside of ordinary limits of chronological time and physical space.

9 Daniel Goleman, *Destructive Emotions: A Scientific Dialogue with the Dalai Lama* (NY: Bantam, 2003), 13.

10 I was introduced to the scientific principle of Least-action Pathway by Dr. Fred Alan Wolf. It is sometimes referred to in science as "principle of least-action." I adapted this in QuantumThink to have us remember that oftentimes our thoughts and actions and attitudes automatically take the path that, although it may conserve energy, actually keeps us from thinking from Infinite Possibility.

11 Joseph Chilton Pearce, *The Biology of Transcendence: A Blueprint of the Human Spirit* (Rochester, VT: Park Street Press, 2004), 131.

12 Adherents.com. website. See also http://www.theologicalstudies.org/classical religionlist.html.

13 "Play of consciousness" is a reference to the early Vedic scriptural teaching idea that consciousness creates reality as we experience it, suggesting the world as a "play." I learned of "play of consciousness" from meditation master Swami Muktananda (1908–1982), previous head of the Siddha Yoga lineage, whose own autobiography is entitled, *Play of Consciousness.*

14 Phil Blazer, *Pioneers of Israel: Modern Day Heroes of the State of Israel*, editor, Shelley Portnoy, (Sherman Oaks: The Blazer Group, 2004), 157.

15 Brian Weiss, Ph.D., *Many Lives, Many Masters* (New York: Simon & Shuster, 1988).

16 A. Robert Smith, "The Rapture: The Gospel of Darby," *Venture Inward*, A.R.E., November/December 2005, 35.

17 Omraam Mikhaël Aïvanhov, *Man's Subtle Bodies and Centres: the Aura, the Solar Plexus, the Chakras ...* (Fréjus: Prosveta USA, 1997).

18 "Heartlight" song lyric written by Neil Diamond, Carole Bayer Sager and Burt Bacharach and performed by Neil Diamond, refers to the adored alien in the movie *E.T.* whose heart "lights" when he connects with people in love and compassion.

PART II—LIVE THE WISDOM

19 Though not exactly the same I would like to acknowledge that this chapter subtitle is "a variation on a theme," a take-off on the Beatles' lyrics from the song "I Am the Walrus" written by John Lennon and Paul McCartney. The Beatles precise lyric is: I am he as you are he as you are me and we are all together. Sony Beatles Ltd (Publisher); Sony/ATV Tunes LLC (Publisher).

20 Greg Rae, "Chaos Theory: A Brief Introduction," online article, http://www.imho.com/grae/chaos/chaos.html.

21 You can watch the amazing classic video *Powers of Ten* created by Charles and Ray Eames for IBM on YouTube, www.youtube.com and search Powers of Ten. This video is a perfect illustration of the Holistic & Holographic nature of our universe.

22 Lewis Carroll, *Alice's Adventures in Wonderland and Through the Looking Glass* (New York: Penguin Group, 1962), 257.

23 National Desk: John Noble Wilford: "At the Core of the Milky Way, The Brightest Star Ever Seen," *The New York Times*, 8 October 1997. Reference is to the Pistol Star.

24 Ibid.

25 Ibid.

26 Albert Einstein and Leopold Infeld, *The Evolution of Physics* (New York: Touchstone, 1967), 31.

27 Many physicists and other thinkers speak of the "possible world," among them Amit Goswami, Fred Alan Wolf, David Bohm, and Ervin Laszlo.

28 Anna Muoio, "Life Is a Juggling Act," *Fast Company*, October-November 1997.

29 Danah Zohar, in collaboration with I.N. Marshall, *The Quantum Self: Human Nature and Consciousness Defined by the New Physics* (New York: William Morrow & Company, 1990), 34.

30 The chamber group we heard that evening is the wonderful South Beach Chamber Ensemble, founder and artistic director, cellist, Michael Andrews who subsequently invited me and my husband to become Board members. We have enjoyed supporting this intimate form of music ever since, using QuantumThinking in our meetings to have it expand and grow. www.sobechamberensemble.org.

31 Cheiro, *Cheiro's Book of Numbers* (New York: Arco Publishing Company, Inc., 1976).

32 Paramahansa Yogananda, *Autobiography of a Yogi* (Nevada City, CA: Crystal Clarity Publishers, 2003), 152.

33 J. Krishnamurti, *Think on These Things* (NY: Harper & Row, 1989), 110.

34 Ibid.

35 Edgar Mitchell, website www.edmitchellapollo14.com

36 Renowned authority in mind-body medicine, Deepak Chopra, discusses this idea.

37 Peter Russell, *Waking Up in Time: Finding Inner Peace in Times of Accelerating Change* (San Rafael, CA: Origin Press, 1998), 5-7.

38 Sarah Rossbach, *Interior Design with Feng Shui* (NY: E.P. Dutton, 1987), ix.

39 Institute of HeartMath® website, www.heartmath.org/research/ri-emotional energetics-intuition-and-epigenetics-research.html.

40 Sri Sri Ravi Shankar is the founder and spiritual head of The Art of Living Foundation, an international nonprofit educational and humanitarian organization, www.artofliving.org.

41 Zack Lynch, who was quoted in Michael Rothschild's *Bionomics* newsletter as a graduate student, is now Founder and Executive Director of Neurotechnology Industry Organization.

42 Dalai Lama and H.C. Cutler, *The Art of Happiness: A Handbook for Living* (New York: Riverhead Books, 1998), 5-6.

43 Norman Shealy, M.D., Live Lecture, The Prophets Conference. Merida, Mexico, (June 20-27, 2000).

44 Ibid.

45 Swami Rudrananda, *Rudi: In His Own Words* (Cambridge, MA: Rudra Press, 1990), 107.

46 Jon Kabat-Zinn, *Wherever You Go There You Are: Mindfulness Meditation in Everyday Life* (New York: Hyperion, 1994), 206.

47 For more information about Body Talk see http://www.bodytalksystem.com.

48 Karl Pribram, Ph.D. with Dr. Jeffrey Mishlove, "The Holographic Brain," *Thinking Allowed: Conversations on the Leading Edge of Knowledge and Discovery*, DVD, 2006.

49 Ibid.

50 Joe Dispenza, D.C., *Evolve Your Brain: The Science of Changing Your Mind* (Deerfield Beach: Health Communications, Inc., 2007) 313.

51 R. McCraty, R. T. Bradley, D. Tomasino, "The Resonant Heart," *Shift*, Issue #5, Noetic Sciences Publications (December 2004-February 2005), 15-19.
    Seminal researchers on the heart field, Institute of HeartMath also "propose that the heart's field acts as a carrier wave for information that provides a global synchronizing signal for the entire body."

52 Roger Nelson, "Global Correlations in Random Data," *Global Consciousness Project, Registering Coherence and Resonance in the World,* an international, multidisciplinary collaboration of scientists, engineers, artists and others, website http://noosphere.princeton.edu.

53 Hunbatz Men, *Secrets of Mayan Science/Religion* (Santa Fe: Bear & Company Publishing, 1990) 25.

54 Colin Barras, "DNA Strands Become Fiber Optic Cables," *New Scientist*, (17:25 12 November 2008).

55 If you want to learn more about the Enneagram a good starting place is the website for the International Enneagram Association, www.internationalenneagram.org.

56 "Zing! Went the Strings of My Heart" song written in 1934 by American Songwriters Hall of Fame songwriter, James F. Hanley (1892-1942).

57 Dennis Overbye, "Music of the Heavens Turns Out to Sound a Lot Like a B Flat," *The New York Times*, (September 16, 2003).
    Jeanna Bryner, "Sun's Atmosphere Sings," website space.com, http://www.space.com/scienceastronomy/070418_solar_music.html, (April 19 2007).

58 Dan Sewell Ward, Ph.D., http://halexandria.org/dward101.htm.
I was introduced to this website two days before I completed the manuscript of this book. A refreshing and comprehensive reference for important knowledge and their intricate relationships.

59 Ani Williams, "Geometry, Music, and Healing," website www.aniwilliams.com/geometry_music_healing.htm.

60 For a mind-blowing "thought" experience on the intricate pattern correspondences of this amazing universe, see: Scott Olsen, Ph.D., *The Golden Section: Nature's Greatest Secret* (New York: Walker Publishing Company, Inc., 2006).

61 Jay Lindsay, The Associated Press, "Sounds of the Sea Have Science Concerned: Increasing Ship Traffic Could Be Jeopardizing Marine Life," *The Associated Press*, on website article www.msnbc.com (April 18 2005).

62 Theodore C. Levin and Michael E. Edgerton, "The Throat Singers of Tuva," *Scientific American*, (September, 1999).

63 M. Shlofmitz and U. Nanda Saraswati, "Lokah," *Lokah: The Ivy Ceiling*, (Ma Bhakti Yoga, LLC: 2008), www.lokahmusic.com.

64 Swami Muktananda. As one of my most significant and great teachers, I have read many of Swami Muktananda's books and have heard him speak both in person and on video and audio recordings. Thus, I cannot recall exactly when or where I heard this story. If you are interested in his work and in the teachings of Gurumayi Chidvilasananda who succeeded him as the current spiritual head of the Siddha Yoga lineage, there is a bookstore link on their website, http://www.siddhayoga.org.

65 We're making a distinction between the Zero-Point State and the scientific term, "zero-point energy" because zero-point energy in science refers to various energy states most typically the electromagnetic zero-point, the ordinary visible light we see with our eyes. As a QuantumThink distinction we are using the term "Zero-Point State" to indicate a state of mind or consciousness.

66 John Hagelin, "Violation of Natural Law: The Source of All Problems," website article, http://www.natural-law.org/ideal_administration/ch01.html.

67 Bernard Haisch, "Brilliant Disguise: Light, Matter and the Zero-Point Field," *Science & Spirit: Exploring Things That Matter* on website, http://www.science-spirit.org, Vol. 10, No. 3, pp. 30-31, September/October, (1999).
Additional notes: *Science & Spirit* magazine is now called *Search*. Also, Bernard Haisch writes similarly about the zero-point field in his book, *The God Theory: Universes, Zero-Point Fields, and What's Behind It All* (San Francisco: WeiserBooks), 2006.

68 To learn more about what is known as The New Energy Movement, see Stephen Kaplan, "New Energy: The Courage to Change—Conference Summary," *Infinite Energy: The Magazine of New Energy Science and Technology*, (Issue 58, September/

October 2004), on website http://www.infinite-energy.com/iemagazine/issue 58/thecouragetochangeconferencesummary.html.

69 If you are interested in reading about various meditation methods, the book is called, *The Experience of Meditation: Experts Introduce the Major Traditions* by Jonathan Shear, Paragon House, 2006.

70 Frederick Travis, Ph.D., "Are All Meditations the Same?: Comparing the Neural Patterns of Mindfulness Meditation, Tibetan Buddhism practice 'unconditional loving-kindness and compassion,' and the Transcendental Meditation Technique," from a talk Dr. Travis presented at the *Science of Consciousness* conference, Tucson, AZ, April 2006, on website http://www.fredtravis.com/talk.html.

Note: Transcendental Meditation became well-known when the Beatles studied with the founder, the late Maharishi Mahesh Yogi. Today the benefits of TM, including restful alertness, higher cognitive performance, better memory, higher creativity, and quicker reaction time, are extensively documented by substantial and substantive scientific research.

71 John Hagelin, Ph.D., Home page of website, http://www.natural-law.org/ideal_administration/index.html.

72 John Hagelin, Ph.D., "Creating Peace" talk from the Miami Prophet's Conference, June 2005, on website Institute of Science, Technology & Public Policy, http://istpp.org/multimedia/prophets_conference.html.

73 Lao Tsu, *Tao Te Ching*, translation by Gia-Fu Feng and Jane English (NYC: Random House, 1972), Eleven.

74 The Associated Press, "Yoga at School Causing Some Stress," published on MSNBC website, http://www.msnbc.com/id/27008935/print/1/displaymode/1098, October 3, 2008.

Eve Conant, "Much Dispute About Nothing: Transcendental Meditation Is Meant to Make Kids Calmer, Happier, But for Some Parents, It's Having the Opposite Effect," on website, http://www.newsweek.com/id/139206/output/print, May 29, 2008.

75 Ibid.

76 Ted Nunn, "American Schools Get a D+ in Violence Prevention," online article on website, April 21, 2009, https://www.change.org/ideas/view/appoint_secretary_of_peace_in_department_of_peace_and_non-violence.

77 There are currently bills in the United States House of Representatives and the Senate for the establishment of a cabinet level Department of Peace for the purpose to create nonviolent, practical solutions to the problems of domestic and international conflict. The effort is supported by The Peace Alliance. For updated statistics of state by state Congressional support, see website http://www.thepeacealliance.org.

78 Jacob Liberman, O.D. Ph.D., *Light: Medicine of the Future* (Santa Fe: Bear & Company Publishing, 1991), 59-62.

79 Jacob Liberman, O.D. Ph.D., *Light: Medicine of the Future*, (Santa Fe: Bear & Company Publishing, 1991), 205.

80 Bernard Haisch, *The God Theory: Universes, Zero-Point Fields, and What's Behind It All* (San Francisco: Red Wheel/Weiser, LLC, 2006) 82.

81 Peter Russell, "Mysterious Light: A Scientist's Odyssey," from *Noetic Sciences Review*, #50, 8-13, 44-47, on website http://www.peterrussell.com/SG/IONS.html.

82 Swami Muktananda, "Nothing but the Self," *Selected Essays* (NYC: SYDA Foundation, 1977, 1995), 159.

83 *The Bhagavad-Gita* 6:32, Translation by Eknath Eswaran, (Tomales, CA: The Blue Mountain Center of Meditation, Nilgiri Press.)

84 Ronald Inglehart,1 Roberto Foa,2 Christopher Peterson,3 and Christian Welzel,4-1Department of Political Science, University of Michigan, 2Department of Government, Harvard University, 3Department of Psychology, University of Michigan, 4School of Humanities and Social Sciences, Jacobs University, Bremen, Germany, "Development, Freedom, and Rising Happiness," *Perspectives on Psychological Science: A Global Perspective*, (Volume 3 Number 4, 1981–2007) 264, on website http://www.worldvaluessurvey.org.
From this website: "Data from representative national surveys carried out from 1981 to 2007 show that happiness rose in 45 of the 52 countries for which substantial time-series data were available. Regression analyses suggest that the extent to which a society allows free choice has a major impact on happiness. Since 1981, economic development, democratization, and rising social tolerance have increased the extent to which people perceive that they have free choice, which in turn has led to higher levels of happiness around the world, as the 'human development' model suggests."

85 Lynne Twist, *The Soul of Money: Transforming Your Relationship with Money and Life* (NYC: W.W. Norton & Company, Inc., 2003), 253.

86 Stuart Zimmerman and Jared Rosen, *Inner Security and Infinite Wealth: Merging Self Worth with Net Worth* (NYC: SelectBooks, Inc., 2003), 8.

87 *The American Heritage® Dictionary of the English Language, Fourth Edition* Copyright ©2007, 2000 by Houghton Mifflin Company. (New York: Houghton Mifflin Company), Updated in 2007, online.

Selected Bibliography and Recommended Reading

The following authors and resources have inspired me and sparked my thinking and provide enlightening, leading edge information and documented research to readers.

Barnett, Lincoln, Foreword by Albert Einstein. *The Universe and Dr. Einstein.* New York: Bantam Books, Inc., 1957.

Begley, Sharon. *Train Your Mind, Change Your Brain: How a New Science Reveals Our Extraordinary Potential to Transform Ourselves.* New York: Random House, 2007.

Bohm, David. *Wholeness and the Implicate Order.* London: Routledge, 1980, 1995.

Braden, Gregg. *The Divine Matrix: Bridging Time, Space, Miracles, and Belief.* Carlsbad: Hay House, Inc., 2007.

Chidvilasananda, Swami. *My Lord Loves a Pure Heart: The Yoga of Divine Virtues.* South Fallsburg: SYDA Foundation, 1994.

Church, Dawson, Ph.D. *The Genie in Your Genes: Epigenetic Medicine and the New Biology of Intention.* Santa Rosa: Elite Books, 2007.

The Dalai Lama XIV, His Holiness. *The Universe in a Single Atom: The Convergence of Science and Spirituality.* New York: Morgan Road Books, 2005.

Dossey, Larry, M.D. *Reinventing Medicine: Beyond Mind-Body to a New Era of Healing.* New York: HarperCollins Publishers, Inc., 1999.

Goldman, Jonathan. *Shifting Frequencies.* Flagstaff: Light Technology Publishing, 1998.

Goswami, Amit, Ph.D. *The Quantum Doctor: A Physicist's Guide to Health and Healing.* Charlottesville: Hampton Roads Publishing Company, Inc., 2004.

Goswami, Amit, Ph.D. with Richard E. Reed and Maggie Goswami. *The Self-Aware Universe: How Consciousness Creates the Material World.* New York: G.P. Putnam's Sons, 1993.

Haisch, Bernard. *The God Theory: Universes, Zero-Point Fields, and What's Behind It All.* San Francisco: Red Wheel/Weiser, LLC, 2006.

Hunt, Valerie V. *Infinite Mind: Science of the Human Vibrations of Consciousness.* Malibu: Malibu Publishing, 1989, 1996.

Institute of Noetic Science. *Shift In Action.* Website: www.shiftinaction.com.

Kaku, Michio. *Hyperspace: A Scientific Odyssey Through Parallel Universes, Time Warps, and the 10th Dimension.* New York: Doubleday, 1994.

Laszlo, Ervin. *Science and the Akashic Field: An Integral Theory of Everything.* Rochester: Inner Traditions, 2004.

Liberman, Jacob, O.D., Ph.D. *Light: Medicine of the Future: How We Can Use It to Heal Ourselves Now.* Santa Fe: Bear & Company, Inc., 1991.

Lipton, Bruce, Ph.D. *The Biology of Belief: Unleashing the Power of Consciousness, Matter, & Miracles.* Santa Rosa: Mountain of Love/Elite Books, 2005.

McTaggart, Lynne. *The Field: The Quest for the Secret Force of the Universe.* New York: HarperCollins Publishers, 2002.

Mitchell, Edgar D., with Dwight Williams. *The Way of the Explorer: An Apollo Astronaut's Journey Through the Material and Mystical Worlds.* New York: G.P. Putnam's Sons, 1996.

Muktananda, Swami. *Mystery of the Mind.* South Fallsburg: SYDA Foundation, 1981, 1992.

Muktananda, Swami. Edited by Paul Zweig. *Selected Essays.* South Fallsburg: SYDA Foundation, 1995, originally published by Harper & Row, 1977.

Pearce, Joseph Chilton. *The Biology of Transcendence: A Blueprint of the Human Spirit.* Rochester: Park Street Press, 2002.

Peat, F. David. *Synchronicity: The Bridge Between Matter and Mind.* New York: Bantam Books, 1987, 1988.

Pert, Candace, Ph.D. *Molecules of Emotion: The Science Behind Mind-Body Medicine.* New York: Touchstone, 1997.

Polich, Judith Bluestone. *Return of the Children of Light: Incan and Mayan Prophecies for a New World.* Santa Fe: Linkage Publications, 1999.

Radin, Dean. *Entangled Minds: Extrasensory Experiences in a Quantum Reality.* New York: Paraview, 2006.

Rosenblum, Bruce and Fred Kuttner. *Quantum Enigma: Physics Encounters Consciousness.* New York: Oxford University Press, 2006.

Russell, Peter. *Waking Up in Time: Finding Inner Peace in Times of Accelerating Change.* Novato: Origin Press, 1992, 1998.

Schwarz, Jack. *Human Energy Systems.* New York: E.P. Dutton, 1980.

Sheldrake, Rupert. *A New Science of Life: The Hypothesis of Morphic Resonance.* Rochester: Park Street Press, 1981, 1995.

Shealy, Norman, M.D., Ph.D., and Dawson Church, Ph.D. *Soul Medicine: Awakening Your Inner Blueprint for Abundant Health and Energy.* Santa Rosa: Elite Books, 1999.

Talbot, Michael. *The Holographic Universe.* New York: HarperCollins Publishers, Inc., 1991.

Targ, Russell and Jane Katra, Ph.D. *Miracles of Mind: Exploring Nonlocal Consciousness and Spiritual Healing.* Novato: New World Library, 1998.

Villoldo, Alberto, Ph.D. *Shaman, Healer, Sage: How to Heal Yourself and Others with the Energy Medicine of the Americas.* New York: Harmony Books, 2000.

Wolf, Fred Alan, Ph.D.

---*The Eagle's Quest: A Physicist's Search for Truth in the Heart of the Shamanic World.* New York: Summit Books, 1991.

---*Matter Into Feeling: A New Alchemy of Science and Spirit.* Portsmouth: Moment Point Press, 2002.

---*Mind Into Matter: A New Alchemy of Science and Spirit.* Portsmouth: Moment Point Press, Inc., 2001.

---*Taking the Quantum Leap: The New Physics for Nonscientists.* New York: Harper & Row Publishers, 1981.

Acknowledgments

Writing the acknowledgments for your first book feels akin to what it must be like to receive your first Academy Award. You want to thank everyone and anyone who ever breathed in your direction and even kiss the ground itself. As this is my first, I want to take the opportunity and luxuriate in the love as far as these pages permit. ♪ **For me, acknowledgment is gratitude.** I appreciate the endless gifts I have received and continue to receive from so many people by virtue of their individuality, kindness, intelligence, awareness and generosity. To you dear readers, I thank you and honor you for reading and enjoying, for thinking and contemplating, for using these principles to have your life and our world be the highest and the best. ♪

    I have had the amazing grace of people who directly played a role in this book becoming an actuality. Five fabulous, powerful women, treasured friends and soul sisters all, contributed their talents, knowledge and resources propelling me to get this published. A million thanks and hugs: to author and pure heart, Lisa Delman, a trailblazer inspiring me to write my proposal and find an agent, and who talked me through the joys and challenges of the writing process; to my birthday twin, preeminent artist, Pedie Wolfond, for offering me the genius and generosity of her art and heart, intuiting the perfect painting for the book's cover, and for surrounding me with her original paintings to energize my writing; to consciousness-raising, ebullient talk show personality, Frankie Boyer, whose enthusiasm for QuantumThink resulted in connecting me to my agent through her friend and author, cutting-edge consultant and quantum soulmate, Faye Mandell. How blessed am I to be able to thank my actual sister, Shelley Portnoy, my forever friend, confidante, coach and comforting *sorella bella,* who freely and willingly spent hours upon hours editing my manuscript, even in the midst of working on her own books. Thank you, Shelley, for your brilliance and extra special sisterly love and support.

    ♪ **Two paths of good fortune led me to my agent,** William Gladstone. Savvy in business and sagacious in life, Bill has been ingeniously instrumental in working through whatever was needed to make the publishing process go smoothly. Thank you, Bill, for everything and for reminding me to "write a good book." ♪ **Much appreciation to the fine people of SelectBooks, Inc.** for their high standard of quality and excellence, saintly patience with me and for their spirit of collaboration. To publisher, Kenzi Sugihara, for sharing his knowledge and keen intellect, and for our lively "debates" where I learned so much. To Nancy Sugihara, whose phenomenal editing expertise made editing enjoyable as we nuanced meaning, grammar, and punctuation. To Kenichi Sugihara, for his marketing prowess and creative ability to masterfully express the essence of my message to the world. To Janice Benight, artist superb, for designing the interior and the cover elegantly and beautifully, capturing the look and feel of QuantumThink, inviting for readers to relax and enjoy "hanging out" on the pages. ᐊᔥ **To dear friend and mentor**, quantum physicist, Dr. Fred Alan Wolf, inspirer and fellow dreamer in upping the ante for humanity, pioneer in the investigation of consciousness while staying true to science, I offer gratitude from my heart and soul for writing an absolutely lucid and enlightening Foreword, for our conversations through the years which always sparked magic for me, and for introducing me to the luminous Sonia. ᐊᔥ **To each one who graciously wrote an endorsement**, I thank you for your generosity and for giving readers the benefit of your experience. ᐊᔥ

To the vitalizing forces of QuantumThink—clients around the world who turn quantum knowledge into living wisdom. ᐊᔥ **Special gratitude to loyal friends for their role in helping to usher QuantumThink into the world:** to Jacob Barrocas, always on the leading edge of thinking and being, for being like family, for your huge appreciation and support of QuantumThink, and for continuously expanding us with your ever-evolving spirit; to Chris Pallas, Handsome Chris, #1 QuantumThinker and dear friend, for dazzling us with your mastery of discipline, listening to QuantumThink distinctions daily for years, and for making us a part of your "intended quantum result" by including us in the ownership of our champion racehorses; to Doug McCraw, inventive thinker and entrepreneur, for your sparks of genius and sparkling spirit and for always taking QuantumThinking to new levels in your life; to William Kantrowitz, for sharing your financial acuity, first-rate fun-loving friendship, and authentic, ongoing engagement in QuantumThink. ᐊᔥ **Sincerest gratitude for your unending support as colleagues, clients, and co-creators:** enlightened bureaucrat, Patsy Stevens; dynamic leader, Linda Lewis; master networker, Cynthia Greenawalt-Carvajal; global visionary, Julie Birtles; evolutionary entrepreneurs, Josephine Gross and Chris Gross, publishers of Networking Times. ᐊᔥ **Heartfelt gratitude to clients who have become friends, each with a plethora of qualities that expand me and the QuantumThink field:** Howard Getson, Dan Schmidt, Rhonda and Bob Bilsker, Mary Leah Weiss, Gayle Hardie, Karen Muller, Liza Spence, Nancy and Paul Pinson, Kathy Bloom, Kathy Erdody-Stumpf, Barbara Braucht, Carole Papazian, Sherry Bellomo, Cathy Wright, Cathy Crenshaw, Becky Patterson, and Ingrid Muller. ᐊᔥ **Abundant gratitude to visionary leaders who use QuantumThink to best advantage in their lives and their organizations, forward thinkers who are changing the world:** Morley Winograd, Keith Cowan, Bob Bickerstaff, Drew Blanchard, Jonathan Davies, Beth Lui, Bernie Ramos, Paul Verrills, Barbara Garvin Kester, Rick Smith, Alan Barnes, Rachel Russell, Kevin Campbell, and Gloria Reese. ᐊᔥ **Sometimes you are lucky to meet kindred spirits who share a common journey and who simply get who you are. Soulful gratitude to:** multi-talented Jeff Hutner of New Paradigm Digest, true to his moniker "cosmic connector" has championed QuantumThink offering ideas, postings, intellect, and witticism. To author and dream-sculptor, Jared Rosen, for reminding me to connect to the soul of my book, for his supportive friendship, and for including me in his book, *The Flip*. To intuitive, Peter Roth, and Debbie, for sharing your wisdom and traveling the cosmic trail with me. To longtime friend, author and creator of the Shadow Process, Debbie Ford, for taking the time to coach and encourage me to get my message out. To Love Lab coach, Rachel Levy, for her beautiful exuberance and excitement that always inspires, and for loving us and QuantumThink. ᴄᴧᴏ **Warmest gratitude to friends who have become QuantumThinkers—great thinkers, global visionaries, and gleaming lights in this world:** Lea and Roy Black, Kathi and Dr. Larry Hurvitz, Steve Tankleff, Lisa and John Tronolone, Claire and Jacob Barrocas, Kelly Painter, Michelina Mottolese, Edgar, Aldo, and Dante, Bryan and Karen Walters, Ben and Maddie, Joanne Weiner, Louise and Bruce Frazey, Jan and Harold Solomon, Mike Smith and wife Joyce, Marcella and Michael Davis, Barbara and Jeff Strauss, Audrey Smith, Valerie Thaler, Pati Baldwin, Christine, Tony, Justin, and Kelly Gold, Issac and Bonita Shoki, Jennifer and Julius Zebede, Sri Michael, Claudia Lewis, Marilyn Seltzer and Ochello, Sherry and Jerry Lee, Beth Davis, Dail and Marshall Adelman, Barry and Arthur Edelson, Siddha Yoga buddies, Ellen Lansburgh, Shabari, Atmika, and Jill Yip Choy. ᴄᴧᴏ **Cheering gratitude to the very special people who have been friends and supportive since the inception of QuantumThink:** to Gail Evans and Alvin Goldstein for sharing their loving spirit, intellectual curiosity, enormous accomplishments, wonderful dinners, and fun times; to William Shanley for sharing mutual appreciation for quantum science, and for deftly producing the original QuantumThink AudioCoach; to Mark Diamond for his electrifying images and for giving me an up front and personal experience of a hologram being created; to the imaginative Kelly Villoch for capturing the essence of QuantumThink in the early graphics; to my beautiful artistic soul sister, Eileen Seitz for the original website painting, *New World View Paradise,* and for supporting me in everything I do. ᴄᴧᴏ **Respectful gratitude to people who were stepping stones for me along the way:** Raleigh Pinskey, who taught me to stay true to my own style; Sam Horn, who took my novice hand and showed me the way of an author; Kim Weiss, who gave me insight into the publishing process; Faye Quam Heimerl who helped me organize my many references; Michael Klar, who with Pedie made sure the cover art was perfect. ᴄᴧᴏ

Loving gratitude to my biggest fans, the foundation of my life—my family. To my sensational, beloved husband, Alan Collins, without whom I cannot imagine how I would have accomplished this. With kind heart, patience, and laughing spirit he assures me, "If I can understand QuantumThink, anyone can." Alan has "translated me" to others and inspired me daily, his expansive mind ever ready to uncap the next limit in our fascinating and often heated conversations colored with "husband-like quirks" that give me food for thought. With his irresistibly resonant English voice he read the manuscript aloud to me countless times so I could get the rhythm, ensuring you would hear pleasing cadence as you read. Thank you, Alan, for your love and devotion to me, to us, and to our work. ᴄᴧᴏ **I must have done something good in a past life because I am surrounded by the greatest family** of individuals who are each brilliant and loving, talented and enlivening, positive and fun, always interested and interesting, and spurring me on. To my adorable and adoring, amazing parents, Lilly and Jack, for the good genes they gave me for thinking, writing, and constancy (at this writing, going into their 70th year of wedded bliss), and for honoring the eternal values of family and goodness. To my mother, vivacious Diamond Lil, I thank you for being my own personal cheerleader, for teaching me to be giving, to love beauty and order, and for showing me by your example that strength, beauty, and an uplifting spirit can coalesce in one person. To my gregarious father, Dadio Jack, I thank you for teaching me through your engineer's sharp mind there's always a way to have things work, for showing me that gentility is commanding, that perseverance gets results, how to captivate an audience, to keep a sense of humor blended with wisdom, and to focus on the bright side and simply enjoy life. Mom and Dad, thank you both for lighting all of us up with your youthful optimism and zest for life. ❧ To my sister, Shelley, thank you for always being there for me, thinking and laughing with me, coaching me through sticky moments, and making family a daily celebration. ❧ To my brother, Al, who demonstrates what it means to be a true gentleman, aptly known as Albie-wan to his friends, whose wisdom is lived, whose nimble mind and humble soul questions and reflects daily; thank you, Bro, for the stimulating thought-provoking conversations, allowing me to "test out" my views and for letting me know in your unique style that you are cheering me all the way. ❧ **Sweetest gratitude to my nieces and nephews, abundant sources of happiness and expansion:** to Alisse and Mark for your forward-thinking minds and compassionately competitive spirit, daring to stretch the envelope of excellence, and to Jessica for your exquisitely bubbling joy in the adventure of life. To Danielle and Steve for your golden hearts as big as the sky, incisive thinking and scintillating wit, and to Jordan for your alluring sweetness, sensitivity and grace. To Katherine and Ryan for your sparkling spirits, regal charm, and natural perfection in all you do, and to Liam for your effervescence, sense of wonder, and for emanating unconditional love; to Hale, for your edgy creative brilliance, insight, and loving warmth. ❧ *Grazie mille* to ichi-ban cousin, Ro, who has been my side-kick and my window onto the world, who has prodded me and lauded me, been my caustic critic and ardent admirer; thank you for knowing it really is all about the love. To her "life," my almost-cousin, the incomparable Howard-san, for keeping me honest and amused with our comedic sparring of new world view principles all these years. ❧ **Humble gratitude for the welcoming interest in my work** from my aunts and uncles, Rhoda, Ruth, Molly, Rosa, Fern and Bev; Joe, Jack, Rayme, and Phil. **Eternal gratitude to the memory of** my grandparents, Rachel and Abe, Eva and Dave, and my in-laws, Anne and Joe, for their devotion and kindness, courage and love; and to the spirit of my uncles, Sy and Seymour, for believing in me. ❧

Some people make you feel good just knowing they are there. Congenial gratitude: to Mel Wolfond, Pedie's amazing husband, philanthropist and all around stellar human being, whose quiet support is felt during our dining-table deliberations; to Devra Ann Jacobs, auspicious proponent of the "now" age, kindred spirit who gave QuantumThink exposure and me lots of experience in keeping writing deadlines for her magazine; to author Nikki Ross, who has offered her insightful support and guidance in having me reach the finish line. To my lifelong friends: the inimitable and fabulous, Sherri Greene; poet-soul Joyce Bershad and smiling husband Stan; forever-young and faithful friend since childhood, Irene Wechsler and fun-loving husband Richard. ꙮ **Collaborative gratitude to our partners, friends and colleagues who put QuantumThink into practice while keeping me engaged in the fullness of life:** to Quantum Racing Team #1 and world class race-horse trainer, Phil Gleaves, Amy, and Sandy who teach me to stay connected to nature; to our champion racehorse, the majestic Mambo Meister, individualist, great soul who teaches me discipline and dignity; to fellow board members of South Beach Chamber Ensemble, Michael Andrews, Holly Berline, Ruth Stoltz, William Handley, and Sandra Walsh who keep the music playing. ꙮ **Extraordinary gratitude to teacher-advisors for their perspective and guidance:** Iris Saltzman, great teacher and dear friend who courageously wove metaphysical principles into practical everyday life before it was acceptable to teach such things; Brenda Brush who has kept me abreast of planetary cycles and how they influence the transformative times we are living through; Jody Rowe Staley who indescribably reflects I am fulfilling my mission; Jill Dahne, who has steered and cheered my book with her gift of seeing; Starr Fuentes, who with crystal clarity confirmed my direction as "right"; Robert Wilkinson, who offered invaluable insight into my soul's purpose; Werner Erhardt, who showed me the importance of distinguishing. ꙮ **Appreciative gratitude to the women and men who kept me feeling beautiful, fit and fresh during the years of my writing,** always showing interest with that ubiquitous question: *How is your book going? Have you finished yet?* Robert Leviyev, magnificent tennis coach who teaches me I can do anything; Rose Macias and Shelly Apperstein, who listened to me expound QuantumThink as they performed miracles with my hair; the lovely ladies of Vzanz who quietly gave me manicures so I could listen to science lectures in my iPhone; to the staff of Oceania, and to Eliana, who beautify my home and work environment. ꙮ **Healing gratitude to:** Renata Miranda, Dr. Mark and Nina Dulberg, Carl Carrozzo, Dr. Steve Friedman, Dr. Lewis Carroll and staff, the counselors of Quick Weight Loss Centers. ꙮ **Daily gratitude to** respected cardiologist and friend, Dr. Leonard Pianko, who brings peace of mind by partnering with me in the well being of my parents, living the wisdom of QuantumThinking by his openness to holistic healing modalities used in tandem with Western medicine. ꙮ **Nightly gratitude to** Jon Stewart and *The Daily Show* for giving me comic relief and daily validation for writing this book. ꙮ **Inestimable gratitude to my great teachers** for their boundless grace, light, and liberation, Swami Muktananda and Gurumayi Chidvilasananda, and to all the Siddhas and ascended masters. ꙮ **Endless gratitude** to divine Infinite Intelligence for selecting me to be the vehicle for this book; I bow in thanksgiving for the honor. ꙮ

INDEX

The Origins of QuantumThink®

I was born to create QuantumThink.

I didn't choose QuantumThink. It chose me.
There was no great single epiphany, no miraculous transformative moment or circumstantial crisis (thank God) *that-changed-my-life-forever*. It has been a gradual, steady awakening. I stood gazing at myself in our hallway mirror at the age of four and pinched the skin on my arm, becoming *aware* for the first time, of Self and of Life. My questioning began.

At age fifteen, I confiscated my older brother's and sister's college texts; Sartre, Camus, Kant and Kierkegaard penetrated my psyche. I attempted learn-by-photos Yoga *asanas* (postures), not really understanding what meditation was about, but intuiting there was something important here. During the Viet Nam war I read a lamentable newspaper story about a young draftee that touched me indelibly. I wondered, "How did I land in a world where people were actually serious about inventing weapons to kill one another?" There was something wrong with this picture, *this entire reality*. Furthermore, no one was talking about this or a bunch of other things either. It was the Emperor's New Clothes. Surely, I couldn't be the only one who was seeing this duplicity? Call me naïve, sophomoric. I prefer *that* to being resigned that "this is the way it is."

I wondered what contribution I would make, what *could* I make—in such a world. At that tender teen age, I was clear that whomever I came into contact with, even strangers passing wordlessly on the street; that I was influencing them (and them, me) because our energy fields were mixing. (*How did I know this?*) I didn't have the way to articulate those thoughts at that time. My task was decided. I could only give at the level to which I developed myself.

Today scientists have proven we are each an aspect—an entry point, actually—into a nonlocal mind, a unified field of consciousness, of Infinite Intelligence. The Beatles knew this: *I am he as you are he as you are me and we are all together.* With awareness, we can tap its endless wisdom, and become unique channels of that wisdom, projecting it to others from the radio of our own being. Our job is to make sure there is no static in the transmission.

Spellbound by the possibility of an evolution in awareness, I set forth. Through my speaking and writing I discovered I could make the connection for people between the reality we truly desire and access to our power to create it. It happens not because of me, but through me; because of natural laws, sacred and divine cosmic principles operating without exception throughout this vast magical universe and therefore within you and me.**

—Dianne Collins

About the Author, Dianne Collins

One of the foremost thought leaders of our time, Dianne Collins is an original thinker dedicated to people living spirited, joyful and effective lives. She is a master of translating ancient wisdom into modern quantum terms that work in business and personal affairs in practical, transformative ways.

Dianne consults executives in the world's leading corporations as well as enterprising entrepreneurs and celebrities, students and evolutionaries in the groundbreaking system of thinking she created, QuantumThink®. Her unique, entertaining style enables people to effortlessly apply exciting new principles and big ideas into their lives, breaking the mold of limited thinking, commanding a life of creative freedom, experiencing the enchantment of universal wisdom lived daily.

Dianne holds a degree in Philosophy from the University of Miami, and is a lifelong student of leading edge thinking and practices, from physics to metaphysics, always with the intent to awaken awareness, expand thinking, and enhance the joy of life. She lives with her husband and business partner, Alan, in their condo on the beach in south Florida.

Opportunities to QuantumThink®

To keep QuantumThinking in your awareness you are invited to receive a free weekly inspirational and thought-provoking email message, "A QuantumThink Moment" available from the website. You can also start a conversation with Dianne on her blog, "The Answer." If you are interested in mastering QuantumThink you can participate in live coaching programs. Visit www.diannecollins.com.

QuantumThink can be successfully applied to any area of life—to global, industry, company and/or social solutions and projects—and for personal and professional effectiveness. Dianne Collins and Alan K. Collins offer private consulting, corporate teleseminars, and public teleseminars open to individuals around the world. All QuantumThink programs are designed for you to achieve relevant, real-time business and/or personal results while deepening your experience and mastery of QuantumThink. For more information visit www.diannecollins.com.